1 & 2 KINGS
A Commentary in the Wesleyan Tradition

*New Beacon Bible Commentary

1 & 2 KINGS
A Commentary in the Wesleyan Tradition

Karen Strand Winslow

BEACON HILL PRESS
OF KANSAS CITY

Copyright 2017 by Beacon Hill Press of Kansas City

Beacon Hill Press of Kansas City
PO Box 419527
Kansas City, MO 64141
www.BeaconHillBooks.com

ISBN 978-0-8341-3561-1

All rights reserved. No part of this publication may be reproduced, stored in a retrieval system, or transmitted in any form or by any means—for example, electronic, photocopy, recording—without the prior written permission of the publisher. The only exception is brief quotations in printed reviews.

Cover Design: J.R. Caines
Interior Design: Sharon Page

Unless otherwise indicated all Scripture quotations are from the *Holy Bible, New International Version*® (NIV®). Copyright © 1973, 1978, 1984, 2011 by Biblica, Inc.™ Used by permission. All rights reserved worldwide. Emphasis indicated by underlining in boldface quotations and italic in lightface quotations.

The following version of Scripture is in the public domain:
The King James Version of the Bible (KJV).

The following copyrighted versions of Scripture are used by permission:
The *New JPS Hebrew-English Tanakh* (NJPS), © 2000 by The Jewish Publication Society. All rights reserved.
The *New Revised Standard Version Bible* (NRSV), copyright © 1989 National Council of the Churches of Christ in the USA. All rights reserved. Emphasis indicated by italic.

Library of Congress Cataloging-in-Publication Data
Names: Winslow, Karen Strand, 1952- author.
Title: 1 & 2 Kings / Karen Strand Winslow.
Other titles: First and Second Kings
Description: Kansas City, MO : Beacon Hill Press of Kansas City, 2017. |
  Series: New Beacon Bible commentary | Includes bibliographical references.
Identifiers: LCCN 2016058162 | ISBN 9780834135611 (pbk.)
Subjects: LCSH: Bible. Kings—Commentaries.
Classification: LCC BS1335.53 .W56 2017 | DDC 222/.507—dc23 LC record available at
https://lccn.loc.gov/2016058162

The Internet addresses, email addresses, and phone numbers in this book are accurate at the time of publication. They are provided as a resource. Beacon Hill Press of Kansas City does not endorse them or vouch for their content or permanence.

DEDICATION

To Dale, the best husband, father, preacher, pastor, and friend; and to my children, Karmelle, Luke, and Benjamin, their spouses and their children, who bring me great laughter.

COMMENTARY EDITORS

General Editors

Alex Varughese
> Ph.D., Drew University
> Professor of Biblical Literature
> Mount Vernon Nazarene University
> Mount Vernon, Ohio

Roger Hahn
> Ph.D., Duke University
> Dean of the Faculty
> Professor of New Testament
> Nazarene Theological Seminary
> Kansas City, Missouri

George Lyons
> Ph.D., Emory University
> Professor of New Testament
> Northwest Nazarene University
> Nampa, Idaho

Section Editors

Robert Branson
> Ph.D., Boston University
> Professor of Biblical Literature
> Emeritus
> Olivet Nazarene University
> Bourbonnais, Illinois

Alex Varughese
> Ph.D., Drew University
> Professor of Biblical Literature
> Mount Vernon Nazarene University
> Mount Vernon, Ohio

Jim Edlin
> Ph.D., Southern Baptist Theological Seminary
> Professor of Biblical Literature and Languages
> Chair, Division of Religion and Philosophy
> MidAmerica Nazarene University
> Olathe, Kansas

Kent Brower
> Ph.D., The University of Manchester
> Vice Principal
> Senior Lecturer in Biblical Studies
> Nazarene Theological College
> Manchester, England

George Lyons
> Ph.D., Emory University
> Professor of New Testament
> Northwest Nazarene University
> Nampa, Idaho

CONTENTS

General Editors' Preface	11
Acknowledgments	13
Abbreviations	15
Bibliography	19
Table of Sidebars	23
Maps	23

INTRODUCTION — 25
   A. Overview of Content — 25
   B. Authorship, Sources, Date, Provenance, Audience, Occasion, Purpose, Sociological/Cultural Issues, Textual History — 27
   C. History and Geography of the Period — 29
   D. Geography, Settlement Patterns, Statehood and Extent of Israel's Boundaries according to the Biblical and Extrabiblical Texts and Archaeology — 32
      1. Geography and Settlement of the Land — 32
      2. The Extent of Jerusalem's Domination according to Archaeologists — 35
      3. Using the Bible with Archaeology — 39
      4. Inscriptions — 39
   E. Genre, Structure, Literary Outline — 40
   F. Theological Themes — 41
   G. Hebrew Text Traditions — 43

COMMENTARY — 45

THE BOOK OF FIRST KINGS — 45

   I. SOLOMON'S ASCENSION AND REIGN: THIRD AND LAST KING IN THE UNITED MONARCHY; SETTING: JERUSALEM: 1 KINGS 1:1—11:43 — 45
      A. Solomon Ascends to the Throne of David (1:1-53) — 47
         1. Abishag Attends to a Dying David (1:1-4) — 49
         2. Adonijah "Assumes" the Throne (1:5-10) — 50
         3. Nathan and Bathsheba Persuade David to Name Solomon King (1:11-40) — 52
         4. Adonijah Responds to Solomon's Accession (1:41-53) — 54

- B. Solomon Eliminates His Opponents (2:1-46) — 56
  1. David Orders Solomon to Keep the Law and to Avenge Him (2:1-12) — 57
  2. Bathsheba Requests Abishag for Adonijah's Wife (2:13-25) — 61
  3. Solomon Establishes His Reign (2:26-46) — 61
- C. Solomon Expands Israel (3—11) — 65
  1. Solomon Marries and Asks Yahweh for Wisdom (3:1-15) — 67
  2. Solomon Displays His Wisdom to All Israel (3:16-28) — 70
  3. Solomon Adds Officials, Land, Wealth, and Honor (4:1-34 [4:1—5:14 HB]) — 71
  4. Solomon Builds a Temple for Yahweh (5:1—6:38 [5:15—6:38 HB]) — 73
  5. Solomon Builds Royal Houses (7:1-12) — 78
  6. Solomon Completes the Temple (7:13-51) — 79
  7. Solomon Dedicates the Temple of Yahweh (8:1-66) — 82
  8. Yahweh Warns Solomon of Covenant Conditions (9:1-9) — 92
  9. Solomon Repays Hiram of Tyre (9:10-14) — 94
  10. Solomon Enslaves Canaanites for His Building Projects and Hires Israelites as Soldiers and Foremen (9:15-28) — 95
  11. Solomon Parades Wisdom and Wealth to the Queen of Sheba (10:1-13) — 99
  12. Solomon Acquires Silver, Gold, and Horses from Egypt (10:14-29) — 101
  13. Solomon Worships Other Gods and Yahweh Responds (11:1-13) — 103
  14. Yahweh Raises Adversaries against Solomon (11:14-25) — 107
  15. Ahijah Promises Jeroboam an Enduring Covenant with Conditions (11:26-40) — 108
  16. Solomon Dies and Is Buried (11:41-43) — 109

II. **THE DIVIDED MONARCHY AND FALL OF ISRAEL: 1 KINGS 12:1—2 KINGS 17:41** — 111
- A. Jeroboam Becomes King over the Tribes of Israel (12:1—14:20) — 111
  1. Israel Requests a Lighter Yoke but Rehoboam Promises a Heavier Yoke (12:1-11) — 113
  2. Israel Rebels and Makes Jeroboam King (12:12-24) — 114
  3. Jeroboam Builds Two Golden Calves to Keep Israel from Jerusalem (12:25-33) — 116
  4. The Man of God Prophesies against Jeroboam's Apostasy (13:1-34) — 119
  5. Ahijah Prophesies against Jeroboam's Dynasty (14:1-20) — 123
- B. Kings of Judah and Israel (14:21—16:28) — 127
  1. Rehoboam, Abijam, Asa Rule Judah (14:21—15:24) — 127
  2. Nadab, Baasha, Elah, Zimri, and Omri Rule Israel (15:25—16:28) — 132

- C. Ahab's Apostasy and Elijah's Prophecy (16:29—22:53 [22:54 HB]) — 136
  1. Ahab Marries Jezebel and Establishes Baal Worship (16:29-34) — 140
  2. Elijah Predicts Drought and Revives the Widow's Son (17:1-24) — 140
  3. Elijah Reveals the Power of Yahweh and Anoints Elisha (18:1—19:21) — 143
  4. Ahab Defeats the Arameans (20:1-43) — 152
  5. Jezebel Murders Naboth and Gives His Vineyard to Ahab (21:1-29) — 154
  6. Ahab Wars with the Arameans and Dies (22:1-40) — 157
  7. Jehoshaphat Rules Judah and Ahaziah Rules Israel (22:41-53 [41-54 HB]) — 161

THE BOOK OF SECOND KINGS — 165

- D. Prophetic Ministries of Elijah and Elisha (2 Kgs 1:1—13:24) — 165
  1. Elijah Denounces Ahaziah before Ascending to Heaven (1:1—2:12) — 165
     a. Elijah Denounces Ahaziah (1:1-18) — 165
     b. Elijah Ascends to Heaven (2:1-12) — 167
  2. Elisha Dons the Mantle of Elijah, Helps Prophets and Mothers, Confronts and Replaces Kings (2:13—9:13) — 169
     a. Elijah's Authority Resides in Elisha (2:13-25) — 169
     b. The Revolt of Moab (3:1-27) — 171
     c. The Destitute Widow (4:1-7) — 174
     d. The Shunammite and Her Son (4:8-44) — 175
     e. The Healing of Naaman, the Aramean (5:1-27) — 178
     f. The Lost Ax Head (6:1-7) — 185
     g. Chariots of Fire (6:8-23) — 186
     h. Famine in Israel Caused by Ben-Hadad's Final Siege (6:24—7:20) — 188
     i. Restoration of the Shunammite's Land (8:1-6) — 193
     j. The Murder of Ben-Hadad (8:7-15) — 194
     k. The Kings of Judah, Jehoram and Ahaziah (8:16-29) — 197
     l. Jehu Anointed King of Israel (9:1-13) — 199
  3. Jehu Slaughters Ahab's Family, Judah's Royalty, and Baal Worshippers (9:14—10:36) — 201
  4. Athaliah Murders Her Grandsons and Claims the Throne of Judah for Six Years (11:1-21 [1—12:1 HB]) — 209
  5. Joash of Judah Repairs the Temple (12:1-21 [2-22 HB]) — 213
  6. Elisha Dies after Prophesying Limited Victory for Israel over Aram (13:1-25) — 215
- E. The Dynasties of Israel and Judah until Assyria Invades (14:1—17:41) — 219
  1. Judah Has a Few Good Kings (14:1-22; 15:1-7, 32-38); Israel's Kings Follow in the Sins of Jeroboam (14:23-29; 15:8-31) — 220
     a. Amaziah's Reign in Judah (14:1-22) — 220
     b. Jeroboam II's Reign in Israel (14:23-29) — 223

   c. Azariah's Reign in Judah (15:1-7)   224
   d. The Reigns of Zechariah, Shallum, Menahem, Pekahiah, and Pekah of Israel (15:8-31)   225
   e. The Reign of Jotham in Judah (15:32-38)   227
  2. King Ahaz of Judah Alters the Altar after Submitting to Assyria (16:1-20)   227
  3. Assyria Captures Samaria and Deports Israelites (17:1-6)   230
  4. Israel Is Destroyed for Sinning against Yahweh Their God and Ignoring His Prophets (17:7-23)   232
  5. Assyria Resettles Israel with Other Captives, and Syncretism Prevails (17:24-41)   234

III. JUDAH TO THE BABYLONIAN EXILE: 2 KINGS 18:1—25:30   239

 A. Hezekiah Serves Yahweh and Is Besieged by Assyria (18:1—20:21)   241
  1. Hezekiah Ascends to the Throne of Judah and Does Right like David His Father (18:1-8)   241
  2. Assyria Captures and Exiles Israel (18:9-12)   243
  3. Yahweh Delivers Jerusalem from Assyria (18:13—19:37)   243
  4. Yahweh Heals Hezekiah (20:1-11)   248
  5. Hezekiah Receives Babylonian Envoys; Isaiah Responds (20:12-21)   250
 B. Manasseh and Amon Abandon Yahweh and Rebuild the Local Shrines (21:1-26)   251
 C. Josiah Reforms Judah according to the Book of the Law (22:1—23:30)   256
  1. Josiah Hears the Words of Yahweh (22:1-20)   258
  2. Josiah Responds to the Words of Yahweh (23:1-30)   261
 D. Egypt Controls Judah (23:31-37)   271
 E. Babylon Takes Exiles, Overruns Judah, and Razes Jerusalem (24:1—25:30)   272
  1. Jehoiakim and Jehoiachin Face Nebuchadnezzar (24:1-17)   274
  2. Zedekiah Rebels and Jerusalem Falls to Babylon (24:18—25:21)   277
  3. The Aftermath of Judah's Exile to Babylon (25:22-30)   281
   a. From Gedaliah to the Flight to Egypt (25:22-26)   281
   b. Epilogue (25:27-30)   282

GENERAL EDITORS' PREFACE

The purpose of the New Beacon Bible Commentary is to make available to pastors and students in the twenty-first century a biblical commentary that reflects the best scholarship in the Wesleyan theological tradition. The commentary project aims to make this scholarship accessible to a wider audience to assist them in their understanding and proclamation of Scripture as God's Word.

Writers of the volumes in this series not only are scholars within the Wesleyan theological tradition and experts in their field but also have special interest in the books assigned to them. Their task is to communicate clearly the critical consensus and the full range of other credible voices who have commented on the Scriptures. Though scholarship and scholarly contribution to the understanding of the Scriptures are key concerns of this series, it is not intended as an academic dialogue within the scholarly community. Commentators of this series constantly aim to demonstrate in their work the significance of the Bible as the church's book and the contemporary relevance and application of the biblical message. The project's overall goal is to make available to the church and for her service the fruits of the labors of scholars who are committed to their Christian faith.

The *New International Version* (NIV) is the reference version of the Bible used in this series; however, the focus of exegetical study and comments is the biblical text in its original language. When the commentary uses the NIV, it is printed in bold. The text printed in bold italics is the translation of the author. Commentators also refer to other translations where the text may be difficult or ambiguous.

The structure and organization of the commentaries in this series seeks to facilitate the study of the biblical text in a systematic and methodical way. Study of each biblical book begins with an ***Introduction*** section that gives an overview of authorship, date, provenance, audience, occasion, purpose, sociological/cultural issues, textual history, literary features, hermeneutical issues, and theological themes necessary to understand the book. This section also includes a brief outline of the book and a list of general works and standard commentaries.

The commentary section for each biblical book follows the outline of the book presented in the introduction. In some volumes, readers will find section ***overviews*** of large portions of scripture with general comments on their overall literary structure and other literary features. A consistent feature of the commentary is the paragraph-by-paragraph study of biblical texts. This section has three parts: **Behind the Text**, **In the Text**, and **From the Text**.

The goal of the **Behind the Text** section is to provide the reader with all the relevant information necessary to understand the text. This includes specific historical situations reflected in the text, the literary context of the text, sociological and cultural issues, and literary features of the text.

In the Text explores what the text says, following its verse-by-verse structure. This section includes a discussion of grammatical details, word studies, and the connectedness of the text to other biblical books/passages or other parts of the book being studied (the canonical relationship). This section provides transliterations of key words in Hebrew and Greek and their literal meanings. The goal here is to explain what the author would have meant and/or what the audience would have understood as the meaning of the text. This is the largest section of the commentary.

The **From the Text** section examines the text in relation to the following areas: theological significance, intertextuality, the history of interpretation, use of the Old Testament scriptures in the New Testament, interpretation in later church history, actualization, and application.

The commentary provides **sidebars** on topics of interest that are important but not necessarily part of an explanation of the biblical text. These topics are informational items and may cover archaeological, historical, literary, cultural, and theological matters that have relevance to the biblical text. Occasionally, longer detailed discussions of special topics are included as **excursuses.**

We offer this series with our hope and prayer that readers will find it a valuable resource for their understanding of God's Word and an indispensable tool for their critical engagement with the biblical texts.

Roger Hahn, Centennial Initiative General Editor
Alex Varughese, General Editor (Old Testament)
George Lyons, General Editor (New Testament)

ACKNOWLEDGMENTS

Dr. Bob Branson and Dr. Alex Varughese asked me to write this commentary on 1—2 Kings after I had responded to a couple of papers in the Biblical Studies section at the Wesleyan Theological Society meeting at Duke Divinity School in 2008. I agreed to do so because I wanted to be immersed in Kings and the scholarship it has provoked over the centuries. I wanted to write a commentary from a Wesleyan perspective and be part of this larger project. I have often taught the books of 1—2 Kings in classes on the Old Testament at Seattle Pacific University, Greenville College, and Azusa Pacific University and was familiar with them. But a commentary would demand that I observe them more closely, word by word in Hebrew, with even more attention to the history of this period and the works of others who have explored these books.

The sabbatical provided by Azusa Pacific University in 2010 helped my progress through 1 Kgs 1—11, and two Accomplished Scholars awards for release of class units moved me forward through subsequent sections. Continuing to teach these books in the classroom turned my students into conversation partners who heard and read some of my discoveries as I commented on these texts and contemplated their application to the present. I am grateful to my 2008-14 students at Azusa Pacific Graduate School of Theology, now Azusa Pacific Seminary.

I am especially grateful to my section editor, Bob Branson, with his suggestions, keen eye, and tireless checking of Scripture citations. I felt throughout that this was a team effort and that made it fun. As always, I appreciate my husband's support, and I expect him to preach from Kings many, many times in the future, using this commentary. My kids and grandkids give me, on a daily basis, sometimes through Skype, rewards for work well done. As my grandchildren increase in size and number, my happiness grows.

Once again, I want to thank my father, Clarence Andrew Strand, who has always loved me and shows it. Finally, I thank God. I remember all your mercies to me, your words, your leading, and your light on the way; and I am grateful.

Karen Strand Winslow

ABBREVIATIONS

With a few exceptions, these abbreviations follow those in *The SBL Handbook of Style* (Alexander 1999).

General

→	See the commentary at
AD	anno Domini (precedes date; equivalent to CE)
ANE	ancient Near East
BC	before Christ (follows date; equivalent to BCE)
BCE	before the Common Era
ca.	circa
CE	Common Era
ch	chapter
chs	chapters
DH	Martin Noth's Deuteronomistic History
Dtr	Deuteronomistic Historian/Historians
Dtr¹	the early producer and redactor of 1—2 Kings who lived during Josiah's reign
Dtr²	the exilic redactor of 1—2 Kings
DtrH	Deuteronomistic History (the Former Prophets—Joshua, Judges, 1 and 2 Samuel, 1 and 2 Kings)
ed.	edition, editor, edited by
eds.	editors
e.g.	*exempli gratia*, for example
esp.	especially
etc.	*et cetera*, and the rest
Gk.	Greek
HB	Hebrew Bible
Heb.	Hebrew
i.e.	*id est*, that is
lit.	literally
LXX	Septuagint
mg.	margin
MS(S)	manuscript(s)
MT	Masoretic Text (of the OT)
n(n).	note(s)
NT	New Testament
OT	Old Testament
passim	here and there
sg.	singular
Syr.	Syriac Version
Vg.	Vulgate
vol(s).	volume(s)
v(v)	verse(s)

Modern English Versions of the Bible

NIV	New International Version (2011)
NRSV	New Revised Standard Version

Print Conventions for Translations

Bold font	NIV (bold without quotation marks in the text under study; elsewhere in the regular font, with quotation marks and no further identification)
Bold italic font	Author's translation (without quotation marks)

Behind the Text:	Literary or historical background information average readers might not know from reading the biblical text alone
In the Text:	Comments on the biblical text, words, phrases, grammar, and so forth
From the Text:	The use of the text by later interpreters, contemporary relevance, theological and ethical implications of the text, with particular emphasis on Wesleyan concerns

Ancient Sources

Old Testament

Gen	Genesis	Dan	Daniel		
Exod	Exodus	Hos	Hosea		
Lev	Leviticus	Joel	Joel		
Num	Numbers	Amos	Amos		
Deut	Deuteronomy	Obad	Obadiah		
Josh	Joshua	Jonah	Jonah		
Judg	Judges	Mic	Micah		
Ruth	Ruth	Nah	Nahum		
1—2 Sam	1—2 Samuel	Hab	Habakkuk		
1—2 Kgs	1—2 Kings	Zeph	Zephaniah		
1—2 Chr	1—2 Chronicles	Hag	Haggai		
Ezra	Ezra	Zech	Zechariah		
Neh	Nehemiah	Mal	Malachi		
Esth	Esther				
Job	Job				
Ps/Pss	Psalm/Psalms				
Prov	Proverbs				
Eccl	Ecclesiastes				
Song	Song of Songs/Song of Solomon				
Isa	Isaiah				
Jer	Jeremiah				
Lam	Lamentations				
Ezek	Ezekiel				

(Note: Chapter and verse numbering in the MT and LXX often differ compared to those in English Bibles. To avoid confusion, all biblical references follow the chapter and verse numbering in English translations, even when the text in the MT and LXX is under discussion.)

New Testament

Matt	Matthew
Mark	Mark
Luke	Luke
John	John
Acts	Acts
Rom	Romans
1—2 Cor	1—2 Corinthians
Gal	Galatians
Eph	Ephesians
Phil	Philippians
Col	Colossians
1—2 Thess	1—2 Thessalonians
1—2 Tim	1—2 Timothy
Titus	Titus
Phlm	Philemon
Heb	Hebrews
Jas	James
1—2 Pet	1—2 Peter
1—2—3 John	1—2—3 John
Jude	Jude
Rev	Revelation

Apocrypha

Bar	Baruch
Add Dan	Additions to Daniel
Pr Azar	Prayer of Azariah
Bel	Bel and the Dragon
Sg Three	Song of the Three Young Men
Sus	Susanna
1—2 Esd	1—2 Esdras
Add Esth	Additions to Esther
Ep Jer	Epistle of Jeremiah
Jdt	Judith
1—2 Macc	1—2 Maccabees
3—4 Macc	3—4 Maccabees
Pr Man	Prayer of Manasseh
Ps 151	Psalm 151
Sir	Sirach/Ecclesiasticus
Tob	Tobit
Wis	Wisdom of Solomon

Old Testament Pseudepigrapha

Liv. Pro.	*The Lives of the Prophets*
Mart. Ascen. Isa.	*The Martyrdom and Ascension of Isaiah*

Josephus

Ant.	*Jewish Antiquities*

Mishnah, Talmud, and Related Literature

B. Bat.	*Baba Batra*
Ta'an.	*Ta'anit*

Secondary Sources

ABD	*Anchor Bible Dictionary* (see Freedman)
ANEP	*Ancient Near Eastern Texts in Pictures Relating to the Old Testament* (see Pritchard)
ANET	*Ancient Near Eastern Texts Relating to the Old Testament* (see Pritchard)

BA	*Biblical Archaeologist*
BAR	*Biblical Archaeology Review*
BDB	*A Hebrew and English Lexicon of the Old Testament* (see Brown)
DCH	*The Dictionary of Classical Hebrew* (see Clines)
IDB	*Interpreter's Dictionary of the Bible* (see Buttrick)
ISBE	*The International Standard Bible Encyclopedia* (see Bromiley)
JBL	*Journal of Biblical Literature*
JSOT	*Journal for the Study of the Old Testament*
JSOTSup	Journal for the Study of the Old Testament Supplement Series
NIDB	*New Interpreter's Dictionary of the Bible* (see Sakenfeld)
TDOT	*Theological Dictionary of the Old Testament* (see Botterweck)

Greek Transliteration

Greek	Letter	English
α	alpha	a
β	bēta	b
γ	gamma	g
γ	gamma nasal	n (before γ, κ, ξ, χ)
δ	delta	d
ε	epsilon	e
ζ	zēta	z
η	ēta	ē
θ	thēta	th
ι	iōta	i
κ	kappa	k
λ	lambda	l
μ	mu	m
ν	nu	n
ξ	xi	x
ο	omicron	o
π	pi	p
ρ	rhō	r
ρ	initial *rhō*	rh
σ/ς	sigma	s
τ	tau	t
υ	upsilon	y
υ	upsilon	u (in diphthongs: au, eu, ēu, ou, ui)
φ	phi	ph
χ	chi	ch
ψ	psi	ps
ω	ōmega	ō
ʽ	rough breathing	h (before initial vowels or diphthongs)

Hebrew Consonant Transliteration

Hebrew/Aramaic	Letter	English
א	alef	ʾ
ב	bet	b
ג	gimel	g
ד	dalet	d
ה	he	h
ו	vav	v or w
ז	zayin	z
ח	khet	ḥ
ט	tet	ṭ
י	yod	y
כ/ך	kaf	k
ל	lamed	l
מ/ם	mem	m
נ/ן	nun	n
ס	samek	s̱
ע	ayin	ʿ
פ/ף	pe	p; f (spirant)
צ/ץ	tsade	ṣ
ק	qof	q
ר	resh	r
שׂ	sin	ś
שׁ	shin	š
ת	tav	t; th (spirant)

BIBLIOGRAPHY

Ackroyd, Peter R. 1981. The Succession Narrative (so-called). *Interpretation* 35:383-96.
Alter, Robert. 2013. *Ancient Israel: Former Prophets: Joshua, Judges, Samuel and Kings*. New York: Norton.
Alter, R., and F. Kermode. 1990. *The Literary Guide to the Bible*. Cambridge, MA: Belknap Press of Harvard University Press.
Althann, Robert. 1992a. Gedaliah (Person). Page 923 in vol. 2 of *The Anchor Bible Dictionary*. Edited by David Noel Freedman. 6 vols. New York: Doubleday.
———. 1992b. Josiah (Person). Pages 1016-18 in vol. 3 of *The Anchor Bible Dictionary*. Edited by David Noel Freedman. 6 vols. New York: Doubleday.
Andersen, Francis I. 1966. Socio-Juridical Background of the Naboth Incident. *Journal of Biblical Literature* 85, 1:46-57.
Auld, A. G. 1986. *I & II Kings*. Philadelphia: Westminster.
———. 1994. *Kings Without Privilege: David and Moses in the Story of the Bible's Kings*. Edinburgh: T&T Clark.
Auld, A. G., R. Rezetko, et al. 2007. *Reflection and Refraction: Studies in Biblical Historiography in Honor of A. Graeme Auld*. Leiden: Brill.
Baker, David W. 1992. Tarshish. Pages 331-33 in vol. 6 of *The Anchor Bible Dictionary*. Edited by David Noel Freedman. 6 vols. New York: Doubleday.
Bergen, Wesley. 1999. *Elisha and the End of Prophetism*. Journal for the Study of the Old Testament Supplement Series, 286. Sheffield: Sheffield University Press.
Berlyn, P. 2007. The Rebellion of Jehu. *Jewish Bible Quarterly* 35, 4:211-21.
Berridge, John. 1992. Jehoiachin (Person). Pages 662-63 in vol. 3 of *The Anchor Bible Dictionary*. Edited by David Noel Freedman. 6 vols. New York: Doubleday.
Botterweck, G. Johannes, Helmer Ringgren, and Heinz-Josef Fabry, eds. 1974—2006. *Theological Dictionary of the Old Testament*. Grand Rapids: Eerdmans (*TDOT*).
Branson, Robert D. 2009. Judges: *A Commentary in the Wesleyan Tradition*. The New Beacon Bible Commentary. Kansas City: Beacon Hill Press of Kansas City.
Bright, John. 2000. *A History of Israel*. 4th ed. Louisville, KY: Westminster John Knox.
Bromiley, Geoffrey W., ed. 1979-88. *The International Standard Bible Encyclopedia*, Fully Revised. 4 vols. Grand Rapids: Eerdmans (*ISBE*).
Brown, F., S. R. Driver, and C. A. Briggs. 1907. *A Hebrew and English Lexicon of the Old Testament*. Oxford: Oxford University Press (BDB).
Buttrick, George A., and Keith Crim, eds. 1962-76. *Interpreter's Dictionary of the Bible*. 5 vols. New York: Abingdon (*IDB*).
Clines, David J. A., ed. 1993—2014. *The Dictionary of Classical Hebrew*. 9 vols. Sheffield: Sheffield Phoenix Press (*DCH*).
Cogan, Mordechai, and Hayim Tadmor. 1988. *II Kings: A New Translation with Introduction and Commentary*. The Anchor Bible. New York: Doubleday.
Cooper, Alan M. 2005. Baal. Pages 1380-90 in vol. 3 of *Encyclopedia of Religion*. Edited by Lindsay Jones. 2nd ed. 15 vols. Detroit: Macmillan Reference USA.
Coote, Robert B. 1992. Siloam Inscription. Page 24 in vol. 6 of *The Anchor Bible Dictionary*. Edited by David Noel Freedman. 6 vols. New York: Doubleday.
Cross, Frank Moore, Jr. 1973. Themes in the Books of Kings and the Structure of the Deuteronomistic History. Pages 274-89 in *Canaanite Myth and Hebrew Epic*. Cambridge: Harvard University Press.
Dever, William G. 1984. Gezer Revisited: New Excavations of the Solomonic and Assyrian Period Defenses. *Biblical Archaeologist* 47, no. 4: 206-18.
———. 2001. *What Did the Biblical Writers Know and When Did They Know It?* Grand Rapids: Eerdmans.
DeVries, Simon J. 1985. *I Kings*. Word Biblical Commentary 12. Waco, TX: Word Books.

Dolphin, Lambert, and Michael Kollen. 1995. First and Second Temples in Jerusalem, last modified June 16, 2000. http://www.templemount.org/theories.html.
Eissfeldt, Otto. 1965. *The Old Testament: An Introduction*. New York: Harper & Row.
Emerton, J. A. 1976. Examination of a Recent Structuralist Interpretation of Genesis 38. *Vetus Testamentum* 26:79-98.
———. 1979. Judah and Tamar. *Vetus Testamentum* 29:403-15.
Endres, J. C., W. R. Millar, et al. 1998. *Chronicles and Its Synoptic Parallels in Samuel, Kings, and Related Biblical Texts*. Collegeville, MN: Liturgical Press.
Evans, Carl D. 1992. Manasseh, King of Judah. Pages 497-98 in vol. 4 of *The Anchor Bible Dictionary*. Edited by David Noel Freedman. 6 vols. New York: Doubleday.
Fewell, Dana. 1986. Sennacherib's Defeat: Words at War in 2 Kings 18:13—19:37. *Journal for the Study of the Old Testament* 34:79-90.
Finkelstein, Israel. 2006. *David and Solomon: In Search of the Bible's Sacred Kings and the Roots of the Western Tradition*. New York: Free Press.
Finkelstein, Israel, and Neil Silberman. 2001. *The Bible Unearthed: Archaeology's New Vision of Ancient Israel and the Origin of Its Sacred Texts*. New York: Free Press.
Freedman, David Noel, ed. 1992. *The Anchor Bible Dictionary*. 6 vols. New York: Doubleday (*ABD*).
Friedman, Richard E. 1980. The Tabernacle in the Temple. *Biblical Archaeologist* 43:241-48.
Gaines, Janet Howe. 2000. How Bad Was Jezebel? *Bible Review* 16:05. Also available at http://www.biblicalarchaeology.org/daily/people-cultures-in-the-bible/people-in-the-bible/how-bad-was-jezebel/.
Gaster, T. 1975. *Myth, Legend and Custom in the Old Testament*. Evanston, IN: Harper & Row.
Goodfriend, Elaine Adler. 1992. Prostitution: Old Testament. Pages 508-10 in vol. 5 of *The Anchor Bible Dictionary*. Edited by David Noel Freedman. 6 vols. New York: Doubleday.
Grayson, A. Kirk. 1992a. Historiography: Mesopotamian Historiography. Pages 205-7 in vol. 3 of *The Anchor Bible Dictionary*. Edited by David Noel Freedman. 6 vols. New York: Doubleday.
———. 1992b. Mesopotamia: Assyria. Pages 733-55 in vol. 4 of *The Anchor Bible Dictionary*. Edited by David Noel Freedman. 6 vols. New York: Doubleday.
Gruber, Mayer. 1983. The qādēš in the Book of Kings and in Other Sources. *Tarbiz* 52:167-76 (in Hebrew).
———. 1986. Hebrew qĕdēšāh and Her Canaanite and Akkadian Cognates. *Ugarit-Forschungen* 18:133-48.
Hallevy, Raphael. 1958. Man of God. *Journal of Near Eastern Studies* 17, no. 4: 237-44.
Handy, Lowell K. 1992. Serpent, Bronze. Page 1117 in vol. 5 of *The Anchor Bible Dictionary*. Edited by David Noel Freedman. 6 vols. New York: Doubleday.
Hanson, K. C. 2012. The Mesha Stele, last modified July 10, 2012. http://www.kchanson.com/ANCDOCS/westsem/mesha.html.
Hayes, J. H., and P. K. Hooker. 1998. *A New Chronology for the Kings of Israel and Judah and Its Implications for Biblical History and Literature*. Atlanta: John Knox Press.
Heider, George C. 1992. Molech (Deity). Pages 896-97 in vol. 4 of *The Anchor Bible Dictionary*. Edited by David Noel Freedman. 6 vols. New York: Doubleday.
Hens-Piazza, G. 2006. *1-2 Kings*. Nashville: Abingdon.
Hess, Richard S. 1992. Chaldea (Place). Page 886 in vol. 1 of *The Anchor Bible Dictionary*. Edited by David Noel Freedman. 6 vols. New York: Doubleday.
Hobbs, T. R. 1985. *Second Kings*. Word Biblical Commentary 13. Waco, TX: Word Books.
———. 1992. Menahem (Person). Pages 692-93 in vol. 4 of *The Anchor Bible Dictionary*. Edited by David Noel Freedman. 6 vols. New York: Doubleday.
Holloway, S. W. 1992. Kings, Book of 1-2. Pages 69-83 in vol. 4 of *The Anchor Bible Dictionary*. Edited by David Noel Freedman. 6 vols. New York: Doubleday.
Hunt, Melvin. 1992. Jezreel. Page 850 in vol. 3 of *The Anchor Bible Dictionary*. Edited by David Noel Freedman. 6 vols. New York: Doubleday.
Kitchen, K. A. 2003. *On the Reliability of the Old Testament*. Grand Rapids: Eerdmans.
Krauss, R., and D. A. Warburton. 2006. Chronological Table for the Dynastic Period. Pages 490-99 in *Ancient Egyptian Chronology (Handbook of Oriental Studies)*. Edited by Erik Hornung, Rolf Krauss, and David Warburton. Leiden: Brill.
LaBarbera, Robert. 1984. The Man of War and the Man of God: Social Satire in 2 Kings 6:8—7:20. *Catholic Biblical Quarterly* 46, 4:637-51.
Leithart, Peter. 2006. *1-2 Kings*. Brazos Theological Commentary on the Bible Series. Grand Rapids: Brazos Press.

Lemaire, Andre. 2010. Solomon & Sheba, Inc. *Biblical Archaeology Review*. 36:01: 54-59.
Levenson, Jon D. 1981. From Temple to Synagogue: 1 Kings 8. Pages 143-66 in *Traditions in Transformation: Turning Points in Israel's Faith*. Edited by Baruch Halpern and Jon D. Levenson. Winona Lake, IN: Eisenbrauns.
———. 1993. *The Death and Resurrection of the Beloved Son: The Transformation of Child Sacrifice in Judaism and Christianity*. New Haven: Yale University Press.
Long, Burke O. 1981. A Darkness between Brothers. *Journal for the Study of the Old Testament* 19:79-94.
———. 1984. *1 Kings; with an Introduction to Historical Literature*. Grand Rapids: Eerdmans.
———. 1991. *2 Kings*. Grand Rapids: Eerdmans.
Mare, W. Harold. 1992. Kidron, Brook of (Place). Pages 37-38 in vol. 4 of *The Anchor Bible Dictionary*. Edited by David Noel Freedman. 6 vols. New York: Doubleday.
McKenzie, S. L. 1991. *The Trouble with Kings: The Composition of the Book of Kings in the Deuteronomistic History*. Leiden: Brill.
Mead, James K. 1999. Kings and Prophets, Donkeys and Lions: Dramatic Shape and Deuteronomistic Rhetoric in 1 Kgs XIII. *Vetus Testamentum* 49:191-205.
Megiddo Expedition. http://megiddo.tau.ac.il/index.html.
Mercer, Mark K. 2002. Elisha's Unbearable Curse: A Study of 2 Kings 2:23-25. *Africa Journal of Evangelical Theology* 21, 2:165-98. *ATLA Religion Database with ATLA Serials*, EBSCOhost.
Meyers, Carol. 1992. Temple, Jerusalem. Pages 350-69 in vol. 6 of *The Anchor Bible Dictionary*. Edited by David Noel Freedman. 6 vols. New York: Doubleday.
Milgrom, Jacob. 2008. *Encyclopaedia Judaica*. http://www.jewishvirtuallibrary.org/jsource/judaica/ejud_0002_0003_0_03145.html.
Nelson, Richard D. 1981. Josiah in the Book of Joshua. *Journal of Biblical Literature* 100:531-40.
———. 1987. *First and Second Kings*. Atlanta: John Knox Press.
Newsom, C. A., and S. H. Ringe. 1992. *The Women's Bible Commentary*. London: SPCK; Louisville, KY: Westminster/John Knox Press.
Noth, Martin. 1943 (English translation, 1981). *The Deuteronomistic History*. JSOT Supplement (Book 15). Sheffield: Sheffield Academic Press.
———. 1960. *The History of Israel*. London: Black.
Panitz-Cohen, Nava, and Robert A. Mullins. 2016. Aram-Maacah? Aramaeans and Israelites on the Border: Excavations at Tell Abil al-Qameh (Abel-beth-maacah) in Northern Israel. Pages 139-68 in *In Search for Aram and Israel: Politics, Culture, and Identity*. Edited by O. Sergi, M. Oeming, and I. J. de Hulster. *Orientalische Religionen in der Antike* (ORA) 20. Tübingen: Mohr Siebeck.
Pinnock, Clark H. 1990. *Tracking the Maze: Finding Our Way through Modern Theology from an Evangelical Perspective*. San Francisco: Harper & Row.
Pritchard, J. B., ed. 1954. *Ancient Near Eastern Texts in Pictures Relating to the Old Testament*. Princeton: Princeton University Press (*ANEP*).
———, ed. 1969. *Ancient Near Eastern Texts Relating to the Old Testament*. Princeton: Princeton University Press (*ANET*).
Provan, I. W. 1997. *1 and 2 Kings*. Sheffield: Sheffield Academic.
Rendsburg, Gary. 1986. *The Redaction of Genesis*. Winona Lake, IN: Eisenbrauns.
Rofé, Alexander. 1988. The Vineyard of Naboth: The Origin and Message of the Story. *Vetus Testamentum* 38, 1:89-104.
Römer, Thomas. 2007, 2009. *The So-Called Deuteronomistic History: A Sociological, Historical, and Literary Introduction*. London: T&T Clark.
Rosenbaum, Jonathan. 1992. Hezekiah King of Judah. Pages 189-92 in vol. 3 of *The Anchor Bible Dictionary*. Edited by David Noel Freedman. 6 vols. New York: Doubleday.
Rost, L. 1982. *The Succession to the Throne of David*. Historic Texts and Interpreters in Biblical Scholarship 1. Translated by M. D. Rutter and David M. Gunn. Sheffield: Almond.
Sakenfeld, Katharine Doob, ed. 2006-9. *New Interpreter's Dictionary of the Bible*. 5 vols. Nashville: Abingdon (*NIDB*).
Sanders, John. 1998. Pages 268-79 in *The God Who Risks: A Theology of Divine Providence*, 2nd ed. Downers Grove, IL: InterVarsity Press.
Schmitz, Philip C. 1992. Topheth (Place). Page 601 in vol. 6 of *The Anchor Bible Dictionary*. Edited by David Noel Freedman. 6 vols. New York: Doubleday.

Schniedewind, William. 1995. *The Word of God in Transition: From Prophet to Exegete in the Second Temple Period*. Journal for the Study of the Old Testament Supplement Series 197. Sheffield: Sheffield Academic.

———. 1996. Tel Dan Stela: New Light on Aramaic and Jehu's Revolt. *Bulletin of the American Schools of Oriental Research* 302:75-90.

———. 2004. *How the Bible Became a Book*. New York: Cambridge University Press.

Seitz, Christopher. 1991. Pages 476-85 in *Zion's Final Destiny: The Development of the Book of Isaiah; A Reassessment of Isaiah 36-39*. Minneapolis: Fortress.

Shanks, Hershel. 2008. Sound Proof: How Hezekiah's Tunnelers Met. *Biblical Archaeology Review* 34:05: 50-57.

———. 2009. Newly Discovered: A Fortified City from King David's Time: Answers—and Questions—at Khirbet Qeiyafa. *Biblical Archaeology Review* 35:01: 38-43.

Solomon, Ann. 1985. Jehoash's Fable of the Thistle and the Cedar. Pages 114-32 in *Saga, Legend, Tale, Novella, Fable. Narrative Forms in OT Literature*. Journal for the Study of the Old Testament Supplement Series 35. Edited by G. W. Coats. Sheffield: Sheffield Academic.

Sperling, David. 1992. Bloodguilt. Page 764 in *The Anchor Bible Dictionary*. Edited by David Noel Freedman. 6 vols. New York: Doubleday.

Spina, Frank Anthony. 2005. *The Faith of the Outsider: Exclusion and Inclusion in the Biblical Story*. Grand Rapids: Eerdmans.

Stager, Lawrence E. 1982. The Archaeology of the East Slope of Jerusalem and the Terraces of the Kidron. *Journal of Near Eastern Studies* 41, no. 2: 111-21.

Strata. 2010. Radiocarbon Dating Confirms Egyptian/Israelite Chronology. *Biblical Archaeology Review* 36:05: 16-17.

Sweeney, Marvin A. 2001. *King Josiah of Judah: The Lost Messiah of Israel*. New York: Oxford University Press.

———. 2007. *1 and 2 Kings: A Commentary*. London: Westminster John Knox.

Tarler, David, and Jane M. Cahill. 1992. David, City of. Page 62 of pages 55-67 in vol. 2 of *The Anchor Bible Dictionary*. Edited by David Noel Freedman. 6 vols. New York: Doubleday.

Thiel, Winfried. 1992. Athaliah. Pages 511-12 in vol. 1 of *The Anchor Bible Dictionary*. Edited by David Noel Freedman. 6 vols. New York: Doubleday.

Thiele, E. R. 1983. *The Mysterious Numbers of the Hebrew Kings*. Grand Rapids: Eerdmans.

Ussishkin, David. 2010. Jezreel—Where Jezebel Was Thrown to the Dogs. *Biblical Archaeology Review* 36:04: 33-42, 75-76.

Van Winkle, Dwight. 1989. 1 Kgs xiii: True and False Prophecy. *Vetus Testamentum* 39:31-43.

Varughese, Alex. 2008. *Jeremiah 1-25: A Commentary in the Wesleyan Tradition*. Kansas City: Beacon Hill Press of Kansas City.

Walsh, Jerome T. 1992. Elijah. Pages 464-65 in vol. 2 of *The Anchor Bible Dictionary*. Edited by David Noel Freedman. 6 vols. New York: Doubleday.

Weinfeld, Moshe. 1972. The Worship of Moloch and the Queen of Heaven and Its Background. *Ugaritische Forschungen* 4, 133-54.

Wesley, John. n.d. *Notes on the Bible*; access at: www.ccel.org/ccel/wesley/notes.html or www.biblestudytools.com/commentaries/wesleys-explanatory-notes or http://wesley.nnu.edu/john-wesley/john-wesleys-notes-on-the-bible/1-2 Kgs.

White, Marsha. 1994. Naboth's Vineyard and Jehu's Coup: The Legitimation of a Dynastic Extermination. *Vetus Testamentum* 44, 1:66-76.

Wiggins, Steve. 2007. *A Reassessment of Asherah with Further Considerations of the Goddess*. Piscataway, NJ: Gorgias Press.

Winslow, Karen Strand. 2005. *Early Jewish and Christian Memories of Moses' Wives: Exogamist Marriage and Ethnic Identity*. Lewiston, NY: Edwin Mellen Press.

———. 2012. God's Covenant Partners in the Bible. Pages 49-51 in *Relational Theology: Issues and Implications*. Edited by Karen Strand Winslow, Thomas J. Oord, and Brint Montgomery. Eugene, OR: Wipf & Stock.

———. Forthcoming 2017. Akedah as Apologia: The Function of Genesis 22 for Second Temple Jews. In *Orthodoxy and Orthopraxis: Essays in Tribute to Paul Livermore*. Edited by Douglas R. Cullum and J. Richard Middleton. Toronto: Clements Publishing Group, Inc.

Wiseman, D. J. 1956. *Chronicles of the Chaldean Kings (626-656) in the British Museum*. London: British Museum.

Zorn, Jeffrey R. 1992. Elath (Place). Page 429 in vol. 2 of *The Anchor Bible Dictionary*. Edited by David Noel Freedman. 6 vols. New York: Doubleday.

TABLE OF SIDEBARS

Sidebars	Location
Bloodguilt	1 Kgs 2:5-6
LXX Additions	Behind the Text for 1 Kgs 12:1—14:20
Archaeological Finds at Dan	1 Kgs 12:28-29
The Donkey and the Lion	1 Kgs 13:23-25
The Indictment of Jeroboam	From the Text for 1 Kgs 13:1-34
Asherah	Behind the Text for 1 Kgs 16:29—22:53 [22:54 HB]
Kings and Prophets—Divided Kingdom 931—586 BC	1 Kgs 22:51-53 [52-54 HB]
Moabite Stone	2 Kgs 3:4-8
Child Sacrifice	2 Kgs 3:26-27
The Kings Named Ben-Hadad	Behind the Text for 2 Kgs 8:7-15
The Tel Dan Inscription	Behind the Text for 2 Kgs 9:14—10:36
The Babylonian Chronicle	2 Kgs 19:36-37
The Text of the Siloam Inscription	2 Kgs 20:20-21

MAPS

Maps	Location
Map 1, Tribal Allocations	30
Map 2, Early Israel and Neighboring Peoples	33
Map 3, Geography of Israel	34
Map 4, The Divided Kingdom and Neighboring Nations	38
Map 5, Israel and Judah: The Divided Kingdom	118
Map 6, Assyrian Empire	236

INTRODUCTION

A. Overview of Content

Whereas the books of 1 and 2 Samuel report how and why Israel became a monarchy and continue the story of David, 1 and 2 Kings, as the name implies, focus on the subsequent kings of Israel and Judah and their relationships to prophets and other nations. David's story comes to a conclusion in 1 Kgs 1—2, where he is depicted as rising one last time to name Solomon as his successor. David ruled a kingdom that he procured from Saul's supporters, and which he united through negotiations, political astuteness, and shrewd marriages, as well as successful battles. Despite his failures and foibles as a father, covenant keeper, and ruler, David is acclaimed as the ideal king of Israel throughout the Scriptures.

Yahweh's promise in 2 Sam 7:15-16 to David that one of his sons would forever sit on the throne was fulfilled beginning with Solomon and lasted through 2 Kgs 25:1-7, the reign of Zedekiah (586 BC), whom the Babylonians deposed. As 2 Kings concludes, Zedekiah's nephew, Jehoiachin, who had been exiled to Babylon in 597 BC, was brought out of prison to eat at the Babylonian king's table. This may have provided other exiled Jews with a bit of hope for their own circumstances. Indeed, many of the exiles in Babylon were not captives or slaves but were allowed to own homes and live in their own communities.

First and Second Kings are the final books in the section called the Former Prophets in the Hebrew Bible and are preceded there by Joshua, Judges, and 1—2 Samuel. The Former Prophets section is followed by the Latter Prophets, which together form the middle division of the Hebrew Bible: Prophets. The second section of the Hebrew Bible is settled between Torah and Writings. The title Former Prophets underscores the significance of prophets and prophecy to Israel's story as it continues in Joshua—2 Kings. Prophets appear throughout the books of Kings to guide kings back to the covenant and to warn them of impending disaster if they fail to obey. First and Second Kings provide the contexts for the messages of preexilic prophets Amos, Hosea, Isaiah, Micah, Nahum, Habakkuk, Zephaniah, and Jeremiah. The books bearing their names make sense only when read with the background that 1 and 2 Kings provides. Some specific examples of this include 2 Kgs 16, which provides the setting for Isaiah's prophecy to King Ahaz in Isa 7. Isaiah appears to King Hezekiah in 2 Kgs 20, and the prophet Jonah is mentioned in 2 Kgs 14:25 (although this passage does not allude to the events of the book of Jonah).

The purpose of these prophetic books about the kings of Israel is to teach later generations of God's people that adhering to Yahweh and the stipulations of the covenant will bring peace and prosperity to the community of God. Any hope of returning to the land or remaining there rests on the choices of living listeners to repent and walk in the ways of Yahweh, as revealed through his prophets, including especially Moses (see Deut 34). This is the repeated message of Deuteronomy, the last book in the Torah division of the Hebrew Bible. The Former Prophets carries this ideology through to its closing verses.

The first chapters of 1 Kings depict the unruly manner in which David's kingdom was transferred to his son Solomon, whose mother was Bathsheba, the wife of Uriah, the loyal soldier whom David had killed. The characters in this drama are familiar from 2 Samuel, but as Solomon's generation thrived and then passed, the story becomes populated with new principals who maneuvered for position as the monarchy gave way to a divided kingdom—Israel in the north and Judah in the south. The narrative of 1 and 2 Kings continues with interwoven accounts of the development and demise of these two nations. In Judah, a descendant of David continued his dynasty; in Israel, numerous dynasties peppered the list of kings. The two kingdoms interacted, as allies or enemies.

The narrator uses Deuteronomy's standards to evaluate the kings of both Israel and Judah, beginning with Solomon. Deuteronomy 17:14-20 is a set of guidelines for kings that is an indictment of Solomon and the other kings who ignored the stipulations of the Mosaic covenant as described in Deuteronomy and other places throughout the Torah (Genesis—Deuteronomy). Did the kings keep a copy of the Law before them and read it all the days of their lives, learning to fear Yahweh, and observing all the laws and statutes, neither turning aside from it nor exalting themselves above the members of their community? Did they acquire many wives for themselves or silver or gold or horses from Egypt? First Kings 11 demonstrates how closely Solomon fit Deut 17's instructions about what a king should not do.

Whereas 1 and 2 Samuel are comprised of stories that illustrate the Deuteronomistic theme—Saul is a clear example—the narrator makes few explicit remarks to that effect (1 Sam 8:11-18 and ch 12 are exceptions). However, 1 and 2 Kings not only produce stories to demonstrate Deuteronomistic principles but also summarize the rule of each king according to these standards, which prohibit graven images, worshipping at shrines outside of Jerusalem, and syncretism (worshipping other gods together with Yahweh). The narrator blames Jeroboam, the first king of Israel after the schism under Rehoboam (Solomon's son), for making his people sin by establishing worship of two golden calves (1 Kgs 12:25-33). The narrator ultimately credits the downfall of both nations to their kings' failures to keep the covenant with Yahweh, which demanded service to Yahweh alone and social justice.

B. Authorship, Sources, Date, Provenance, Audience, Occasion, Purpose, Sociological/Cultural Issues, Textual History

The books of Kings cover four hundred years of Israel's history, 970—562 BC, recounted from a theological perspective through a Deuteronomistic lens, as mentioned above. By using the past—the experiences of the ancestors—Jewish scribes taught their people (including future generations) how to be and remain the people of God. From this perspective, unnamed Jewish scribes produced an account of four centuries of the monarchy, which is occasionally confirmed by texts of the Assyrians, Babylonians, and Egyptians. The scribes responsible for 1 and 2 Kings are appropriately considered "producers," because these books are the result of the creation, selection, supplementation, and creative redaction of ancient sources throughout the preexilic (900—586 BC), exilic (586-536 BC), and postexilic (536—ca. 333 BC) eras. They were produced in order to create an identity-confirming history and theology for Israel.

Martin Noth (1943) designated the Former Prophets collection of the Hebrew Bible as the Deuteronomistic History (DH). He chose this label based on linguistic formulae, common chronology, and on how this division emphasizes the theme of Deuteronomy: those who keep the Mosaic covenant will prosper; those who defy its terms will be stricken with famine, war, exile, and destruction (Deut 27:11-29; compare Lev 26). Noth believed the Deuteronomistic emphases comprised a cohesive work that became the foundation for the final form of the books of the Former Prophets—the DH was not a later overlay. In his view, the work was written during the exile by a single author using previous sources and traditions. Most scholars have accepted Noth's theory in general, but they debate the date of writing and the theory of a single author. The books of Kings represent the Deuteronomistic unity of theme but also display literary unevenness and multiple redactions.

Thus, subsequent scholars increasingly posit that the production of the DH (hereafter: DtrH) was more complex: a series of redactional levels both before and after the exile, although no extant documents provide extratextual evidence for multiple layers of composition and redaction. The theory of multiple redactions is credible because, before the text was fixed, it was shaped and handled by generations of scribes for whom this story held great significance as they made theological and pedagogical sense of Israel's past for the sake of the present and future. (See the Introduction to Judges in this commentary series [Branson 2009, 26-30]; McKenzie 1991, 4-19, esp. 17-19, 117-34; Holloway 1992, 72-73, 82 and further bibliography there.)

Large sections of Kings (and 2 Samuel) were formed by cohesive narratives that may have been earlier oral and written traditions: the court history (2 Sam 9—20; 1 Kgs 1—2), the narrative on the reign of Solomon (1 Kgs 3—11), and the prophetic narratives (1 Kgs 17:1—2 Kgs 8:15). At the end of many summaries of kings' reigns within 1—2 Kings, readers are directed to consult now lost (nonextant) royal court archives used as sources for Kings. They include: "the book of the annals of Solomon" (1 Kgs 11:41); "the book of the annals of the kings of Israel" (1 Kgs 14:19; 15:31); "the book of the annals of the kings of Judah" (1 Kgs 14:29).

During the production period, these texts were subject to shaping, editing, expansion, subtraction, and commentary as they were promulgated—orally and in writing. Ultimately, through this process, they were authorized, preserved as Scripture, and eventually transmitted without intentional changes. We know from analysis of the texts at Qumran (300 BC—AD 68) that the copying of biblical texts before the turn of the era (among the Qumran scribes) was a more fluid practice than afterward. The extant copies from later and outside of Qumran do not differ from each other in spelling and word order. It is thus assumed that they became fixed and were carefully copied up through and subsequent to the time of the Masoretes (AD fifth—tenth centuries).

The final redaction of Kings, and that of the Former Prophets, or Deuteronomistic History (DtrH), cannot be before 562 BC when Jehoiachin was released from his Babylonian prison (2 Kgs 25:27-30). It could, of course, be later. Twenty-five years later (536 BC), the Persians conquered Babylon and allowed the Jews (and other Babylonian captives) to return to their homelands, directing officials and funds to restore political and physical structures, including the essential literature (see Ezra-Nehemiah). The postexilic handlers of the traditions found in 1 and 2 Kings included those among the community of previously exiled Jews who rebuilt the temple in the province of Persian Yehud (Judah), with the Torah (Genesis through Deuteronomy) as their constitution. They did not have a king, and their establishment within the land depended upon the support of Persian authorities for the practices and traditions of previously displaced peoples, which included literary culture. Priests and scribes laid up the scrolls they had produced in archives in this second temple and brought them out for public reading and instruction.

In the Hebrew Bible, 1 and 2 Kings was one book and does not appear divided in Hebrew manuscripts until the Biblia Rabbinica version of 1516-17, probably following some Greek manuscripts in which 1 and 2 Samuel and 1 and 2 Kings comprise the four books of Kings. The rabbis who contributed to the Talmud (*B. Bat.* 15a) ascribed the books of Kings to Jeremiah. Indeed, the book of Jeremiah contains clear Deuteronomistic agendas that remind readers of editorial comments in 1 and 2 Kings and Deuteronomy itself.

C. History and Geography of the Period

Whereas Egypt dominated Canaan during the fifteenth through thirteenth centuries BC, in the middle of the twelfth century BC (the close of the Late Bronze Age), Egypt weakened, allowing the tribal confederation and nascent monarchy of Israel to develop, a story told from Israel's perspective in Joshua, Judges, and 1 and 2 Samuel, as well as the books of Kings. Other small kingdoms in the area—Philistia, Syria, Phoenicia, Ammon, Edom, and Moab—also emerged. The books of Kings refer to these peoples' battles with the kings and commanders of Israel's armies over borders, property, and resources, as well as to the coalitions they sometimes formed against the greater nations that began to harass all of them. Assyria and Babylon, the eventual superpowers to the northeast that figured prominently in the respective collapses of Israel and Judah, appear at crucial points in 2 Kings, as does Egypt.

The biblical text provides the only extant and cohesive account of Israel/Judah during this period and explains why Saul, David, and Solomon ruled all the tribes, but Solomon's son Rehoboam and his descendants ruled Judah, which absorbed Benjamin and Simeon. Kings implies that Judah and Israel were fairly evenly endowed states, but archaeological excavations of settlements, inscriptions, and artifacts demonstrate that the northern kingdom, Israel, was wealthier, more centralized, and more powerful than Judah until the eighth century BC, when it was conquered by Assyria (722 BC).

At that time Ahaz became king and submitted to Assyria, buying time to grow, prosper, and gain autonomy. Jerusalem grew from 10 acres to 150 acres and its population from one thousand to twelve thousand, according to estimates of Nahman Avigad, Ronnie Reich, and Eli Shukron, who excavated the Jewish quarter and the city of David (Finkelstein 2006, 129). Israel, on the other hand, was besieged by Shalmaneser V of Assyria and conquered by his successor, Sargon II. Some Israelites were deported and others fled south to Judah in the last quarter of the eighth century BC. In addition, 2 Kgs 17:24, as well as Aramaic and cuneiform texts, announce the arrival of immigrants to Samaria and Bethel.

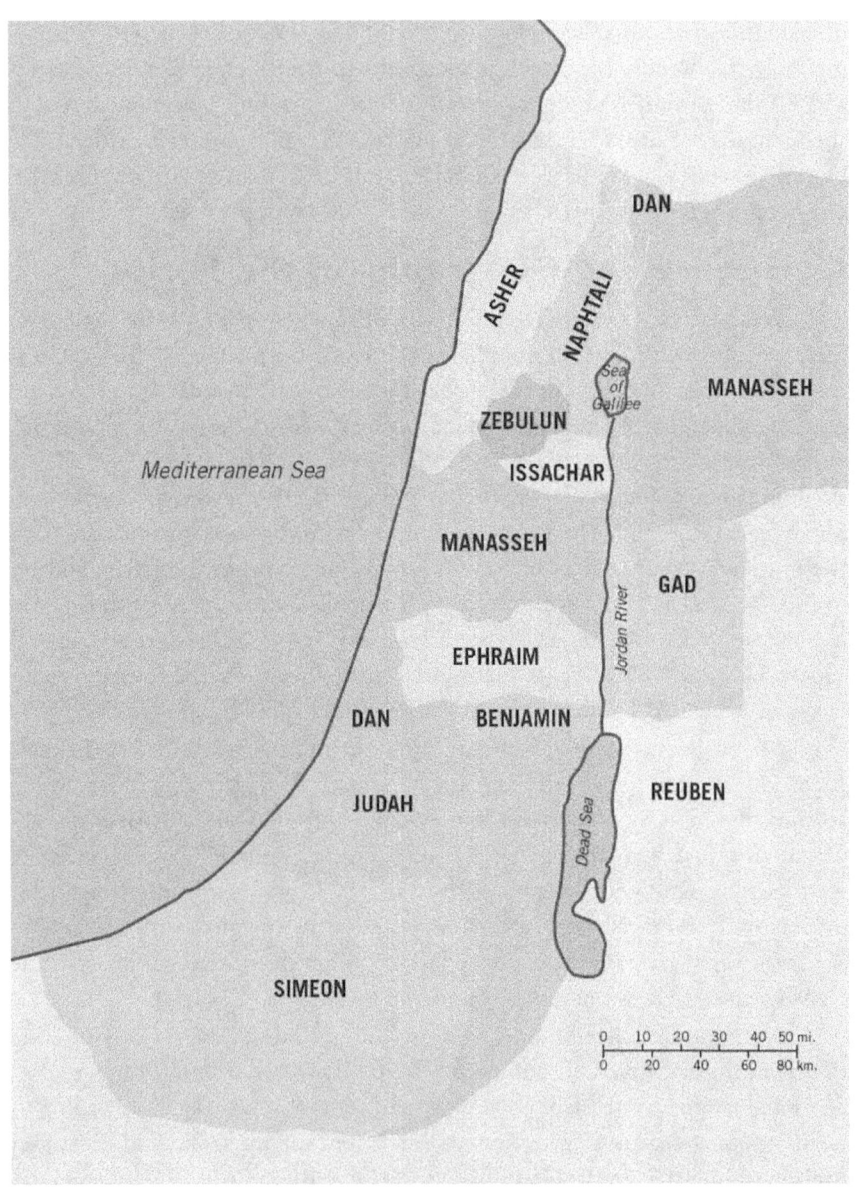

Map 1, Tribal Allocations

With Assyria's protection and the influx of southern Israel refugees, Judah expanded. The consequent thriving economy and widespread literacy during this period left evidence in the archaeological record of a centralized government and its building programs.

Finkelstein claims that Samuel and Kings were written during this period, believing that only during a time of widespread literacy could such accounts have been written (2006, 128-34). However, widespread literacy is not necessary for court scribes to write annals and other royal records, which were used by the scribes to develop the written account of 1 and 2 Kings during the reigns of Hezekiah, Josiah, and during the exile. In addition, we know wider literacy existed in the tenth century BC (Iron Age IIA) from the inscription found at Khirbet Qeiyafa in the Valley of Elah. It has five lines of text totaling fifty letters and was found in the walls of a fortified city also dating to the tenth century BC. The inscription is written in proto-Canaanite script—the longest inscription of its kind—but the language is Hebrew. According to Garfinkel, who led the excavation, the words "don't do," "king," "judge," and "servant" are all legible. This Hebrew inscription predates the other ostracon by one hundred years or more (Shanks 2009). This find also addresses the controversy among archaeologists over the abilities of David and Solomon to establish a state or kingdom at that early date.

To return to our discussion of the eighth century BC, during the reign of Ahaz's son Hezekiah, workmen hewed the Siloam Tunnel and inscribed the story of its completion on its bedrock wall. The reform of Hezekiah, which eventuated in his rebellion against Assyria, is confirmed by the excavation of dismantled sanctuaries and altars in the countryside and settlements outside of Jerusalem. This nationwide religious reform would have integrated the refugees from Israel with Judah's population. When the reform led to revolution, Hezekiah paid dearly with the loss of people, towns, and fields. Jerusalem remained, and Hezekiah was forced to pay tribute, as both 2 Kgs 18 and Sennacherib's Prism attests.

Manasseh, Hezekiah's son, adopted a compliant stance with Assyria and it paid off. In the seventh century BC, he expanded agriculture to the desert of the Dead Sea in order to feed the people and pay the heavy taxes to Assyria. He reestablished copper mines, trade with other Assyrian-controlled states to the south, some Arabic, and built towns along the caravan routes. Judah flourished under Manasseh's long reign but began to falter when his grandson, Josiah, died at the hands of Pharaoh Necho of Egypt in 609 BC. Josiah had become king as a child and, when grown, continued Judah's expansion. He also initiated a religious reform in the late seventh century BC, like his great-grandfather Hezekiah had in the eighth. During this period, Assyria weakened and withdrew, while Egypt was on the rise, even as far as Philistia to the west of Judah. No explanation is given in Kings for Josiah's death at Megiddo. Twelve years later, Babylon dominated the area, laid siege to Jerusalem, and captured King Jehoiachin and other nobles. In 586 BC, Babylon burned the temple and its city to the ground and marched more Judahites to Babylon, beginning the period of exile described in the last chapter of 2 Kings.

Some events described in the books of Kings correlate with the same events mentioned in tenth through sixth century BC Egyptian, Assyrian, and Babylonian datable accounts of this period, which are then used to date the dynasties and wars of Israel and Judah. In this discussion, I will refer to a number of these extrabiblical texts, some of which have been unearthed by archaeologists in the last century. The information in these ancient texts may be compared not only to biblical testimony found in Kings about the history of Israel but also to the results of archaeological surveys concerning the land's geography.

D. Geography, Settlement Patterns, Statehood and Extent of Israel's Boundaries according to the Biblical and Extrabiblical Texts and Archaeology

1. Geography and Settlement of the Land

Egyptian cuneiform texts from the Amarna archives and dated to the fourteenth century BC demonstrate qualities of the topography and politics of the land of Canaan that later and gradually became dominated by Israelites. When Egypt controlled the region's fortified city-states, the vassal leaders wrote to Pharaohs Amenhotep III and Akhenaten, complaining of tension with shepherds (Shosu), outlaws (Apiru), and one another, such as the northern vassal, Labayu (Finkelstein 2006, 69). In one of these Akkadian letters, Abdi-Heba of Jerusalem appealed to Egypt for help in protecting his villagers from raiders who roamed the mountains and woods and attacked the peasants, while attracting some of them to their bandit ranks. Abdi-Heba's depiction of life in the highlands (later the territory and kingdom of Judah) reflects what geographers and archaeologists know about this region's persistent physical characteristics.

Nomadic shepherds and bandits, as described in the Amarna letters, co-existed with and sometimes tormented peasants of scattered settled villages in the Judean hill country centuries before and during the time of David. Jerusalem, the site of much of the action of Kings, was an ancient city, continuously occupied from before 3500 BC. It is located in the highlands of northern Judah or near the center of the united Israel. Along with Hebron and Bethlehem, Jerusalem lies on a rather isolated highland north-south plateau, the terrain of which is woody, rugged, and rocky and whose soil is poor and rainfall limited. To the southwest of Jerusalem is the Shephelah, a series of populated, fertile foothills. East of Jerusalem, the hills drop to desert, the Dead Sea, and the Jordan valley, an arid land of cliffs, canyons, and caves. The Beersheba valley lies south of Jerusalem and Hebron, and its climate is more moderate. As the

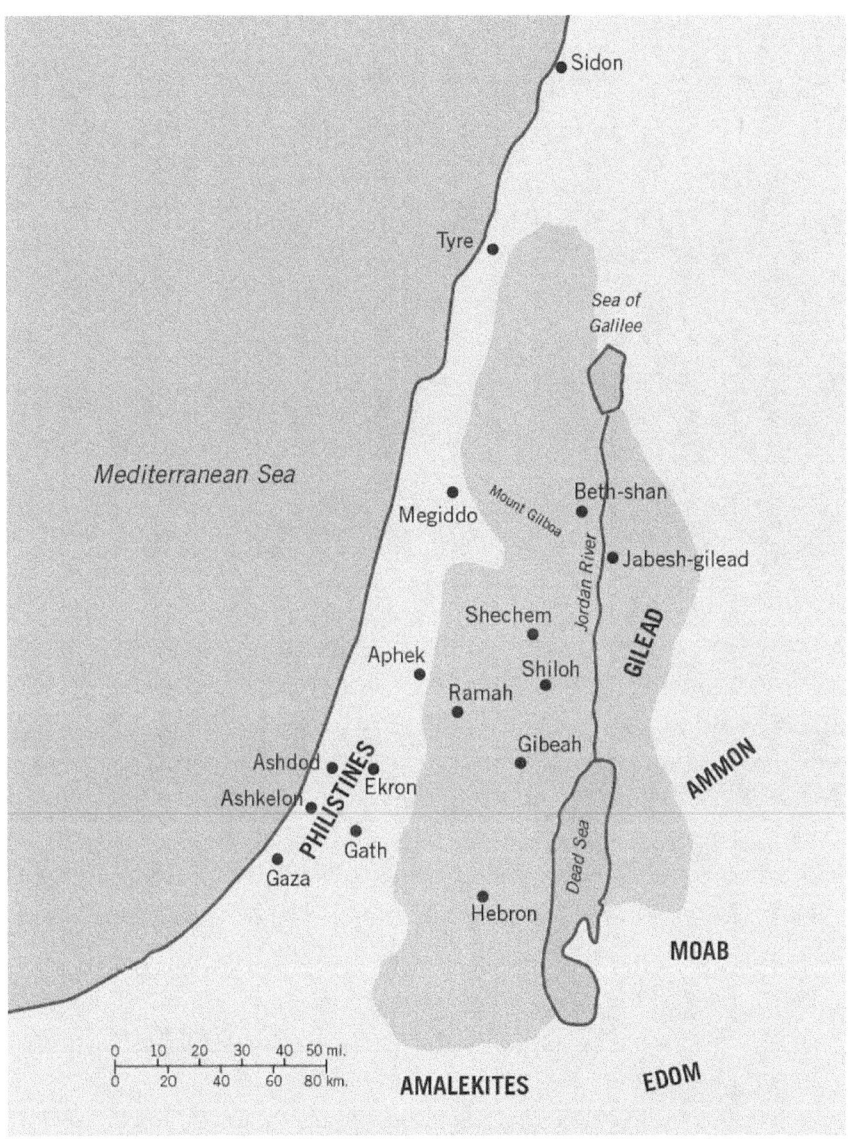

Map 2, Early Israel and Neighboring Peoples

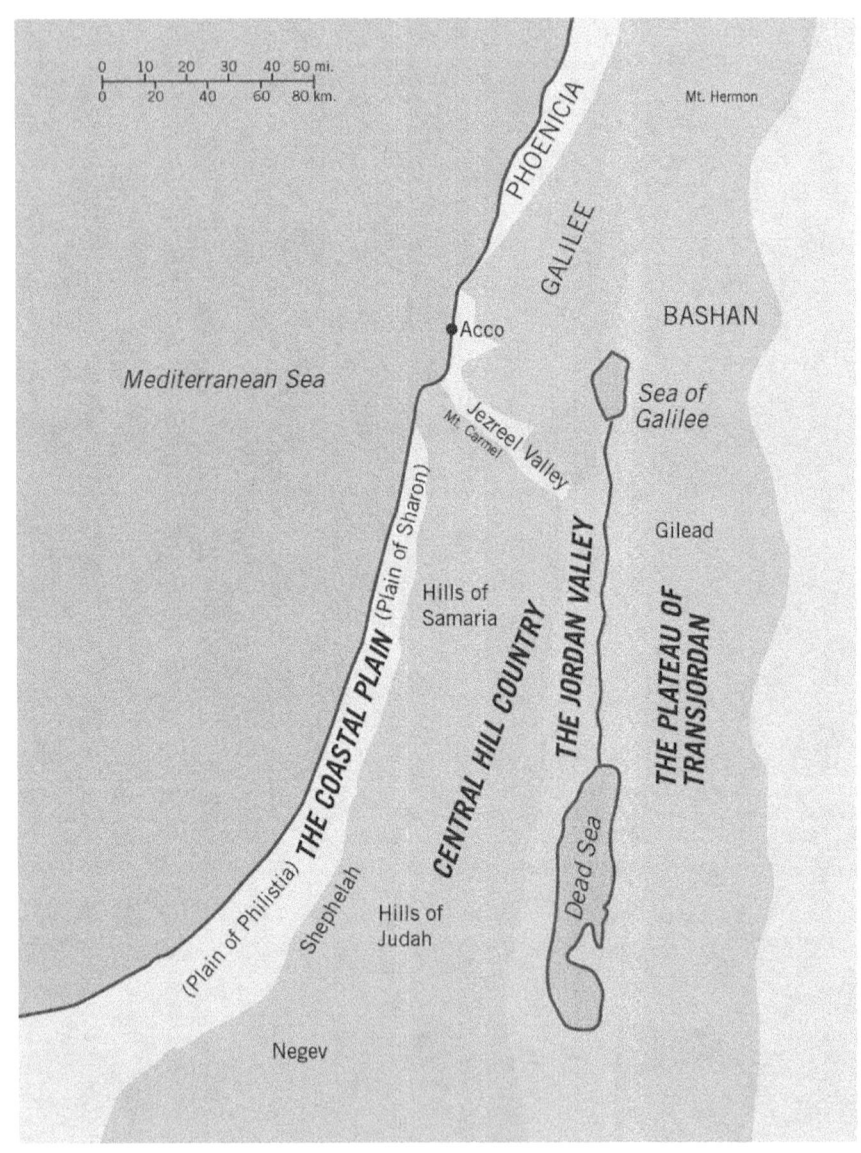

Map 3, Geography of Israel

Late Bronze Age passed into Iron Age I (twelfth century BC), the hill country of Judah's population was around five thousand.

The area belonging to what became the northern kingdom, "Israel" in the books of Kings, was comprised of the Joseph tribes, as well as Issachar, Zebulun, Asher, Naphtali, and Dan. This region was less isolated, more populated, with predictable rainfall. Israel's economy prospered throughout the late tenth and ninth centuries BC. The excavation of structures such as monuments, palaces, and walls provide evidence of a government, armies, and storage facilities (Finkelstein 2006, 99). According to Kings, the Omride dynasty of Israel built Samaria as their capital, and excavations at the city indicate that it became an important center in the early ninth century BC. Other palaces, stables, monuments, and gates were built throughout Israel by Omri and his descendants.

2. The Extent of Jerusalem's Domination according to Archaeologists

A debate among archaeologists and biblical scholars centers on whether Solomon's administration in Judah was centralized enough to build the city gates that preceded those of Omri. Was Solomon's Jerusalem the capital of a "state," or does the archaeological evidence establish that it should be considered a "chiefdom" and not as organized and powerful as Kings depicts? Attempts to answer this question by archaeologists and biblical historians are based on extensive research across the land surfaces "from Dan to Beersheba" (1 Kgs 4:25 [5:5 HB]).

Israeli and American archaeologists have painstakingly surveyed many biblical sites to study the settlements of the Iron Age, the context for the story told in Samuel—Kings (Iron I [1150—900 BC] and Iron II [900—586 BC]; compare Dever 2001, 127; Finkelstein and Silberman 2001, 114). Archaeologists interpret Iron Age evidence differently and write contrasting accounts of Judah's and Israel's history based on their interpretations. The differences among archaeologists' interpretations are not as great as those among biblical scholars and historians who avidly debate the nature of the evidence and what it means.

How artifacts, extrabiblical texts, and analysis of Iron I-II settlements relate to the biblical text of Kings will be discussed here with reference to differing interpretations of the evidence and how it relates to the biblical account. I will introduce an example of one of the primary conflicts about the historiography of Kings, which concerns the size, wealth, and centralization of Solomon's reign and has implications for understanding the relative strength of Israel and Judah and their dynasties.

During Iron I (twelfth to tenth centuries BC), the archaeological record of twenty settlements in the Judean hill country around Jerusalem assigns to them a population of around five to ten thousand. The highlands north of Jerusalem (Gibeon, Shechem, the Jezreel valley, and Shiloh), in contrast, expanded to a population of over forty thousand, supported by their cultivation of grain, grapes, and olives (Finkelstein 2006, 68). This area's settlements, associated in the biblical text with Saul, were destroyed and abandoned in the late tenth century BC (930 BC and following), whereas the settlements in the northernmost regions of the highlands (Israel) and those across the Jordan in the area of Gilead also grew in number and remained occupied until the eighth and seventh centuries BC.

This destruction, revealed through surface surveys and deep excavation of a few sites, is related to two texts—one from the Bible (1 Kgs 14:25-26) and one found on the Hypostyle Hall in the temple of Amun at Karnak in Egypt. The biblical text claims that Pharaoh Shishak of Egypt took away the treasures of the temple and the king's palaces in Jerusalem in the fifth year of Rehoboam or 926 BC. The Karnak wall relief shows Pharaoh Sheshonq I of Egypt (who ruled in the tenth century BC) smiting figures labeled by place names that include Megiddo of the lowlands, the Israelite area north of Jerusalem, and many other sites, but no towns of Judah—no Jerusalem.

Most archaeologists and biblical scholars identify Sheshonq I with the Shishak of 1 Kgs 14:25 (see 1 Kgs 11:40; 2 Chr 12:2-4; compare 1 Kgs 9:15). They theorize that his campaigns, which occurred between 950 and 900 BC, represent Egypt's attempt to reassert power over Canaan/Israel during a period when older Canaanite groups and later Israelite settlements had begun to thrive (Finkelstein 2006, 78).

First Kings 14:25-26 does not mention the destruction of surrounding areas, but rather allows that Shishak took all the treasures of Jerusalem. Did Shishak perhaps offer Rehoboam terms of peace through tribute of all the treasures in Jerusalem on his way north to burn other towns? On the other hand, why would Shishak have not mentioned this triumph on the inscription at Karnak? We should recall here that the text claims that Solomon married the daughter of Pharaoh (1 Kgs 3:1).

Remains of uniquely treated pottery at the three gate sites of Hazor, Gezer, and Megiddo have been dated to the tenth century BC or before because they lie in a layer of destruction attributed to Shishak (Dever 2001, 134-36). These gates are featured in the debate over the centralization of Solomon's government and its influence. We will refer only to the six-chambered Gezer Gate here in order to relate its excavation to Shishak's / Sheshonq I's rampage over the settlements north of Jerusalem, beyond the northern border of Judah in Saul territory (mentioned above). Gezer is not one of those towns but lies to the west of Jerusalem near Philistia. First Kings 9:16 asserts that a pharaoh (probably Siamun, the next to the last king of the Twenty-first Dynasty) had destroyed Gezer and given it to his daughter as her "sending away" gift when she married Solomon early in his reign; so Solomon rebuilt Gezer.

Because of a traditional consensus on the date of Shishak's campaign, 925 BC, the destruction layer at Gezer is assumed to have been caused by him; thus its pottery is assigned to that time and before. By implication, then, this gate was built and used between 970 and 930 BC, the traditional date of Solomon's reign (Dever 2001, 134). If Solomon could build well-engineered gates such as these in areas far outlying Jerusalem, then he was a head of a centralized, organized, and wealthy state, as the Bible describes. Thus, we have independent, archaeological witnesses to the biblical account of a unified and far-reaching state under Solomon. William Dever and others use these conclusions in the debate against the "minimalist/revisionist" claim that Solomon never existed and Kings was not written until the late Persian period, or the milder version: if Solomon lived, he headed a small, nonthreatening chiefdom like his father, David.

Nonetheless, another prominent archaeologist, Israel Finkelstein, claims that using the pottery to date the well-crafted Gezer Gate is circular. If we are seeking a date for Shishak's campaign to verify the biblical account (Egyptian texts of the Twenty-first to Twenty-second Dynasties are fragmentary), we cannot use the "tenth century BC" pottery, which is dated on the basis of a destruction attributed to Shishak in 925 BC. A destruction layer exists, but we cannot demonstrate who did it or when, so we cannot date the pottery found there. Nonetheless, Finkelstein places Shishak in the mid-late tenth century BC and is convinced that Shishak campaigned in this area to revive Egyptian influence over a traditional Canaan (including Megiddo and the emerging chiefdom Tel Masos [2006, 76-77]). At Megiddo, where traditional Canaanite artifacts were found in and under a layer of destruction, a stele set up by Shishak claims victory over the city. Could not this witness be extrapolated to Gezer? Both cities are listed in Shishak's Karnak inscription as having been burned by him.

Finkelstein believes Shishak did not mention Jerusalem (1 Kgs 14:25-26) because it was too small to be a threat to him, whereas he was threatened by the densely populated and expanding territory associated with Saul north of Jerusalem (ibid., 80). In other words, in aligning the Karnak list with the biblical account of Saul's military crusades, Finkelstein affirms the biblical basis for the strength of an expanding northern entity that threatened Egypt, but not the biblical view of an empire for Solomon. The strength of Saul's territory was thus thwarted by Egypt, while David's descendants in Judah were left alone. He suggests that Jerusalem's king at the time of the Shishak raids was a "passive partner" in an "Egypto-Philistine alliance" (ibid., 84). Perhaps this alliance was aided by the fact that Rehoboam's father had married an Egyptian princess and Rehoboam gave Shishak all his riches (1 Kgs 3:1; 14:25-26). This earlier alliance is significant, as is the fact that no record of violence at Jerusalem or among the Philistine cities exists. These cities, like Jerusalem, show no evidence of destruction during the late tenth century BC, unlike the communities in territory associated with Saul.

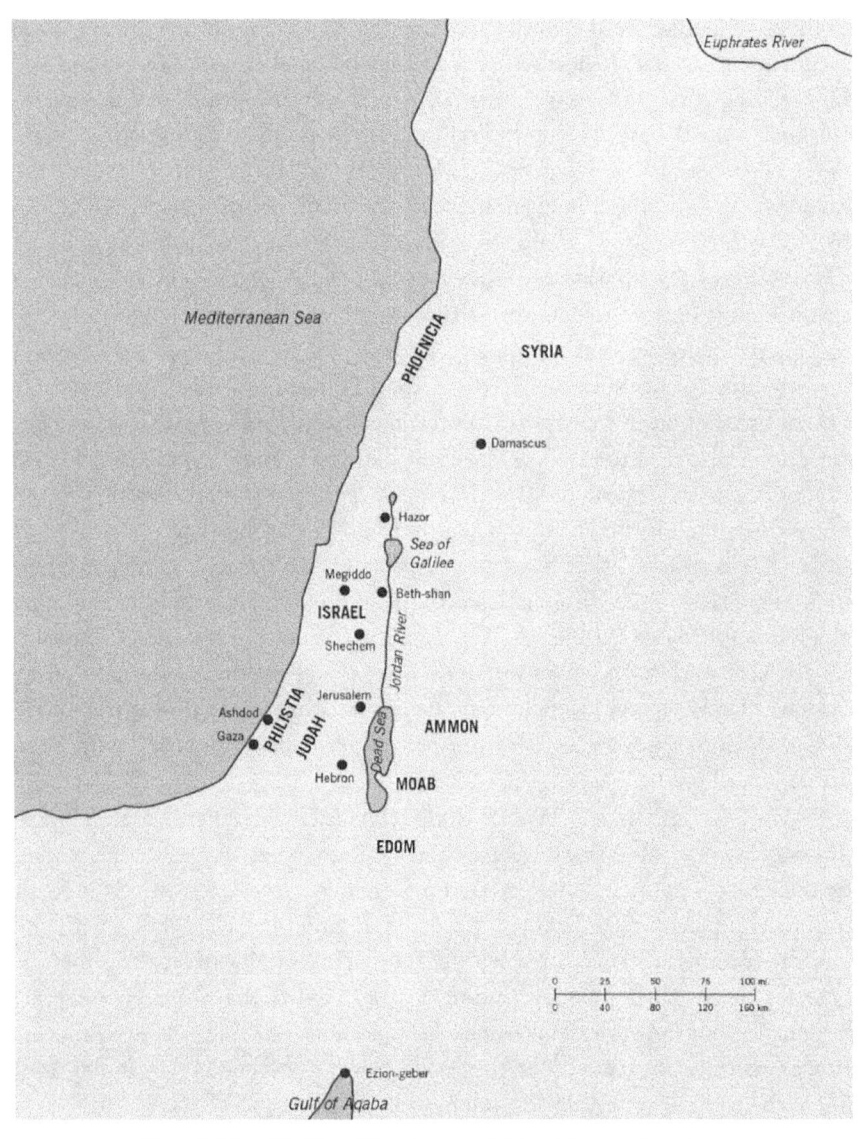

Map 4, The Divided Kingdom and Neighboring Nations

3. Using the Bible with Archaeology

Finkelstein and Dever represent archaeologists who consider the Bible to be an important source of Israel's history and use the Bible as a supplement to archaeological endeavors, but not always to the same effect. Dever affirms a strong centralized government of Judah in the mid-late tenth century BC, organized and wealthy enough to build cities, gates, and horse stables such as those found at Gezer. On the other hand, Finkelstein's excavation of settlements in the Judean hill country have convinced him that Jerusalem was more like a village during this time and did not control a centralized state until the time of Hezekiah in the ninth century BC. Since the story of Kings was written from a Judean perspective, with influence from Israelite refugees after the fall of Samaria around 722 BC, he believes that the writers "remembered" Solomon's glory as greater than it could have been.

Although neither archaeologist accepts the Bible as strictly history, both are convinced it contains a good deal of historical material. They disagree on which aspects of Kings represent history and which are more stylized. Dever claims that the biblical account of a centralized government under Solomon is reflected in the archaeological evidence. They concur that the latter shows the biblical writers and editors lived in the preexilic, exilic, and postexilic periods, not in the late Persian and Greek periods, as the minimalist school argues. The latter—represented by Philip R. Davies, Niels Lemche, and Thomas Thompson—insist that ancient Israel and its literature was a creation of fourth- and third-century BC Jews who were influenced by the great literature of the Greeks to make their own. They attempt to rest their case on archaeology as well but have made the mistake of denying independent references to the Judean monarchy, such as that found in the Tel Dan inscription. Some minimalists have suggested the inscription is a planted forgery and others ignore it (Dever 2001, 30, 128-30), but archaeologists and epigraphers affirm its authenticity (Finkelstein 2006, 261-66).

4. Inscriptions

Tel Dan is the site of the northernmost settlement of the kingdom of Israel and has been excavated for remains of Middle Bronze through Iron Age cities. Gila Cook, who was working there in the summer of 1993, found an Aramaic inscription from the ninth century BC just outside the city gates, which contains a line that mentions the slaying of the Israelite king Joram (847-842 BC), *and* a son of the "House of David, Ahaziahu." The black basalt inscription is ascribed to Hazael of Damascus, who ruled in 835 BC, around the time the lines were chiseled. The inscription from Tel Dan is the first extrabiblical witness to "the house of David," and it confirms that David was the founder of a dynasty that included his descendant Ahaziah, who lived a century later.

The 2 Kgs 9:14-27 account of the battle, which also describes the death of both kings, ascribes the assaults to the traitor Israelite general Jehu, who, as an eventual result, became king of Israel. Thus, the Tel Dan inscription credits a king of Aram, probably Hazael, who calls himself the son of the Aramaic god Hadad, with overpowering both kings. The biblical text, however, credits Jehu, an Israelite king, with destroying the house of Ahab. Jehu is depicted as a kneeling vassal paying tribute to the Assyrian king Shalmaneser III on the Black Obelisk found in Nimrud in Iraq and presently resides in the British Museum in London. This Assyrian text calls Jehu a "son of Omri," which is ironic given the biblical account of his destruction of the house of Omri.

First Kings 20—22 describes the attack by Syria upon the Israelite capital of Samaria, during Ahab's reign, although he is not the hero of this particular battle. The Kurkh Monolith of Shalmaneser III of Assyria (responsible for the Black Obelisk of 841 BC) lists Ahab as a participant in the battle. Tiglath-Pileser III's annals of 734 BC mention Ahaz of Judah, and annals of Shalmaneser V and Sargon II announce the fall of Samaria. In addition, the deportation of Jehoiachin is reported in Babylonian cuneiform accounts. The sack of Jerusalem was paralleled by the razing of other Judean cities, which archaeological excavations have consistently verified.

This discussion provides a glimpse of the use archaeologists make of artifacts, surveys, and excavations. They interpret their discoveries and relate them to the biblical story, sometimes affirming biblical reports, sometimes denying them, while hypothesizing over the agendas of the biblical authors to remember history and traditions the way they have, especially when they do *not* comport with the history reconstructed through the archaeological evidence. Their interpretations of the latter sometimes conflict with one another, and their willingness to use the Bible as a resource for the history of Israel varies.

Similarly, biblical scholars access the extrabiblical references to Israel and Judah obtained by the archaeologists and produce different conclusions on the veracity of the specifics found in Kings. Nonetheless, the combination of the ancient narrative found in Kings with even older pottery and inscriptions not only provides raw material for reconstructing Israel's history but also helps in constructing the theology of the biblical text as it now stands.

E. Genre, Structure, Literary Outline

After a lengthy account of Solomon's reign (1 Kgs 1—11, ca. 970 BC), 1—2 Kings is organized into a narrative that traces the parallel dynasties of kings of Israel and Judah until both are rendered obsolete. The narrative is a theological history, which includes dialogues, character sketches, speeches, prayers, prophetic oracles, and evaluative overviews, written from a mostly Judahite perspective. A formulaic feature occurs at the beginning and end of each king's reign. The first year of the king of one nation is aligned to the corresponding year within the reign of the king of the other nation. They are evaluated according to whether they did good or evil in the eyes of Yahweh.

When they died, the kings were buried and succeeded by their sons, or, sometimes in Israel, the leader of a coup, who began a new dynasty.

First and Second Kings' chronology between ca. 930 BC and ca. 560 BC cannot be easily reconciled with itself and other dating standards of this period. However, we should not stumble over the problematic arithmetic, because this literature is primarily theological with a historical foundation. It uses history to advocate covenant commitment, wholehearted devotion to the God of Israel, and submission to God's requirements for leading God's people as emphasized by prophets. For those interested in the dates of kings, scholars offer a variety of explanations, some of which are grounded in differences among and corruptions in the extant textual traditions, and the probability that copyists sought to correct suspected errors (Holloway 1992, 76). The dating discrepancies do not affect Kings' explanations for a dynasty remaining or dissolving, nor the order of the kings within each dynasty and kingdom. The dating systems of the scholars attending to these matters do not vary by more than a few years.

F. Theological Themes

First and Second Kings carries forward the focus on the Davidic covenant that 2 Sam 7 introduced as a perpetual dynasty. These books ultimately treat the trauma that unfolded when the dynasty of David first lost the throne of Israel (922 BC) and finally the throne of Judah as well (586 BC).

At the outset of Kings, however, David's son Solomon took up the mandate to build a house for the name of Yahweh, which had been an aspect of the Davidic covenant announced to him by Nathan the prophet (2 Sam 7:13). Solomon initiated the temple project when he responded to Hiram of Tyre's good wishes by asking for cedars from Lebanon. This temple is central to chs 5—10 of 1 Kings, which detail how its materials were acquired and then fashioned into a magnificent structure. The temple of Solomon was viewed as the place for God's name, eyes, and heart (1 Kgs 8). These terms represent God's presence and demonstrate that his house was a place of prayer. Although Israel's God, Yahweh, cannot be confined to a building made with hands, he agreed to place his name there and turn his attention to all who prayed within or toward the house that Solomon built.

The temple took the place of the wilderness tabernacle and came to be viewed by Israel as a place that mediated between heaven and earth. It mirrored the heavenly dwelling place of God and influenced the order of the universe. Although these themes were developed in later Jewish literature, they were grounded in Solomon's blessings and prayers of 1 Kgs 8.

When Yahweh consecrated the temple in ch 9, he also warned Solomon that the temple would fall to ruin if he or his sons failed to submit to the Law, the Torah. Every listener and reader is thus warned as well. If the temple should become desolate, all will know why. It would not be because Yahweh failed but because the kings had broken their covenant with Yahweh. Understandable then, but nonetheless tragic, was the temple's loss at the hands of Babylon at the end of 2 Kings. A ruined temple accompanied the defeat of the Davidic dynasty and preceded their exile to Babylon (2 Kgs 25).

Nonetheless, the theology and practices (prayer, festivals, and sacrifices) that permeated the first temple built by Solomon endured among the Jews who restored and preserved the second temple in the restoration period. The Jerusalem temple was the center of nascent Judaism, and the priorities of its priests and scribes eventually served to authorize the texts that became more and more important to Jews.

Regardless of the extent and nature of the texts underlying Kings before and during the exile, we can be certain that during the postexilic period, the Jews were determined to affirm their renewed identity as people who worshipped Yahweh alone through their rituals, teachings, and texts. Postexilic Jews developed the concept of Scripture, authoritative, sacred, and inspired teachings and texts. Scripture included Israel's story from the very beginning, all of which demonstrated God's creation of, and love and provision for, a people with whom to dwell (see Exod 40; Lev 26:11-12; 1 Kgs 8:12, 22-30; Ezek 37:26-28; Rev 21:3). When the people were besieged, dispersed, enslaved, destroyed, and/or exiled, when the temple was burned and the king dethroned, where was Yahweh? Could Yahweh go with them to Babylon or abide with the people without a temple and holy of holies?

The books of 1 and 2 Kings answer these and other questions such as: Why were Israel and Judah divided, dispersed, and exiled? Was their God, Yahweh, weaker than the gods of Assyria and Babylon? Had he forgotten or broken the covenant made with Israel at Sinai through Moses or with David at Jerusalem?

Confirmed by contemporary prophetic oracles, 1 Kings argues that Yahweh was not weak and neither had he broken the covenant. First and Second Kings demonstrates that the kings and leaders, beginning with Solomon, failed by leading the people to apostasy (serving other gods) by ignoring covenant obligations and abusing the poor and weak. The curses of the covenant (Deut 27—28 and Lev 26) would come to pass after Yahweh had mercifully sent prophets and delayed judgment. When the leaders' evil became as great as that of the Amorites whom Yahweh had removed before their ancestors, Yahweh used other nations to expel them from the land as well (Gen 15:16; Deut 28:45-47; 29:24-28 [23-27 HB]).

Whereas 1 and 2 Kings imparts a Deuteronomistic explanation for the demise (Israel) and exile (Judah) wrought by other nations, hope is also implied, though not as explicitly as in the prophetic oracles of the period. If the survivors returned to Yahweh and renewed their covenant obligations, Yahweh would forgive their sins, restore them to health, and reestablish them in their land (1 Kgs 8:46-53).

The books of Kings also answer the questions: What is prophecy? Who is a true prophet? How can prophecy be tested? For people who were *limping upon two divided opinions* (1 Kgs 18:21) by serving Baal, Yahweh was willing to display his power. The Mount Carmel contest Elijah arranged dramatically revealed that Baal was no god at all. On the other hand, the text indicates that the significance of prophecy lies in the words of direction for the prophets, and of correction for kings and people (1 Kgs 19:11-18). Elijah and Elisha not only produced signs of Yahweh's power but also demonstrated his compassion to the widows and orphans of the land.

G. Hebrew Text Traditions

The scrolls of the library at Qumran included manuscripts of the Jewish Scriptures that were one thousand years older than the oldest previously available. However, Qumran's text of Kings is fragmentary, unlike that of the books of Samuel, and does not resolve the issue of the significance of the old Greek versions for reconstructing the earliest stages of the Hebrew text of Kings. The Qumran caves have portions of 1 Kgs 1, 3, 12, and 22 only. The Masoretic Text's (MT) order is not followed in the Kings of the LXX, and the latter often adds extra information or midrashic detail that puts Solomon in a better light than he appears in the MT. The Aramaic *Targum Pseudo-Jonathan* adheres to the MT without expansions and interpretations. This commentary follows the MT with attention to the other versions. For a detailed list of variants from Greek translations to each passage, see DeVries 1985.

COMMENTARY

THE BOOK OF FIRST KINGS

I. SOLOMON'S ASCENSION AND REIGN: THIRD AND LAST KING IN THE UNITED MONARCHY; SETTING: JERUSALEM: I KINGS 1:1—11:43

OVERVIEW

We learn in 2 Sam 12:24 that Solomon was the second son of Bathsheba and David, the first, the son of David's adultery, having died as a newborn (vv 15-23). Yahweh loved Solomon, naming him Jedidiah, as he conveyed to Nathan the prophet (v 25). Nonetheless, this son is always called "Solomon" (Hebrew: *Shlomo* [*šĕlōmô*] from *Shalom* [*šālôm*]), man of peace, the name his mother and/or father gave him (NIV: "they"; in the Hebrew text, the read version is "she called him," while the written is "he called him" [v 24]). The traditional Hebrew text, which is used as a basis for translation (along with several versions of the Greek text [LXX]) is called the Masoretic Text (MT). The MT records the ancient practice of reading the Scriptures aloud to the congregation by the vowels placed under the consonants and notes in the margin. "She called" is in the margin here. The read version is usually the more traditional, known text because the written version could have been miscopied or intentionally changed (as is probably the case here).

The story of Solomon's reign begins in 1 Kgs 1 when his older brother, Adonijah, who assumed he would be king, held a great feast and did not invite Solomon. At the urgent prompting of Nathan and Bathsheba, a failing David named Solomon king and ordered him to kill men against whom David held grievances. Before doing so, Solomon killed his brother Adonijah (ch 2) and thus he began his "peaceful" reign violently.

Solomon married the daughter of the king of Egypt before asking Yahweh for wisdom at the high place of Gibeon (ch 3). Pleased with this request, God also promised riches and honor. The remainder of this narrative section outlines Solomon's administration, the extent and wealth of his empire, his alliances with other nations, his fame as a wise man, conscripting laborers from Israel and Syria, building his home, then erecting and dedicating the temple to Yahweh (chs 4—8).

After these things, Yahweh appeared again to Solomon, reminding him of covenant obligations and promises (ch 9). Solomon continued building, using forced labor from Israel and slaves from other nations (ch 9). The visit from the Queen of Sheba and another report of Solomon acquiring horses and chariots from Egypt (ch 10) emphasize his fame as a wise and wealthy ruler, who was also ignoring Yahweh's requirements for a king of Israel (Deut 17:14-17).

The narrator seems to favor Solomon's achievements until the all-important summary of Solomon's reign in 1 Kgs 11. This sharply accuses Solomon of apostasy before prophesying adversaries during his lifetime and a divided kingdom after his death. However, a closer reading shows that throughout chs 3—11, the author retains a tone of cool judgment, peppered with qualified praise. By describing Solomon's marriage to an Egyptian, acquiring horses from Egypt, instituting forced labor, building his own house in twice the time it took to build Yahweh's house, and amassing great wealth, the storyteller has implicated Solomon as a king who failed to keep the statutes for a king of Israel set forth in Deut 17:14-17. Thus, even before his foreign wives "turned his heart after other gods" (1 Kgs 11:4), we notice a third king of Israel who began his reign in humility, increased in prowess, and then set himself outside of the covenant laws of Yahweh. In this way Solomon's reign is comparable to those of Saul (1 Sam 9—10; 13—31) and David (1 Sam 16—17; 2 Sam 11—12).

As noted in the Introduction, scholars posit multiple redactions of Kings that may explain differences in authorial perspectives on Solomon throughout these chapters. However, in chs 3—11 the narrator (final redactor) is circumspectly progressing toward ch 11 (where his overtly disappointed stance is similar to that found in Neh 13:26). God's appearances to Solomon in 1 Kgs 3 and 9, and the notice that Yahweh loved him (2 Sam 12:24) make Solomon's apostasy all the more egregious. "The Lord became angry with Solomon because his heart had turned away from the Lord, the God of Israel, who had appeared to him twice" (1 Kgs 11:9).

Furthermore, Solomon's turning away from the law of God did not necessarily begin when he was old. Before we are told he loved God and walked in God's ways, we are told that he made covenants with the king of Egypt sealed by marrying Pharaoh's daughter, whom he kept in the city of David until he had finished building his own house and the house of Yahweh. Even the order of that statement in 1 Kgs 3:1 implies a perspective on Solomon's priorities: his own house is listed first (thirteen years to build [1 Kgs 7:1]), then Yahweh's house (seven years to build [1 Kgs 6:37]).

A. Solomon Ascends to the Throne of David (1:1-53)

BEHIND THE TEXT

Because 1 Kings continues the story of David and the establishment of a monarchy in Israel, 1 and 2 Samuel, Judges, Joshua, and Deuteronomy are all relevant to understanding 1 and 2 Kings. The early audiences of this book were aware of the traditions found in these books, as well as those about the patriarchs (1 Kgs 18:36), Moses (1 Kgs 18:4), and Horeb (1 Kgs 19).

Especially pertinent to 1 Kgs 1—11 are several Deuteronomistic passages: Deut 17:14-20 (as mentioned above), 1 Sam 8:11-18, and 2 Sam 7. In the latter, the prophet Nathan conveyed this promise to David: "The LORD himself will establish a house for you . . . I will raise up your offspring to succeed you . . . I will establish the throne of his kingdom forever . . . Your house and your kingdom will endure forever before me" (2 Sam 7:11-13, 16). This raises expectations not only for David's immediate successor, Solomon, but also for a lasting Davidic dynasty. Since 1—2 Kings concludes with the throne and all Jerusalem in ruins, the unconditional nature of Yahweh's promise to David is questioned and qualified, not only in Kings and in Chronicles' subsequent retelling of the story, but in the Psalms and Latter Prophets.

As literary critics have noted, 1 Kgs 1—2 concludes the larger narrative complex that began in 2 Sam 9—20 (Eissfeldt 1965, 270, 271, 277). The intervening chapters (2 Sam 21—24), which recount incidents, songs, and people connected to David's reign, seem to interrupt an otherwise coherent document. In 1926 Leonhard Rost labeled 2 Sam 9—20 with 1 Kgs 1—2 "the Succession Narrative," because he understood it as a political document explaining how Solomon achieved the throne (DeVries 1985, 8-9). Other scholars who label this section "The Court History of David" more persuasively claim that "the theme of the end cannot be cast over the entire work, which incarnates other important meanings" (Long 1981, 79; Ackroyd 1981, 383).

The court history part I (2 Sam 9—20) features characters that reappear in 1 Kgs 1—2 to place Solomon on his father's throne. The story of an established King David in 2 Sam 9—20 is framed by the closing verses of 2

Sam 8 and 2 Sam 20, which are nearly parallel synopses of his reign over all the tribes. Second Samuel 8 ends with a summary of David's reign and a list of the king's military commanders (Joab and Benaiah), the recorder and secretary, and the priests (Zadok, David's sons, and Abiathar, son of Ahimelek [the MT reverses father and son here, but in every other place, Abiathar is called the son of Ahimelek, who is the son of Ahitub]; see 1 Sam 22:3-20; 23:6; 30:7; and 2 Sam 20:25). Second Samuel 20 concludes by listing Joab, Benaiah, Zadok, and Abiathar. This list also includes Adoram, who is in charge of forced labor, and suggests connections between David's census (2 Sam 24) and the corvée (forced labor), which divides the kingdom later. All of these characters named here figure prominently in the 1 Kgs 1—11 account of Solomon's accession and reign. The first three sons born to David at Hebron—Amnon, son of Ahinoam of Jezreel (1 Sam 25:43); Kileab, son of Abigail (1 Sam 25:1-42); and Absalom, son of Maakah—participate in this story by their absence, which makes Adonijah the eldest as David lay dying (see 2 Sam 3:2-5).

The court history includes the cryptic narrative about how David acquired Bathsheba (daughter of Eliam) as a wife, which is followed by Nathan's proclamation of Yahweh's verdict on David's adultery and murder of Bathsheba's husband. "Therefore the sword shall never depart from your house, for you have despised me, and have taken the wife of Uriah the Hittite to be your wife" (2 Sam 12:10 NRSV; see 11:1—12:15). Second Samuel 12:24-25 reports that Solomon was conceived when David consoled Bathsheba after the death of their first son (whose death was part of the judgment against David). Nathan the prophet was sent to announce that Yahweh loved Solomon (Jedidiah). According to 2 Samuel, Solomon was Bathsheba's second son after Nathan (see 2 Sam 5:14-16), but 1 Chr 3:1-8 lists Solomon as the fourth son of Bathshua (daughter of Ammiel).

David practiced a policy of noninterference with several of his sons, if not all his children, although their violent and subversive actions disturbed him. He did not punish Amnon for raping Tamar (2 Sam 13—14). The LXX adds a reason: *because he loved him for he was his firstborn.* This led to Absalom avenging Tamar himself by killing Amnon. Compare this to Jacob in the case of Dinah's rape and the response of Simeon and Levi (Gen 34), which is like that of Absalom. Although Jacob was disturbed by Dinah's brothers' slaughter of the Hivites, he could not do anything about it after the fact. David could have, but failed to bring Absalom to justice for his murder of Amnon and sought to protect him, even when Absalom attempted to overthrow his father (2 Sam 13—18). Joab, David's military chief, killed Absalom (2 Sam 18).

The court history reports another rebellion against David, that of Sheba, which Joab and a wise woman of the northern Israelite city of Abel suppressed. In pursuit of Sheba, Joab killed Amasa, whom David had appointed as commander of the army in Joab's place (2 Sam 20:1-22). Amasa had been Absalom's military chief in the latter's conspiracy against David!

The court history does *not* include any mention of which son should rule Israel after David's death. Adonijah, David's son by Haggith, was David's oldest remaining son when 1 Kings begins. He was born in Hebron, as were his now deceased elder brothers (Amnon, Kileab, and Absalom) and younger brothers (Shephatiah and Ithream) (2 Sam 3:2-5; 1 Chr 3:2). In 1 Kgs 1:11-31, Adonijah, Nathan, and Bathsheba are center stage strategists by turn who seek to fill the throne of Israel soon to be vacated by a failing David. He had not told anyone who the next king should be.

1. Abishag Attends to a Dying David (1:1-4)

IN THE TEXT

■ **1-4** As the drama of 1 Kings opens, the lights on King David are rapidly dimming. The book begins by depicting David as very old, very cold, and impotent. **Old and well advanced in days** is a phrase used only about the childless Abraham and Sarah (Gen 18:11) and Joshua (Josh 13:1; 23:1).

The pericope about Abishag, the beautiful Shunammite maiden brought by David's servants to warm him in his bed (**to be his attendant** [*sokenet*]), sets the stage for Adonijah's move. It illustrates David's advanced age and disorientation and affirms that his days of sexual potency were over. A *sokenet* is someone who benefits, profits, is useful to, or is used by another. See Ps 139:3 describing Yahweh's familiarity with the ways of the psalmist. Here David did not "know" her physically; soon we learn that he did not "know" about Adonijah's feast, interpreted as a claim to the throne.

Situated at the beginning of this story, Abishag's appearance also demonstrates the connection between David's physical prowess and his ability to rule. The king's servants saw that even a beautiful virgin could not compel the king to sexual potency, although they retained her to serve him in other ways. She will serve the conclusion of the story about Adonijah. In 2 Kings another woman from Shunem enters the narrative to sustain the prophet Elisha, providing him with a place to stay in her home (4:8-37).

The author proceeds to tell a story as a scriptwriter and comes close to providing stage directions. As readers of a script, we must not fall for the schemes of the characters as we watch their words and maneuvers. Information found in the dialogues is not giving us more details on what actually happened but is showing us the character's intentions and rhetorical skill. Rarely in Kings do we hear the narrator's take on Yahweh's or the characters' intentions, memories, or thoughts, but we can observe—as in a play—what the characters do and say and how they relay the messages they are given. When the narrator does provide commentary or judgment, we should be all the more attentive to the perspective offered.

2. Adonijah "Assumes" the Throne (1:5-10)

BEHIND THE TEXT

Nathan's confidence in approaching Bathsheba and her confidence in going to David suggests she was David's primary wife. The background for the 1 Kgs 1—2 narrative is supplied by 2 Sam 11—12, where we observe an indolent King David, rising from his afternoon nap while all the other kings and his own armies are at war. From his elevated palace patio, he saw Bathsheba bathing and inquired after her. Even after learning she was the wife of one of his mighty men, David used his authority as king to shun the law of Yahweh and commit adultery. When he learned she had thus become pregnant, he brought back her husband, Uriah, who refused to sleep with his wife while the armies of Yahweh were camped in the fields. David's next ploy was to have Uriah carry a note to Joab, which instructed Joab to have Uriah killed in battle. As distasteful as this was to Joab, he obeyed after a fashion. Bathsheba became a widow, whom David then married. The child of David's adultery died, but Solomon was born soon afterward. Bathsheba, Uriah, and Joab were pawns in the hands of a lustful, scheming, murderous king.

Yahweh was not pleased. He sent Nathan to convict David with a parable (2 Sam 12), which the callous king did not understand, until Nathan pronounced: "You are the man!" (v 7). He proceeded to describe the consequences of David's sins: "Now, therefore, the sword will never depart from your house, because you despised me and took the wife of Uriah the Hittite to be your own" (v 10). Although David recognized his sin, the consequences came. The narrator construes the subsequent events in David's life as outcomes of or related to his sins, including the birth and reign of Solomon. Without David committing adultery and murdering Uriah, Bathsheba would not have become his wife. Without Bathsheba, Solomon would not have been born. Without Bathsheba's intervention with Nathan, David would not have named this younger son to succeed him. On one level, Solomon is an example of God bringing good out of evil (see Gen 50:20), and it fits the pattern of an unexpected younger-son leader, exalted by God. However, on another level, he is an illustration of the sword continuing to reside in David's house (1 Kgs 2).

Unlike David's other wife, Abigail (1 Sam 25), Bathsheba could not stop David from killing her husband, but she could save her son Solomon by placing him on the throne of Israel. The possibility that Solomon was endangered by Adonijah and his supporters has some precedent in the conspiracy of David's son Absalom, who went to great lengths to wile the throne away from his father, taking over David's palace and wives, then fighting David, until he was killed by Joab (2 Sam 15—18).

Although we know from 2 Sam 12:24-25 that Yahweh loved Bathsheba's Solomon, naming him "Beloved of Yahweh," we find no hint that David swore to Bathsheba that Solomon would succeed him in all of the court history. We are to understand that Nathan was convinced he and Bathsheba were doing what was required to save Solomon and themselves.

IN THE TEXT

■ **5-6** David's eldest remaining son, Adonijah (fourth born), assumed that he would be the next king, habitually exalting himself. By juxtaposing the account of David's impotence, unrelieved by Abishag, the text implies that Adonijah made a move to assume the throne because David's death seemed imminent. The narrator's practice of citing Adonijah's mother underscores the competition between Haggith and Bathsheba. "Haggith" is a name derived from *hgg* as is the noun "feast," whereas Bathsheba means "daughter of the oath." Both names foreshadow the events of this chapter.

Adonijah would have been expected to succeed David from the human perspective, for he was the remaining firstborn, was handsome, and would not expect any objections from the king, because his father had never **grieved him** (v 6) by questioning him at any time about anything (perhaps including Adonijah's assumption that he would be king). However, because of the stories of Amnon and Absalom, we are suspicious about Adonijah's looks and David's practice of neglecting to guide him. Handsome Adonijah reminds us of his handsome brothers, all of whom were now dead. Furthermore, we know from David's anointing story (1 Sam 16) and the Genesis accounts of Isaac, Jacob, Joseph, and Ephraim that elder brothers are often set aside in favor of younger brothers.

■ **7-8 Adonijah conferred with Joab**, David's general and nephew (2 Sam 2:13-32; 3:22-31; 8:16; 10; 11:1, 6-25; 12:26-31; 18; 19:5-7 [6-8 HB]; 20; 24), and Abiathar, one of David's priests (1 Sam 22:20-23; 23:6-9; 30:7; 2 Sam 8:17; 15:24, 29-36). These strong supports were eventually toppled by the shrewdness of the prophet Nathan and Bathsheba, Solomon's mother.

■ **9-10** Adonijah held a sacrificial feast, to which he invited the royal officials and all of his brothers except Solomon. Notice that the text says: **He invited all his brothers, the king's sons . . . but he did not invite . . . his brother Solomon**, thereby drawing attention to the exclusion of *this* brother and their rivalry. The other brothers of Adonijah were not in danger, especially since they all chose to eat and drink at his feast. Adonijah also pointedly excluded the prophet Nathan and Benaiah, a warrior of valor whom David had placed in charge of his bodyguard and who was the commander of the Kerethites and Pelethites (2 Sam 23:20-23; see also 2 Sam 8:18; 20:23; 1 Chr 27:5-6).

Although Adonijah probably expected his father to affirm his celebration and confirm him as king (as Joab and Abiathar did), the narrator does not say that Adonijah proclaimed himself king. In the next section, Nathan will report to both Bathsheba and David that Adonijah did so (in the shape of questions).

3. Nathan and Bathsheba Persuade David to Name Solomon King (1:11-40)

IN THE TEXT

■ **11-14** This section plays like a carefully crafted drama with stage directions. In the first scene, after noticing that Adonijah had invited some of the court principals to a sacrificial feast but not others, the prophet Nathan contacted Bathsheba. Her task? Compel David to place her son Solomon on the throne immediately. In so doing, Nathan orchestrated Adonijah's downfall.

Whereas in 2 Sam 12:1-14 and 25, Nathan was sent by Yahweh with words against David, here Nathan acts on his own initiative by *asking* Bathsheba if she had heard a report that Haggith's son had become king without David knowing it. By naming Adonijah's mother, Nathan raised the issue of rivalry between wives of David. He advised her to ask the king if he had not sworn to her that her son Solomon would succeed him. Nathan's move in response to Adonijah's feast may be for the sake of their survival, not ambition for the throne itself. In any case, Solomon's survival required that David name him to the throne.

Nathan also told Bathsheba to ask David why Adonijah had become king, although they both affirmed that David did not know about this. David could not know about this, because, in the first place, Adonijah was not king; and, in the second, David was not aware of much, including Adonijah's feast for his supporters (1 Kgs 1:11). Nathan and Bathsheba's recital of what David did not know (vv 11, 18) and later what David had not allowed Nathan to know (supposedly [v 27]) underlines his neutralized position already foreshadowed by the disclosure that the king did not know Abishag (v 4).

■ **15-21** Although Nathan told her to ask questions (vv 11-13), when the next scene opens, Bathsheba entered, bowed, knelt, and made statements. **You yourself swore to me . . . "Solomon your son shall be king after me . . ." But now Adonijah has become king, and you, my lord the king, do not know about it** (vv 17-18). She did not ask as per Nathan: "Why then has Adonijah become king?" (v 13). In biblical literature, differences between the original message and the report are significant (see 2 Sam 11, the foundation for this account).

By asserting that David had previously sworn to her **by Yahweh your God** that Solomon would be king, the woman once victimized by David's lust and position persuaded him to swear that Solomon would sit on David's throne. Bathsheba then declared to David that **all the eyes of Israel** were on the aged king, waiting for David to announce his successor (1 Kgs 1:20). She verified that she and *her* son would be counted offenders and thus endangered when David died. She was counting on the closeness of their ties, as Nathan had, that David would be motivated to act out of concern, first for her and then for her son. Bathsheba made pronouncements that stirred David to act kingly. She did not ask questions.

The claim that David swore that her son would be king is presented here as a ruse of Nathan's, enforced by Bathsheba, to coerce the king to name Solomon to be his successor. This becomes more apparent as the story unfolds. We are to understand that Nathan was convinced he and Bathsheba were doing what was required to save Solomon and themselves.

■ **22-27** The next scene opens when Nathan entered David's chambers while Bathsheba was still speaking; she did not leave. Nathan bowed to the ground, then *questioned* the king, which serves to verify part of what Bathsheba had reported: that Adonijah was king, performing kingly functions of sacrifice and feasting with his supporters who were saying: **Long live King Adonijah** (v 25). This is *not* in the narrator's report of the feast, but only in Bathsheba and Nathan's reports to the king. We are not to understand that Nathan is providing a particular that the narrator did not supply, but that Nathan is purposefully adding this provocative element to *provoke* the king to act. Nathan was also careful to attest to the truth that he, David's **servant**, along with Zadok, Benaiah, and Solomon, David's **servant**, were not invited. Nathan "wondered" if King David brought this about without telling his **servants**: himself and Solomon.

Nathan, however, *did not* attempt to corroborate Bathsheba's claim that David had promised her that Solomon would be king; this was something only Bathsheba could have known. Since we know that Nathan told Bathsheba to inform ("remind") David that her husband had made this oath to her, we also know that this was Nathan's scheme to save their lives, which would have been endangered if David confirmed Adonijah as his successor. Adonijah's mistake, then, was in not inviting Nathan and Solomon to join the festivities, thereby reinforcing a division between two competing groups.

■ **28-35** The king is then shown to muster himself and rise to this indubitably royal occasion, convinced by Bathsheba's claims concerning a previous oath and the potential threat to her. He believed her and followed her lead in "remembering" his oath, credible within a relational context. He did not wonder what would then happen to Adonijah, the son he never disciplined or guided. He clearly made his choice for Bathsheba and her son over Haggith and her son.

David grasped the strength to respond to the crisis presented to him by Bathsheba and Nathan and imperiously began ordering people about. He called Bathsheba to himself and swore (for the first time) by Yahweh that he would cause Solomon to sit on his throne (vv 29-30). He took an oath for the sake of the "daughter of an oath" (Bathsheba). She responded by bowing low again, kneeling, and honoring him with her gratitude and blessing: **May my lord King David live forever** (v 31). This is not intended to be ironic but to reflect her deepest blessing on his posterity, not himself personally.

David told her to call for a trio of kingmakers: priestly (Zadok), prophetic (Nathan), and military (Benaiah) leaders. These were the very men

Nathan had told him were not invited to Adonijah's recent feast, and all of whom would have been counted as offenders if David had chosen to support Adonijah's claim to the throne. Nathan, no doubt, was also still in the room, but King David told Bathsheba to call him, as if he was not. The narrator shows us David's confusion, but he also depicts David's ability to respond to this crisis and perform the crucial function that he had heretofore neglected. David's directives were clear. He told Nathan and Zadok to settle Solomon on the royal mule, anoint him at the spring of Gihon, blow the trumpet, and follow him to David's own throne, where he would sit as ruler (*nāgîd*) over Israel and Judah in David's place (v 35). David gathered his waning strength to designate this younger son, Solomon, to be the next king of Israel and Judah.

■ **36-40** Benaiah (his name means "Yahweh has built") responded to David's appointment of Solomon with a prayer that Yahweh would confirm David's choice and bless him with an even greater throne. Zadok was silent but obedient, taking Solomon with Nathan and Benaiah's troops, the Kerethites and Pelethites, to the Gihon spring, anointing him, sounding the trumpet, claiming Solomon to be king and rejoicing. The Gihon is a spring associated with the founding of the city of Jerusalem and appears in Gen 2:13 as one of the rivers watering Eden. Solomon's coronation thus occurred at the center of the Judahite world.

4. Adonijah Responds to Solomon's Accession (1:41-53)

IN THE TEXT

■ **41-48** David avoided naming a successor until his hand was forced, but he made no apologies for placing Solomon on the throne instead of Adonijah. This fact was not lost on Adonijah and his guests when they learned the news.

Jonathan arrived at Adonijah's feast while the trumpet was blasting (vv 41-42), which followed the anointing and preceded the people's proclamation, Solomon's occupation of the throne, and the congratulations in David's room (vv 47-48). Yet Jonathan reported the king's proclamation as if he had been in David's bedchamber, at the Gihon spring, and in the throne room; and had returned to David's bedchamber to watch David bow and bless Solomon. Thus, Jonathan reported as if he had already witnessed everything, serving here as an omniscient narrator and emphasizing the irrevocability of Solomon's ascension to the throne.

■ **49-50** When his guests therefore scattered, Adonijah sought asylum at the **horns of the altar** (v 50) and an oath from Solomon, perceiving that Solomon would count him as an offender. This gives further credence to the precarious positions of Nathan, Bathsheba, and Solomon if David had supported Adonijah, the elder brother, who had assumed he would be king. If Adonijah feared for his life when his brother was named king, so also Solomon's life may have been in danger if Adonijah became king at David's death.

■ **51-53** Adonijah's demand while **clinging to the horns of the altar** (v 51) prompted Solomon to appear and speak onstage for the first time. Clearly, Adonijah was on notice to monitor his aspirations and mind all of his behavior. The spotlight will remain on King Solomon, to whom Adonijah must bow. But Adonijah did not stay home.

FROM THE TEXT

With Solomon's accession, we are reminded of the younger sons in Genesis, who overcame their elder brothers through guile, sheer determination, abuse, and/or providential circumstances. These occurred in scenes in which their fathers and often mothers were prominent. Consider Isaac over Ishmael, Jacob over Esau, and Joseph's sons over all of Leah's sons. For both Isaac and Jacob, their mothers had a hand in the younger brother's advancement. Sarah cast out Ishmael and Hagar; Rebecca initiated the deceit required for Jacob to "steal" Esau's blessing. Like David, Isaac was very old, blind in fact; and Rebecca used his handicap to convince him that Jacob was Esau. Similarly, Nathan and Bathsheba used David's senility to compel him to name Solomon king.

Consider also the means by which Ephraim was placed over Manasseh. In Gen 48:14-20, Jacob brusquely performed the firstborn's blessing on Ephraim, Joseph's younger son. Establishing a younger brother as the inheritor of promises and property countered convention. Solomon had an older brother with the right of primogeniture. Could the younger-brother narratives of Genesis function as a defense of Solomon's claim to the throne? The traditions about David remind us of other stories in Genesis. The explicit parallels lead some scholars to argue that certain Genesis accounts of the patriarchs were written to parody David's weaknesses. (See Rendsburg 1986; Emerton 1979, 403-15; and Emerton 1976, 79-98.)

By the events that unfold in this chapter and the next, we might infer that David should have named his successor sooner. His failure to do so must be added to his neglect of other matters, such as bringing—in his own lifetime—justice for the murders of Abner and Amasa by Joab (2 Sam 2—3; 20). However, David probably expected his oldest remaining son to be king after he died. Furthermore, David had reason to worry about fratricide and patricide. He had lost Amnon and Absalom violently, and Absalom had nearly stolen the kingdom from him while pursuing him to the death.

In any event, David seemed to have been stunned to inaction following his adultery, murder, and confrontation with Nathan. We are told only what the narrator wants us to know, but he implies an omission on David's part, left ultimately to interpreters to puzzle out.

Although noted above, the contrast between 1 Kgs 1:11-40 and 2 Sam 12:1 in regard to God's initiative with Nathan is worth emphasizing here. In 2 Sam 12, Yahweh sent Nathan to confront David after he had killed Uriah and acquired a pregnant Bathsheba. In 1 Kgs 1, God did not send Nathan to approach Bathsheba or David. Whereas Yahweh told Samuel to anoint Saul and David (1 Sam 8:22; 10:1-2; 16), David responded to the orchestration of Nathan and Bathsheba to order the anointing of Solomon. God was remarkably absent from all of these proceedings, except when used by the characters to stand behind alleged and authentic oaths (1 Kgs 1:17, 29-30).

After 2 Sam 12, God did not appear again as a speaking figure or through a prophet until he appeared to Solomon in a dream at Gibeon in 1 Kgs 3:5-14. Neither did any character consult God for wisdom or direction, although Benaiah (who became Solomon's "hit man") called upon God to ordain David's appointment and to be with King Solomon (1:36-37). As it turned out, the warning that the sword would not depart from David's house (see 2 Sam 12) may have also implied that God would withdraw into the background until called upon. On the other hand, we must not forget God's promise to David in 2 Sam 7:12: "When your days are over and you rest with your ancestors, I will raise up your offspring to succeed you, your own flesh and blood, and I will establish his kingdom."

B. Solomon Eliminates His Opponents (2:1-46)

BEHIND THE TEXT

This chapter has three sections: David's charge to Solomon followed by his death (vv 1-12), Bathsheba's visit to her son to relay Adonijah's request for Abishag as his wife (vv 13-22), and Solomon's response (vv 23-46). This includes killing Adonijah, banishing Abiathar the priest, as well as fulfilling David's orders to punish Joab and Shimei.

David's last words to Solomon echoed those of Joshua to Israel when he prepared to "go the way of all the earth" (Josh 23:11-14). Joshua 1:7-9 and Deut 17:14-20 also stand behind David's charge to his son and successor, Solomon, "man of peace." In these passages, Yahweh spoke through Moses and Joshua, counseling the leaders of Israel to be strong (*ḥāzaq*) and keep the Law mediated through Moses. The prosperity and continued existence of Israel—and now Solomon—depended upon reading and observing all that is in the Torah of Moses; this is the repeated message of the Deuteronomist (→ Introduction).

When Yahweh promised David an enduring dynasty in 2 Sam 7, he promised that he would establish David's own son forever. This passage describes the founding occasion for the Davidic covenant clearly refers to Solomon, who would build a house for Yahweh. The wrongs of this son are mentioned, which implies ignoring the commandments, but the book of the law is not specified in 2 Sam 7, as it is in later evocations of this covenant. Although this son would be punished for his sins, he would not be removed from the throne, according to 2 Sam 7. This contrasts to David's words to Solomon in 1 Kgs 2:1-4 and the admonitions to all other kings, for whom law keeping is the condition for continuing on the throne.

In the same breath that David used to adjure his son to keep the charge of Yahweh written in the law of Moses, he demanded revenge by Solomon against men whom David had not brought to justice (Joab), or to whom he had shown mercy (Shimei [2 Sam 15:5-8; 19:16-23]). This included Joab's brash and selfish murders of Abner and Amasa (2 Sam 3:17-39; 17:25; 19:23; 20:4-10). David may also have been motivated to assign Joab to death because he had killed Absalom when the latter had become David's enemy (2 Sam 18:5-15, 33 [5-15; 19:1 HB]).

When Adonijah asked for Abishag as a wife, we see further allusions to the practice of a new king taking over the wives of his predecessor. It was a power play. See 2 Sam 3:7-11 regarding Saul's commander Abner who was accused of taking Saul's concubine Rizpah, and 2 Sam 16:20-22, which led to Abner turning Israel over to David. This lies behind Solomon's immediate outraged response in this section, which includes killing Adonijah and Joab and exiling Abiathar from the priesthood.

I. David Orders Solomon to Keep the Law and to Avenge Him (2:1-12)

IN THE TEXT

■ **1-4** David had been roused to vigorously proclaim Solomon king in the presence of Bathsheba, Zadok, Nathan, and Benaiah, but before he died he rose of his own initiative to speak forcefully to Solomon. Using many of the same words Yahweh had spoken to Joshua after Moses' death, David charged his successor to keep (*šāmar*) all of the ways, statutes, commandments, ordinances, and testimonies as they were written in Moses' law *so that* he would prosper. These Deuteronomistic terms set the Davidic covenant, as transmitted to Solomon, within that framework. Law keeping was a condition for prospering (→ Introduction).

Furthermore, David's reiteration of Yahweh's promise in v 4 contains the important condition not found in 2 Sam 7:12-16. The 2 Sam 7 covenant was about the son (sg.) of David who would build a house for Yahweh, Solomon, not subsequent descendants. The son mentioned in 2 Sam 7 would be punished for wrongs without removal from the throne (vv 14-15). The contrast is with Saul, whom Yahweh removed from the throne of Israel. But the Deuteronomist depicted David telling Solomon (1 Kgs 2:4) that Yahweh had said *if your sons* [plural] *guard their way to walk before me faithfully . . . [then] you shall not fail to have a man on the throne of Israel*. If David's descendants were faithful, *then* Yahweh would establish the word Yahweh had spoken to David concerning his throne. Thus, as the story now stands, David disclosed a conditional version of the covenant immediately before he died and applied those conditions to Solomon and all subsequent descendants.

The forever quality of the 2 Sam 7 covenant lends itself to David's application of it to subsequent sons; he uses "forever" three times. Whereas 2 Sam 7 does not mention law keeping, here David emphasized law keeping as the condition of the covenant to Solomon. Dtr's David used all the terms for Yahweh's commandments with conditional clauses. The conditional nature of this rendering of the Davidic covenant is critical for understanding 1 and 2 Kings' interpretation of Israel's history, although the unconditional nature of the 2 Sam 7 version is necessary for understanding some of the exilic psalms and prophets (e.g., Ps 89 and Habakkuk).

■ **5-6** Then, as the text now stands, David shifted gears. From concerns for the covenant of Yahweh, he turned to demanding Solomon to wreak vengeance upon both friend and foe; or, in his understanding, to bring justice. Joab had been David's loyal commander through thick and thin, but not without self-interest. When Joab suspected (rightly) that David was relieving him of his command in favor of Abner or Amasa for political purposes, Joab killed both of them. Joab bore an additional grudge against Abner, the commander of Saul's supporters, for killing his brother (in time of war). Joab had led Abner to step outside of Hebron, a city of refuge, before he killed him (2 Sam 3:26).

In both cases, David needed to retain Joab as commander (for Joab had murdered his qualified replacements), but to do so was to act in his own self-interest as Joab had done. Joab's actions had brought bloodguilt to David's dynasty even though David had tried to distance himself from Joab's murders (2 Sam 3:31-39; 19:13 [14 HB]; 20:4-13). This is clearer in the LXX (proto-Lucianic recension) where the blood on *his* (Joab's) waist, sandals, and feet (MT and English) are rendered *my* (David's) belt and sandals. This older and more difficult reading clarifies David's concern that Solomon must begin his reign by settling the scores that David could not and would not do.

Bloodguilt

When Solomon ordered Benaiah to slay Joab as the latter grasped the horns of the altar in the tent of meeting, he expressed the concept of bloodguilt and the means for its removal (1 Kgs 2:31-32). Solomon sought to rid his father's dynasty of the guilt Joab brought upon it when he shed the "innocent blood" of two men (v 31; "without cause" [NRSV]). Although David had not overtly ordered Solomon to slay his commander Joab, he strongly implied as much, indicating great bitterness over the deaths of Abner and Amasa. "[Joab] killed them, shedding their blood in peacetime as if in battle, and with that blood stained the belt around his waist and the sandals on his feet" (v 5). The guilt upon David's dynasty could be returned to Joab's own head only by executing him. This account represents the idea that the altar would provide shelter from execution. Exodus 21:12, 14 also hints at this notion: "Whoever strikes a person mortally shall be put to death. . . . But if someone willfully attacks and kills another by treachery, you shall take the killer from my altar for execution" (NRSV). Solomon ordered Joab slain *at the altar* as he grasped its horns!

Earlier, closer to the times of their deaths, David attempted to put the blood of Abner and Amasa on Joab's family (and remove it from himself) with words. These words were not sufficient (see 2 Sam 3:28-29). David did not want Solomon's reign to begin without fully avenging Abner and Amasa. Joab could not die a natural death.

In an earlier account, Saul was considered guilty for slaying Gibeonites. The land suffered famine until the innocent deaths were expiated. David accommodated the demands for blood of the Gibeonites, demonstrating again the concept of bloodguilt (2 Sam 21:1-14). But stories such as this are not without nuance. Within the world of the story, a certain primitive sense of justice resulted from the slaying of Saul's sons to pay for the sins of their father. On another level, the stark senselessness of blood for blood strikes the reader when Rizpah, the matriarch, cares for the bodies of her slain sons and nephews through all seasons. The rain did not fall on the land until their bones were buried with those of Saul and Jonathan at the tomb of Saul's father Kish. "After that, God answered prayer in behalf of the land" (v 14).

Another example is the story of Rahab in Josh 2. The Israelite spies told Rahab that they would bear on their heads the blood for any of her family members who stayed indoors yet were killed by the invading Israelites. If the family of Rahab went outside, "their blood [would] be on their own heads" (v 19).

In these and other stories and laws referring to unjustified killing or negligence, the Hebrew term for blood (*dām* or its plural *dāmîm*) is used. Although such acts leave the perpetrators guilty and their blood must be shed to avenge innocent blood, no term for "bloodguilt" is found in the Hebrew. "Bloudgyltynesse" entered the English language through Coverdale's 1535 translation of Ps 51:14 [16 HB] (Gaster 1975, 56-73; Sperling 1992, 764).

The Hebrew term for blood in guilt-charged contexts is translated "bloodguilt" by the NIV translators (1973 edition) in Joel 3:21 [4:21 HB] and Ps 51:14 [16 HB]. The NRSV uses the term "bloodguilt" much more often for the concept of unjustified killing/negligence (Exod 22:2-3 [1-2 HB]); Num 35:27; Deut 21:1-8; 22:8; 1 Sam 25:26; compare v 31; 2 Sam 21:1-14).

When the guilty were executed for sins that did not involve murder or negligence leading to death, their blood was *on them*. Asserting that blood was *upon* one's "head" (2 Sam 1:16) or *at* one's "head" (1 Kgs 2:37) are other ways to express this. This meant that they were at fault for their deaths, not their executioners. See Ezek 33:5. See also Lev 20:27 regarding the execution of persons who divine by means of ghosts or familiar spirits.

The foundation for bloodguilt is the view that innocent blood cries out for vengeance (Gen 4:10) or is avenged by Yahweh (Isa 26:21; Ezek 24:7) or is rejected by the earth, pollutes it, or will cause perpetrators to perish (Jonah 1:14). Since accidental killing also results in bloodguilt, the killer may be slain by the kinsman redeemer (*gō'ēl* [Num 35:26-27; Deut 19:4-10]). Unintentional killings may be atoned for by the natural death of the high priest (Num 35:25, 28), but the killer was confined to a city of refuge to protect him from the *gō'ēl* (Num 35:9-11;

Deut 4:41-43; 19:1-13; Josh 20:1-3). The village nearest the body of the slain must perform a ritual to symbolically wash away the blood of the slain and thus deny any complicity (Deut 21:1-9). See Gaster 1975, 56-73; Sperling 1992, 764; and Milgrom 2008.

In any case, throughout the story of the early monarchy, the narrator included Joab's strengths and weaknesses as he did for Saul, David, and Solomon. Joab had been almost as loyal to David as he was to himself, choosing the shrewder course and advising David to do the same. When David asked his commanders to deal gently with Absalom, who was out to kill and replace him (2 Sam 18:5), Joab ignored David and killed David's enemy. When David heard that Absalom was dead, he was so distraught that his loyal troops would have scattered had not Joab directed David to powder his nose and show his face in gratitude for their support (19:2-9 [3-10 HB]). Nonetheless, in the end, David disregarded Joab's service and remembered his crimes. We are led to wonder if Bathsheba and Nathan's report concerning Joab's alignment with Adonijah may have been one of the reasons David set Adonijah aside in favor of Solomon. Joab supported Adonijah, so he chose the son associated with Bathsheba and Nathan and against the son associated with Joab. In his last breath, David dropped on Solomon the role of retaliator for wrongs Joab had committed long ago.

■ **7** David remembered the generosity of Barzillai and willed Solomon to reward him by caring for his sons (see 2 Sam 19:31-39 [32-40 HB]).

■ **8-9** David also recalled the man who had cursed him on his way out of Jerusalem when Absalom was headed there (2 Sam 16:5-14). He ordered Solomon to slaughter this same Shimei, a supporter of Saul's family. Apparently David's promise of mercy to Shimei only lasted so long as his own life; he clearly held a grudge—or apprehension—that trumped his promise of clemency. When David had been returning to Jerusalem, he knew he needed the support of all of the tribes, especially Benjamin. When preparing Solomon for the crown, he was not only operating out of personal rancor but also may have believed he was clearing the opposition for his younger son. David technically kept his promise to Shimei; he himself had never used a sword to slay Shimei (2 Sam 19:15-23 [16-24 HB]).

■ **10-12** See the nearly identical reckoning of David's reign in 2 Sam 5:4-5, which adds David's age at the time of his accession. After David's charges to Solomon, David **rested with his ancestors** (1 Kgs 2:10), a formulaic term used for the death and burial of subsequent kings. David was the first king to be **buried in the City of David**. He probably was not buried with Jesse and Obed, who died before there was a city of David (see 1 Sam 17:12; 22:3). Solomon sat on his throne, firmly established at this point, because David, who had named him to be his successor, died. First Kings 2:46 repeats the formula after Solomon carried out David's charges, and then some. Co-regency seemed to be operating while David was still alive, for Solomon did not act as king until David died, excepting his royal verdict on his brother Adonijah (1 Kgs 1:50-53).

2. Bathsheba Requests Abishag for Adonijah's Wife (2:13-25)

IN THE TEXT

■ **13-18** This is the last time Bathsheba appears onstage in the drama that Adonijah provoked by exalting himself. Just as Solomon was named to the throne as a result of Adonijah's feast at En Rogel, so Solomon began to carry out David's orders and establish his kingdom as the result of another aggressive move by Adonijah. The narrator leaves it up to readers to determine if Adonijah intended to make a boldly defiant play for the throne, as Solomon saw it, or simply wanted Abishag as a "consolation prize." Notice that even after his flight to the horns of the altar, Adonijah still declared to Solomon's mother that the kingship had been his and ***all Israel had turned to him to make him king*** (v 15). Once again he left out Nathan, Bathsheba, Benaiah, and Solomon, who obviously did not want him to be king! Adonijah piously admitted that Solomon was king through Yahweh and he remained under Solomon's ruling: "if evil is found in him, he will die" (1:52). King Solomon was the judge of that.

■ **19-21** Bathsheba may have been fully aware that Adonijah's request for Abishag would be judged evil by Solomon when she went to Solomon with his request. She hardly would have had any sympathy for Adonijah, given what had transpired. Could she have hoped that Abishag would not become Solomon's wife if she was the wife of Adonijah?

■ **22-23** Though he clearly honored his mother, Solomon was outraged. In his agitated and sarcastic response to Bathsheba, Solomon mentioned Abiathar the priest first, then Joab as those who would receive the kingdom with Adonijah. This is a prelude to what will follow.

■ **24-25** Solomon swore by Yahweh with the words of David (vv 2-4) and Nathan (2 Sam 7:13-15) to answer Adonijah's request for a wife with death. He immediately ordered Benaiah to slay his brother.

3. Solomon Establishes His Reign (2:26-46)

BEHIND THE TEXT

Abiathar was one of David's priests with Zadok (1 Sam 22:20-23; 2 Sam 8:17). He was the only son of Ahimelek and had escaped the sword of Doeg the Edomite, while his father, along with all his brothers and the entire town of Nob, had been slaughtered at Saul's command at Gibeah. Saul was incensed because Ahimelek had given David the sword of Goliath and the priestly bread (1 Sam 21:2-10 [3-11 HB]; 22:9-23). See also 1 Sam 23:6-9; 30:7; 2 Sam 8:17; 15:24, 29-36). Abiathar fled to David, who had promised to protect him. The narrator concludes that Abiathar's ultimate exile fulfills finally the prophecy against the house of Eli, spoken first by an unnamed man of God and then by the young Samuel (1 Sam 2:27-36; 3:11-14).

Joab had shared the trials and triumphs of David, as catalyst of David's military successes, along with several political fiascoes. He brought Absalom back to Jerusalem when he knew David was grieving over him. Knowing what David's reaction to Absalom's death would be (death to the messenger), he cautioned Ahimaaz, the son of Zadok, against taking that role (2 Sam 18:19-32). Joab had been scandalized over David's order, sent by the hand of Uriah, that he cause Uriah's death in battle, but he did it (ch 11). Ultimately, however, Joab's life ended at the word of his longtime king, fellow warrior, and uncle. This is unexpected after reading the summary of David's supporters and officials in chs 8 and 20, which lists Joab, Benaiah, Zadok, and Abiathar as colleagues of David.

IN THE TEXT

■ **26-27** Solomon did not punish any of his other brothers who had supported Adonijah. Neither did he set out to obey his father or see to his own grudges until Adonijah made a claim on Abishag. But once this occurred and Solomon had put Adonijah under Benaiah's sword, he also confronted his father's priest, Abiathar, the sole survivor of the Nob massacre, with whom David had had no quarrel. But Solomon did. He removed Abiathar from the priesthood, confining him to Anathoth, in the tribal territory of Benjamin. This was the birthplace of Jeremiah many generations later.

■ **28** News of the exile of Abiathar and the death of Adonijah propelled Joab to the **horns of the altar** in the tent of Yahweh. Some ancient texts say that Joab had not supported *Solomon* (instead of the MT's "Absalom"). Solomon might be the more original because Joab killed Absalom, so readers would hardly need to be reminded that Joab did not support his rebellion. Furthermore, this passage is about Joab's relationship to Solomon within the context of Solomon dealing with the supporters of Adonijah. We wonder what would have become of Joab if he had supported Solomon, given his past murders under David still stained David's dynasty.

■ **29-31** Joab's entry into **the Tent of Yahweh** to grasp the horns of the altar prompted Solomon to order Benaiah to strike Joab there, not the other way around. Although Benaiah hesitated and told Joab that the king had ordered Joab to come out, Solomon had no qualms about violating the sanctuary.

■ **32-35** Solomon mimicked David's fervor as evidenced by his energized speech to Benaiah here, which underscores the bloodguilt that Joab had brought to David's *dynasty* and not merely to Joab and David. Thus the narrator closes out Joab's colorful life with Solomon's crisp demand that Benaiah fulfill Joab's "prediction": "I will die here" (v 30). To review Joab's variegated life, see 2 Sam 2:13-32; 3:22-31; 8:16; 10; 11:1, 5-25; 12:26-31; 18; 19:3-6 [4-7

HB]; 20; 24. (→ "Bloodguilt" sidebar at Behind the Text above, and commentary under 1 Kgs 2:5-6.)

After this, Solomon replaced Joab (who must have been nearly as old as David) with Benaiah; he also replaced the priest Abiathar with Zadok. Zadok's descendants will figure prominently as priests in the generations to come through the time of Qumran and Jerusalem in the first century AD.

■ **36-38** Solomon continued to execute David's orders by turning to Shimei, the Benjamite, who had cursed David when he was retreating from Jerusalem. Shimei had begged for mercy when David returned (2 Sam 16:5-14; 19:15-23 [16-24 HB]). David had said Solomon should *wisely* (read *shrewdly*) determine how to bring Shimei to a bloody end (1 Kgs 2:9). Solomon did so through his scheme to confine Shimei to Jerusalem. The Kidron brook is east of Jerusalem, and on the way to Bahurim, Shimei's home, north of Jerusalem.

■ **39-46a** An increasingly verbal Solomon explained at length to Shimei why he deserved death for retrieving his servants who fled to Gath (probably west of Jerusalem). He then sent Benaiah to strike him with his sword. While Shimei did not cross the Kidron, he did go out from Jerusalem. Solomon had hired eyes to watch his every move, waiting for the pretext by which he might slay him. Solomon's self-blessing when pronouncing death to Shimei is Dtr's echo of 2 Sam 7:12, 13, and 16 (1 Kgs 2:45) and seems grandiose on this occasion, as if Shimei was an opponent inciting a rebellion. With Shimei dead, Solomon had eliminated David's real and perceived adversaries and anyone associated with Adonijah. We are not told whether Solomon showed kindness to Barzillai's sons as David had charged (v 7; see Ezra 2:61 and Neh 7:63).

■ **46b** The kingdom was now *firmly* established in Solomon's hands. Dtr's conclusion of Solomon's accession narrative parallels v 45. It recalls, albeit rewording, v 12, "so Solomon sat on the throne of his father David, and his rule was firmly established," which was the narrator's notice of the transition from David to Solomon.

FROM THE TEXT

The narrator, and consequently the reader, is predisposed to be sympathetic toward Solomon because of the preceding attention to Nathan the prophet and Bathsheba, the stolen and bereaved wife, in the extended story. However, in 1 Kgs 1—2, the reader detects a subtle tone of judgment on David's dynasty, which now includes Solomon, as the author links the events that emboldened Solomon to overcome perceived and real opposition. These events flow from omissions on David's part, as well as from his own crimes against a woman, her husband, and Yahweh. David's directives to Solomon call to mind Jesus' parable about the servant whose great debts had been forgiven but immediately throws in prison a fellow servant who owed him a small amount (Matt 18:23-34).

David had failed to bring Joab to justice (as well as Amnon and Absalom) while he was on the throne, and he had regularly avoided intervening in the lives of his children. However, the narrator never reports that David had neglected to discipline Solomon as he had the sons who were handsome, spoiled, and now dead, and we are given no description of Solomon's appearance. We can reasonably presume that David's practice with his older sons carried over to Solomon; he neglected him. Indeed, we are treated only to a single interaction between David and Solomon, found here, when David orders Solomon to enact his version of justice concerning past offenses.

Recall that Bathsheba called Solomon *her* son when she affirmed they would be counted as offenders should Adonijah become king (1 Kgs 1:21). In like manner, the man of peace, Solomon, counted everyone that supported Adonijah as offenders who must be eliminated. According to this chapter, both David and Solomon eschewed mercy, even given under oath (to Shimei). The narrator is not complicit in this ruthlessness. After recounting bloodshed and exile in retaliation for past crimes, he announces: **thus the kingdom was established in the hand of the man of peace!** (2:46). He clarifies that Adonijah was the only victim of Solomon who made a move against him. Once Adonijah was dead, Solomon should have had little to fear from the aging Joab, the priest Abiathar, and the Benjamite, Shimei, who was confined to Jerusalem and away from his tribe. Thus, the narrator imposes the irony.

Furthermore, we are not told that Solomon was kind to Barzillai's sons, as ordered by David. The notice in Ezra and Nehemiah might lead us to surmise that they did not come to royal court. Solomon was willing to bring down gray heads in blood to establish his rule, but not to do kindness. On the other hand, threats to a king were real, especially in the time of transition, and especially since the king was a younger, and possibly underage, son. (See 2 Sam 20:1-2 and 1 Kgs 12 when the men of Israel split away from the Judahites for minor and substantial reasons, respectively.)

As in ch 1, God is absent from the action onstage. This absence is all the more pronounced when his name is used in the mouths of the characters to swear, to bless, or to refer to his laws and ways, which are ignored. No one consults God for wisdom, although this will change in ch 3, in which Solomon humbly recognizes the enormity of the task of ruling God's people and seeks a **hearing heart** with the faith of a child. Thus the chaotic circumstances described in chs 1—2 bring to Solomon the opportunity to walk in God's ways. A very different succession account appears in 1 Chr 28—29. There David and God both actively set Solomon on the throne with blueprints and furnishings for the temple in his hands.

Like God, Solomon was behind the scenes in 1 Kgs 1 and silent while absorbing his father's charges (2:1-9). He spoke for the first time to Adonijah in 1:53, then at length in response to Bathsheba's relaying of Adonijah's request for Abishag. With every vengeful act he spoke more. Benaiah is the actor who physically established Solomon's kingdom while obeying Solomon, who was, except in the case of Abiathar, obeying David, not God.

As we follow Solomon's life, we will continue to track a series of ironies that are interwoven with God's mercy and grace. Before the events recounted in 1 Kgs 1—2, Solomon was born and named "He is peace." But he was conceived after his mother's first husband was murdered. Solomon was a consolation to Bathsheba (after the death of his brother) and especially loved by God. Thus, we gain a glimmer of hope for the sorry situation kindled by David's lust and callousness.

Most biblical characters—like David, Joab, Nathan, and Solomon—operated out of self-interest. But their stories also reveal moments or months of devotion to God, compassion, fierce loyalty, and heroism. Even when they neglected to seek God or follow his ways, we see that God is willing to work with the results of muddled and fractious transactions. God expects people to fight for their own and others' survival and uses the outcomes. Consider the manager of Jesus' parable in Luke 16:1-9 who is commended for his shrewdness in taking care of himself. The shrewdness depicted in Solomon's story, however, excluded mercy and discernment in judgment, which are products of godly wisdom. Nonetheless, as described in the next chapter, God will bless Solomon's awareness of his need for God's wisdom in order to govern God's people.

C. Solomon Expands Israel (3—11)

BEHIND THE TEXT

Second Samuel 7:8-17, which announces a son of David on the throne, is an enduring divine foundation for the Davidic dynasty in Judah and Jerusalem and for the books of Kings, especially Solomon's legacy in Judah. Solomon, and not any other son of David, came to the throne when David named him king at the instigation of Nathan and Bathsheba. A divine and prophetic selection of Solomon to be king is absent; the references to Yahweh in 1 Kgs 1—2 simply sanction what people had already done or were about to do. In ch 3, God honors Solomon's humility and youthful devotion to him and legitimates Solomon's kingship by theophany. God finally speaks into Solomon's story.

The traditional date of Solomon's accession is from 970 to 960 BC, and the date of his death is between 930 and 920 BC (see Dever 2001, 134, among many others). Certain scriptures synchronize Solomon's rule with Hiram of Tyre (1 Kgs 5:1-12 [15-26 HB]; 9:10-14; 2 Chr 2:3-16 [2-15 HB]) and Shishak of Egypt (1 Kgs 11:40). Depending on the date of Solomon's accession, the king of Egypt at the beginning of Solomon's reign was Siamun (986-967 BC) or Psusennes II (967-943 BC), the last two pharaohs of Egypt's Twenty-first Dynasty. One of these or Shishak (Sheshonq I, 943-922 BC) was the pharaoh who captured Gezer from the Philistines and gave it to his daughter, Solomon's wife (1 Kgs 9:16). Siamun was the first king of Egypt known as "pharaoh," and inscriptions and reliefs show that he made incursions into Philistine coastal territories, but so did Shishak (see Krauss 2006, 493). Evidence for the standard dating of the Egyptian dynasties (based on king lists from Egypt, Assyria, and Babylon correlated with astronomical events) has been confirmed by accelerator mass spectrometry (AMS). Samples of plant material taken from reliable archaeological contexts were subjected to AMS, and the results support the validity of the previously constructed chronologies, with minor adjustments (Strata 2010).

Evidence of the Deuteronomistic Historian's (Dtr's) interpolations or glosses throughout Kings, beginning with ch 3, includes: an instructive tone, "Yahweh" for deity (instead of "Elohim" or "God"), familiar formulae (e.g., "love for Yahweh," "walking in the ways or statutes of his father David"), fidelity to the dynasty of David, and explaining in order to harmonize unorthodox (according to Dtr) practices. In ch 3, the latter include Solomon's Egyptian marriage alliance and his worship at Gibeon. Dtr "knows" that Jerusalem was the proper place to sacrifice and pray. Dtr inserts these glosses into earlier accounts of Solomon's empowerment by God (the dream theophany) and his building projects, gleaned from an earlier document, "the book of the annals of Solomon" (DeVries 1985, 48-49).

3—11

God promised Israel's ancestors that their descendants would be as numerous as the sands of the sea (Gen 13:16; 15:5; 22:17; 26:4; 28:14). So they became during Solomon's rule, according to 1 Kgs 4. Likewise, their borders expanded according to the patriarchal promises (Gen 12:7; 13:14-15; 15:18-21; Josh 1:4). Nonetheless, a more sobering passage underlying Solomon's rule is 1 Sam 8:10-17, in which Samuel warned Israelites demanding a king (vv 4-20) that the king would drain them of children and crops and even enslave them. Although the narrator does not accuse Saul or David of these abuses, this describes exactly what King Solomon did (1 Kgs 4 [4:1—5:14 HB], 9, 10, and 12).

The earlier accounts of the kings of Judah and Israel in the books of Kings are paralleled in 1—2 Chronicles, whose authors used Kings (and other materials) as written sources. The contrasts between 1—2 Kings and 1—2 Chronicles demonstrate the Chronicler's agenda to make relevant his received traditions to his postexilic community, especially through revisions and excisions of his primary source, Kings. Recognizing that Chronicles is a postexilic midrash on Kings, scholars tend to avoid consulting it for historical details about the characters, events, and descriptions of kings. Nonetheless, it provides insights into scribal concerns of the restoration period and has been shown to transmit historical memories that were not included by the redactors of Kings.

1. Solomon Marries and Asks Yahweh for Wisdom (3:1-15)

IN THE TEXT

■ 1 As Solomon had secured his kingdom through eliminating opponents, so he solidified its standing among the nations through marriage alliances. The first (in significance if not chronologically) was with Egypt. The narrator introduces Solomon's reign with his marriage to Pharaoh's daughter and claims that the duration of her tenure in the city of David depended upon the completion of Solomon's building projects, which included her own home. This notice casts a shadow over the narrator's explanation that Solomon's wisdom, riches, and honor were gifts from God. Egypt was, for Israel, the place of bondage to which Israel should never return, even for horses (Deut 17:16). According to Deut 17:17, Israel's king "must not take many wives, or his heart will be led astray." Why, then, did Solomon go to Egypt for a wife? A politically astute reason exists, of course. His rule, now secured from internal opposition, began with his marriage to a foreign princess, which is the first of many foreign alliances. It foreshadows the shrewd nature of his policies that promote peace and prosperity, calm and commerce. The verse also forecasts the construction of his house, Yahweh's house, and the walls around Jerusalem, which are described in 1 Kgs 5—7.

■ 2 The mention that Solomon had not yet built the house of Yahweh explains why he and the people sacrificed at the principle shrine at Gibeon, one of "the shrines." The local shrines (*bāmôt*) were not necessarily high places, although that is how they are usually translated; the root is "back" (DeVries 1985, 50-51). These places of sacrifice became rivals to the temple once it was built, and Dtr qualified their use as necessary during the period before Solomon built the house for the name of Yahweh on the site of **the place Yahweh God will choose** (Deut 12:4-7 and passim). David was never depicted as worshipping at the local shrines.

■ 3 Solomon loved Yahweh. This verse is the introduction to the Gibeon story, the shrine at which Solomon sacrificed and burnt incense. This practice was perceived to be an understandable exception to Solomon's devotion to Yahweh and walking in the statutes of David. Throughout the Gibeon sacrifice-dream-theophany scene, the terms "Yahweh" and "Elohim" are used interchangeably for deity in the Hebrew text (NIV: "the LORD" and "God").

■ 4 Gibeon was **the great shrine**, the **most important** place of sacrifice. David had built a tent for the ark in Jerusalem, but until Solomon went there after his experience at Gibeon, we have no account of anyone sacrificing there. Its greatness in size and popularity may have been the reason Solomon went there instead of to the tent that housed the ark in the city of David. Gibeon (modern El Jib) was seven miles northwest of Jerusalem. Joshua 9 tells the story of Gibeon, the story of an adept people group willing to be subjugated by Israel to survive. Second Chronicles 1:3-13 says Moses' tent of meeting was at Gibeon (but not the ark) and that Solomon took a great multitude of officials with him. The Chronicler's version seems to be a further attempt to legitimate Solomon's practice of sacrificing outside of Jerusalem.

■ **5** Solomon's dream theophany is comparable to other appearances of God in the Torah, Joshua, and Judges. However, Yahweh did not appear and speak to Solomon through men or angels—or directly—as he did to Abraham, Hagar, Rebekah, Jacob, Moses, Joshua, and Gideon. Here he **appeared** and spoke **in a dream**. God had used dreams to address or guide earlier characters as represented in Gen 20:3 (Abimelek); 28:12 (Jacob); 31:24 (Laban, the Aramean); and 37 and 41 (Joseph and Pharaoh, but God did not speak; dreams revealed the future). Several of the dreamers were foreigners. Nonetheless, God's invitation to Solomon in a dream reveals God's love for him (1 Kgs 3:5; see also 2 Sam 12:24-25) and explains Solomon's later astuteness in managing his people, region, and resources. The dream theophany also explains why Solomon became so wealthy and famous: these were God's gifts.

■ **6** These are Solomon's first and only words to Yahweh his God outside of his lengthy Deuteronomistic prayer of temple dedication in ch 8. Here Solomon significantly construed Yahweh's **kindness** (*ḥesed*) to David as conditioned upon David's faithfulness to God. This is an allusion to 2 Sam 7 and to the many other times in David's life that he depended on God. Solomon was fully aware of the favorable consequences of ***walking truthfully, righteously, and with integrity before and with God***. Solomon knew the rule for himself: that while obedience brings God's blessings, disobedience withdraws them.

■ **7-9** Solomon continued, in the words of Dtr, aligning himself with his father as God's servant. Solomon had been crowned, as he claimed, even though he was a young boy or small lad, who did not even know (in our idiom) "left from right" (lit. "how to exit or enter"). He humbly claimed youth, inexperience, and helplessness in seeking a ***hearing heart*** (v 9) to govern God's chosen, numerous, and difficult people. The word *šmʻ* (meaning "hear" [v 9]) also means "obey."

Solomon sought this hearing (obedient) heart in order to judge between ***good and evil***, the same formula used for the tree in Eden (Gen 2—3). The term "heart" in Hebrew is the place of judgment and volition, similar to "mind," the seat of understanding, in English. When his actions in the previous chapter are recalled, Solomon's humility here is incongruous. On the one hand, in obeying his father David, he had "humbly" submitted to his father's orders, but these were also in the interest of securing his own kingdom. He coldly added to David's orders, lashing out with temerity against older companions of his father, who were at his mercy, which he failed to show. This chapter, however, seems to abandon the nature and activity of the previous one; this one is about how Solomon loved Yahweh, walked in his ways, and asked for discernment for the sake of governing Israel.

■ 10 The narrator reports concerning Solomon's request: **the thing was good in the eyes of Yahweh**. The formula "good and evil" reminds us that the woman and the man in the garden (Gen 3) were commanded not to eat of the tree of the knowledge of good and evil. However, Solomon's request shows that the contexts in which good and evil appears nuance the meanings. In Genesis, God used the trees in the garden to make an implicit conditional covenant: all the trees are available to you, except this one. With a command against eating from a certain tree, human free will could be represented in story form. When humans ate and attained the knowledge of good and evil, God did not want them to eat from the tree of life also, for then they would live forever. In contrast, Solomon asked God for the ability to *judge* between good and evil in order to *judge* God's difficult people. Anyone familiar with Israel's story knows how difficult a people they were. See, for example, Num 11:10-15, which depicts Moses' sense of the burden of God's people.

■ 11-14 God granted and rewarded this unselfish request with incomparable riches and honor. The pleasing position of Solomon reflected by his primary heart's desire was enough for God to grant him wisdom, understanding, riches, and honor. For a long life, however, God reiterated the condition: you must **walk in my ways and obey my statutes and commands**. A **hearing heart** (v 9), a receptive heart, is wise (*ḥākām*) and understanding (*nābôn*). For God, in giving wisdom and discernment, said, **I will do as you have spoken** (v 12). In these attributes, Solomon will stand alone.

■ 15 Solomon's immediate return to *Jerusalem* to worship indicates another way for the narrator to mitigate his "unorthodox" sacrificing at Gibeon and the theophany there. Solomon's appearances before the ark of the covenant and his sacrifices for his household in Jerusalem enfold that city into the theophany at Gibeon. Solomon turned his face toward Jerusalem from this time forward.

Solomon and David (Judahites) offered sacrifices, without Dtr's censure, even though they were not from the priestly tribe of Levi. Neither was Saul (a Benjamite) denounced by Samuel (an Ephraimite) for sacrificing, but for not waiting for him to appear before he sacrificed (1 Sam 13:8-14). Priestly writers from later eras confined sacrificing to Levites and later to Levitical Zadokites, but Samuel and Kings were not reworked to comply with these priestly concerns.

FROM THE TEXT

The monarchy in Israel's story was fraught with ambivalence from its inception. In 1 Sam 8 and 12 the narrator reports that it was not God's ideal, although he was willing to go along with it. Solomon inherited this nascent kingdom, the kingdom of his father David. Although appearances of God are rare throughout this account, in ch 3 God finally appeared in a dream to help

King Solomon, to enhance his rule, and to bless him. This theophany aligned Solomon's rule with the kingdom of God, but the two were never identified.

Solomon responded to God by seeking a practical and necessary gift from God, the ability to rightly judge his people, discerning good from evil. Pleased with this humble, selfless request, God also gave him the things a young king might have been expected to seek: riches and honor. In the light of this text, how much more should we, knowing that the request for a ***hearing heart*** pleased God, ask God for the same as we are required to discern right from wrong. To do so indicates our respect for those we lead, our humility before God, and our faith in God to speak to us, provide understanding, and help us obey.

In Matt 6:33, Jesus told his listeners on the mountain that when they seek first *God's* kingdom and *God's* righteousness, then food, drink, and clothing would be given as well. Furthermore, Jesus promised the poor and hungry crowds that they could seek and obtain the kingdom and righteousness of God, which is both far less and far greater than the kingdom of men. Jesus taught that God's kingdom was and is available to everyone and is found on the opposite path of those who seek wealth (Matt 6:24). In so doing, they could be like the lilies of the field, whose clothing far outclassed Solomon's. The context of this sermon in Matthew points the way for Jesus' followers to determine how to gain God's kingdom and righteousness, thus it is filled with practical wisdom and social holiness, as well as spiritual blessings.

2. Solomon Displays His Wisdom to All Israel (3:16-28)

BEHIND THE TEXT

This narrative illustrates Solomon's God-given ability to govern his difficult people, to understand and judge right from wrong, to distinguish what is good from what is disastrous. This account of the prostitute whose son was stolen by her housemate is linked to the previous pericope by juxtaposition and conclusion. The final verse claims that when all Israel heard the king's verdict they saw that his ability to bring justice to everyone was from God and fulfilled God's promise of 3:11-12. This is the purpose of the story for its later receivers as well; a grieving mother and an endangered child appeared before a king whose inner wisdom reunited them, to our relief and awe.

IN THE TEXT

■ **16** The narrator makes no apologies that ***women of prostitution*** had access to the king of all Israel. They **stood before** him, the lowest of the low, without bowing low as Queen Bathsheba had done before both David and Solomon (ch 1).

■ **17-21** One woman presented the case, which was promptly refuted by the other. The mother of a four-day-old infant would indeed recognize her own baby! But the first woman could have been lying in order to acquire a live child. No witness could be called, for no **stranger** (client) was in the house with them; they were alone. No further investigation was possible.

■ **22** The two continued their dispute as they stood before the king. The bare-bones report allows us to imagine the anguish of the women, both bereaved until a judgment could be determined. The (here unnamed) king must render justice for them based on what they said and who they were, real mother of the living son and pretender, who had lost a son.

■ **23-25** The king summarized the dispute, and then resolved it by observing how the women reacted when he abruptly ordered that the living son be sawn in half and his parts distributed to both women.

■ **26** Both of the women were mothers, but one had a far different reaction to the king's order than the other. The Hebrew says, literally, her *wombs grew hot* (the plural of *raḥam* ["womb"] means "compassion," a mother's compassion, and *kāmar* means "kindled" or "inflamed"; see Gen 43:30; Hos 11:8). *We* know this woman was the mother of the living son because the narrator tells us. But Solomon only knew which woman would be the best parent and surmised she was the mother of the living son. One can understand a mother wishing to save her child's life at any cost, but it is harder to fathom anyone, especially a recently bereaved mother, endorsing the death of a child so that both housemates could be equally desolate.

■ **27** The king based his judgment on the callousness of the second responder as much as on the compassion of the first. In his ruling, he echoed the latter's pleas as a command: **do not kill him**!

■ **28** Solomon's God-given wisdom to administer justice in difficult situations is hereby illustrated. He had prayed for a *hearing heart* at the beginning of this narrative. At the end of it, through the story of the bereaved mother, all Israel stood in awe before the king and saw the divine wisdom that was within his inner being to render justice.

3. Solomon Adds Officials, Land, Wealth, and Honor (4:1-34 [4:1—5:14 HB])

IN THE TEXT

■ **1 All Israel** marveled at Solomon's wisdom to bring justice (3:28) and Solomon ruled **all Israel**. **All Israel** had made Solomon's father king through a treaty between Abner and David (whose tribe of Judah had made him king at Hebron years before [2 Sam 2:4; 3:1-20; 5:1-5]). Later Israel (tribes outside of Judah) reconfirmed David as their king after Absalom and Sheba's rebellions (19:9-15). This term, **all Israel**, implies unity on the one hand but disunity on the other. Often **all Israel** refers to everyone but the people of Judah (see 1 Kgs 12:16), for the tribes of Israel named after the twelve sons of Israel/Jacob were always aware of their composition, that is, family groups and land holdings.

They recognized also that kings from Judah did not govern without prejudice. The narrator distinguishes Israel and Judah even when describing the united kingdom (v 20).

■ **2-6** The Israel of Solomon was governed by his council of officials (*śārîm*): priests, army commanders, and administrators. It included two sons of Nathan and four priests, including Abiathar whose story of exile is told in ch 2. A number of the names link Solomon's rule to that of David. We will meet Adoniram again.

■ **7-19** The list of district governors from the north (Israel) who fed Solomon's household and stables includes two sons-in-law of Solomon. Only a few of the providing regions are identified as tribal: Ephraim, Issachar, Benjamin, and perhaps Asher. All have unclear boundaries. DeVries attends to each name, demonstrating how the list is relatively early, reflecting the tribal religion of Israel's recent past (1985, 70). The last unnamed district governor was over Judah, according to the LXX and a reconstructed MT. The first Judah at the end of v 19 dropped out because of the next Judah that begins the sentence of v 20 through a process of haplography (an accidental omission when the same word appears twice and together [here] or the same word ends two consecutive lines of a manuscript). Thus, the list should conclude with v 19*b*: **There was one governor over the district of Judah**. This governor is unnamed.

■ **20-23 [20—5:3 HB]** Before the abundant provisions are detailed, the editor inserts a summary comment about the population, happiness, and boundaries of Israel *and* Judah. This comment assumes that **Israel** stands for all the tribes except Judah. Earlier, Israel's opponents numbered as the sand of the sea (Josh 11:4; Judg 7:12; 1 Sam 13:5), but Israel's enemies had been overcome by God's might (and the wise counsel of Hushai [2 Sam 17:11]). The kingdoms from the Euphrates on the east to the land of the Philistines on the west and down to the border of Egypt on the south paid tribute and served Solomon. This serves to announce the fulfillment of God's promises to Israel's ancestors (Gen 15:15; 22:17; 32:12 [13 HB]). The kingdom was stable and prosperous because it was wisely administered *and* because God was fulfilling ancient covenant promises. The Hebrew version transmitted in our English Bibles indicates that Solomon's wealth also came from outside of Israel, from kingdoms that paid him tribute. The Greek versions are shorter and rearrange the material.

■ **24-25 [5:4-5 HB]** The Hebrew says that Solomon ruled over all regions *across* **the Euphrates River**, indicating the standpoint of the writer who must have been residing east of the Euphrates, in Babylon. Most translators use **west** to translate '*br* instead of *across*, the correct term. Tiphsah lay on the upper Euphrates (to the northeast) and Gaza is on Philistia's west coast. Solomon controlled all the kingdoms (or city-states) between the Euphrates, Philistia, and Egypt and had peace with these people. From 1 Kgs 3:1 and ch 11, we learn that Solomon's marriage alliances brokered such peace. The picture here is of Solomon and his nation residing in contentment and prosperity at the center of the world. Micah 4 also envisions a fig tree for everyone in the last days made possible through peace and the knowledge of Yahweh. Dan is on the northern border of Israel, and Beersheba is near the southern border of Judah.

■ **26-28 [5:6-8 HB]** The horses and their stables are numbered to prepare for the announcement of barley and straw provided for them by the district officers who also served the king's table. Topically, 4:22-23 [5:2-3 HB] and 4:26-28 [5:6-8 HB] belong with 4:1-19, which is how this chapter appears in the LXX. The lists may come from "the book of the annals of Solomon" (DeVries 1985, xliv, 66). This nonextant book is mentioned in 1 Kgs 11:41 and is obviously one source for this book. But the final rendering is chiastic; the expansions about Israel and Judah's greatness, happiness, and peace under Solomon is interwoven with the details of their prosperity and the officials in charge of distribution.

■ **29 [5:9 HB]** This verse speaks again of **sand**, this time referring not to the numbers of people in Israel and Judah (v 20) but to Solomon's God-given **wisdom and very great insight** and his ***broad heart, which was like the sand on the sea shore.***

■ **30-31 [5:10-11 HB]** Solomon's wisdom surpassed the wise men from the east and from Egypt, places that cultivated wisdom. Some of the other named men (Ethan, Heman, Kalkol, Darda) are also listed in 1 Chr 2:6 as sons of Zerah (son of Judah and Tamar [Gen 38]). Heman prophesied on musical instruments (1 Chr 25:1-6). Heman and Ethan produced Pss 88 and 89. "Sons of Mahol" means cantors, choristers, and/or dancers. Solomon exceeded the wisest and most talented of famous artisans and sages, both inside and outside of Israel across time.

4:26-34

■ **32-33 [5:12-13 HB]** Not only was Solomon a prolific sage and musician, but he was a scientist—an observer and namer of the natural world, ranging from the greatest to the smallest creatures and plants.

■ **34 [5:14 HB]** Solomon, the center of this particular world, shared his observations about all of life to those who came to listen. Solomon had asked for a ***hearing heart*** when God invited a request (3:7-9). One of the results of God's granting of his prayer was that kings, queens, and delegates from all nations came to hear him.

4. Solomon Builds a Temple for Yahweh (5:1—6:38 [5:15—6:38 HB])

BEHIND THE TEXT

The most significant underlying passages for Solomon's preparation, blueprints, and actual construction of the temple in Jerusalem are those describing the tabernacle that Moses built in the wilderness (Exod 25—27; 30:1—31:11) and 2 Sam 7, God's message to David that his son would build him a house. The detailed descriptions of both tabernacle and temple, different as they are in size and material, both include a holy of holies and cherubim set within the inner sanctuary. In fact, everything used to build and furnish the tabernacle and the temple has religious significance. And, most importantly, both were viewed as places for God to dwell (Exod 25:8; 40; 1 Kgs 8), although Dtr is careful to affirm that God's presence cannot be affixed to a single site.

The temple focus of 1 Kgs 5 and 6 continues in ch 7 at v 13, which turns to Huram, a bronze worker from Tyre. Solomon hired Huram to cast two crowned columns, the molten sea, stands, basins, pots, shovels, latticework, and other vessels. Huram's work paralleled that of Bezalel and Oholiab, who crafted the metal vessels of the wilderness tabernacle (or tent of meeting), described in Exod 31:1-11. One obvious difference between the building of the wilderness tabernacle and Solomon's temple is that every detail of the former is ordered by Yahweh. He did not, however, direct the framing or furnishing of the temple.

Excavations of temples in Syria and present-day Israel are relevant to the Jerusalem temple, which cannot be excavated. Canaanite and Hittite temples from the Late Bronze and Iron Ages have features that are described in these chapters. There is a vast literature on this subject, much of which is referred to by Carol Meyers (1992, 350-69).

The 1 Kings arrangement of temple construction texts, including ch 7, seems confusing with its foray into Solomon's other building projects at 7:1-12. Thus the LXX reorders the material. But there is logic to the Hebrew-English ordering of this process. An early version that relied upon available records preserved in "the book of the annals of Solomon" was redacted with expansions from later periods, including that of Dtr. Through a thorough study of the Hebrew terms translated "cubit" (variations of *'mh*) here and at Exod 26—28, DeVries finds six extracts from "the book of the annals of Solomon," some of which are architectural records that the writer of 1 Kings cited verbatim (1985, 91-93). In 6:11-13 Yahweh is depicted as acknowledging the project with the reminder that Solomon's obedience would be the condition on which Yahweh would dwell with the people.

The account first describes the temple, its external framing, a three-story storage structure wrapping around it, and then its internal finishing, including the inner court (6:2-37). Then the palace complex is outlined (7:1-8), followed by a description of the methods for shaping the costly stones at the quarry for the foundation of the temple (vv 9-12). At this point Huram, the bronze worker, is introduced and the vessels and furnishings that he molded for the temple (vv 13-47). The NIV uses Huram, as he is called in 2 Chronicles, perhaps to avoid confusion with King Hiram of Tyre.

IN THE TEXT

■ **1-2 [15-16 HB]** King Hiram of Tyre, a city in Phoenicia, the region on the west coast to the north of Israel, was not one of those kings who had heard of

Solomon's great wisdom. Rather, he had heard that Solomon had succeeded David, whom *he had loved* (v 1 [15 HB]). Thus, this passage could easily follow ch 2 and may have originally. These verses introduce Solomon's desire to build a temple for Yahweh based on the fact that Solomon was surrounded on every side by peace, clearly affirmed by the preceding material.

■ **3-4 [17-18 HB]** Solomon responded to King Hiram's envoy by conveying his intentions to build a temple for *the name of Yahweh*, his God; the first time this construct is used in the narrative. It may have been employed by the redactor to disabuse people of the notion that Yahweh would actually live in a house of cedar, which the dedication prayer of 1 Kgs 8 takes great pains to disavow (v 27). Solomon directed Hiram to order the logging of cedars in his region. Hiram had sent cedars for the building of David's house, and by this David *knew that God had established him on his throne* (2 Sam 5:11-12).

The Chronicler depicts David preparing materials for the temple that Solomon would build, using cedars that King Hiram had already sent (1 Chr 22:1-4). He repeatedly confirms that David autonomously made Solomon king well before he died, so intent was David on helping Solomon build the temple. But this is the Chronicler's later construal. First Kings says that David did not know which son would rule after him until Nathan and Bathsheba informed him. According to 2 Sam 7, David wanted to build a temple but did not begin storing materials for it. In Kings, David did not speak to Solomon until he was dying and his words were not concerned with the temple but with bringing justice to those to whom David had shown mercy and/or who might be dangerous to Solomon.

Solomon told King Hiram that David could not have built a house for "the name of Yahweh" because of enemy harassment. (Compare 1 Chr 28:3: David should not build Yahweh a house because David had shed blood.) However, 2 Sam 7:1 and 9 claim that *after* God had given David rest from his enemies (and a cedar home) David supposed the ark needed a house of cedar. Yahweh had responded without saying why David should not build him a house (temple), only that Yahweh had never needed or wanted a house in the past, nor did he at this time. David's son would build Yahweh's house. This was followed by the promise that Yahweh would build David a lasting house (dynasty) instead (7:12-13).

Nonetheless, Solomon reported to Hiram that David's enemies had hindered him from building the temple, whereas Solomon had no adversary (śāṭān) or risk of disaster. (For other uses of śāṭān, see 1 Sam 29:4 and 2 Sam 19:22 [23 HB].) This statement explains the positioning of this passage immediately after affirmations of Solomon's peaceful relations (based on his dominance) with his neighbors far and wide (1 Kgs 4:20-24 [20—5:4 HB]).

■ **5-6 [19-20 HB]** The precedent for Solomon's order of cedars was King Hiram's gift of cedars for David's house. Hiram clearly had dominion over the loggers of Sidon and the region of Lebanon where the cedars grew. The

Chronicler indicates that David acquired cedars from Lebanon for the temple through Hiram before David died (1 Chr 22:1-14). The Chronicler also includes a parallel account to this one: the story of Solomon ordering cedars from Hiram (2 Chr 2:1-16 [1:18—2:15 HB]).

■ **7-12 [21-26 HB]** In any case, Yahweh's house remained to be built, and the flourishing King Solomon began when he procured cedars of Lebanon from King Hiram, who was happy to comply in exchange for food for his household continually. This arrangement, involving huge quantities of food and timber, was confirmed by a state treaty.

■ **13-18 [27-32 HB]** As noted above, the term **all Israel** usually does not include Judah. If this is the case here, the thirty thousand forced laborers (who felled logs four months of the year in Lebanon under Adoniram) did not include Judahites. The foundation stones for the temple were quarried and dressed where they were extracted by eighty thousand stone masons and then transported by seventy thousand others, making them costly indeed. The fine stones observed today at the temple site were placed there centuries later by Herod long after Solomon's costly foundation stones were crushed or buried underground.

This text implies that these laborers and their foremen included foreigners and possibly men from Judah by mentioning them separately from the thirty thousand "shift workers" from Israel. The Chronicler specifies that these workers were conscripted from resident aliens who had been counted in the Davidic census (2 Chr 2:17 [16 HB], with reference to 2 Sam 24:1-9).

The notice of the provenance of the workers and the burden of their labor foreshadows one of the reasons for the permanent split of **all Israel** from Judah after Solomon's death. His son Rehoboam's decision to oppress the northern tribes more than Solomon had done provoked the rallying cry: "To your tents, Israel! Look after your own house, David!" (1 Kgs 12:16).

■ **6:1** The Hebrew term translated **temple** is simply *the house* (*habayit*). The order of the description of the temple's construction links Solomon's temple to the wilderness tabernacle (→ Behind the Text for 1 Kgs 5:1—6:38 [5:15—6:38 HB], above). Furthermore, the solemn introduction to this material dates the onset of the project in terms of Israel's exodus from Egypt, the house of bondage. This great round number (12 x 10 x 4) puts Israel's tenure in Egypt too early (fifteenth century BC instead of the more likely twelfth century BC), given Solomon's mid-tenth century BC reign. Its significance may be found in the Deuteronomistic redactor's wish to recall Yahweh's deliverance of his people and the Passover. Israel had experienced a long period of freedom as the people of God without a temple and most of it without a king. On the one hand, this means that they could endure without either; on the other, that it was high time for God's people to be prosperous enough to build Yahweh a house of cedar and costly stones. Still, we must wonder, did God need a house?

■ **2-6** A cubit is one and one half feet and the notes to the NIV give the dimensions of the temple in feet and meters. The three chambers of this stone building, lined with cedar, were covered with a cedar roof and grounded on a rock threshing floor (see 2 Sam 24) covered with cypress wood (1 Kgs 6:15; NIV: "planks of juniper"). The three stories were surrounded by rooms at each level. Each level was supported by a *ledge* (v 6; Heb.: "ribs") laid horizontally from the outer wall; v 6 lists the widths of the three levels of side rooms. The strong outer walls were wider at the base to compensate for the side-room surround, the widths of which were progressively narrower. A tripartite plan was the style of Aramean, Canaanite, and Phoenician temples during the Late Bronze and Early Iron periods, the age of Saul, David, and Solomon (Meyers 1992, 350-69, esp. 355; Sweeney 2007, 110; DeVries 1985, 98).

■ **7** The verse interrupts the description of the side chambers. As noted earlier, the finished stones were dressed where they had been excavated and then brought to the construction site. In Deut 27:5-6, Moses told the people to build an altar of whole stones upon which no iron tool had been wielded. However, in this case, tools were used on the temple stones, but not at the temple site. No hammer, chisel, axe, or iron tool was heard on-site.

■ **8-10** The temple was entered on the south side and its middle and third levels were reached through winding stairs. The side rooms described above are mentioned here again.

■ **11-13** The tone of Yahweh's message to Solomon is that of toleration of the temple, acceptance of his efforts on the condition of his obedience to the Torah. He reminded Solomon that his adherence to the decrees, regulations, and commands was far more important for the fulfillment of Yahweh's promise than a temple made with hands. If Solomon would observe these conditions (the verbs are: *walk, do,* and *keep* [v 12]), **Yahweh would establish for Solomon the words that he had spoken to David**, and Yahweh would live with his people. Although this may be implied, Yahweh still did not promise to live in the house that Solomon was building, but rather to live among his people, which was his intent in the wilderness. In fact, this was why God delivered this people from Egypt in the first place! (See Exod 40.) This insertion may be the Deuteronomistic reminder that God did not need man-made structures to live among obedient and contrite people (Isa 57:15). Recall that he told Saul in 1 Sam 15:22 that he desired obedience, not sacrifice.

■ **14-20** The comment about Solomon completing *the house* (1 Kgs 6:14) may serve as a summary of the previous presentation. But it also introduces the description of its interior finish, including the inner sanctuary (*dĕbîr*) or holy of holies for the ark, set apart at the end of the long hall (vv 16-19). Solomon established this place for the ark of the covenant of Yahweh, which consistently represented the presence of Yahweh. The high point of Solomon's dedication of the temple was the settling of the ark into its place by the priests

(1 Kgs 8:3-11). The walls of the most holy place (*dĕbîr*) were gold, while the altar was finished in cedar.

■ **21-22** The inside of the temple was paneled in cedar, according to 6:18, but this later expansion idealizes the entire temple as overlaid with gold, including the altar.

■ **23-29** The earlier version of the temple's features continues with a description of the fifteen-foot wingspan of the gold cherubim, which stood side by side within the inner sanctuary (the holy place), a thirty-foot spread. Cherubim (sg.: cherub) were fashioned onto the mercy seat of the ark (see Exod 37:6-9). Images of cherubim, flowers in full bloom, and palm trees were also carved into the walls and doors of the interior room and on the walls of the outer rooms of the temple. These were images of fruitfulness and, most significantly, Eden. (For a description of cherubim, see Ezek 1:10-11.)

■ **30** Verses 29 and 30 of 1 Kgs 6 are from the same late gilding hand as vv 21-22, 27, and 32-35, all of which can be identified linguistically by the use of the perfect with the conjunctive *waw* ("and," "but," "indeed").

■ **31-36** Like most of the descriptions above, this account of the embellished olive wood and juniper doors, the inner courtyard, and the time parameters of the temple's construction reflect the early version of this passage, which was probably adapted from the records found in the now nonextant "book of the annals of Solomon." (For vv 32-36, → vv 23-29.)

■ **37-38** The month of Ziv (flowers), when Solomon began to build, is an old Canaanite name for a spring month. Likewise for Bul (rain), the final month, which is in the fall. The temple of Solomon thus took seven years and six months to complete. During the Babylonian exile, the beginning of the Jewish year was moved to spring, thus Ziv was called the second month and Bul (now Heshvan) the eighth month as it is here (see Auld 1986, 42). Previous to this, Israel's calendar had begun in the fall, but this is also true today. The commemoration of the Jewish New Year is on the first of Tishri, the seventh month (in the fall), and that is when the year number is increased. The "first month" of the Jewish calendar is the month of Nissan in the spring when Passover occurs.

5. Solomon Builds Royal Houses (7:1-12)

IN THE TEXT

■ **1** This verse belongs with 6:38*b*. Thus: ***And he built it [in] seven years and his [own] house Solomon built [in] thirteen years; and he finished all of his house.*** The Hebrew word order shows that the durations of the construction of both houses are intentionally juxtaposed. The NIV conveys the meaning with **however**. The NRSV uses "his own house" to express the significance of the Hebrew word order. Solomon's house is mentioned as among his other building projects again in 7:8, but without detailed descriptions of it in either place. Since it (or all of them) took thirteen years to build, it probably surpassed the temple, unless he commissioned far fewer laborers for its construction, which seems unlikely. Solomon acquired a very large family to shelter lavishly. DeVries and Sweeney find support for a location of Solomon's house adjacent to and south of the temple with an entrance to the temple's inner court (DeVries 1985, 102; Sweeney 2007, 112). Thus the entrance to the temple on the south side would have faced Solomon's home.

■ **2-5** The **Palace of the Forest of Lebanon** is described in some detail here and later in 1 Kgs 10:17, 21 (paralleled in 2 Chr 9:16, 20). No indication of where it was built in relation to the other buildings is given. The **Forest Hall**, obviously made of cedar, was much larger than the temple and would have been used for large public gatherings.

■ **6-8** Cedar from Lebanon also covers the **throne hall**, which was also known as the **Hall of Justice**, Solomon's residence, and that of his primary wife, Pharaoh's daughter.

■ **9-12** The writer was taken again with the huge and costly stones of the magnificent outer walls of all of Solomon's buildings and the courtyard walls that surround all of them. Unlike the finished-at-quarry pristine stones for the temple, these stones were permitted to be dressed on-site. The great court of v 9 is described in v 12.

6. Solomon Completes the Temple (7:13-51)

7:2-22

IN THE TEXT

■ **13-14** Solomon continued his construction of the temple by hiring Huram, who was, like his father had been, a bronzesmith from Tyre. King Hiram had supplied Solomon with cedars and workmen, and this artisan Huram cast the bronze work for the temple. He was the son of an Israelite woman from the tribe of Naphtali, but, other than offering assurance of this connection, the narrator makes no apologies for the foreign influence on the temple.

■ **15-22** The text continues to provide architectural details using ancient terms, here concerning Huram's bronze work. He began by casting the twenty-seven-foot-high pillars that stood at the temple's entrance, named **Jakin** (*he establishes*) and **Boaz** (*in strength*) (v 21). Read from north to south (or right to left as one reads Hebrew) they say: *in strength he establishes*. These are topped with lattice-embellished crowns or capitals that increase their height to slightly less than thirty-five feet. The temple building was forty-five feet high. The pomegranates and lilies symbolized fertility reminiscent of Eden's orchards and gardens, and the pillars (eighteen feet around) represent the stability of the pillars thought to be the foundations of the land, mountains, and all creation (see Job 9:5-6; 26:11; Pss 18:15 [16 HB]; 75:3 [4 HB]; 82:5; Isa 24:18; Mic 6:2).

■ **23-26** The thick bronze Sea symbolized another aspect of creation (Gen 1), and its water functioned to purify the priests entering the temple (Lev 8:6). It may also have been used to wash the organs of the sacrificial animals (Lev 8:21; 9:14). Twelve bronze bulls facing outward toward each point of the compass supported the fifteen-foot-across reservoir, which could have held up to eleven thousand gallons of water (each bath is thought to convey around five gallons of water). The bronze Sea was placed near the entrance to the temple on the southeast corner (1 Kgs 7:39).

■ **27-45** The **movable stands** (or carts) for the ten water basins—all of hammered bronze—were embellished with more cherubim, as well as lions and cattle. They could have been used to fill the bronze Sea and to hold water for purification and other necessary cleansing. Huram also made pots, shovels for the ashes of sacrifices, bowls for libations and to hold the blood sprinkled on people and altar (see Exod 24:6-8; 29:16; Lev 1:5; 7:14).

■ **46-47** The writer explains where the bronze casting occurred—a foundry for melting and pouring the metal was situated in the clay pits of the banks of the Jordan River. The mention that they were not weighed leaves the impression that weighing temple vessels would have been customary, with those weights included in the records, but the sheer numbers precluded doing so.

■ **48-50** The focus has been on the bronze casting of Huram, as commissioned by Solomon, yet, in this list, the narrator affirms Solomon *made* gold implements of the holy place, without naming the goldsmith, who certainly would have been as accomplished as Huram. This set of gold vessels and veneers complete the account with attention to the inner sanctuary and underscore Solomon's great wealth. Compare these verses to 6:16-35 (which are different) and Exod 27 and 38 (which are similar, although the vessels there are of bronze (Exod 27:2-3). They seem to be a later addition, as DeVries suggests (1985, 111).

■ **51** The temple preparations David had made and the holy things he had stored, according to the Chronicler, seem to be alluded to here, although they have not been mentioned before in Samuel or Kings. The statement may come from "the book of the annals of Solomon" as well. Furthermore, we might surmise that the **treasuries**, a term used for the first time, were the storage rooms and galleries described in 1 Kgs 6:5-6 and 10 that surrounded each level of the temple on three sides.

FROM THE TEXT

Few sermons are centered on the details of the temple, but the writers of these scriptures were clearly concerned with the temple's function and beauty—its observable, tangible, physical features. These descriptions derive from some of the earliest sources represented in the Bible and indicate the importance of keeping such records. They remind us of our own physicality and our need for icons to help us focus on the God who wants to dwell with us. The people who entered the temple chambers were moved to awe over the holiness of God, who was not too proud to show up in buildings made by human hands. The layering of text upon text about the costly cedars, bronze, and gold raises a question to be answered in the rest of the story: what will happen to Solomon's temple and its accoutrements when the generations pass?

Where was the temple? Details of the design and decor, furnishings and utensils are provided in 1 Kgs 6—7, but not the location relative to the Jerusalem of the day. Second Chronicles 3:1 refers to the census narrative of 2 Sam 24:16-24 (in which David buys the threshing floor of Araunah) and marks it (and Moriah) as the site of Solomon's temple. Nonetheless, we can surmise that Solomon's additions to Jerusalem were north of the city of David (Zion) on the southeast side of the hill of Ophel outside of the wall of Ophel. The Ophel hill was directly adjacent to the Kidron valley. The first scriptural mention of Ophel occurs in 2 Chr 27:3, not in Kings, and refers to King Jotham's building projects.

Archaeologists and historians have argued for temple sites directly under, as well as just north, south, and east of the Dome of the Rock. (For a concise summary, see Dolphin and Kollen 1995.) In any case, 1 Kings implies that Solomon's structures were built outside of the city of David (2 Sam 5:11-12; 1 Kgs 3:1). Thus, the temple was not at the center of the city but in an empty space and thus disconnected from any shrines of the Jebusites or David's palace.

Although identifying the site was not a priority for the writer, he was careful to describe the sort of stones used, where and how they were dressed, distinguishing the treatment of the temple stones from those used for Solomon's other buildings. Unlike the stones for the altar of Deut 27:1-8, the temple stones were treated and shaped, but not at the temple site. No one heard the sounds of tools scraping, clanging, or crashing against stone. Thus, the temple retained the nature of that first altar built for inscribing the Law: that of stones carried and settled one upon the other.

7:13-51

One reason for the thirteen years necessary for the building of Solomon's home, halls, and courts may have been that their stones were cut on site while the temple's stones were predressed at the quarry. However, the narrator stresses the nature of the great stone blocks for both types of structures *and* compares the length of time for building them without making such a connection.

The predressed stones symbolized nature and creation, as did the elaborate carvings and impressions in bronze of fruits and flowers. The pillars at the temple entrance and the great bronze Sea seem to be an attempt to parallel the stability of Solomon's reign with the firm foundations of the created world. If Solomon wished to imply this, God wished to disabuse him of the notion by appearing to Solomon after he had begun building the temple. God reminded him that the laws God had given for serving Yahweh alone were the way his promise to David would be fulfilled. A temple was acceptable *if* obedience ensued. God would dwell with his people if his statutes were followed by the king (1 Kgs 6:11-13).

Although God had ordered every detail of the tabernacle's construction in Exodus, God has not appeared in Kings as the initiator or director of this endeavor, just as God had not directed the installation of Solomon as David's successor. Observed across the range of narratives that comprise the Torah and Former Prophets, God has slipped from his place as primary mover of the action. Nonetheless, God intervened in Solomon's life. Just as God came alongside of Solomon in 1 Kgs 3:5, so God appeared to him after he began building the temple to acknowledge the project and remind him of his priorities (6:11-13). Each time God appeared to Solomon, he reminded him that the fulfillment of God's promise to David, and to him, was conditioned upon his submission to God's laws. God intended to use Israel's monarchy to preserve justice and peace in the land.

This is not to imply that the Scriptures, in every place, blame the institution of monarchy for God's withdrawal from center stage. During the judges period, without a king, the tribes lived in chaos for the most part. Deuteronomy 17:14-20 expects a king who will submit to God's laws. Furthermore, God selected both Saul and David and spoke to them through prophets. God spoke to Solomon twice in this section and will speak again. He does not leave his people alone and will bless their endeavors if they acknowledge and obey him.

7. Solomon Dedicates the Temple of Yahweh (8:1-66)

BEHIND THE TEXT

After Solomon brought all the vessels and furnishings that David had set apart into the house of Yahweh, he prepared to bring up the ark that was in Zion as well. This entailed innumerable sacrifices by the elders, tribal heads, family leaders, and all the men of Israel whom Solomon had assembled in Jerusalem for this purpose. Once that was accomplished, Solomon delivered a series of public prayers and blessings that emphasized the past foundation of the temple in the will of David and its future role as a place toward which people who were suffering could pray. Solomon's prayers were followed by sacrifices of peace and fellowship.

Sacrifices and possible references to the Festival of Sukkot (Booths) in the seventh month frame the Deuteronomistic theology extended by Solomon's announcements and prayers. Except for 2 Kgs 17, no other passage is as rife with Deuteronomistic concerns. Solomon, like Moses, Joshua, and Samuel before him, is the mouthpiece for Dtr (DeVries 1985, 121). Yet 1 Kgs 8 is also comprised of material both earlier and later than that of Dtr^1 and Dtr^2 (→ Introduction). DeVries identifies the earliest strata as ancient "sacred story" and the latest redaction as postexilic expansions that use late terms and/or explain earlier terms, such as the name of the month "Ethanim" (1985, 122-23).

The subunits of this chapter may be identified as follows:
- Verses 1-9: All Israel gathered and sacrificed as their priests attached the ark of the Sinai/Horeb covenant to the temple in Jerusalem.
- Verses 10-13: A cloud identified with the glory of Yahweh filled his new house, and Solomon invited Yahweh to live forever there.
- Verses 14-21: Solomon announced the historical and theological foundation for this temple.
- Verses 22-53: Solomon requested God's attention to seven potential conditions: oaths, enemy oppression, land fertility, natural disasters, foreigners' prayers, war, captivity.
- Verses 54-61: Blessings.
- Verses 62-66: All Israel sacrificed, celebrated, and departed from Jerusalem.

As in the previous passages regarding temple construction, the question of Yahweh's dwelling place appears in this chapter: can Yahweh live in a house made with hands? (→ 1 Kgs 5:3-4 [17-18 HB]; 6:1, 11-14.)

In this chapter, the ark and the tent of meeting are both brought up to the Temple Mount after the completion of the temple and its vessels. The ark is placed under cherubim in the holy of holies. As central features of this account, these wilderness productions connect for Israel and all later receivers of these traditions Solomon's building, furnishing, and consecration of the house of Yahweh to Moses and the Sinai/Horeb covenant.

When Yahweh had delivered Israel from Egypt, he brought them to the mountain (Sinai) or Horeb (the term used by Dtr) where he made a covenant with them based on this monumental act of grace (Exod 19:1-5). However, Yahweh prohibited any man-made monuments to represent him (20:1-5), which the people quickly violated. Aaron accommodated their request for a visual representation of the god(s) who brought them from Egypt (32:1-6). In the meantime, Yahweh had called Moses up to the mountain to detail a tabernacle, an ark of the covenant, the table, and lampstand, all tangible icons that would help these people serve the God who had freed them from bondage, the "iron-smelting furnace" (1 Kgs 8:51). So, while they were not permitted to make or bow to any likeness of a creature or thing, Yahweh was instructing Moses in patterns and procedures for a hands-on sensory style of worship involving an assortment of materials—animal, vegetable, and mineral. All these things would help Israel practice their gratefulness, their repentance, and their devotion to Yahweh, as well as to experience God's forgiveness and presence with them.

When providing careful descriptions of patterns and materials, Yahweh directly told Moses to have the people make him a sanctuary so that he could live with them (Exod 25:8-9). Although David's desire to build Yahweh a house grounds Solomon's projects, they are not the result of explicit words from Yahweh indicating he wanted a place to dwell. However, the wilderness traditions clearly establish the tabernacle and the mercy seat of the ark as a place for Yahweh to dwell and to meet Moses.

The Jerusalem temple and Yahweh's fidelity to the house of David are the focal points of this chapter. They exist on the condition of the kings' adherence to the commands of Yahweh. Although their failures to do so were anticipated, with consequent trauma and exile, so was Yahweh's mercy and restoration.

Scholars differ on whether the references to exile and potential restoration in this chapter are Josianic (Dtr¹) and refer to the Assyrian exile of the northern tribes, Israel, or whether they were written during the Babylonian exile (Dtr²). During the Assyrian exile, a son of David was still on the throne of Judah and would stay there *if* he would abide by the laws of Yahweh. The house of Yahweh was still standing in Jerusalem during the times of Hezekiah and Josiah, for the poles of the ark were still observable from the nave, the place just outside of the holy of holies (1 Kgs 8:8). In addition, it was toward this house the exiles must turn and repent (vv 47-50). Sweeney presumes this means the house was still standing when this was written (2007, 130), while Levenson argues that it means turning to pray toward the place the temple had stood (1981, 143-66, esp. 157-64).

Ultimately, the prayers of Solomon in this chapter apply to any and every period of exile or Diaspora, including that of Babylon. God's people could pray without a temple; God would hear from heaven wherever they were. Within the context of multiple sacrifices in this passage, Solomon affirms that the temple is a place of prayer and God's people can pray with or without a temple as the rabbis affirm after the Romans destroy the last temple of the Jews in AD 70.

IN THE TEXT

■ **1** The chapter begins with **King Solomon** summoning **the elders of Israel**, among other leaders. The term **elders of Israel** first appears in Exod 3:16 and reflects the ancient tribal league, indicative of "the sacred story" of temple consecration that is the core of this account. The core story is supplemented with Dtr's supplements and later expansions, as mentioned above. The purpose of this summons was to bring up **the ark of Yahweh's covenant**, a phrase used also by Dtr at 1 Sam 4:5 and 1 Kgs 6:19. Once it reaches its destination, the ark would continue to symbolize Yahweh's presence as it had in the wilderness when it was constructed, through the conquest of Joshua (Josh 3; 6; 8:30-35), and at Shiloh (1 Sam 1—3). But not until 1 Kgs 8:6 does the narrator identify the destination of the ark. Here we are to picture the leaders of Israel going to the ark in Zion.

■ **2** In this verse, King Solomon *gathered each man of Israel.* The festival refers to Sukkot (Booths) in the seventh month on the fifteenth day (Ethanim, the old Phoenician/Canaanite name, was changed to Tishri). Sukkot is described in Lev 23:33-43 and Num 29:12-38 and referred to elsewhere throughout the Torah, the Prophets, and the Writings. Solomon moved the ark and consecrated the temple eleven months after he had finished the building (1 Kgs 6:38).

■ **3-4** The priests conveyed the ark with the tent of meeting and its vessels, but the Levites are included in 8:4. The wilderness tent has not been mentioned in Samuel—Kings, although 2 Chr 1:3-13 says Moses' tent of meeting was at Gibeon (→ 1 Kgs 3:4). Samuel—Kings described a tent that David had made for the ark, a different tent (2 Sam 6:17; 1 Kgs 2:29-30). The text is silent about what happened to the tent of meeting, but, on the basis of its measurements, Richard E. Friedman suggests that it was placed within the holy of holies (1980, 241-48). Such a move, however, would have been significant enough to mention. In any case, the tent of meeting could have fit into the holy of holies.

■ **5 King Solomon** and the summoned congregation of Israel sacrificed before the ark, apparently after the priests had placed it in the courtyard outside of the house of Yahweh. During this occasion, all the people were sacrificing, including Solomon. This assembly may have included women and children, or it may refer to those described in vv 1-4, priests, Levites, and each Israelite man, only males.

■ **6-8** The priests settled the ark inside the house of Yahweh, beneath the wings of the new cherubim in the **shrine room** (*dĕbîr*), which is the **holiest of all holy places**. The Hebrew says: **The priests brought the Ark of Yahweh's covenant to its place, to the shrine room of the house, to the Holy of Holies, to [rest] under the wings of the cherubim**. This way we can picture the progression. The ark came with great fanfare from Zion (the city of David where David had made a tent for it), to the temple courtyard, where all could see and sacrifice before it, to the most inner room, to the cherubim and was set underneath their wings.

The ark had been around! Recall with Israel on this occasion the other journeys of the ark as told in Samuel (Shiloh [1 Sam 3:3]; Ashdod, Gath, Ekron, Beth Shemesh, and Kiriath Jearim [1 Sam 4:3—7:1]; briefly to Gibeah [1 Sam 14:18]; Obed-Edom's house [2 Sam 6:1-12]; Zion [2 Sam 6:13-19]). This temple was meant to be the ark's final resting place.

By the command of Yahweh through Moses, the ark had been designed to contain the two stone tablets of commands from Horeb/Sinai and to be the place of meeting between Yahweh and Moses (see Exod 24:12—25:22). "There I will meet with you, and from above the mercy seat, from between the two cherubim that are on the ark of the covenant, I will deliver to you all my commands for the Israelites" (25:22 NRSV).

The poles inserted in the rings of the ark are described in 25:12-15. The notice that they remained there in the author's time is an affirmation of the command in v 15 that the poles remained in the rings of the ark, as well as of the fact that the ark, its poles, the holy of holies, and of course the temple itself still existed. Thus, this text could not have been written during the Babylonian exile after the temple had been destroyed. Later redactors of this material did not change this line, but it dropped out in the Greek versions produced much later.

■ **9** Horeb is Dtr's designation for the mountain and a sign of his hand. Similarly, Deut 10:5 claims that the ark contained the tablets. Compare the priestly texts of Exod 16:33 and Num 17:10-13 [25-28 HB], which indicate the reasons a pot of manna and Aaron's flowering and fruiting staff were kept in the tent of meeting. They do not claim they were in the ark itself (but see Heb 9:4).

■ **10-11** The cloud settling on the tabernacle in Exod 40:35 demonstrated Yahweh's presence. The appearance of the cloud of Yahweh in the newly constructed tabernacle was the climax of his acts of deliverance and covenant making in Exodus. He had formed a people with whom to dwell, and he had them construct a physical place, a tabernacle, where he manifested himself to Israel. From then on, they would follow the cloud's movements in order to know when and where to go (Exod 40:36-37). So also Solomon's temple is blessed with the cloud representing **the glory—the weight**—of Yahweh; the work of Solomon was honored by a visible demonstration of Yahweh's life among Israel. The cloud of Yahweh's glory (or weight) filled the temple only after the priests came out from the sanctuary. They were so overwhelmed by it that they could not **stand to serve**. Similarly, Moses and Aaron were not able to enter the tent in the wilderness because of the cloud and the glory of Yahweh except at appointed times (Exod 40:35; Lev 16:2-13).

■ **12-13** Solomon's response to the temple filled with Yahweh's glory cloud was a potent and enigmatic statement that aligned Yahweh's stated place to dwell with the house Solomon had built. He seemed to invite Yahweh to move from **thick darkness** or **dripping gloom** (*ărāpel*) to this exalted house forever. **Surely I have built an exalted house for you, a place for you to rest forever**. The Hebrew term that the NIV translates **dark cloud** (*ărāpel*) is different from the Hebrew term for "cloud" in vv 10-11 and in Exod 40 (*ānān*). However, Ps 97:2 is among the scriptures that associate the two terms: **Clouds and thick darkness are all around him** (see also Ezek 34:12; Joel 2:2; and Zeph 1:15). Scriptures such as Exod 20:21 convey the tradition of Yahweh dwelling in *ărāpel*, "thick darkness": "Moses approached the thick darkness where God was." Other passages that associate God's home with **thick darkness** are: Deut 5:22; 2 Sam 22:10-12; Ps 18:9-11 [10-12 HB]. Second Chronicles 6:1-2 is the parallel passage to 1 Kgs 8:12-13. Other uses of *ărāpel* are in Isa 60:2; Job 3:6; 23:17; and 38:9. The LXX emends this passage considerably (see Sweeney 2007, 132).

■ **14-15** The order of the Hebrew is important here as it is in the progression of the ark to its new resting place in the holy of holies. **The king turned his face** *around and he blessed the whole congregation of Israel, and the whole congregation of Israel stood, and he said: "Blessed is Yahweh the God of Israel who spoke by his mouth with David my father and by his hand fulfilled it saying . . ."* The king who had been facing the cloud of Yahweh and the temple turned all the way around to face Israel. He blessed them and they stood. Then he blessed Yahweh. This is followed by a historical prologue to his series of prayers for Israel of the present and the future.

■ **16-19** Solomon insisted that Yahweh did *not* choose a city for a temple for his name, but rather he chose a king, David. Since David was chosen by Yahweh, he favored David's desire to build a temple for his name but gave that task to David's son. This emphasis on Yahweh's choice of David, not a city, must be remembered together with Deuteronomy's repeated phrase regarding Israel's future place of sacrifice: **The place Yahweh God will choose** (e.g., Deut 12:5-6, 11-13, 14, 18, 26; 15:20; 16:2; 26:2). No city is named in these passages either, but they do insist that God would choose a place. The logic of Solomon's claim that Yahweh had instead chosen a king proceeds like this: the chosen king, David, chose to build a temple; Yahweh delayed this procedure to the time of David's son. This son, Solomon, chose the place: Jerusalem, on a hill outside of the city of David. But Yahweh's fidelity to David is the underpinning of Solomon's subsequent prayer that Yahweh would faithfully respond to prayers in or toward this temple.

The recurring phrase *a house for God's name* echoes Yahweh's words to David through Nathan in 2 Sam 7:13 and is repeated throughout the chapter. David wanted to build a house for the ark of God (2 Sam 7:2). Yahweh said in response (v 5): "Are you the one to build me a house to dwell in?" In v 13 he states that David's son would build a house for his name.

8:16-21

In sum, in 2 Sam 7, Yahweh interprets shelter for the ark as a house for himself and later claims this will be for his name, as does Solomon throughout this passage. The temple of Solomon, according to this chapter, was a house for the ark, for Yahweh, and for Yahweh's name. In 2 Chr 2:6 [5 HB], Solomon asserted to Hiram/Hiram of Tyre that the house would be (no more than) "a place to burn sacrifices before him" [Yahweh]. But see also 2 Chr 6:2, which quotes 1 Kgs 8:13, claiming that this house is "a place for [Yahweh] to dwell forever." This will be discussed further below.

■ **20-21** Solomon portrayed himself as the heir and fulfillment of the Davidic promises and as the connector of the Exodus traditions (represented by the ark and the tent of meeting) to the temple in Judah. Two things had been fulfilled and they must be understood together. First, a son of David had indeed ascended to the throne of Israel, as promised. Second, this son built the temple for the name of Israel's God, Yahweh, a fulfillment of Yahweh's promises to the man he chose to rule Israel (2 Sam 7:13). Furthermore, the purpose of this temple had been fulfilled: it provided a place for the ark, which held the tablets of the covenant Yahweh made with Israel in the wilderness. Thus,

Solomon's speech effectively ties the ark produced by the freed slaves of the Exodus period to the temple he built. This had the effect of emphasizing the unity of the tribes and the traditions of all Israel, even though the place was in Jerusalem of Judah. See Ps 132.

■ **22-23** *Solomon stood in front of the altar of Yahweh and opposite (facing) the whole gathering of Israel and spread his hands toward the sky.* Then he addressed Yahweh, the God of Israel and proclaimed: *no one of gods in the sky above or on the land beneath is like you for keeping the covenant and the loyal love with your servants who walk before you with all their hearts.* This parallels Deut 4:39 and Josh 2:11.

■ **24-26** As he continued, Solomon further stressed his assertion of 1 Kgs 8:20: that Yahweh had kept his covenant promises to David. Then he added the request that Yahweh continue to keep this promise. He acknowledged that Yahweh had fulfilled by his hand (in Solomon's time) what he had promised by his mouth (in David's time [v 24]). This grounded his request that Yahweh keep his promise that one of David's sons would be on the throne of Israel. Solomon here recognized the condition that these sons walk before Yahweh as David had (v 25; → 1 Kgs 3:11-14; 6:11-14). This compares to 1 Kgs 2:4; 9:4-5, but contrasts to 2 Sam 7, which does not allow for the removal of a son of David from the throne for any reason. The Deuteronomistic redactor paved the way for understanding why a son of David did not rule the northern tribes, Israel, and eventually was removed from the throne of Judah.

■ **27** Lest anyone think that Yahweh could be confined to this temple, that he in fact really lived in this temple on earth, this verse demonstrates that Solomon recognized that Yahweh was too great to be housed by even the highest layers of the heavens. Since Yahweh's presence had just been manifested through the cloud, Solomon certainly had evidence that Yahweh honored this place with his presence. Nonetheless, the exilic Dtr (Dtr² in Cross's terms [1973, 278-85]) indicates the magnificence of this house and Solomon's desire that Yahweh live there (1 Kgs 8:13), as well as the temple's limitations before Yahweh. Israel's God is too big to be sheltered among stones and cedar.

■ **28-30** Acknowledging that Yahweh does live in the heavens, Solomon prayed that the place Yahweh designated for his name would be a meeting point between Israel and Yahweh. He asked Yahweh to respond to all the prayers prayed in and toward this place, and assumed these would be prayers of repentance.

■ **31-32** Verses 31-53 convey seven cases, particular situations, concerning which Solomon prayed that Yahweh would hear from heaven. The "if" or "when" is the case, the "then" is Yahweh's desired response—hearing, forgiving, and restoring.

(Case 1) This petition is an allusion to the practice of making oaths before the altar of Yahweh in the temple after an accusation has been made. A similar case may be found in Deut 17:8-13 with the Levitical priests (at the place Yahweh would choose) performing the judgment. Solomon asked that the verdict enacted be Yahweh's, that it be just, so that the guilty be punished, not the innocent. Thus, Solomon's first petition concerned justice within the community of Israel.

■ **33-34** (case 2) Enemy oppression, which is the result of Israel's sin, is one aspect of this case. The other is Israel's repentance *in this house*. Under these conditions, Solomon implored Yahweh to restore them to their land. The implication is that they are in captivity, so it is not clear how they would be able to pray *in this house*. However, this problem is treated in the next petition.

■ **35-36** (case 3) Again, Israel's repentance was a necessary condition, this time for relief from drought caused by their sinning. Solomon prayed: if they prayed *toward* this place, then God would hear them, forgive, teach, and send rain. The sinning and suffering people needed to be taught and retaught of Yahweh's ways. Torah is a noun form of the Hebrew verb "teach."

■ **37-40** (case 4) The catchall petition concerning cases of famine, plague, drought, disaster, or disease is similar. If and when the afflicted prayed *toward* this house, Yahweh was asked to forgive, with a Deuteronomistic caveat: ***render each one according to his ways*** (v 39). All of Solomon's petitions presume the characteristic retribution ideology of Dtr: sinning leads to disaster; obedience leads to blessing. Although the corollaries to these are different, they may be derived from retribution ideology: disaster is the result of sinning, and blessing indicates obedience.

■ **41-43** (case 5) Another common theme of Deuteronomy concerns hospitality to the resident alien (*gēr*; see Deut 1:16; 5:14; 10:18) and the foreigner (*nāk rî*; see Deut 14:21; and esp. 29:22 [21 HB], which uses the same phraseology as here). Solomon requested that the prayers of non-Israelites who come to live among Israel on account of Yahweh's name be answered so that all nations will revere him. This was the purpose of the ***smitings*** or plagues in Egypt as well (Exod 7:5).

■ **44-45** (case 6) Israel has traveled to besiege another land and they pray toward the city of the temple, then support their cause, that is, give them victory. This is the first mention of a city Yahweh had chosen. This petition indicates this text had to emerge from preexilic times in Israel.

■ **46-51** (case 7) These verses represent the case of Israel's captivity. They are far from their land, not because they are the aggressor but because they have been exiled and enslaved because of their sin. Under the condition that they fully repent and pray this time **toward the land** (and the city and temple), then Yahweh should hear and forgive given his history of delivering them beginning with their enslavement in the iron furnace of Egypt (Deut 4:20; Jer 11:4).

The petition is that Yahweh would **uphold their cause** and cause their conquerors to **show them mercy**, no request for deliverance or a return to their land as in 1 Kgs 8:33-34. Because these verses seem to indicate an awareness of both the Babylonian exile and a still standing temple and city, Sweeney (among others) argues that the text had to have been written before those were razed; it anticipates exile, but not the Babylonian exile (2007, 130). Levenson believes otherwise, citing evidence that Solomon's prayer is produced by Dtr², the exilic redactor (1981, 143-66).

■ **52-53** Solomon concluded his prayer with a further request that Yahweh always heed Israel's prayers, whom he had elected **from all the nations** to be his **inheritance** (v 53), reminding him of Moses and the exodus (Lev 20:24, 26).

■ **54-61** Solomon had been kneeling before the altar and now stood to bless the people. Binding his temple to the Mosaic covenant (1 Kgs 8:56) and the ancestors (v 58), Solomon's blessings reinforce Dtr themes of rest (Deut 12:9; 25:19; Josh 21:41-44; 23:1; 2 Sam 7:1) and obedience to the covenant. Solomon was concerned that Yahweh would support Israel's causes and their daily needs so that he would be known by all nations. Again we hear the desire that all the earth know that Yahweh is God, there is no other, which was the reason for Yahweh showing his mighty arm and outstretched hand in Egypt (Exod 6:7; 7:5, 17; 8:6, 10, 22 [2, 6, 18 HB]; 9:14, 29; 10:2; 11:7; 14:4, 18).

■ **62-64** The sacrifices and offerings were the means by which the center of the temple's courtyard was consecrated (1 Kgs 8:64). They also became the food the celebrants ate (vv 62-63). The meat of the well-being/peace offerings was eaten by people and priests, while the fat was offered to Yahweh by burning it on the altar (Lev 3:3-5, 9-11, 14-16). More than one hundred thousand people could have been fed over the fourteen-day celebration period (Sweeney 2007, 136, n. 127). The whole burnt offerings and the grain offerings atoned for the guilt of the priesthood and the sanctuary (Num 18:1).

■ **65** Just as the celebration of Sukkot (Booths) introduced this day of temple consecration, so also it concluded it. This was a unique occasion. Normally Sukkot lasted seven days, but this year, because of the temple dedication, the celebration lasted two sets of seven days. Israelites from the northern boundary near Syria to the southern boundary near Egypt were present.

■ **66** The Hebrew of v 66 says Solomon sent the people away on the eighth day: **On the eighth day he sent away the people, and they blessed the king, and they went to their tents rejoicing and sound of heart concerning all the goodness that Yahweh had done for David his servant and for Israel his people.** This was the eighth day of the second set of seven days (see 2 Chr 7:9; → 1 Kgs 8:2 and notes about Sukkot in Behind the Text for 1 Kgs 8:1-66, above). The narrator was careful to bind this time of joy and blessing to David, again demonstrating Yahweh's fidelity to him. The prosperous Solomon distributed the meat from the peace offerings to the people, but he did not give out bread and raisin cakes like David had done after he brought the ark to Jerusalem (2 Sam 6:17-19).

FROM THE TEXT

In his blessing and prayer, Solomon referred to the temple he was dedicating as the place for God's name, Yahweh (→ 1 Kgs 8:16-19, 20-21, 28-30, 41-43). This may be Dtr's attempt to resolve Solomon's question: **For will God really dwell on earth?** This chapter says yes and no. Yahweh had signified his presence with the glory cloud and the ark in the holy of holies, which represented his ancient and continued covenant sojourn with Israel. Solomon affirmed that the temple was a place for God's name, because Yahweh had said his name would be there (v 29), and it would be a site to which all people may pray. God had not needed a house in the past, and he could not be confined there. Thus, although Solomon did not allude to a time without a temple here, Dtr's implication is that should the temple ever be lost, Yahweh would remain. Although tangible symbols of God's initiative and response to Israel could help the people serve him, no building or its demise could enhance or detract from God's essence and presence.

One way Israel served God after the temple was built was to hold the three festivals there (see 1 Kgs 9:25). The males of Israel were commanded to walk to the temple in Jerusalem three times a year during the pilgrimage festivals: Sukkot (Booths), Pesach (Passover), and Shavuot (Weeks); see Exod 23:14-17; 34:18-23; Deut 16. Women and children were not obligated to go, but they could if strength permitted. (Later rabbinic discourse excluded women, minors, the disabled, and *tumtum,* the doubly sexed. But such discussions occurred during a period when the temple no longer existed.)

The pilgrimage festivals were highpoints of the year. They were not quiet, austere spiritual retreats, but crowded and noisy celebrations of Israel as God's people. The abundant sacrifices accompanying the movement of the ark in 1 Kgs 8 necessitated sights, sounds, and smells unknown to most contemporary urban and suburban people, especially in the Western world. Worship of Yahweh, from the wilderness era through the temple era, was fraught with substantial physical elements so unlike the mostly mental and spiritual exercises of religion in the Protestant tradition. Israel's reminders of their walk before God were bloody and fiery and oily and wet, as well as made of gold, bronze, cedar, and finished stones.

We are surrounded by icons of our culture's gods on our highways, televisions, computer screens, cell phones, and paper media. Ubiquitous advertising demands that we listen, look, and consider how this or that might taste, look, and make us popular, rich, or happy. Yet we've been taught to retreat from icons that would physically remind us of God.

Israel did not worship its temple or its ark; the sacrifices were offered in service to (worship of) God. Similarly, when we create tangible objects (art) and music to bring us into God's presence and remind us of previous times that God has spoken to us, we are recognizing our own physicality and need for signs and symbols of our relationship to God. Such symbols can mediate God's presence to us. We need reminders of God's provision, for then we remember and are grateful.

Knowing, as Solomon did, that God does not need a house, and that no man-made edifice can accommodate God (1 Kgs 8:12-13, 27; Acts 17:24), we still need to be reminded that God lives within us (1 Cor 6:19-20). Physical objects can show us that as we walk in God's ways, we bring God's presence, love, and light into our communities.

8. Yahweh Warns Solomon of Covenant Conditions (9:1-9)

BEHIND THE TEXT

In his opening line, the narrator directs the reader back to Gibeon where Yahweh appeared to Solomon for the first time in a dream at night (1 Kgs 3:1-15). We are thus invited to compare these two theophanies to Solomon. At the Gibeon altar, before Yahweh appeared, Solomon had sacrificed one thousand burnt offerings. This time, before Yahweh appeared, Solomon offered innumerable sacrifices as the ark proceeded to the Temple Mount (8:5), and 22,000 oxen and 120,000 sheep after his dedicatory prayer and blessing (v 63). Before the Gibeon theophany, Solomon had obeyed David's orders, established his kingdom, and married the daughter of Pharaoh (2:10—3:3). Before this theophany, Solomon had built the temple, palaces for himself and his Egyptian wife, and expanded the borders and trade opportunities of his kingdom (9:1). At Gibeon (ch 3), Solomon was a young, new, humble king; at Jerusalem (ch 9) Solomon was seasoned; he had ruled for twenty years (6:37; 7:1; 9:10) and was at the midpoint of his reign.

In both cases, Yahweh responded to Solomon's requests and worship with promises and conditions, using David's language from 1 Kgs 2:1-4: Solomon must walk in Yahweh's ways and keep his laws as David his father had done. At Gibeon, keeping the commandments was the condition for a long life (3:14), whereas in Jerusalem (9:1-9) it was the condition for a perpetual Davidic dynasty as David had made explicit (2:4; see also 6:12).

With this final appearance of Yahweh to Solomon, we are reminded that his success and that of his sons continued to rest on obedience to Yahweh. The conditions repeated in this section also look to the future, preparing the audience for Israel's division and removal from the land. They will know that Solomon and his sons had been thoroughly warned of the results of neglecting the commands of Yahweh.

IN THE TEXT

■ **1-3** The cloud and glory of Yahweh had filled Yahweh's new house (compare 8:10-11) (there is no mention of fire from heaven consuming the sacrifices as in the parallel passage of 2 Chr 7:1). First Kings 9:2 claims that this is the second appearance of Yahweh to Solomon and it is after the manner of Yahweh's appearance to him at Gibeon (ch 3). In 6:11-13, however, the word of Yahweh *happened to Solomon* (v 11) with a similar purpose. This third theophany seems to be taken by Dtr as different from—perhaps less immediate than—the theophanies described here and at Gibeon (see 11:9). Nonetheless, the message to Solomon in 6:1-13 included the conditions we find here, with the message that Yahweh condoned the temple project and promised to dwell with his people, *if* Solomon walked in the commandments. In 9:1-3, Yahweh granted Solomon's request that Yahweh put his name (8:20, 29, 44, 48) and his eyes (8:29, 52) there in order to heed the prayers prayed in and toward this house. He also added that his heart would always be there. This then was Yahweh's part of a clear conditional covenant.

■ **4-5** The rest of this section (9:4-9) reaffirms Solomon's obligations for maintaining a successor on the throne of Israel. Verses 4-5 represent a shortened version of David's instructions to Solomon before he died, which were also fraught with exhortations to keep the commandments (1 Kgs 2:1-4; see also 1 Kgs 3:14 and Deut 17:18-20).

■ **6-9** This section outlines the disaster that would befall Israel and this house (temple) if Solomon and his descendants did not keep the commandments and if they served and *bowed before* other gods. The list is short and less graphic than the curses of Deut 28, but it is no less severe: Israel would lose its land and temple, as well as its Davidic king.

■ **7** **Cut off** is the term for abrupt and permanent removal, and is used throughout the OT to refer to the literal severing of hands or head from a person's body, but more often as a curse, as in removal from community or from life itself. Here it is Israel who would be cut off from the land. In addition, Yahweh would *send away from his face* (or *dismiss from his presence*) this house he had set apart for his name. Israel would be mocked. **Send away** is the term used for divorce, but it does not have to mean destruction.

■ **8-9** The Hebrew and Greek say *and this house will be exalted*, but text critics believe that the original word may have been "ruins" (as in Targum and Peshitta, the Syriac versions) and emended to say "exalted" (also used at 2 Chr 7:21). The context is disaster for Israel and the temple, not exaltation, so if the temple remained in some form, it was deserted, defaced, and/or stripped so as to incite awe and horror in each spectator. Those who *happened upon this house* would ask why Yahweh did this to this land and this house. The awestruck would be answered according to the closing words of Yahweh to Solomon: Israel's apostasy (v 9). Yahweh had brought their ancestors out of Egypt, but if they repaid him by turning to worship *other* gods, Yahweh, their erstwhile benefactor, would cause this disaster. And this would make perfect sense to every onlooker. With this ominous notice, the focus on the construction and dedication of the temple is concluded.

Although Solomon's response to this "second" appearance of Yahweh seems lacking, it is found in 9:25, which parallels his response in 3:15. It has been separated from Yahweh's words to him by intervening information about Israelite cities for Hiram's gold, Solomon's slaves, armies, fortifications, and the move of Pharaoh's daughter to her new home in the neighborhood that included the Temple Mount (9:10-24).

After the Gibeon theophany, Solomon did not return to Gibeon, but to the ark in the city of David in Jerusalem to offer up the two kinds of offerings mentioned in v 25. Solomon offered up whole offerings and peace offerings three times a year on the altar he had built for Yahweh (in the temple courtyard). As we shall see, the writer includes Solomon's faithful worship of the speaking God in both cases, but in ch 9, Solomon's faithful response is mitigated by a series of reports about policies and incidents that are subtly critical of Solomon's decisions and practices.

9. Solomon Repays Hiram of Tyre (9:10-14)

IN THE TEXT

■ **10** The formula that appears in this verse indicates a shift from all that had occupied Solomon throughout his first twenty years as king to his next twenty years. The latter half of his reign was exemplified by relationships with other royalty, resident aliens (whom he forced into slavery), foreign wives, and adversaries. In other words, Solomon was in decline, although allusions to his problematic—from a covenant standpoint—policies occur throughout 1 Kgs 2—7.

■ **11-14** These verses furnish the rest of the story of Solomon and Hiram, Solomon's royal supplier of cedars from Lebanon and juniper (1 Kgs 5:6-8 [20-22 HB]). Here the materials include juniper and gold. Hiram was not impressed with the cities of Galilee (***the land of the Galil***) that Solomon gave him; he found them worthless. The narrator connects ***they were not pleasing in his eyes*** with what they are subsequently called: **Kabul** (see Josh 19:27); the name sounds like the Hebrew word *kebal*, which means "like nothing." First Kings 5:9-10 [23-24 HB] indicates that Solomon had provided Hiram's land with food in repayment for the timber. We learn in 9:14 that Hiram "paid" for this region with "120 talents of gold." Apparently Solomon decided he needed gold more than he needed the land and more than he cared for the Israelites living there. We are not told what happened to them. When Solomon ceded twenty northern Israelite cities to Tyre, a Phoenician-Canaanite city, he was returning portions of Israel to Canaan. He gave away the land that Yahweh had given Israel to descendants of the Canaanite inhabitants.

The Chronicler is unwilling to affirm the loss of some lands of Israel to the Phoenician king. Second Chronicles 8:2 suggests that Hiram gave Solomon cities that Solomon then settled with Israelites.

10. Solomon Enslaves Canaanites for His Building Projects and Hires Israelites as Soldiers and Foremen (9:15-28)

BEHIND THE TEXT

Solomon's relationships with non-Israelites—for good or ill—continue to be highlighted in this section. Solomon's consistent policy of forced labor is interwoven with references to Solomon's alliance with the Egyptian Pharaoh and his daughter. Whereas in Egypt Israelite slaves were abused by their overseers, under Solomon, Israelites act as overseers of Canaanite slaves. Solomon has become like Pharaoh.

IN THE TEXT

■ **15** This verse is a reminder that Solomon used **forced labor** for his building projects, which included not only the temple and palaces but also the Millo and the wall around Jerusalem. The Millo is not defined in the Bible (it probably means "filling"), but it may be "the stepped stone structure," so labeled by archaeologists, which connects the lower city of David to the Temple Mount (see Judg 1:29; 2 Sam 5:9; 1 Kgs 11:27; 2 Kgs 12:21 [22 HB]).

Hazor is a city in north Galilee near Aram (Syria). Megiddo is also north of Jerusalem overlooking the Valley of Jezreel. This site was inhabited from approximately 7000 BC to 586 BC, but not since. Gezer is eighteen miles west and slightly north of Jerusalem near the coastal plain on the road to Egypt, which intersects the road to Jerusalem. It was continuously occupied from the Bronze Age to the Hellenistic period. All three places demonstrate features of similar fortifications (walls and gates) dated to the tenth century BC, but not all archaeologists agree that they should be attributed to Solomon. (For a full discussion of these sites throughout their long history, see http://megiddo.tau.ac.il/index.html; Dever 1984, 206-18; Finkelstein and Silberman 2001, 135-42; Stager 1982, 111-21.)

■ **16** The Deuteronomistic redactor interrupts his list of Solomon's ambitious construction projects around Israel and Judah to describe how Gezer came to be Solomon's. According to Josh 10:33, Joshua had defeated the king of Gezer, but Judg 1:29, the less optimistic version of Israel's settling of Canaan, charges the tribe of Ephraim with failing to drive out the inhabitants of Gezer. This view comports with 1 Kgs 9:16, which claims that an Egyptian king (possibly Pharaoh Siamun), the father of Solomon's wife, killed the Canaanites controlling the city, destroyed it, and gave this city as a *sending away gift* to his daughter (i.e., her dowry). It was up to Solomon to rebuild the ruins. (→ Behind the Text for 1 Kgs 3—11, above.)

■ **17-19** Solomon's construction projects ranged from the city of **Tadmor** (v 18), south of the Dead Sea, through northern Lebanon, and included establishing protective cities: Baalath (8 miles west of Jerusalem), Beth Horon (11 miles northwest of Jerusalem), as well as coastal storage cities for his chariots and military. Tadmor is in Syria, 140 miles northeast of Damascus.

■ **20-21** As the transitional verse (v 15) indicates, this is the account of Solomon's slave labor, and here we learn the identity of his slaves. The list here includes not the seven nations of Deut 7:1 and Josh 3:10, or the six of Deut 20:17 (it lacks the Girgashites), but rather five nations. It excludes both the Girgashites and the Canaanites. Solomon acted as a pharaoh to these people. Just as the Egyptian king forced the resident aliens to build great storage cities for him (Exod 1:11), so also Solomon enslaved the natives of this land. The parallels between the two oppressive rulers are obvious. But is the writer triumphal, applauding the reversal of fortunes for Israel and her king, or is he subtly maligning Solomon's programs?

■ **22-23** Although 1 Kgs 5:13-15 claims that Solomon conscripted labor from the tribes of Israel for his building projects, these verses say that Solomon drafted Israelite men into his armies and hired them as foremen over the people of the land he had enslaved. Israelites thus became the taskmasters (see Exod 1:11-14). The descendants of the enslaved people became like the Egyptian taskmasters who had oppressed their ancestors, just as Solomon became more like Pharaoh. The writer, however, was not explicit in making these connections; they are subtle and he seems to be most concerned with insisting that Solomon did not enslave Israelites, so he differs from Pharaoh in this regard.

■ **24** By referring to Solomon's acquisition and restoration of Gezer in 1 Kgs 9:15-16, the narrator reminds us again that Solomon had married Pharaoh's daughter. Here he does so by repeating that she had been living in the city of David with Solomon until her palace was built (3:1). The narrator wants to underscore that she moved. Once her palace was complete, she **went up** (*'āltâ* from *'lh* means to "to go up") to the newly formed temple district that contained the ark in the holy of holies, the temple, the new heart of Jerusalem, Judah, and all Israel. The picture painted here is of an Egyptian princess fully embraced by the king of Israel in Jerusalem, a king who was acting more and more like the pharaoh of Exod 1—12. (→ 1 Kgs 3:1.)

Compare 2 Chr 8:11, which claims Solomon brought his Egyptian wife up because of the holiness of the city of David, given that the ark resided there. This, however, ignores the going up of the same ark to the temple of Solomon before Pharaoh's daughter went up to her nearby home (as well as the fact that she had resided in David's city for many years). Thus, Pharaoh's daughter was enfolded by Solomon into Israel, although this does not mean she or his other wives adhered to Yahweh. After this remarkable move, Solomon built the Millo. (→ 1 Kgs 9:15, above.)

If the Millo is the now excavated high and wide terraces that led from the lower city to the Temple Mount and Solomon's royal headquarters, it may have divided these parts of Jerusalem. In other words, the Millo may have been a barrier between the old lower city and the new higher complex. It may have separated the royal court and the priests from the people, instead of enabling easier access between the city of David and Solomon's administrative, royal, and religious center. First Kings 11:26-27 says that Solomon's Millo and his closing the gap in David's city was the reason Jeroboam later rebelled against Solomon. (See Sweeney 2007, 146.)

■ **25** This verse seems to naturally follow 9:9. The appearance of Yahweh to Solomon, subsequent to his temple dedication and prayer (9:1-9), confirmed that Yahweh sanctified this house and would keep his eyes and heart there forever. This, along with the warning against apostasy and reference to Solomon's customary sacrifices at the altar completed the house more finally and theologically than the notice of 7:51.

Paralleling once again 1 Kgs 3, which describes Yahweh's first appearance to Solomon following his offerings at Gibeon and his marriage to Pharaoh's daughter, this verse outlines Solomon's custom of offering up (Heb. root: *'lh*) whole offerings three times a year during the pilgrimage festivals (→ From the Text for 1 Kgs 8, above). Notice that the same Hebrew term is used for Solomon's Egyptian wife's move *up* to her new home near the temple and Solomon's sacrificing. The Hebrew verb *'lh* means both **going up** and **offering up**; it is the root of the word for "steps." It is also used in the modern era for the immigration of Jews to Israel from anywhere outside of Israel (the Diaspora). Ascending to a higher place (and Jerusalem is always considered to rest above the rest of the earth) or lifting up an object (such as an animal to an altar) is the sense of *'lh*.

Thus, Solomon **fully completed the temple**. Recall that the writer said that temple construction was complete at 6:38 and 7:51. But here the confirmation of the temple's completion *follows* the formal dedication day, God's covenant-affirming response, Solomon's building projects in Jerusalem and around the land, the **going up** of his Egyptian wife, his building of the Millo, and institutionalizing the annual festivals.

Thus, we come to the end of Solomon's establishment of the temple; it is finished. As noted above, v 25 topically belongs after v 9, but Dtr has chosen to precede it with a demonstration of Solomon's affinities with Egyptian pharaohs, most notably the oppressive Pharaoh of Exodus, foreshadowing Solomon's apostasy as registered in ch 11. Thus, Dtr aligns the first and second appearances of Yahweh to Solomon as he weaves in reminders of Solomon's Egyptian marriage and his regular service to Yahweh at the temple. Solomon's rule has a shadow side even before he constructs altars to his wives' gods and serves them.

■ **26-28** Verses 26-28 fit topically with 15-23, but Dtr inserted vv 24-25 between them. Solomon relied on Hiram of seafaring Phoenicia once again, this time to service his new fleet of ships far south of Israel in Edom at the east coast of the **Sea of Reeds**. This partnership produced gold from Ophir, far more than the 120 talents that Hiram had paid Solomon to balance the gift of twenty Israelite cities (v 14).

Ezion Geber/Elath is at the southernmost point of Edom, the northern shore of the **Sea of Reeds**, crossed by the Israelites from the west as they left Egypt, another reminder of Exod 1—11. It is mentioned in Deut 2:8 and 2 Chr 8:17, while Ophir is noted for its gold in several biblical passages (1 Kgs 10:11; Job 22:24; 28:16; Ps 45:9 [10 HB]; and Isa 13:12). Ophir's location is not known, but tradition places it in various sites in northern Africa. (See Josephus [*Ant.* 8.164] and Sweeney 2007, 146.)

FROM THE TEXT

The final form of this chapter depicts God as still "in Solomon's court," on his side, willing to support and bless him. God, in 9:1-3, meets Solomon, accepting the temple and promising to answer Solomon's prayers. God's promise to put his name, eyes, and heart there was God's part of this implicit covenant between God and Solomon. This was an innovation upon the founding covenant with David's dynasty. God's appearance here was newly provoked by Solomon's building of this house, moving the ancient ark there, and praying, blessing, and dedicating it. However, the terms go back to David, especially as indicated by vv 4-5, which outline *again* Solomon's part: he must be faithful to the ancient commands in order to remain on the throne of Israel. Solomon was well warned about the dangers of apostasy, not only for Israel, but for this house Solomon had just built (vv 6-9).

While this chapter goes on to depict Solomon as faithful to his God in regard to sacrificing during the festivals (v 25); it also continues to portray him as an enterprising trader and empire builder who made alliances with Phoenician and Egyptian rulers while enslaving remaining Canaanites. John Wesley said that Solomon could have destroyed these Canaanites because he had the power to do so, but that Torah's ban against them did not apply to later generations (*Explanatory Notes*, on 1 Kgs 9). The narrator makes no explicit judgment of Solomon's policies but implies he appreciates the fact that Solomon did not enslave Israelites. Nonetheless, the reader grows increasingly uncomfortable by reminders of Solomon's foreign alliances and his social and commercial practices.

Since this chapter claims that the fortified cities, as well as Jerusalem's temple and royal halls, were constructed by slaves, we remember Pithom and Rameses of Exod 1:11. Twice we are reminded of Solomon's wife, Pharaoh's daughter, and Solomon himself reminds us of Pharaoh. Thus, the picture of Solomon, while glowing in ch 8, is cast with shadows here, shadows that deepen as the narrative progresses. In addition to his attention to the temple and its cult, Solomon was clearly just as focused on making Israel flourish in the eyes of the world.

11. Solomon Parades Wisdom and Wealth to the Queen of Sheba (10:1-13)

BEHIND THE TEXT

The visit of the Queen of Sheba demonstrates the far-reaching fame of Solomon and Yahweh. She claimed that her firsthand experience of Solomon's wisdom and wealth was even greater than all she had heard. Compare this passage to Exod 18:1 in which we learn that Jethro, the priest of Midian (another outsider), heard about the wonders against Egypt wrought by the saving hand of Yahweh on behalf of Israel (Exod 18:9-11). The result for Jethro, as for the queen, affirmed confidence in Yahweh's blessing of Israel.

The Sheba pericope was inserted into the longer report of Solomon's acquisition of gold, almugwood, gems, apes, peacocks, and so forth, by means of his fleet manned by Hiram's sailors and Israelites (1 Kgs 9:26-28; 10:11-22). The writer summarizes in v 23: **King Solomon was greater than all the kings of the land in riches and wisdom**. The queen's visit highlights both Solomon's wisdom and his wealth; but its context, the description of Solomon's avenues for gaining goods from across the seas, emphasizes his prosperity alone. We sense his growing appetite for worldly treasures.

Sheba probably refers to the kingdom of Saba, which was located on the southeast coast of the Red Sea in modern southwest Saudi Arabia and Yemen. It thrived from the eleventh century BC to the third century AD, trading spices and gold. Arabian queens are mentioned in Assyrian texts of 800 to 600 BC. An inscription dated to 600 BC that mentions trade with "the towns of Judah" was found recently. This is, however, several centuries after the time of Solomon (see Lemaire 2010).

Josephus and Ethiopian traditions have identified Sheba with Ethiopia on the west side of the *Sea of Reeds*, across from Saba. This is based on legends that the long ruling dynasty, which ended in 1974, was descended from Menelik, the son of Makeda (the Queen of Sheba) and Solomon (see Sweeney 2007, 149-50). As Wesley notes, the commodities mentioned here associate Sheba with Saba more than with Ethiopia (*Explanatory Notes*, on 1 Kgs 9). Ancient Saba may have included both regions and the *Sea of Reeds* between them.

The land of Sheba is mentioned a number of times in the Bible in connection with trading spices and gold (Job 6:19; Isa 60:6; Jer 6:20; Ezek 27:22) and alluded to more often. Jesus cites this visit to proclaim his superiority to Solomon, saying: "The Queen of the South will rise at the judgment with this generation and condemn it; for she came from the ends of the earth to listen to Solomon's wisdom, and now something greater than Solomon is here" (Matt 12:42; compare Luke 11:31).

IN THE TEXT

■ **1-3** In this chapter, we have an account of the queen of the South hearing about Solomon's alliance with Yahweh. Solomon's fame had spread so far and was so impressive that a queen from the ends of the earth traveled by camel caravan to test his wisdom and see if his wonders comported with what she had heard (see 4:34 [5:14 HB]). Just as Jethro heard and came (Exod 18:1-11), so also the Queen of Sheba heard and came.

The report was *according to the name of Yahweh*, which may mean that she had heard of Solomon's reliance upon the name of Yahweh. The visit narrated here is not merely a wisdom tale about two royals posturing before one another about their mental and physical goods. The fame of Yahweh as reflected in Solomon is central to the story. Recall the prayer of Solomon at 1 Kgs 8:60: *so that all the peoples of the earth will know that Yahweh is God, there is no other.* The purpose of the *smitings* (plagues) of Egypt was so that Israel, the pharaoh, and the whole earth would know that Yahweh was the only god (Exod 9:16; see also 1 Sam 17:46).

Her caravan included a host of soldiers and was loaded with gold, gems, and spices that she gave to Solomon (and he, in turn, filled her coffers with "all she desired" [1 Kgs 10:13]). But the queen was not merely loaded with treasures; her mind was filled with difficult questions, which Solomon satisfactorily answered.

■ **4-9** The quantity and quality of Solomon's wisdom, house, food, servants, clothing, seating, and offerings at the temple exhausted the queen. Nonetheless, her energetic response during her visit indicates that her former incredulity was replaced with astonishment over his accomplishments. It concludes with a blessing on Solomon's wives and servants who have the opportunity to hear his wisdom regularly. She blessed Yahweh as Dtr would have (and did), with affirmations of Yahweh's role in placing Solomon on his throne, and remembering Yahweh's **love for Israel** and his purposes for establishing **justice and righteousness** (v 9). In Deuteronomy, Israel was selected to be God's people for no other reason than that he loved them. Outside of Deuteronomy, love terminology is not common (see Deut 4:37; 10:15; 15:16; 23:6 [7 HB]; 30:3; 33:3; compare Exod 15:13 in the Song of Moses).

■ **10 and 13** The Queen of Sheba gave Solomon gold, gems, and spices, the latter in unparalleled abundance. But Solomon was not to be outdone. He gave her whatever she asked (1 Kgs 10:13). Testing, repeated mention of renown, exchange of goods, observations, blessings is typical of Wisdom literature (see Prov 23:1-2; 25:1-7).

■ **11-12** The writer interrupts the Sheba account with another general gold report in 1 Kgs 10:11-12. Gold holds the various aspects of this chapter together. These verses remind us that the Phoenician king enabled the transfer of gold to Solomon, as well as gems and almugwood. Like the spices of Sheba (v 10), so was the almugwood (juniper or sandalwood) harvested and shipped by King Hiram, never seen in such quantity again.

12. Solomon Acquires Silver, Gold, and Horses from Egypt (10:14-29)

IN THE TEXT

■ **14-17** The **666 talents** of gold (v 14) that Solomon acquired in one year was in addition to that which came from outside sources (v 15). This is slightly over the sum of the amounts mentioned in this section at 9:14, 28 and 10:10. Recall that the decor and the floors of the temple were gilded and the vessels used there were gold (6:20-21, 28-35). Solomon also made various sizes of shields from the gold and placed them—perhaps on display—in the large Palace of the Forest of Lebanon described in 1 Kgs 7:2 (paralleled in 2 Chr 9:16, 20).

■ **18-20** The gold Solomon continued to acquire was also used to cover his great ivory throne. The narrator believed that no other king had ever owned such a fine throne. The narrator speaks in superlatives about spices, almugwood, and now Solomon's throne. Whereas the Jerusalem temple and its courtyard were filled with cherubim, including the mercy seat of the ark of the covenant (→ 1 Kgs 6:23-38), no such creatures adorned the steps and sides of Solomon's throne. It was flanked by fourteen lions, the symbol of the tribe of Judah. Although the narrator does not mention it here, Solomon's lions may be connected to Gen 49:8-10:

> Judah, your brothers will praise you;
> your hand will be on the neck of your enemies;
> your father's sons will bow down to you.
> You are a lion's cub, Judah;
> you return from the prey, my son.
> Like a lion he crouches and lies down,
> like a lioness—who dares to rouse him?
> The scepter will not depart from Judah,
> nor the ruler's staff from between his feet,
> until he to whom it belongs shall come
> and the obedience of the nations shall be his.

Models of Egyptian and Phoenician thrones have been found, and they include cherubim-like creatures flanking them in the place of Solomon's throne's lions (e.g., the sarcophagus of King Hiram of the Phoenician city Gebal of the tenth century BC [later Byblos, now Jubayl of Lebanon]).

■ **21-22** Notice Solomon's abundance of gold and his disdain of silver, it was so common. The Tarshish (NIV: **trading**) ships of Solomon went to ports in India and Africa to acquire animals, silver, and more gold. Tarshish may be a reference to the Phoenician colony in southern Spain or to ships with oars (Baker 1992, 331-33). (See 2 Chr 9:21; Jonah 1:3.)

■ **23-25** This summarizes what the writer has exemplified so far in this chapter: Solomon surpassed every other king in the world in regard to riches and wisdom and popularity; he was sought by everyone. All who came to him brought him tribute or offerings for the temple.

■ **26-29** In spite of a sort of coda in the previous verses, Dtr cannot resist returning to Solomon's accumulation of silver, gold, horses, and chariots acquired from Kue (Que) and Egypt. He also sold horses to the Hittites and Arameans. Kue is north of Phoenicia and Syria in Cilicia (which includes Tarsus) and was known for breeding horses.

Once again, Dtr leads us to recall the suitable Israelite king depicted in Deut 17:14-20. This king would *not* return to Egypt for horses: "for [Yahweh] has told you, 'You are not to go back that way again'" (v 16); nor should he "accumulate large amounts of silver and gold" (v 17). Although, as we have seen in 1 Kgs 3—11, Solomon was greater in regard to riches and wisdom than any other king; he was *not* the prescribed king of Deut 17:16-20:

The king, moreover, must not acquire great numbers of horses for himself or make the people return to Egypt to get more of them, for [Yahweh] has told you, "You are not to go back that way again." He must not take many wives, or his heart will be led astray. He must not accumulate large amounts of silver and gold. When he takes the throne of his kingdom, he is to write for himself on a scroll a copy of this law, taken from that of the Levitical priests. It is to be with him, and he is to read it all the days of his life so that he may learn to revere [Yahweh] his God and follow carefully all the words of this law and these decrees and not consider himself better than his fellow Israelites and turn from the law to the right or to the left. Then he and his descendants will reign a long time over his kingdom in Israel.

Through this allusion to Deut 17, we have been prepared for Solomon's other great breach: marrying a multitude of foreign women along with Pharaoh's daughter. In the next passage, ch 11, the tone shifts from admiring and neutral descriptions of Solomon's unsurpassed wisdom, wealth, and fame (albeit peppered with controlled criticisms), to full-on attack mode. Nonetheless, chs 3—10 are the basis for Solomon's longstanding reputation as the greatest and wisest Israelite king. According to Dtr here, he enlarged Israel's borders, formed alliances with neighboring nations, established trade, fortified cities, and built the temple to Israel's god, Yahweh. And yet, the writer introduced Solomon's wisdom by the humble example of a maternity case that two prostitutes brought to him.

FROM THE TEXT

Solomon is the representative of the wisdom tradition in Israel. Tradition ascribed to him the book of Proverbs, a collection of wisdom sayings from both before and after the Babylonian exile, and Song of Songs, an extended love poem that refers to the pageantry of Solomon's wedding several times and his "vineyard" once. Solomon's reputation for wisdom continued through the time of Jesus, who, speaking of himself, said that he was wiser than Solomon (Matt 12:42).

As the Introduction points out, controversy rages among archaeologists and biblical scholars over the accuracy of the biblical portrayal of Solomon's "empire" as described in 1 Kgs 4—10. Archaeology bears out building programs across the land at Hazor, Gezer, and Megiddo with their six-chambered gates, often ascribed to Solomon. But, in Jerusalem, tenth century BC evidence of a great royal city is lacking, even taking into account later stripping by the Egyptian king Shishak, destruction by Assyria and Babylon, Herod's massive temple built upon the Temple Mount, and the Dome of the Rock, which allows for no excavation of the site. (For a detailed discussion, → Introduction, D. Geography, Settlement Patterns, Statehood and Extent of Israel's Boundaries According to the Biblical and Extrabiblical Texts and Archaeology.)

The theological question that lingers over chs 3—10 is: did Solomon consult God regarding his international alliances, slave labor, building projects, and commerce? He had asked for a ***hearing heart*** when God appeared to him first (1 Kgs 3:9); did he continue to listen to God throughout his reign over Judah and Israel? Was he using God-given wisdom when he acquired gold from Ophir and horses, chariots, and a wife from Egypt? Did he allow God to direct him in matters of governance and thereby walk in the ways of the commands of which he was so often reminded?

And this is our challenge. Solomon offered sacrifices regularly but failed to obey (see 1 Sam 15:22). Do we walk in the paths cut for us by the Scriptures and God's Spirit as we plan and proceed in the matters of family and work? Is any effort mundane or outside of God's purview? Do we practice our faith as avidly outside of church and times of formal worship as we do inside? Do we remember that we are always living before God? Or do we extend our boundaries and expand our wealth as much as we are able without regard to limits that would safeguard the rights of others?

13. Solomon Worships Other Gods and Yahweh Responds (11:1-13)

BEHIND THE TEXT

This chapter must be read in its entirety (11:1-43) and with the preceding material in order to understand the interconnections among Solomon, David, and the nations with whom they were allied and against whom they waged war. Second Samuel 8—12 recounts David's interactions with the nearby nations (Moabites [8:2], Ammonites [10:1-19; 12:26-31], Edomites [8:13-14], and Arameans [8:3-12; 10:1-19]).

Like Solomon, David had been allied with Hiram of Tyre, a Phoenician/Sidonian (see 2 Sam 5:11-12). Sidon stands for Phoenicia generally and Sidon was called a "mother city of Tyre" on ancient coins. Solomon's Egyptian connection, namely his marriage to Pharaoh's daughter, has been stressed since 1 Kgs 3 and reinforced in the previous two chapters. We learn in ch 11 that Solomon's alliance with Egypt did not obstruct Pharaoh from harboring Solomon's enemies, but Solomon became so much like Pharaoh on theological and literary levels that one of Solomon's adversaries, Hadad, was posed against him as a Moses figure.

The Deuteronomist's judgment of Solomon found in this chapter is inexplicable without its foundation in Deut 17:14-20, a portion of which is quoted above in the comments on 1 Kgs 10:26-29. The connection between Solomon's wives and the seven nations prohibited for intermarriage in Deut 7:1-6; 23:4, 8-9 [5, 9-10 HB] is less straightforward, as we shall see.

11:1-13   Apostasy (worshipping other gods) was the basis for concerns about exogamy (intermarriage). Yahweh in Deut 7 and Exod 34:15 warned Israel that intermarriage with certain people groups already in the land could turn themselves and their children to other gods. This was the problem with Solomon marrying women who were not Israelites. The concern in Deuteronomy was over apostasy incited by potential intermarriage with the local people. There was no reason to prohibit intermarriage with people that Israel would not be around, even though the bordering nations also worshipped other gods. A king had the wherewithal to cross boundaries in order to marry out, and Solomon's exogamy led to his apostasy. Solomon intentionally married women of outlying people groups to promote peace and commerce, and then he also chose to worship other gods. In spite of the constant reminder that Solomon had married an Egyptian, no specific mention is made of Solomon worshipping Egyptian gods, apart from the general comment of 1 Kgs 11:8.

Exogamy in the OT is both encouraged and banned. The crucial and consistent difference is whether the exogamy represents apostasy or faithfulness to Yahweh. Did she (and the concern is with wives) preserve the people of God (Tamar in Gen 38); did she know the ways of Yahweh (Zipporah in Exod 2; 4:24-26); did she confess faith in Yahweh (Rahab in Josh 2); was she loyal to Yahweh and his people (Ruth)? Other evidence that the concern is not "racial" or "ethnic" is found in Deut 21:10-14, which legislates the procedures by which foreign captive women might be married to Israelite men. However, Ezra 9—10 illustrates an attempt by postexilic leaders of the Jews to restrict intermarriage, even between exiled Jews and those who had been left behind, and those of mixed heritage.

IN THE TEXT

■ **1-2** The restrained handling of Solomon's practices and policies is set aside here. The writer bluntly announces that Solomon disobeyed Yahweh by taking wives from nations who worshipped other gods. This includes not only Pharaoh's daughter, whom we have known about all along (1 Kgs 3:1; 7:8; 9:16, 24), but also many, many other foreign wives. Clearly, Egypt was Solomon's most important alliance and Pharaoh's daughter was his primary wife. The other royal wives may not have been daughters of kings. The love language is like that of Deuteronomy where Dtr, the Deuteronomistic redactor, assured Israel that they were beneficiaries of Yahweh's provision because he **loved** them (v 1). (→ 1 Kgs 10:4-9.) This time, however, Dtr depicts Solomon *clinging* to his foreign wives **in love** (v 2).

The list of nations with whom Solomon cemented bonds through marriage is not the same list as that found in Deut 7:1-6, although the writer alludes to this passage (and Exod 34:15). There Yahweh prohibited Israelite marriage with people of the land they were about to occupy: Hittites, Girgashites, Amorites, Canaanites, Perizzites, Hivites, and Jebusites. Hittites are the only people that appear on both lists: nations under the Deuteronomy ban and nations of the wives of Solomon. (The Hittites occupied land on the northern border of Canaan, but also inside; see Gen 23.) Solomon's wives did not come from the internal, Canaan people groups, but from outlying nations with whom David also had alliances, and/or bloody conflicts (2 Sam 8—12: Moabites, Ammonites, Edomites, and Sidonians).

Like Egypt, the origin of Solomon's first wife, these nations were previously established on the borders of Canaan and *not* among those prohibited for intermarriage (except the Hittites). But they did worship other gods, which was the concern of Deuteronomy (→ Behind the Text for 1 Kgs 11:1-13, above).

Deuteronomy 23:4-7 prohibits Ammon and Moab from entering "the assembly of [Yahweh]" (v 8) because they did not support Israel on their way and they hired Balaam to curse them (literally until after the tenth generation, but the text may imply forever). Verses 8-9 order Israel against hating Edomites (their kinsmen) and Egyptians (who hosted them). They must allow children of the third generation to join Israel. From each of these nations, Solomon took wives.

■ **3-6** The depiction of seven hundred royal wives and three hundred concubines is schematic, as is Job's perfect family, which included seven sons and three daughters. Solomon's large harem shows his potency for making peace, establishing trade relations, creating wealth, and producing children.

At the same time, Dtr indicates that the first step Solomon took toward apostasy was to take foreign wives. Although Solomon is blamed for marrying them, building altars, and sacrificing to other gods, his wives are blamed for turning the aging Solomon away from Israel's God, Yahweh. From a political perspective, he may have done this to continue peaceful relations with his "religious" wives and their people.

Here we learn why David (vv 4, 6), in spite of his grievous sins, is the exemplar for Dtr; he never followed after other gods. The proscriptions against exogamy were put in place to avoid this, Solomon's great sin. He became the paradigm for demonstrating that marrying foreign wives who worship other gods leads to apostasy. Nehemiah 13:26 implies that if wise Solomon was turned away from Yahweh by intermarriage, how much more could this be the case for others.

■ **7-8** The Phoenician Ashtoreth (goddess of love and war) and the Ammonite Molek or Milcom (thought to require child sacrifice [Lev 18:21; 2 Kgs 23:10]) are singled out here. ***Then*** Solomon built a shrine on a hill facing Jerusalem to the god of the Moabites, Chemosh, and to Molek and to the gods of all his other wives who served their gods through incense offerings and sacrifices. Singling out these gods is a way of calling attention to his wives from among the royal houses of Phoenicia, Ammon, and Moab. Nonetheless, the narrator emphasizes Solomon's multiple apostasies by informing us that he did the same thing for *all* of his wives who sacrificed and burned incense to them, just as Solomon did three times a year to Yahweh (see 1 Kgs 9:25).

What an egregious turn of affairs! Solomon sacrificed to Yahweh at a shrine at Gibeon outside of Jerusalem before the temple was built; but once Yahweh appeared to him, he sacrificed before the ark of Yahweh in Jerusalem (1 Kgs 3:15). Soon Solomon set about building the temple, which he elaborately consecrated to Yahweh (chs 5—9) with sacrifices and prayer. But, in his old age, he built shrines to other gods near Jerusalem!

■ **9-10** No wonder ***Yahweh flared*** against Solomon! Yahweh had appeared to him twice (3:5-14; 9:2-9) and spoken to him (6:11-13) to warn him against apostasy, basing the perpetuity of Solomon's rule upon his faithfulness to Yahweh alone. Although Deut 17 knows of a law scroll that the Israelite king should copy and read all the days of his life, 1 Kings insists on Solomon's direct experiences with Yahweh as the basis for the subsequent division of Israel and loss to David's house. As he aged, he did not remain steadfast to serve Yahweh alone but had turned to follow after other gods *and serve them*. He was made more culpable by the fact that **Yahweh, the God of Israel . . . had appeared to him twice** and commanded him concerning this very matter. This explicit condemnation of Solomon as a covenant breaker with no excuse sets the stage for the specific consequences that follow for Solomon and his descendants—the kingdom would be torn from them.

■ **11-13** *And Yahweh said: Because it will be this way with you and you have not kept my covenant and statutes which I commanded you, I will certainly tear the kingdom from you and give it to your servant.* Yahweh gave up hope on Solomon. Nonetheless, Yahweh would reserve a portion of Israel to remain with Solomon's son because of his promise to David (2 Sam 7 and reiterated to Solomon several times), and also because he had chosen Jerusalem. For the first time in Deuteronomy—Kings, *Jerusalem's* divine election is made explicit.

Jerusalem was not only the place David had conquered, built a home, and settled the ark. It was not only the city in which Solomon had decided to build the temple and state buildings. It was also the place *Yahweh* chose. Verse 13 of 1 Kgs 11 thus identifies Jerusalem as the identity of the place mentioned throughout Deuteronomy with the phrase **the place Yahweh God will choose** (Deut 12:4-27; 14:23-25; 15:20; 16:1-17; 26:2; 31:11; and Josh 9:27). And for the sake of Jerusalem and his promise to David, Yahweh would give Solomon's son one tribe. Whereas up to here in 2 Samuel—1 Kings, Jerusalem had emerged as selected, conquered, acquired, rebuilt, and embellished by David and Solomon, in these verses, Yahweh claims his choice of Jerusalem.

14. Yahweh Raises Adversaries against Solomon (11:14-25)

■ **14-23** Solomon's disregard for the ways of Yahweh ensures a reign marred with rivals and rebels, raised up by Yahweh. The first was Hadad of Edom, whose life parallels that of Joseph and Moses in Genesis and Exodus (see other royal Edomite Hadads in Gen 36:31-43). This alignment increasingly condemned David's army (through Joab) of becoming oppressive and cruel to outsiders as Pharaoh had been.

Edom lies southeast of Israel and is associated with the descendants of Jacob's slightly older twin, Esau (Gen 25, 27, 32). When their mother, Rebekah, was distraught over the wrestling within her womb, Yahweh responded to her inquiry by announcing that she carried two nations who would struggle with each other, one or the other dominating. Although Gen 25:23 is usually translated as "the older will serve the younger," the verse refers to *nations* of greater and lesser numbers and significance, not the brothers. Its syntax is ambiguous as to which will serve the other, implying continual power struggles. This is borne out in the biblical encounters between the *nations* of Edom and Israel.

This passage refers to David's aggression against the Edomites among his other wars as told in 2 Sam 8:13-14. David killed eighteen thousand Edomites and put garrisons throughout all of Edom and enslaved them. Verses 15-16 describe Joab's "cleanup" operation afterward; not only burying the dead, but also killing every male in Edom. This is an allusion to Pharaoh's death warrant for every male infant of Israel in Exod 1—2.

A young Hadad, like Moses, was saved from the slaughter, fleeing from Midian to Paran to Egypt, all significant places in Moses' and the Israelites' sojourn when they fled Egypt (Exod 2—3; Num 10:11-12). For Hadad, Egypt was the place of refuge where he was treated like Joseph when Yahweh "was with him" (Gen 39:3, 6, 21, 23). Hadad married the sister of Pharaoh's wife, and his son, like Moses, grew up in Pharaoh's household. Just as Moses told his father-in-law (who had given him refuge and a wife) that he wanted to visit his people after hearing Pharaoh died, so Hadad requests permission to return to Edom when he heard that David and Joab were dead. The implication is that Hadad returned to Edom, led his people, and opposed Solomon as an adversary.

■ **24-25** Another **adversary** (*śāṭān*) raised by God was Rezon, who came to rule Aram (Syria) on Israel's northeast border. For use of the term "adversary," see Num 22:22; 1 Sam 29:4; 2 Sam 19:22 [23 HB]. In later texts, the adversary (*śāṭān*) is depicted in heavenly court scenes: Job 1—2; Zech 3:1; 1 Chr 21:1. This adversary is also associated with the wars of David that expanded Israel's hegemony (2 Sam 8:3-8). Rezon must have fled Hadadezer before David's slaughter of the Arameans who came to help the men of Zobah, a region north of Aram. In the later stage of his life, Solomon, the man of peace, was harassed on all sides.

15. Ahijah Promises Jeroboam an Enduring Covenant with Conditions (11:26-40)

BEHIND THE TEXT

Jeroboam became the first king of the northern division of Solomon's kingdom when it split. Through the prophet Ahijah, Yahweh promised to Jeroboam an enduring dynasty as he built for David. This covenant was clearly conditional as was the Davidic covenant as it was reiterated to Solomon. *If* Jeroboam would follow the way of Yahweh, *then* he would have a dynasty like David. Second Samuel 7's iteration of the Davidic covenant included an unconditional aspect: even if David's sons sinned, God would punish, but not take the throne from them. But no hint of that exists here; obedience to the laws was the clear condition for the enduring dynasty of Jeroboam.

IN THE TEXT

■ **26-28** The young and able Ephraimite, Jeroboam, was selected by Solomon as a taskmaster over the tribes of Ephraim and Manasseh during their forced service for Solomon's building projects. Calling them **the tribes of Joseph** (v 28) reminds us that Joseph's rise to power and provisions for his brothers led them to reside in Egypt, to which Jeroboam would flee from Solomon.

■ **29-36** Ahijah's announcement that Yahweh would give Jeroboam the ten tribes to be torn from Solomon's dynasty led him to rebel against Solomon (v 27). Like other prophets who reenacted Yahweh's word using garments and symbolic gestures, Ahijah demonstrated his message by throwing off his new robe and tearing it into twelve pieces, symbolizing the tribes of Israel. He ordered Jeroboam to take ten of them. Through Ahijah, Dtr repeats Yahweh's indictment of Solomon and Yahweh's determination to punish him for apostasy, while keeping the promise to David of a perpetual dynasty. For the second time, we are told of Yahweh's loyalty not only to David but also to Jerusalem, the city **I have chosen** (v 32; → 1 Kgs 11:13, above). Thus the unconditional aspect of the promise to David shifts from a dynasty in *Israel* (2 Sam 7) to one that will remain in *Jerusalem*.

■ **37-39** Yahweh demonstrated his hope in Jeroboam by offering magnificent promises to the young man, noted for his abilities by Solomon. Yahweh would be with him, give him Israel, and cause his dynasty to endure *if* he would listen, walk, and do right by keeping Yahweh's laws. The **not forever** punishment of David's descendants (1 Kgs 11:39) indicates hope on the part of Dtr that Israel would be reunited under the house of David in the future.

■ **40** We are told in v 27 that Jeroboam rebelled against Solomon because of this incident. This implies that Jeroboam began actively rebelling after reporting it (Ahijah and Jeroboam were alone in open country [v 29]). The result was Solomon's attempt to kill Jeroboam so that he fled to the protection of King Shishak of Egypt as another adversary of Solomon taking shelter from Israel in Egypt, as did Hadad (vv 14-23). Israel had become so like the house of bondage from which their ancestors had fled that Egypt became a place of respite for those out of favor in Israel (see Exod 1:8). Israelites enslaved by Solomon for part of the year (1 Kgs 5:13-18 [27-32 HB]) and resident aliens enslaved at all times (9:20-22) had no such respite from their labors.

16. Solomon Dies and Is Buried (11:41-43)

■ **41-43** A regnal formula, void of further judgment, reports the end of Solomon's life and introduces his son Rehoboam. Rehoboam came to the throne without the drama of Solomon's accession. Other sources for Solomon's story include "the book of the annals of Solomon," which includes accounts of his wisdom. First Kings 1—11 is a theological account of Solomon's life and works, depicted as a mixture of good and evil, humility and pride, devotion and apostasy, promise and disappointment.

FROM THE TEXT

Chapter 11 emphasizes that Solomon's primary failure was his apostasy, his service to other gods. But the previous chapters show that, throughout his entire reign, he had become like the Egyptian pharaohs in his treatment of his subjects, both insiders and outsiders to Israel (1 Kgs 5, 9). Sometimes subtly, sometimes overtly, Solomon is additionally indicted for breaking every rule found in Deut 17:14-20. He acquired horses from Egypt, many wives, and great quantities of silver and gold. This often-cited passage in Deuteronomy may well have been written in order to indict Solomon, for its final redaction was likely after Solomon's reign.

As a young monarch, he had humbly sought the discernment to govern God's people well, a ***hearing heart***. But he failed to heed Yahweh's reminders about full, undivided devotion. By the end of Solomon's story he had become an anti-model of wisdom. He did not use his God-given wisdom to govern himself. Solomon allowed his pursuit of peace through marriage alliances to drive his agenda, building temples for the gods of his wives. Thus Solomon brought idolatry to Israel and established it in Jerusalem. Chapter 11 repeats that Solomon's apostasy was the reason the kingdom divided, lest we place too much blame on Rehoboam's later failure to listen to his older advisers (12:13). Nonetheless, the division occurred through political machinations under Rehoboam, and to that story we now turn.

II. THE DIVIDED MONARCHY AND FALL OF ISRAEL: 1 KINGS 12:1—2 KINGS 17:41

A. Jeroboam Becomes King over the Tribes of Israel (12:1—14:20)

BEHIND THE TEXT

In the MT, the primary basis of translations of the Jewish Scriptures and Christian OT, the story of King Jeroboam I is framed by the last verse of ch 11 and 1 Kgs 14:21, both about Rehoboam, Solomon's son and successor. First Kings 11:43 announces his ascension to his father's throne without intrigue or fanfare, but, in the subsequent section, Rehoboam made decisions that led to the fragmentation of the kingdom. This resulted in Jeroboam's rule over the northern tribes, called "Israel" and even "all Israel" by Dtr.

First Kings 12—14 also focuses on Jeroboam, who first appeared as an excellent worker and then as an adversary of Solomon in 1 Kgs 11. The brief account of Rehoboam's story is introduced by the Judahite king formula: name, father, length of reign, mother's name, and evaluation of his rule by Dtr in 1 Kgs 14:21. The LXX inserts this at 11:43.

LXX Additions

The Greek versions of Jeroboam's story rearrange and elaborate on it. For example, the LXX claims that Jeroboam's mother was a harlot after whom he named a city he built, Sarira in the hills of Ephraim. This associates him with ambitious Abimelek and his failed kingship of Judg 9. The LXX also says that he returned to Israel when he heard of Solomon's death and was with the northern tribes before their meeting with Rehoboam (1 Kgs 12:1). Jeroboam is thereby an instigator of the revolt (1 Kgs 11:43; 12:24). First Kings 12:20 in the MT says that Jeroboam returned *after* the revolt. For many other LXX alterations, see Sweeney 2007, 164-67.

We were told in ch 11 why David's house would rule over only a tenth of Israel: Solomon's apostasy. We know that Yahweh selected Jeroboam as a covenant recipient to rule the northern tribes and that his story is fraught with allusions to Moses and David. Jeroboam was given the opportunity to head a lasting dynasty if he kept the statutes and laws of Yahweh, and we sense that God had high hopes for him (see 1 Kgs 11:37-39). In ch 12, we see how the prophecies against Solomon's dynasty were implemented through human choices; God had a reason for tearing the tribes from the dynasty of Solomon, but political scrabbling (reflecting human choices) provided the means.

Places and motifs of Israel's earlier story reappear in this account of the emergence of a separate, autonomous kingdom. Egypt, from whence Jeroboam returned, had been a place of refuge for the patriarchs as well. This allusion to Egypt also recalls the oppression of Israel by the Egyptians and a reminder that Jeroboam fled there to escape a Pharaoh-like Solomon! As in Exod 1—2 and 1 Kgs 1—2, so also here, the death of a king, this time Solomon, son of David, ignited hope for relief from oppression (Exod 2:23-25). Shechem, the setting of 1 Kgs 12, is the site of the inauguration that was not. This city/region had been the setting for other crucial events as recounted in Genesis through Judges (Gen 12:6; 33:18-20; 34; Josh 24:32; Judg 8:31—9:49). (→ 1 Kgs 12:1).

Another motif that reemerges here represents tribal cohesion of the northern tribes and the distinction of Judah from them. Even under Kings Saul and David, Israel was a tribal confederation to varying degrees. Each tribe (except the priestly Levites) was allotted a portion of the land. Saul's inauguration as a warrior king loosely united the tribes against the Philistines and other enemies. When he died, David was made king at Hebron by Judah, but he struggled with the house of Saul for seven years before Israel (every other tribe) confirmed his rule over them (2 Sam 3:1, 6, 17; 5:1-5). The cry: "Every man to his tent, Israel!" was shouted by Sheba ben Bikri to reject David's leadership, exemplifying the other tribes' identity apart from Judah (2 Sam 20:1; see vv 1-22).

This Israel-Judah distinction is further magnified when Solomon levied taxes and forced all the tribes into labor except Judah (1 Kgs 4:7-19; 5:13-

18 [27-32 HB]; but see also 2 Sam 20:24, which shows that David placed Adoniram "in charge of forced labor"). Solomon became like Pharaoh, using his people, especially non-Judahites, to support his huge household and to establish cities, forts, and trade with other peoples. Dtr consistently pointed out that Judah was favored and Israel was afflicted, even to the extent that some of Israel's territories were given to Hiram of Tyre (1 Kgs 9:10-14).

And yet all Israel came to Shechem intending to install Solomon's son as king over them. They brought a critical question.

1. Israel Requests a Lighter Yoke but Rehoboam Promises a Heavier Yoke (12:1-11)

IN THE TEXT

■ 1 In this verse, it appears that **all Israel** selected Shechem and notified Rehoboam that this was the place they would inaugurate him; at Shechem they would confirm that he was their king as his father Solomon had been. This confirmation-inauguration was necessary, given their strength and numbers of the northern tribes.

Shechem was last featured in the story line in Judg 9, which tells about "king" Abimelek, Gideon's son, killing many Shechemites, his kin who had made him their king earlier. Shechem is Tel Balata today, near modern Nablus, and is the home of a small community of Samaritans. It was situated in the narrow pass between Mounts Gerizim (to the south) and Ebal (to the north). The tribes entering Canaan under Joshua were told to go there once they crossed the Jordan. There they divided and called out blessings and curses on those who obey and those who break the covenant, respectively (Deut 27:1-26; Josh 8:30-33). A generation later, while Joshua was still alive, Israel renewed the covenant and buried Joseph's bones at Shechem and thus it is of great importance to the Joseph tribes, Ephraim and Manasseh. The Shechemites comprise one of the clans of the tribe of Manasseh (Num 26:31; see also Josh 8:30-33; 24; Gen 32; 33:18-20; 50:25-26; Exod 13:19).

■ 2-3 Jeroboam **was still in Egypt, where he had fled from King Solomon** when he heard about the Shechem gathering. Although 2 Chr 10:2 and the LXX (and the NIV) report that he *returned* from Egypt at that time, 1 Kgs 12:2 (MT) claims that Jeroboam *stayed* in Egypt until the assembly of Israel sent for and called him. He then came and joined the assembly to speak with them to Rehoboam at Shechem. The narrator is not concerned to account for his quick travel time but is concerned to place Jeroboam with the Israelites requesting lighter service from Rehoboam. Alternatively, the text could be underscoring that Jeroboam had settled in Egypt after fleeing there; it was his residence. In any case, Israel summoned him to be their spokesperson while he had sanctuary in Egypt, and he came to Shechem at their call.

■ **4-5** As the condition for their continued support of the Davidic dynasty, Jeroboam and the congregation of Israel asked that Rehoboam lighten the hard service and heavy yoke his father had laid upon them. Rehoboam had the chance to be discerning and to govern wisely. He asked for time to consider their demand while he consulted advisers, but he did not turn to Yahweh or prophets.

■ **6-7** Rehoboam first consulted the elders who had stood before his father as advisers. They attempted to teach Rehoboam diplomacy by wisely pointing out that **Israel will be your servants forever** if you will be a servant to them **today**. They advised him to tell them what they want to hear **today**: **good words**. If he would speak humbly now, the people would be his servants in the future. The elders' answer indicates that they may have opposed Solomon's policy of consistently exacting a heavy toll from his subjects, or they knew this was the answer that would please Israel and thus support Rehoboam and unity. In any case, the elders saw the strength and discontent of Israel and knew that Rehoboam must ease their burdens, or at least promise to do so, in order to retain them as subjects.

■ **8-9** He rejected this advice. Looking for another answer, he turned to **boys** or **children**, those who had grown up with him and still continued in his company.

■ **10-11** The narrator shows his contempt for the new king's young friends by repeating the phrase: **the children who had grown up with him**. These youth prepared a harsh answer to Israel's request that Israel's yoke of service be lightened: **My littleness** or **my little thing** [NIV: little finger] **is thicker than my father's loins** (waist or **genitals**). The obvious meaning is: "Yes, my father's yoke was heavy, but I will add to it! His whips were bad; mine will be worse." Their view of their generation's prowess is clear, as is their contempt for their elders and their northern kin. But their answer was not diplomatic or sensible. It failed to reflect the shrewd strategy behind the elders' advice that Rehoboam present himself humbly as a servant to them as a welcome respite from his father at the beginning of his reign.

2. Israel Rebels and Makes Jeroboam King (12:12-24)

■ **12-14** The focus turns back to Jeroboam and Israel's return to Shechem on the third day for Rehoboam's response. We were warned to expect that he would reply according to the harsh advice of his fellows, **abandoning the advice of the elders** who had his interests at heart. Rehoboam avoided repeating his friends' analogy about his father's loins and his own **littleness**, but he threatened to lay upon the tribes of Israel a heavier yoke and discipline them with **scorpions** (whips with sharp points and stingers). The writer deplores the brutal answer and immaturity of Rehoboam. He was sympathetic to the elders and may have been one of them (see DeVries 1985, 157). The writer of this material is comfortable with the tension between the pronouncements of Yahweh through his prophets (i.e., against Solomon) and the machinations of humans.

■ **15** Although this answer was Rehoboam's choice based on the advice of his peers, the narrator affirms that Yahweh used this scenario to tear the kingdom from him as he had promised to both Solomon and Jeroboam through Ahijah (11:11, 29-39; 12:24). Does this mean the events were orchestrated by God and the players had no alternative? This chapter indicates otherwise: Rehoboam had the opportunity to retain leadership of all the tribes by listening to the elders, acting the humble servant, and speaking graciously to Israel. Nonetheless, Dtr connects the schism wrought by Rehoboam's answer, which was not hasty even though it was imprudent, with Yahweh's promise to punish Solomon's apostasy by giving ten tribes to another. Recall that Yahweh set Saul aside and gave the rule to David, promising him the dynasty, the promise that allowed the Davidic dynasty to continue in Jerusalem.

■ **16-17** The battle cry of Israel as they pulled away from Judah had longer-lasting and farther-reaching results than the one in Sheba's rebellion of 2 Sam 20:1-22. Whereas the narrator wished to point out that those from Israelite tribes living among the towns of Judah were still his subjects, all the rest of Israel, the northern tribes, seceded.

■ **18-19** That Rehoboam did not recognize the secession is shown when he immediately sent out the taskmaster, Adoniram, the officer who would clearly have been most despised by Israel (2 Sam 20:24; 1 Kgs 4:6; 5:14 [28 HB]). The king may have been testing their resolve in the most egregious and cowardly way, a pathetic but fatal attempt to force compliance. When Adoniram was stoned, Rehoboam fled for his own life, such was the anger of Israel against him and the Davidic dynasty he represented. The general dating of this source is indicated by 12:19, **to this day**. It was written before 722 BC when Israel was destroyed by the Assyrians while the house of David was still ruling over Judah.

■ **20** In 12:2-3, Jeroboam heard the news of the Shechem gathering while he was in Egypt: *all Israel sent for and called Jeroboam and he returned*. Here: *all Israel heard that Jeroboam had returned and they sent for and called him and crowned him king*. Israel's rebellion is framed by their selection and summons of Jeroboam, which is reiterated and climaxed as they crowned him king over **all Israel**, clearly a reference to the seceding northern tribes.

■ **21** The claim that only the *tribe* of Judah followed the house of David (v 20) is mitigated here, for we find the *tribe* of Benjamin enfolded into an army with the *house* of Judah to bring *all Israel* back. Benjamin is not only Saul's tribe, but also that of Sheba, who led the rebellion against David after Absalom (2 Sam 20:1-22). Judah was occupying Benjamin's territory at this time and they did not join *all Israel's* secession. Still stubbornly determined to resist losing power over the northern tribes, Rehoboam assembled a large force to restore his kingdom. The army was comprised of the same number of Israelites in Solomon's forced labor corvée, 180,000 (1 Kgs 5:13-16 [27-30 HB]). The reminder that Rehoboam was the **son of Solomon** also underscores Solomon's foundational role in this affair.

■ **22-24** Shemaiah brought an oracle of Yahweh to **Rehoboam son of Solomon** (v 23). Like Moses, Samuel, Elijah, and Elisha, the prophet is called **the man of God** (v 22). His oracle forbade them to fight their *brothers, the people of Israel* (v 24). The reason, *this thing is from me*, may have been news to Rehoboam, but it is not news to the reader. In what turns out to be an unusual response to prophets, Judah and Benjamin obeyed the word of Yahweh and turned away from civil war (compare 1 Kgs 14:30, which depicts continuous war between Rehoboam and Jeroboam).

3. Jeroboam Builds Two Golden Calves to Keep Israel from Jerusalem (12:25-33)

The previous report, 12:1-24, sets up this section's focus on Jeroboam the Ephraimite, which continues through 13:34.

■ **25** Having been crowned in Shechem, the ancient city nestled in the pass between Mount Ebal and Mount Gerizim in the Ephraim mountain range, Jeroboam built it as his capital and then turned toward Peniel to the east and set it up as another administrative city, possibly for governing subjects east of the Jordan. Peniel, a ford on the Jabbok River, was passed by Jacob the morning after his name was changed to Israel and he realized he had been wrestling with God. He named the wrestling site Peniel, meaning *face of God*, and Peniel is the name of the city on or near that site (Gen 32:24-32 [25-33 HB]; see also Judg 8:8-9, 17).

■ **26-27** Jeroboam "forgot" the promises of Yahweh and regarded his rule from a purely human perspective. Like Saul, he was anxious to retain, through his own efforts, what had been given to him by God. Jeroboam feared that Israel would submit to Rehoboam should they continue to travel to Jerusalem to worship. The Deuteronomist ensured that his readers understand that Yahweh planned to use Jeroboam to punish Solomon's apostasy but did not plan for Jeroboam to follow Solomon's ways and fail to keep the laws and statutes (see 1 Kgs 11:33).

■ **28-29** Thus, after consulting advisers, who are not identified but apparently suggested this course, he built worship sites centering on a gold calf at Dan and another one at Bethel. Dan (Tel el-Qadi) is near the source of the Jordan River at the foot of Mount Hermon in the Galil (Galilee).

Archaeological Finds at Dan

An Iron Age four-horned altar was found at Tel el-Qadi (Dan). The site was destroyed in the ninth century BC, rebuilt later, only to be destroyed again by the Assyrians in 722 BC. The Aramaic inscription referring to an Aramean king's defeat of a king from "the house of David" (Ahaz) was also found there. The Aramean king was probably Hazael.

Bethel was first known as Luz (as noted after Jacob's ladder dream [Gen 28:18-22] and in Gen 35 where a very different perspective is given on its purity as a site for an altar to Yahweh). Bethel was also the site of conquest (Josh 8), regret (weeping [Judg 2:1-5]), and war (Judg 20:18). Jeroboam's calves are firmly linked to Aaron's calf by his proclamation that they were Israel's gods who brought them up from Egypt, instantly reminding the readers of that apostasy, which nearly destroyed Israel just after Yahweh had delivered them from Egypt. His words are identical to Israel's proclamation when they saw the calf Aaron had made (Exod 32:1-4). They thus answer the question: "Why did Israel say 'calves' when Aaron made only one calf?" This is the writer's way of underscoring that Aaron's calf and Jeroboam's calves point to each other. Both Aaron and Jeroboam committed grave acts of apostasy by forming sculpted images in the likeness of something on the earth (Exod 20:4).

Commentators remark that Jeroboam did not intend to image Yahweh by means of these calves, but rather to make seats for Yahweh, much as the ark in the Jerusalem temple was Yahweh's footstool (see Sweeney 2007, 177; DeVries 1985, 162-63). Dtr does not inform us of this, however. Whatever Jeroboam intended, he proclaimed: **behold your gods, O Israel, who brought you up from the land of Egypt!** not: "behold the mount of Yahweh." Even if Jeroboam's two golden calves were intended to be a seat for an invisible Yahweh, and not images of Yahweh, as some scholars contend, Jeroboam's actions show his rejection of Yahweh's previous commands and covenant (1 Kgs 11:37-38). The Judahite narrator clearly classified this as a sin.

12:30-33

■ **30-31** In addition to making two golden calves that kept Israel out of Judah on holy days, Jeroboam sinned further by building shrines throughout the countryside and appointing non-Levitical priests, much to the disdain of Dtr (see 1 Kgs 13:34; Exod 12—13; 22:28-30 [27-29 HB]; 34:19-20; Num 3; 8). The likely Levitical status of the writer is disclosed in this description of Jeroboam's establishment of a festival on a new date and of scattered country shrines. Jeroboam is further indicted for not using the Levites living among the northern tribes to function as priests, but selecting anyone (Num 3:11-13, 40-51).

■ **32-33** His illegitimate festival in the eighth month paralleled Judah's celebration in the seventh month of Sukkot, the feast of booths (Exod 23:16; Lev 23:33-42; Num 29:12-39; Deut 16:13-15). The Deuteronomistic redactor is also condemning Jeroboam for rejecting the command to worship at one Yahweh-chosen place (Deut 12:2-8), which the writer knows is Jerusalem (though not identified in Deuteronomy). The books of Samuel and Kings show that David and Solomon chose Jerusalem as the royal residence and temple site and that Yahweh decided to accommodate their prayers and dwell there. The first time Yahweh is depicted as confirming that he had chosen this city is when he promises Jeroboam to tear most of the kingdom from Solomon's son: "Jerusalem, which I have chosen" (1 Kgs 11:32). First Kings 12:33 is the setting for the incidents that follow in ch 13.

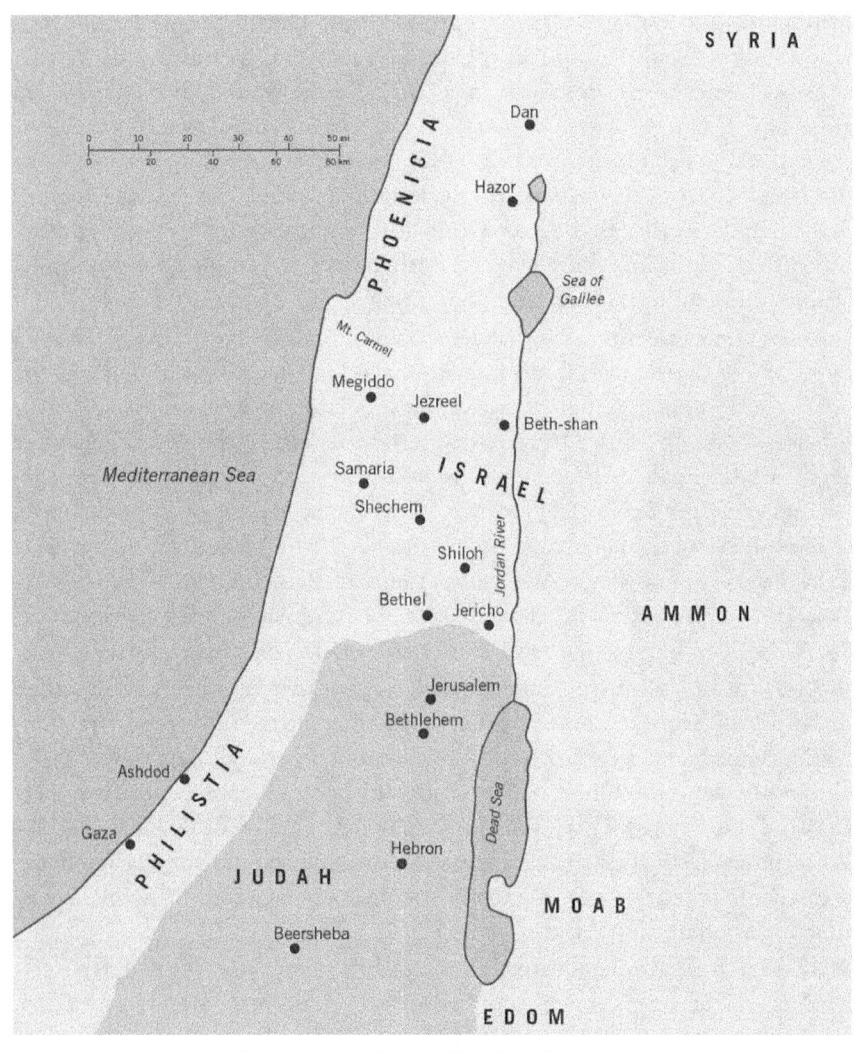

Map 5, Israel and Judah: The Divided Kingdom

The crowning of Jeroboam, the first king of the northern kingdom Israel, fulfilled conditions of Deut 17:14-20. Jeroboam was a king whom Yahweh and Israel had chosen; he was one of their brothers, not a foreigner. He did not acquire many horses, wives, silver, or gold as Solomon had done. However, he became odious to the Levitical priesthood from whom a king of Israel must obtain the Law and make a copy. He failed to keep the Law close to him and thus broke the conditions of the covenant of Yahweh that Ahijah the prophet had transmitted to him (1 Kgs 11:37-38). Furthermore, out of fear of losing the loyalty of his kinsmen, mistrusting Yahweh, he instituted new places of worship, building golden calves at the northern and southern points of his kingdom, Dan and Bethel respectively, and other shrines, to which he appointed non-Levitical priests. This incensed the writer, who could have been a Levite from Judah. This pericope, beginning with 12:25, continues in the next chapter.

4. The Man of God Prophesies against Jeroboam's Apostasy (13:1-34)

BEHIND THE TEXT

This section continues the story of Jeroboam with an account of Yahweh mercifully sending a prophet from Jerusalem to confront him, warn him to desist from practices that violated the conditions of his selection, and urge him to turn back to the commands of Yahweh. Allusions to biblical incidents abound in this narrative. Dtr seems to be aware of a form of written Torah with statutes, which he depicts Jeroboam as transgressing.

IN THE TEXT

■ **1** As Jeroboam (an Ephraimite) attempted to function as a priest himself by burning incense on the Bethel altar, a **man of God** from Judah joined him at Bethel by the command of Yahweh. Throughout this pericope, this Judahite prophet is called the **man of God**, who speaks only **the word of Yahweh**. His words and life became a lesson that Jeroboam failed to heed.

We have seen that Jeroboam invented a worship cult to preserve his own dynasty, showing his faithlessness to the directly revealed commands of Yahweh to him (11:29-39). Saul, David, and Solomon offered sacrifices to Yahweh without censure, but Jeroboam's offering is specifically condemned, as is the entire context for his smoke offering (a priestly prerogative) on a strange altar. This context includes many cult locations outside of Jerusalem, non-Levitical priests, and specifically the Dan-Bethel calves as gathering points for worship. Furthermore, this sets up the northern kingdom for failure at its beginning. In Dtr's view, kings were not to create worship systems but were to submit to the words of Yahweh they had received.

■ **2-3** Addressing the altar, God's man from Judah declared that a later son of David, Josiah, will burn the bones of the non-Levitical priests appointed by

Jeroboam and thus will defile it. The fulfillment of his words is recounted in 2 Kgs 23:15-20. This later narrative explains Josiah's respect for the prophet's tomb and otherwise serves Josianic Deuteronomistic denigrations of the northern nation's cult. The man of God concludes with a sign for Jeroboam that his words are from Yahweh: the altar will break and its ashes pour out.

■ **4-5** As Jeroboam *sent forth* his royal hand to order the seizure of God's man, it withered and froze, indicating his powerlessness in the face of the word of Yahweh. The altar immediately broke and poured forth its ashes as a sign from Yahweh.

■ **6-7** As Aaron once prayed to Moses to restore Miriam, whose skin had become like snow after the siblings challenged Moses' marriage and prophetic uniqueness (Num 12:9-12), so here Jeroboam prayed to the man of God to appeal to Yahweh to restore his hand. Like Moses had then prayed to Yahweh, so also did this prophet appeal to Yahweh, and Jeroboam's hand became his own again, showing that God listened to the prophet. The prophet's prayer for the wayward but fearful king was answered, indicating once again the significance of prophets during the monarchy.

The words spoken against the altar and Jeroboam's cult were given credence by the signs accompanying them (as in the case of the exodus and wilderness experiences of the Israelites). We do not know Jeroboam's motives for inviting the man of God to dine. The man of God's response is important: the commands he reiterates were revealed to him by Yahweh and became the basis for a lesson to Jeroboam and all hearers of these scriptures.

■ **8-10** These are the key verses upon which this entire narrative turns. God's man from Judah was determined to speak to the king only the words God gave him and to fully obey Yahweh's exact directives to him, which he recited to Jeroboam—and to all who hear this story. We are to learn a lesson from it. He delivered the exact words of Yahweh concerning the illegitimate altar and Josiah, a son of David, who would defile it with the bones of the illegitimate priests Jeroboam had established. His response to Jeroboam's invitation was equally firm: no, because the word of Yahweh to him prohibited eating, drinking, and returning to Jerusalem the same way he came. And thus he left by a different road, fully obedient to the commands of Yahweh.

■ **11-15** Sadly for this man of God from Judah, an old and curious prophet heard about his prophecy against Jeroboam and the reasons for his refusal to eat and drink with the king. He sought to test the words of the Jerusalem prophet. Thus, the Judahite prophet's life becomes a parable to teach the dangers of disobeying previous commands of God. The **old prophet** is determined to discover the truth of the other prophet's words against Jeroboam, indeed, to discover true prophecy. He set up a test scenario by which Jeroboam and all who heard the story were assured that the words God's man spoke to Jeroboam were from Yahweh and would come to pass.

■ **16-17** When he was invited home with the old prophet, the Judahite prophet repeated the commands of God to him, which indicated that he decline any food or water in Israel. This may be a textual attack on Israelite worship rites, which include eating and drinking (1 Sam 2:27-29; 9:11-27; Sweeney 2007, 181).

■ **18-19** Apparently because of the old prophet's claim to prophetic credentials, the Judahite prophet believed his lies and followed him home to eat and drink. What would happen next dramatically demonstrated to Jeroboam the authenticity of the words God's man had spoken to him. The deception of the **old prophet** from Bethel further discredits that northern city and its cult.

■ **20-22** *The word of Yahweh happened to* [came to] *the prophet who returned him*. This refers to the **old prophet**, who thereby prophesied against the man of God for disobeying God's words to him and for believing his own lying words that countered God's words. These words of Yahweh against disobeying God's directives will literally ***happen to*** God's man from Judah as will the latter's words happen to Jeroboam.

■ **23-25** The story proceeds in a straightforward manner, without concern to describe the feelings of the doomed **man of God**. We learn that when he rode away on the donkey of the old prophet, he was promptly killed by a lion who stayed by his body along with the donkey, without eating either.

What is the significance of these two animals and their standing together beside the corpse? James K. Mead submits that the donkey is associated with the old prophet, "who rides it, owns it, lends it to the man of God, and uses it to carry the latter's corpse." When God's man from Judah dies, he is on the donkey and carried to his death because of the deception of the old prophet (1999, 204).

Furthermore, throughout Scripture, we see that lions represent Judah and David's dynasty, as well as God's judgment upon those who disobey his voice (1 Kgs 20:36; 2 Kgs 17:25). Also consider all the passages in which Yahweh is like a lion. Mead suggests that the fact that the lion does not eat his prey shows the stark contrast between God's man, who eats but was forbidden from doing so, and the lion, which does not. The lion, as the symbol of an obedient Judah and of Yahweh's judgment, is the model of not eating, another condemnation on the altars at Bethel. In addition, "Yahweh is the lion who has come upon the stage to carry out the sentence" (1999, 204).

The Donkey and the Lion

Mead's case for the association of the donkey with the old prophet is strong, but his claim about the connection between the animal and Jeroboam is less so (1999, 202-3). That the lion represents the judgment of Yahweh is unassailable:

> This suggested identification is strengthened, but also expanded, by the fact that the lion does not eat the man of God's body. It would surely have been natural for the lion to eat its prey, and that action would have secured the prophecy that the body of the man of God would not come

to its ancestral grave. The clue to the lion's abstinence [is] suggested by the repetition of the verb "to eat." [Earlier], the verb is used ten times in relation to Yahweh's prohibition to the man of God; but the verb appears only once [at the end] with the lion not eating anything! (1999, 204; see also Sweeney 2007, 181-82)

■ **26-28** When the old prophet heard that his guest, whom he had deceived, was dead, his test was complete. He pronounced that the man of God's pronouncement against Jeroboam's altar to be true, for death followed the Judahite prophet's disobedience of God's directives to him. By association, his words against Jeroboam and the altar were sure to come to pass. All of this seems coldhearted reasoning over the unnecessary death of God's prophet. However, the old prophet's anguish emerges in the next verses.

■ **29-32** The truth of the words of Yahweh was demonstrated through the lion's attack and thereby the old prophet considered the dead man his own kin. Certain of the Judahite prophet's authenticity, the old prophet clamored to his body and brought it home to bury it in his own tomb and to mourn it, requiring his sons to promise to bury him with God's man. He did this **because the word he proclaimed by Yahweh against the altar in Bethel and against all the temples of the high places in the cities of Samaria . . . shall come to pass.**

■ **33-34** Jeroboam was the target of this entire story, including the final words of the old prophet. This story is a prophetic tragedy that functions as a living parable—a teaching—especially for Jeroboam. Jeroboam had the chance to heed the meaning of this incident and repent. The narrator concludes that this God-selected king of Israel (1 Kgs 11:29-39) continued to sin in spite knowing about the fatal outcome of the Judahite prophet's disregard for minor directives of Yahweh. Thus, Jeroboam would bring disaster on his own dynasty by continuing to make priests for high places of anyone, disobeying previous commands of Yahweh, just as the man of God met a disastrous end for disobeying Yahweh's commands to him.

Nonetheless, the contrast between Jeroboam and the man of God is also clear: Jeroboam sinned out of faithless fear, heeding unnamed advisers (1 Kgs 12:28); God's man sinned because he believed the lies of another prophet. This is a classic case of the principle of *qal vehomer* (lit. "light to heavy"). It means "if x how much more y," also called a fortiori. If a lion would kill God's man who obeyed except when deceived, *how much more* would Jeroboam be punished if he did not cease his willful and consistent defiance of God's conditions for remaining king. (See Van Winkle 1989, 31-43.)

FROM THE TEXT

Once again, we see a case demonstrating that a prophesied outcome is not destined to happen, for this prophecy and the life parable were meant to deter Jeroboam from continuing to sin. It was an impetus for him to repent, to change direction. If even a mostly obedient man of God who failed to obey (as a result of deception) in a negligible matter was dead, and Jeroboam knew this, how great was his own culpability! God's man was deceived into disobeying, but this king had been repeatedly warned about the serious nature of his defiance and yet he continued to sin! Pronouncements of punishment are conditional; they do not have to happen. They are intended to thwart their own fulfillment if their targeted hearers heed them, just as Nineveh heeded the words of Jonah. In this case the prophet paid with his own life to carry a message to the king.

As scripture, this story is a warning for all who hear it. Has God previously revealed commands, calls, expectations, and directives through Scripture, the Holy Spirit, prophets, pastors, teachers, and friends? Of course! And yet we, like Jeroboam, fear losing the positions, roles, and other favors God has so graciously given. We are tempted to manipulate to retain them or to advance ourselves, forgetting God's conditions and his hope that we observe all of his commands, walk in his ways, and do what is right (1 Kgs 11:38).

The Indictment of Jeroboam

Mead expands upon the meaning of the prophet's life for Jeroboam in contrast to the obedient son of David, Josiah.

The man of God moves from obedience, through temptation, into disobedience and ultimately to death.... When seen within the context of the Deuteronomistic material surrounding it (xii 25-33 and xiii 33-34), therefore, the story takes on its larger sense as political rhetoric for Josiah's kingship in and through the indictment of Jeroboam and his reforms. The wicked northern king is unmoved by the events of the chapter, and thus he will find that his own path will follow that of the disobedient man of God, namely, unto destruction. (1999, 196, 205; this article references a number of other scholars who insightfully probe the significance of this passage [191 and passim])

5. Ahijah Prophesies against Jeroboam's Dynasty (14:1-20)

BEHIND THE TEXT

In ch 13, Yahweh used a man from Judah to bring the word of judgment against Jeroboam, not the prophet Ahijah of Shiloh (in Israel), who had presented Yahweh's covenant to Jeroboam in 11:30-39. However, in this narrative Yahweh deployed old Ahijah to reiterate the conditions of that covenant and, on that basis, to deliver once again the message of judgment: Yahweh planned to destroy Jeroboam's dynasty. Even here, Jeroboam rejected the word of Yahweh and refused to change his ways.

IN THE TEXT

■ **1** The occasion for Ahijah's address to Jeroboam is brought about by his sick son and his wife's visit to Ahijah. Jeroboam's sons' names are similar to those of Aaron, who (like Jeroboam) built a golden calf to the shame and punishment of Israel. Abijah (*my God is Yah*) and Nadab were Jeroboam's sons; Abihu (*he is my God*) and Nadab were Aaron's older sons. See Exod 24:1, 9-11, where they saw God; and Lev 10:1-2, where they were consumed for offering unholy fire. Again, this comparison is not accidental; Aaron and Jeroboam both built golden calves, leading Israel to sin (→ 1 Kgs 12:28-29).

■ **2-3** Jeroboam had not forgotten who had pronounced him **king over this people** when trouble struck his home. Shiloh, Ahijah's home, ten miles north of Bethel, was the premonarchy sanctuary of the ark (1 Sam 4). Jeroboam would not be seen going to the prophet himself and did not want his wife to be recognized, so he sent her in disguise and laden with food to obtain a favorable prediction concerning his son. Nonetheless, he did not ask for healing prayer as the Syrian Naaman did in 2 Kgs 5.

■ **4-5** Ahijah was too old to see her, but Yahweh told him that Jeroboam's wife was coming and what he should tell her. The reader does not learn this word of Yahweh until Ahijah addressed her.

■ **6-8** He heard her feet as she entered through the door and he began speaking. Although *she* came to him, Ahijah said: **I am sent to you**, which is what God does to prophets carrying the word of Yahweh. This word of Yahweh for Jeroboam was **a severe thing**, which began with the prophetic formula ***thus says Yahweh*** and reminder that Yahweh is **the God of Israel**. Then he reminded Jeroboam his kingship was based on the condition that he keep it as had **my servant David**. The Judahite perspective recognizes the punishment on the house of David through the torn kingdom, but also that David is the model king for Jeroboam and all subsequent kings of Israel and Judah. (But see the acknowledgment of the exception in 1 Kgs 15:5: David's sin in taking Uriah's wife and life.)

■ **9** Yahweh through Ahijah accused Jeroboam of doing evil more than any before him. **Evil** (*rāʿaʿ*) here is the verb; he has **eviled** or transgressed, done wrong, and thus brought more disaster/harm than any other before him. Jeroboam had few predecessors, but this formula was also used against King Ahab (1 Kgs 21:21) and the nation of Judah (2 Kgs 22:16, 20; Jer 4:6; 6:19; 11:11; etc.]).

This formula displays Yahweh's utter disgust, but it still did not *determine* that the judgment must occur. When Ahab repented after Elijah pronounced this formula and consequent judgment against him, God relented (1 Kgs 21:27-29), indicating the dynamic, relational character of God.

Ahijah went on to say that Jeroboam had not simply failed to do what was right with a whole heart, he had sculpted **other gods** of gold to anger

Yahweh. This shows that Yahweh did not view these calves as a mount for his invisible presence, but rather saw them as evidence of apostasy.

■ **10-11** In turn, as judgment, Yahweh will bring evil (*rā'â*, this time used as a noun) on the house of Jeroboam. This term can mean sinning and provoking Yahweh as Jeroboam had done, and it can also refer to the judgment that Yahweh brings for apostasy and otherwise breaking the covenant. The penalty of cutting off *every* male (***those who piss against a wall***)—bond or free (***bound or released***)—also appears as a judgment formula against Baasha (1 Kgs 16:11) and Ahab (1 Kgs 21:21; 2 Kgs 9:8). This phrase has also been understood to mean "utterly helpless and abandoned" (see DeVries 1985, 179).

The totality of judgment is expressed by terms of consuming as with fire or sweeping away, as well as with graphic examples of Jeroboam's unburied dead: dogs will eat their bodies in the city and birds will eat corpses in the country. This formula stressing that the males of the house of Jeroboam will be cut off from their ancestors by not being buried with them also appears in regard to Baasha, Ahab and his wife, Jezebel, and later rulers of Israel who worship in the shrines Jeroboam established (see, for example, 1 Kgs 16:4; also 1 Kgs 21:19, 23, 24; 22:38; 2 Kgs 9:10, 36).

■ **12-13** Ahijah then addressed Jeroboam's wife concerning their son and the reason she came, but not with a favorable prediction. He pronounced that he would die and be the only son of Jeroboam buried and mourned, ***because Yahweh found something good in him***.

■ **14** Ahijah went on to announce that Yahweh would establish a king of Israel to be the instrument of God's destruction of Jeroboam's dynasty, which, the prophet declared, would begin ***today, now!*** A coup to depose Nadab, Jeroboam's son, would be led by Baasha, whose capital was Tirzah, the city to which Jeroboam's wife returned, a foreshadowing of Baasha's reign and the terror it would bring to Jeroboam's house (→ 1 Kgs 14:17-18).

14:10-15

■ **15** Ahijah, as the spokesman here for Yahweh's Deuteronomistic denunciation of Israel, saw the ***asherim*** (sacred poles; → "Asherah" sidebar at Behind the Text for 1 Kgs 16:29—22:53 [22:54 HB]) that Israel would set up in the future. The Hebrew ***asherim*** (wooden poles or trees) may be related to the goddess by the name Asherah (one of the three Canaanite goddesses) or objects of worship in themselves. At Kuntillet Ajrud on the Negev/Sinai border, at a military post there is an inscription from 900 to 800 BC: "I have blessed you by Yahweh of Samaria and his Asherah."

In any case, such apostasy would lead Yahweh to uproot them, just as the Canaanites before them had been uprooted. They are likened to a feeble reed, one that will sway by the judging wind of Yahweh, finally to be completely torn out of this good land that Yahweh had given to their ancestors. To scatter them beyond the river is an allusion to the Euphrates and their dispersion by the Assyrians in 722 BC.

■ **16** Yahweh through Ahijah blamed Jeroboam for Israel's present and subsequent sinning. He caused them to sin by setting up the disparaged calves as alternatives to worshipping in Jerusalem and by making priests from anyone with no regard to the Levitical priesthood. Nonetheless, Jeroboam reigned as king of Israel until he died twenty-two years after his inauguration.

■ **17-18** When Jeroboam's wife crossed the doorstep in return, her son died. Jeroboam's capitals were Shechem and Peniel (1 Kgs 12:25), but she returned to Tirzah, which would become the capital city of the later Israelite kings: Baasha, Zimri, and Omri. The reference to Tirzah foreshadows Baasha's rule and deposing of the dynasty of Jeroboam (15:29-30), fulfilling Ahijah's words. Tirzah is seven miles northeast of Shechem, identified with modern Tel el-Farah.

The use of a city to foreshadow later events is a technique also deployed in 1 Sam 17:54, which describes David taking Goliath's head to Jerusalem immediately after he cut it off. Jerusalem was still a Jebusite city at that time; David did not conquer it until much later (2 Sam 5:6-7). As in the case of Tirzah here, the mention of Jerusalem well before it became the royal city foreshadows David's conquest and its later status, just as his defeat of Goliath meant that he would indeed be king. Although Western interpreters often do not know what to make of this literary technique, it is not difficult to appreciate, and it illustrates the literary, theological nature of this material.

■ **19-20** This concluding formula will begin to look familiar, for it provides closure to the rule of each northern king with a reference to lost written sources. These seem to be formal royal annals and include details as to each king's wars and rulings (see 1 Kgs 15:31; 16:5, 14, 20, 27; 22:39; 2 Kgs 1:18; 10:34; 13:8; 14:15, 28; 15:11, 15, 21, 26, 31; etc.). This referral to royal archives from which the reader might gain further information is another indication of the theological, prophetic focus of these scriptures.

In the books of Kings, the writer, while selectively relying on written royal annals, tells the reader what he considers to be historically and theologically important. For example, in the remaining material, the writer claims that each northern king followed Jeroboam's religious innovations, without repeating information that he assumes the reader can find in the annals. An indication of his Judahite provenance is the fact that the writer judges each king against David's faithfulness to Yahweh. (The lost records of Israelite and Judahite kings are also referred to in 1 Chr 9:1; 2 Chr 16:11; 20:34; 27:7; and etc.)

FROM THE TEXT

In this section, Solomon's apostasy was joined by Rehoboam's arrogant decisions as the cause for the kingdom's division. Then Jeroboam's egregious infidelity to the commands of Yahweh began the downward spiral of the northern kingdom. These rulers were catapulted to power by God's selection of them (Jeroboam) or on account of their ancestors (Solomon, Rehoboam), but they failed to live according to God's conditions. Although no king's conscience convicted him, God mercifully sent prophets to warn him of impending judgment.

Jeroboam did not fear, honor, or believe God, who appeared to him offering a tremendous covenant promise. When God's living people follow our own fears and rely on advisers or our own choosing to survive, we foolishly defy the counsel God has already provided. We forget God's promises and walk without faith.

Like many biblical texts, this section is a narrative exhortation to leaders, depicting how they can lead entire people groups astray. Moses was judged harshly in Num 20 for his understandable anger that led to words and actions that did not set God apart as holy. He was not allowed to enter the land. Here, out of faithless, fearful motives, Jeroboam committed much more egregious offenses: he set up calves and shrines, made non-Levites priests, and required Israel to sin by worshipping in Dan and Bethel instead of in Jerusalem. His lack of trust in God's promises led God to take extreme measures to warn him against continuing to break the covenant God gave him. As noted in the comments at 1 Kgs 12:26-27 (→), leaders fail when they try to retain, through their own efforts, what is given by God. The writer blames leaders for causing their people to fall victim to judgment. The hope provided by this narrative emerges from God's warnings through prophets, implying that the hearers can change course and thereby avert disaster.

The application of this message might not be obvious to church leaders in an age in which no one sets up physical images and shrines for sacrifices. Nonetheless, church leaders can set up idols to success and appearances of wealth, health, and activity. They may enforce rules and restrictions on God's people that are not based on biblical examples and principles. They become culpable for quenching the Holy Spirit and leading God's people astray. For example, some churches still forbid women to preach, teach, and baptize and thus restrict the spread of the gospel and reject the Spirit's call and anointing on individuals.

14:21—
15:24

B. Kings of Judah and Israel (14:21—16:28)

I. Rehoboam, Abijam, Asa Rule Judah (14:21—15:24)

BEHIND THE TEXT

First Kings 14:25-26 claims that Pharaoh Shishak of Egypt took the treasures from the Jerusalem temple and the king's palaces in the fifth year of Rehoboam, 926 BC (see also 1 Kgs 11:40; 2 Chr 12:2-4; and 1 Kgs 9:16). As noted in the Introduction, the wall relief in the Hypostyle Hall in the temple of Amun at Karnak in Egypt shows Pharaoh Sheshonq I (tenth century BC) smiting figures labeled by place names that include Megiddo and Gezer, regions of Israel north of Jerusalem, and many other sites, none of which are in Judah. Scholars identify Sheshonq I with the Shishak of 1 Kgs 14:25. Remains of pottery at the three gate sites of Hazor, Gezer, and Megiddo lie in a layer of destruction attributed to this pharaoh (Dever 2001, 134-36).

Because no record of violence at Jerusalem or among the Philistine cities exists, historians suspect that Shishak offered Rehoboam terms of peace on his way north in return for tribute from Jerusalem's temple and palaces. Finkelstein suggests that Judah was a "passive partner" in Shishak's "Egypto-Philistine alliance" (2006, 84). This alliance may have been aided by Solomon's earlier marriage to an Egyptian princess (1 Kgs 3:1; 9:16).

Having concluded his treatment of Jeroboam I of Israel in 1 Kgs 14:21—15:24, the narrator turns to Judah and the kings who descended from David and Solomon. The initial choices of Solomon's heir, Rehoboam, were critical to the formation of the northern kingdom and explain his appearance at the outset of Jeroboam's story. Chapter 14's focus on Rehoboam is formulaic and presents a pattern for each of Judah's kings regarding his age, length of reign, mother, and whether he served Yahweh exclusively. The books of Chronicles also use this formula (for example, 2 Chr 12:13). The formula for Rehoboam is slightly different from that used for the later Judahite kings, because Rehoboam came to the throne of Judah before the northern kingdom, Israel, seceded. Thus, the beginning of his reign is not dated in terms of the reign of an Israelite king, as is the case for each subsequent king of Judah before the fall of Israel to Assyria in 722 BC. This formula itself probably came from the book of the annals of the kings of Judah, referred to in 1 Kgs 14:29 (→ 1 Kgs 14:19-20 regarding the book of the annals of the kings of Israel).

The formula for the start of a Judahite king's reign reveals the names of the mothers of Judah's kings. Rehoboam is the son of an Ammonite woman, Naamah, probably of the royal family. She is also mentioned in the formula for the end of his reign at v 31. Naamah is the only named wife of Solomon, and the fact that she came from Ammon underscores Solomon's policy of making peace with his neighbors through marriage.

The relationship of Judah/Israel and postexilic Jews with Ammon is mostly troubled. See, for example, Gen 4:22 (Lamech and his daughter Naamah are from the line of Cain); 19:37-38; Deut 2:19, 37; 23:3-5 [4-6 HB]; Judg 10:7-9; 1 Sam 11; 14:47; 2 Sam 11:1—12:31 (Joab was fighting the Ammonites while David stayed home to procure Bathsheba and murder Uriah). Of particular significance is Neh 13:23-26, which describes Nehemiah's distress at seeing male Jews marry Ammonite women (among others) when they had been restored to the land under Persia. His response was to claim that Solomon was made to sin by marrying foreign women.

IN THE TEXT

■ **14:21** The Judahite Deuteronomistic Historian (Dtr) underscores the holiness of Jerusalem: he claims that Yahweh selected this city for the home of his name. However, the chosen place was carefully left unnamed in the book of Deuteronomy, for, in the world of the story the speaker, Moses, could not have known that Jebus would become the royal temple city. In Kings, however, Dtr had freedom to emphasize Jerusalem's pride of place among all the towns of the tribal territories. Not only did David conquer it and build it into the royal city, not only did Solomon build the temple and invite Yahweh to place his name there and honor all the prayers in and toward it, but *Yahweh* had chosen it. Thus, Dtr emphasized that Yahweh required that Judah and all Israel worship there and there alone.

■ **22-24** The annals' formula frames an expansion on Rehoboam's sins described. The narrator does not blame the king's Ammonite mother for Judah's sins but claims that they were worse than any committed by their ancestors, such as Solomon, who instituted the worship of his wives' gods, including Molek (Milcom), the god of the Ammonites (1 Kgs 11:1-8). Solomon's apostasy was the reason the kingdom was torn from him (vv 11-13), and his apostasy was connected to his foreign wives, one of whom was Rehoboam's Ammonite mother. Thus, Rehoboam's apostasy is more understandable than Solomon's, to whom Yahweh had appeared (more than) twice (v 9). Not only was his mother an Ammonite, but his Judahite father, the son of David, worshipped other gods.

The claim that Judah's sins were worse than those of Judah's ancestors is a serious indictment given the horrors Israel committed during the judges period, when they did what was right in their own eyes. Judah's sins under Rehoboam are not listed as crimes against their own people (see Judg 19) but rather as sins that provoked Yahweh to jealousy, following the Canaanite rituals of worship.

This text implies that this included male prostitutes (*qĕdēšîm*, set apart ones). Scholars rely on Deut 23:17 [18 HB] to explain the activity of the *qĕdēšîm*, which specifically proscribes against female and male set apart ones. This ordinance is juxtaposed with prohibitions against bringing fees earned by regular male and female prostitutes in Deut 23:18 [19 HB]. Rehoboam's grandson, Asa, will expel the *qĕdēšîm* (1 Kgs 15:12).

■ **25-28** Shishak's entrance into this scene and his stripping of Jerusalem's gold, which had been so lavishly spread around by Solomon, may be considered punishment for Judah's sins. Rehoboam quickly replaced the gold shields with those of bronze, which accompanied him when he entered the house of Yahweh. Clearly, he did not abandon Yahweh's temple, but he added places of worship and implements of the service of other gods, such as country shrines and **asherim**, sacred poles. (→ 1 Kgs 14:15 and "Asherah" sidebar at Behind the Text for

1 Kgs 16:29—22:53 [22:54 HB].) The 1 Kings account is sparse compared to the expanded, later version of 2 Chronicles, which includes Rehoboam's repentance to explain theologically how Judah survived Shishak's raid.

■ **29-31** This is the formula used in Kings/Chronicles for the end of the reign of each king of Judah, except for the repetition of the queen mother's name, which does not appear for other kings. Although Rehoboam listened to the prophet and did not ignite a war between Judah and Israel when the latter broke away (1 Kgs 12:22-24), apparently the nations skirmished with each other regularly throughout Rehoboam's reign.

He died four years before Jeroboam, king of Israel. Second Chronicles 11:5-12 expands upon Rehoboam's building activities, indicating Rehoboam's efforts to fortify Judah's cities against encroachment by Israel.

There are two unrelated Abijahs in proximity in chs 14—15: the first Abijah is the ailing son of Jeroboam (14:1), while King Abijah (NIV and 2 Chr 11:20-22) is the king of Judah, son of Rehoboam and father of Asa. King Abijah is called Abijam in most Hebrew manuscripts at 1 Kgs 14:31—15:7. In Chronicles' later rendering of this account, Abijam's name is spelled Abijah, to make the more orthodox meaning: "my father is Yahweh"). Abijam means "my father is Yam," the sea-god, known through Ugaritic texts. We will call him Abijam here.

■ **15:1-5** Some scholars question whether Abijam's mother (Rehoboam's wife) was the daughter of David's son Absalom (2 Sam 13—19) or another man with a similarly spelled name. Second Chronicles 13:2 says that "Abijah's" mother (Rehoboam's wife) was Micaiah, the daughter of Uriel of Gibeah (Maakah in NIV, see NIV footnote). This conflicts with 2 Chr 11:20-22, which parallels 1 Kgs 15:2 here, adding that Maakah, daughter of Absalom, was Rehoboam's favorite wife and bore him "Abijah" (Abijam in 1 Kgs 15). Rehoboam (Absalom's nephew) could easily have married Absalom's daughter (his cousin).

The notice of the reign of Abijam, son and heir of Rehoboam, is almost entirely formulaic, with the exception of a discursus on the merit of David as the reason for sinful Abijam to remain on the throne for three years. Such loyalty to David again demonstrates the pro-Judah stance of the writer who is also cognizant of David's sin (stealing Uriah's wife, then killing him [2 Sam 11]). The mention of David's sin, however, may be a gloss by a redactor who recognized that the audience was acquainted with David's failures.

■ **6-8** Some Hebrew and Syriac manuscripts refer to war between Abijam and Jeroboam in v 6, as in v 7, which makes sense here. But most Hebrew manuscripts say Rehoboam instead of Abijam in v 6. This may be an earlier reading but an error that later manuscripts corrected. These verses represent the typical reference to the annals, the death, and the name of successor to conclude a Judahite king's reign.

■ **9-10** Asa, Abijam's son, reigned much longer. He is said to have the same mother as his father had, which scholars explain in various ways. As noted above, 2 Chr 13:2 refers to a different mother, Micaiah of Gibeah, for Abijam. Sweeney suggests that Rehoboam may have married Micaiah of Gibeah, Saul's territory, as a unifying political move. When she died, she was replaced as queen mother by Maakah, daughter of Absalom, whose mother was Maakah of Geshur (2 Sam 3:3; Sweeney 2007, 191). Geshur was a city in northern Galilee, which became vulnerable to raids by Aram/Syria, reported later in this passage. Alternatively, Maakah, Absalom's daughter, may have been Asa's grandmother who retained the queen mother role until he deposed her for idolatry.

■ **11-14** As part of his reform, which included the removal of male prostitutes and idols, Asa removed Maakah from her elevated role as queen mother because of the pole she had set up for Asherah, the Canaanite fertility goddess. He cut down and burned this **repulsive image for the worship of Asherah** in the Kidron valley much as Josiah would later do to idols and other objects that Judahites used to serve other gods (2 Kgs 23:4-7). Before Josiah, another reforming king, Hezekiah, also cut down Asherah poles and removed the shrines (18:4). Although Asa did not remove the shrines scattered throughout the countryside, Dtr gave the long-reigning, reformer king a good evaluation, comparing his heart and his actions to David's. (→ "Asherah" sidebar at Behind the Text for 1 Kgs 16:29—22:53 [22:54 HB].)

■ **15** Apparently Abijam and Asa refashioned gold, silver, and vessels to replace those that Shishak had seized. They had stored them in their own homes until Asa restored them to the temple. Their restoration was a significant aspect of Asa's reign that would enable Asa to combat the advances of Baasha, king of Israel, against Judah (15:19-20).

■ **16-17** Baasha, from the tribe of Issachar (v 27), who had ousted Nadab, Jeroboam's son, threatened Judah by advancing on Ramah of Benjamin, which was only five miles north of Jerusalem. Baasha thereby encroached on Judah's territory and restricted entry to Jerusalem, enlarging Israel's borders.

■ **18-20** In response, Asa made an alliance with Ben-Hadad, the king of Aram (Syria) against Israel by offering him payment of the restored temple treasures in exchange for his support. Asa recalled the treaties of David and Solomon with Aram, requesting that Ben-Hadad break any treaties with Israel, which he did by advancing against Israel's northern borders in Galilee (**Kinnereth**), including the cities of Dan and Abel Beth Maakah in the tribe of Naphtali. The remains of the latter city, now called Tell Abil al-Qamh, are now being excavated by archaeologists, including Robert Mullins of Azusa Pacific University (Panitz-Cohen and Mullins, 2016).

Ben-Hadad's invasion included the region of Geshur (on the east side of Lake Galilee), with whom Judah had been allied since David married Maakah, Absalom's mother (2 Sam 3:3). When this woman's granddaughter (also named Maakah, daughter of Absalom; → 1 Kgs 15:1-5 above) was deposed as queen mother under Asa, the alliance was broken. (See Map 5, p. 118.)

■ **21-22** The result of the Judah-Aram alliance was Baasha's withdrawal from Ramah and return to his capital, Tirzah. Then Judah took Baasha's fortifications of Ramah farther north in Benjamin's territory to Geba and Mizpah to defend Benjamin and Judah against invasion by Israel. This essentially moves the border between Judah and Israel northward, against Baasha's claim that it should be south of Ramah.

■ **23-24** Asa's reign is concluded with the reminder that more information about his achievements can be found in Judah's royal annals. He was an old man when he died and his **feet** or genitals suffered. ("Feet" is sometimes used as a euphemism for genitals, so this may refer to prostate disease, but it can also simply mean an ailment of his thighs, legs, or feet.)

Rehoboam and Abijam slept with their fathers and were buried in the city of David, whereas Asa's death notice underscores his relationship to David, emphasizing the writer's approval of Asa, whose heart and works followed David's, the ideal king. In 2 Chr 14—16's expanded version of Asa's story, however, Asa is remembered for his cruelty to the seer Hanani and others (16:7-10). Jehu, son of Hanani the seer, addresses Jehoshaphat, king of Judah in 19:1-3. The annals of Jehu form a section of the book of the kings of Israel (20:34) and may be a source for both Chronicles and Kings (Sweeney 2007, 197-98, 202).

Although Judah's rulers and people continued to worship at the temple in Jerusalem, they also supported the country shrines erected by Solomon. Until Asa's reign, they set up sacred poles and accepted sacred prostitution. This demonstrates *syncretism*, worshipping Yahweh *and* other gods. This also showed that Judahites worshipped Yahweh at places outside of the temple in Jerusalem. This is a picture of Judah's continuing decline with one bright spot, one good king, Asa, among the first few generations after the northern tribes made Jeroboam king and broke away from the Davidic dynasty.

2. Nadab, Baasha, Elah, Zimri, and Omri Rule Israel (15:25—16:28)

BEHIND THE TEXT

This section accounts for the kings of Israel leading up to and including Omri, the father of the notorious King Ahab. The throne of Israel is subject to bloody coups, which the Deuteronomist usually claims is punishment for sins institutionalized by Jeroboam and not repudiated by each subsequent king—the golden calves in the shrines at Dan and Bethel.

From the Moabite Mesha stone and Assyrian texts, we know Omri was renowned among the surrounding nations. He captured Moabite territory in the mid-ninth century BC (*ANET*, 320-21). Shalmaneser III of Assyria (853-

824 BC) refers to Jehu, the exterminator of Omri's dynasty, as "the son of Omri" (ibid., 282). In addition, Tiglath-Pileser III (744-727 BC) calls Israel the land of Omri (ibid., 284). Other Assyrian texts call Israel "the house of Omri." However, to Dtr, Omri was merely a footnote in his theological narrative; the one who established Samaria as the capital of Israel.

This account begins with Nadab, who was the son of Jeroboam, but deposed and murdered by Baasha. Baasha's son Elah was murdered by Zimri, who in turn killed himself by burning Tirzah when Omri besieged it, after his troops inaugurated him, their general, as king.

IN THE TEXT

■ **25-26** After introducing us to Asa's son and successor Jehoshaphat, Dtr returns to Israel during the time of Nadab, the son of Jeroboam I, whose dynasty was destroyed by Baasha, according to the word of the prophet Ahijah (14:10-11). As is the convention, the beginning of the reign of each king of Israel is dated by the year of the king of Judah; in Nadab's case, this was Asa's second year of a forty-one-year reign. Nadab continued to sin like his father by preserving as worship sites both the golden calves at Dan and Bethel and the non-Levitical priests.

■ **27-28** Baasha of the tribe of Issachar assassinated Nadab, king of Israel, an Ephraimite, indicating tension among the northern tribes, as well as personal ambition. Baasha may have been a commander in Israel's army, led by Nadab, who was attempting to take the Philistine town on the coastal plain (modern Tel Malat). The two Ahijahs mentioned within two chapters are not related: Baasha's father was from Issachar while the earlier Ahijah was a prophet from Shiloh in Ephraim.

Baasha made Tirzah his capital, a hegemony that had been literarily foreshadowed by the "return" of Jeroboam's wife to Tirzah after she had made a secret visit to the prophet Ahijah at Shiloh (→ 1 Kgs 14:17-21). Tirzah is north of Shechem and in the territory of Manasseh, a bit south of the territory allotted to Issachar. However, tribal boundaries were never firm and had been in flux for many decades.

■ **29-30** Baasha's purge of Jeroboam's entire family ensured that no potential heir could claim back the throne. It also fulfilled Yahweh's words of punishment against Jeroboam for inventing and establishing an alternative worship system for Israel (14:10-11). No other branch of government prevented the comprehensive slaughter of the royal family. On the one hand, this is seen as accomplishing Yahweh's pronouncements; on the other hand, Baasha himself would be punished for annihilating Jeroboam's people (16:7).

■ **31-34** Nadab, son of Jeroboam, did not "sleep with his fathers," for he was treacherously murdered. Baasha continued to dispute Israel-Judah boundaries with Judah's king Asa throughout the twenty-four years of his reign, during which time he also continued the cult of Jeroboam's calves.

■ **16:1-4** Here and in subsequent passages, we continue to observe that if a king would change his ways, the judgments of Yahweh would also be altered. The kings were not destined to sin or to be punished. Jehu's (son of Hanani) prophecy against Baasha claimed that Yahweh had **appointed** him **ruler over his people Israel**. This word of Yahweh is remembered in 1 Kgs 16:12. In 2 Chr 19:2-3, Jehu addressed the Judahite king Jehoshaphat. The annals of this prophet Jehu are part of the book of the kings of Israel according to 2 Chr 20:34, and the Jehu history may be the written source for the author of 1 Kgs 14—16 (Sweeney 2007, 197-98, 202).

Yahweh hoped that Baasha would destroy the shrines of Jeroboam, but since he did not, Baasha's dynasty was set for violent destruction. His successors would die without proper burial, unless, we presume from other accounts of prophetic activity, they responded to Jehu's warning by repenting. Jehu's prophecy links this account to those concerning Jeroboam and Ahab (see 1 Kgs 14:11 [Jeroboam] and 21:19-24; 2 Kgs 9:10, 36 [Ahab]).

■ **5-7** The writer's account of Baasha is settled in the conventional fashion by citing the record of his reign in the royal annals. He troubled Asa, king of Judah, and we learned of their skirmishes in 1 Kgs 15:16. Although Baasha's dynasty would not remain, Baasha died peacefully in Tirzah, succeeded by his son Elah. Jehu's prophecy is repeated here, as is Baasha's apostasy and his capital, Tirzah. Notably, in the summary of his life, he is also indicted for his blood purge of the house of Jeroboam! In the final form of the text, the repeat of Jehu's prophecy to Baasha functions to emphasize the oracle of Yahweh.

■ **8-14** Like Jeroboam's son Nadab, Baasha's son Elah reigned only two years before he was assassinated by Zimri, the commander of half of his chariots. This occurred while he was in Tirzah drinking at the home of Arza, the palace custodian, in the twenty-seventh year of Asa, king of Judah. The total destruction of Baasha and Elah's family by Zimri followed, just as Jeroboam's sons and other males were slaughtered by Baasha himself. This time, Baasha and his son suffer for their own sins and **worthless idols** or ***vain things***. Jeroboam and his golden calves are not named here, and this is an aberration.

■ **15-19** Zimri stayed in Tirzah and settled himself on the throne, but not for long—seven days. During his short reign, Zimri functioned as the instrument of destruction of Baasha's dynasty. He hardly had time to ***walk in the path of Jeroboam*** (v 19) before ***all Israel*** made Omri, the general, king (v 16). And yet, Dtr sees Omri's capture of Tirzah and Zimri's self-destruction by fire as punishment for his complicity in Jeroboam's sins. This is a characteristic of the Deuteronomistic editions of Kings (Sweeney 2007, 202).

The forces with Omri (who could not have comprised all Israel, for not everyone supported him, according to v 21) appeared to be dismayed at Zimri's bloody conspiracy, and rushed from Gibbethon to Tirzah to avenge Elah and put Omri on the throne. Gibbethon of the Philistines was the city under attack by Nadab when he was assassinated by Baasha (15:27). It was on the eastern border of the coastal plain (modern Tel Malat) and far from Tirzah. Nonetheless, Omri and his forces made good time.

■ **20** Whereas Zimri was commander of half of the king's chariots, Omri was the general over the army and thus over Zimri. Omri did not conspire against his king or extinguish a dynasty, but was made king by his forces who considered it their duty to punish Zimri, who murdered his master. Jezebel's later reference to Zimri when speaking to General Jehu in 2 Kgs 9:30-31, **Is all well, Zimri, murderer of your master?** indicates that "Zimri" connotes the worst sort of traitor. At that time Jehu had come to Jezebel to kill her after he had slaughtered the king of Judah, Ahaziah, and the king of Israel, Joram, who was her son and the son of Ahab, grandson of Omri.

■ **21-22** The rivalry between the camps of Tibni and Omri lasted for four years, but no mention is made of fighting. We know little about either man, and no information is provided to explain why **half** of Israel made Tibni king. The text does not say Omri or his supporters killed Tibni, only that he died. On the other hand, warfare and assassination may be implied. The absence of specifics about Tibni and the four-year interval when he was king over part of Israel again indicates that this narrative is not intended to be a history as we think of it. In his case, mention is not even made of the royal archives as it is in the case of Zimri, king for seven days. We have the sense that Dtr is rushing the reader along to the narratives about Ahab, the son of Omri, and his wife, the Phoenician princess, Jezebel. These tales are dominated by Ahab's nemesis, the illustrious prophet Elijah.

16:20-28

■ **23** The account of the kings and coups of the northern kingdom, Israel, continues with the narrator's short reckoning of Omri's uncontested twelve-year reign (following the four years after Zimri's death when Tibni was his rival [vv 15-22]).

■ **24** As noted in Behind the Text at the beginning of this section, Omri was a significant player on the stage of nations during the ninth century BC. However, Dtr's treatment of him is formulaic, summed up by the introductory and conclusions typical of those used for other Israelite kings. Omri is credited with buying the hill of Samaria as his capital, a more strategic location than Tirzah in regard to Phoenicia, the coastal nation with whom Israel had trade agreements and marriage alliances. But leaving Tirzah was not without cost, for the Arameans often attacked Israel from the east.

■ **25-28** Omri is also blamed for doing more evil than any king before him, another common formula used by the writer to indicate the evil of the king under review. When any king did not remove the calves of Jeroboam, if he worshipped at their shrines in Dan and Bethel, he is evaluated as an evildoer and the reader is referred to the royal annals for specifics about his affairs. Omri died peacefully, was buried in the city he purchased from Shemer, and was succeeded by his son Ahab.

FROM THE TEXT

Throughout Kings, we often see political moves and motives viewed through a Deuteronomistic lens; the disasters that occur are usually viewed as retribution for sinning and ignoring prophetic warnings. Such is the case for Jeroboam, who was repeatedly warned against his establishment of the shrines at Dan, Bethel, and throughout the region of the northern tribes. This also became true for subsequent kings who did not tear down the calves and shrines. Clearly, these accounts are warnings to future leaders against breaking the covenant with God.

However, the reverse is not implied. These texts are not suggesting that every harmful event, every case of individual or collective suffering, is the result of the sufferer's apostasy or other sin.

In fact, the text clearly demonstrates how targeted prophecy provides meaning to the disasters that befell the kings who broke the covenant. Israel's kings' choices caused innocent people (their descendants and others) to suffer dire consequences. The prophets warned or explained just as the text theologically explains the meaning of disaster in these cases. Other tragedies—illnesses, injuries, deprivation—are not addressed. Thus, no one should use these stories and retributive pronouncements, as Job's friends did, to claim that those who suffer must have sinned.

C. Ahab's Apostasy and Elijah's Prophecy (16:29—22:53 [22:54 HB])

BEHIND THE TEXT

Elijah is a prophet like Moses (see Deut 18:15-22), and his story often alludes to Moses' story. Elijah and Moses fled their homes to analogous places for similar reasons: to hide from kings while supported by outsiders and/or nature (see Exod 2—4). They both were used as instruments of Yahweh's might and led Israel to places of decision (1 Kgs 18—19 parallels Exod 19 and 24). Both forced confrontations between Israel and Yahweh on mountains. In fact, both Moses and Elijah ascend Mount Horeb/Sinai, but at different moments in their ministries: Moses encountered Yahweh to receive and relay Yahweh's words early in his leadership of Israel, while Elijah fled to Sinai to resign (see Walsh 1992, 464-65). Neither prophet had a grave site.

In the previous narratives, the primary sin of Israel—kings and people—was their pilgrimages to Jeroboam's golden calves at Bethel and Dan, which meant their failure to worship Yahweh alone in Jerusalem only. In these chapters, the prophet Elijah was sent to confront Ahab, who added the worship of the Canaanite god "Baal" the building of **asherim** (1 Kgs 14:15), which was even more provocative to Yahweh than Jeroboam's innovations (16:31-33).

No prophet arranged a contest between Yahweh and the non-Levitical priests that Jeroboam established for his sacred sites. Elijah, however, organized a demonstration against the prophets of Baal of Phoenicia, called **Baal Shamen**, lord of heaven.

Baal has appeared across the Pentateuch/Torah and beyond as a place and a person's name (Gen 36:39; Exod 14:2, 9; Num 22:41 [platform/shrine of Baal]; Josh 11:17; 12:7; 15:60, etc.). The term means "owner" (Exod 21:28; 22:8 [7 HB]; Judg 19:22; Isa 1:3 [**master**]; Eccl 5:13 [12 HB]) and "husband" (Exod 21:3, 22; Deut 24:4).

In Num 25, Judg 2—3, 6—9, and throughout 1 and 2 Samuel, Baal is the name of a god of the Canaanites, as in the Ahab-Elijah passages of 1 Kgs 16:29—22:40. The meanings are connected, for places and people are named after the god, or refer to the possession of a quality of the person so named. In Num 25, Baal Peor is god of the place, Peor (or *lord of fire*). Israel was seduced to bow before Yahweh *of fire* at Shittim and was subsequently punished when Yahweh's anger kindled against them; see also Deut 4:3.

Information about Canaanite gods at Ugarit in the second millennium BC, including seven Baals and Asherah, comes from the Ras Shamra site (Late Bronze III, ca. 1365—1180 BC; Level I.3 of the Ras Shamra excavations). These ancient religious documents represent the development of a cuneiform alphabetic script during the reign of Niqmad II (ca. 1360-1330 BC). They were preserved on clay tablets in the library of the high priest, which was located on the acropolis near the two temples of Dagon and Baal. These include prayers and liturgies, lists of sacrificial offerings, mythological material, divinations, dedicatory inscriptions, and lists of gods (Cooper 2005, 1380-90).

In these lists, three *Il*'s (all associated with the father god El) are followed by Dagon, then the seven Baals. The first is the Baal who dwells in the "heights" or "recesses" of Mount Sapan, which was probably the Baal temple found at Ugarit. Baal (the Akkadian Adad) was the mountain and rain/storm god whose full title in the mythological texts is "prince, lord (*Baal*) of the earth." He is called "most powerful one" (*aliyan*), "high one" (*aliy*), and "rider of the clouds." Baal represents the divine power that is immanent in the world (Cooper 2005, 1380-90).

Baal's adherents sought from him rain and fecundity of land and people. The residents of Canaan, including the tribes and kingdoms of Israel and Judah, sought to survive by serving the god of the land who was believed to cause its fertility. This is evident in the premonarchial tribal period, as recounted in Judges, when Gideon's father built an altar to Baal and an Asherah, which Yahweh ordered Gideon to pull down and burn (Judg 6:25-32).

Many parallels may be drawn between the public incidents perpetrated by Gideon and Elijah, who both contended against Baal and for Yahweh. Gideon was given a new name as a consequence of his obedience to Yahweh: Jerub-Baal: *Let Baal contend against him*. Notice the meaning of Elijah: *Yahweh is my*

God. Both passages reasonably point out that a god should have the ability to hear and defend himself.

The Sidonian/Phoenician god of Jezebel, King Ahab's wife, was Baal Shamem, *lord of the heavens.* Ahab not only served this Baal but also made the *Asherah* (fem. sg. ending), who appears in this narrative with 400 prophets, mentioned after the 450 prophets of Baal. Many of the forty occurrences in the Bible use the alternate forms of *Asherim* (masc. pl. ending), and *Asherot* (fem. pl. ending). As noted above, Asherah was known as a cultic object by Israel and Judah long before Ahab's marriage to Jezebel (Judg 6:25-32; 1 Kgs 14:15). Although Solomon had established sacred sites for the gods of his wives and served them, Asherah and Baal are not mentioned in the Dtr's indictment against him in 1 Kgs 11:5-8, 33.

In the ancient Ugaritic texts found at Ras Shamra, Asherah is the queen mother, consort of the god Il or El, not Baal (who is said to be the son of Dagon [and also Il/El]). She is connected to the sea, not with trees (Wiggins 2007, 262). Biblical references that imply that Asherah was a goddess or juxtapose the terms "Baal" and "Asherah" do not demonstrate an assumption that Asherah was the consort of Baal, contrary to the annotations in many translations. In the Ugarit tablets, Baal's consort is Anath, who rescues him from the underworld, which brings the spring rains to the land.

In the Torah and Judges, Asherah is not associated with a goddess, but with wooden cultic objects that were stylized, built, erected, made, or planted (once) near shrines or altars. Deuteronomy 16:21 says: **You will not plant for yourself an asherah, any tree beside the altar of Yahweh your God which you will make for yourself.** Commands to burn or cut down every Asherah are found in Exod 34:13; Deut 7:5; 12:3, all of which have other markers of the Deuteronomistic redactor (Dtr).

While little mention is made of Asherah by the classical prophets, the context for Dtr's attention to Asherah in Kings is found in Hos 4:13. This verse proclaims Yahweh's disgust with Israel's worship; people and priest sacrificing "on the mountaintops and . . . hills, under oak, poplar and terebinth, where the shade is pleasant." In 1—2 Kings, Asherah are located at such sites (see 1 Kgs 14:23; 2 Kgs 17:10; compare Jer 17:2). The condemnation of both Jeroboam and Rehoboam in 1 Kgs 14:15, 22-24 was partially based on their erection of **asherim upon every high hill and under every luxuriant tree.** This demonstrates that both Judah and Israel had hilltop/grove shrines at the beginning of their division into two nations. When a king made Asherah/asherot/**asherim** (along with shrines outside of Jerusalem) Yahweh's anger flamed out against Israel and Judah; when a king destroyed them, he was commended (→ sidebar, "Asherah," below).

Ahab's worship of Baal and making the Asherah pole created an untenable situation for Elijah, who intervened by dramatically demonstrating that Yahweh, unlike Baal, could hear, respond, and provide direction for Israel. The

Elijah/Ahab narratives flesh out Deut 11:13-17, which predicts rain for those faithful to Yahweh alone and drought, famine, and eventually exile for those who served other gods. Like other narratives in the books of Kings, this one illustrates Deuteronomy's blessing and curse theme repeated clearly and often: those who served Yahweh alone would receive rain, those who serve other gods would suffer drought and famine.

Asherah

"Amaryau says: say to my lord: Is it well with you? I bless you by Yhwh of Teman and by his asherah. May he bless you and keep you and be with my lord . . ." Inscription found in 1975-76 by Z. Meshel at Kuntillet Ajrud, modern Ḥorvat Teman in the Sinai, a remote site used as a stopover for caravans.

The inscriptions on storage jars found at Kuntillet Ajrud include blessings that include these phrases: "I bless you by Yhwh of Teman and his asherah" and "I bless you by Yhwh of Samaria and his asherah." The two inscriptions show that Yahweh was known in both Samaria and Teman (Edom), in the north and south. See Isa 63:1: *Who is this coming from Edom, with red garments from Bozrah*; and Hab 3:3: *God [Eloah] comes from Teman, the Holy One from Mount Paran* (Wiggins 2007, 205).

Steve Wiggins (who has written the most comprehensive studies of biblical, Ugaritic, Mesopotamian, Phoenician, and Hebrew references to the Asherah [Athirat]) does not find that these inscriptions prove that the term "asherah" refers to a goddess of trees or that it refers to Yahweh's wife or consort (as W. Dever and D. N. Freedman claim). However, the inscriptions attest to the presence of "his asherah" in these two locations, which seem to indicate that the Asherah of Yahweh are geographically bound (Wiggins 2007, 205).

While it is difficult to determine from some biblical contexts whether "asherah" refers to a goddess or a sacred tree or pole, the inscriptions have far less context to help. Without a context for these blessings, we cannot conclude if they are social conventions or indicative of priestly cults of Yahweh and a consort Asherah or Asherah poles at these sites. Wiggins cites studies of blessings to show that inanimate objects (such as poles) may be used as agents of blessing and that greetings invoking the language of divine blessing may be social conventions. "If they are mere greetings, they may imply no more about the religion of Israel than 'God bless you' does" (206).

Another similar Asherah inscription from Khirbet el-Qôm lends itself to multiple translations because its surface was marked and its syntax is unusual (190-97). Wiggins concludes that "it should not be used to provide evidence that Yahweh had a consort in Judah" (196). He also stresses that, while Ugaritic texts indicate that at Ugarit Asherah was the consort of the god Il (not Baal) and a mother goddess, she cannot be decisively connected to trees or groves (268-69).

1. Ahab Marries Jezebel and Establishes Baal Worship (16:29-34)

IN THE TEXT

■ **29-30** The narrative about Ahab's reign begins with the Israelite king formula along with the notice that Ahab's evil surmounted that of all the previous kings of Israel. So far the sins of Israel's kings increased with each one. Omri sinned more than all those before him, but Ahab **did more evil** than Omri, his father. Ahab's son Joram (his second son to succeed him) would be better than Ahab, for he would remove the Baal pillars, but would follow in Jeroboam's sins (2 Kgs 3:1-3).

■ **31-33** During his twenty-two-year reign, Ahab continued in the ways of Jeroboam as had his predecessors. But his sins were worse because he married Jezebel and worshipped her god, Baal (in Phoenician, Jezebel means "where is honor?"). Jezebel was the daughter of Ethbaal (which means "with Baal"), the king of Tyre and Sidon from 887 to 856 BC. This marriage was similar in purpose and effect to Solomon's marriages to many non-Israelite princesses; it brought peace and trade to the region. Peace and trade, however, were never worthy of Dtr's praise. For, like Solomon's wives, Jezebel brought her god.

Like Solomon, Ahab served his wife's god. He made a temple and altar for Baal and Asherah in his capital city, Samaria. Although Baal was not new to Israel (see Judg 6), Jezebel and Ahab revived, even instituted, Israel's worship of this storm god. We cannot assume, however, that Jezebel compelled Ahab to make Asherah. It appears he added this to his other sins (→ Behind the Text for 1 Kgs 16:29—22:53 [22:54 HB], "Asherah" sidebar above, and 1 Kgs 15:11-14).

■ **34** The rebuilding of Jericho by Hiel of Bethel (site of the gold calf in the southern shrine of Israel) during Ahab's reign prompted this reminder of Jericho's destruction by Joshua when the tribes invaded Canaan and took over the land. After Jericho fell to the circling tribes, Joshua pronounced a curse against anyone who would rebuild it—the loss of two sons (Josh 6:26). Its destruction was to be total; the only things saved from it were precious metals and Rahab's family. Because of Joshua's curse, everyone was to fear undertaking its reconstruction. The notice of the fulfillment of the word of Yahweh—immediately after the narrator introduced Ahab and Jezebel and immediately before we meet Elijah—sounds an ominous note for anyone who takes Yahweh's words lightly. (See Map 5, p. 118.)

2. Elijah Predicts Drought and Revives the Widow's Son (17:1-24)

■ **1** Elijah is not introduced as a prophet but simply as **the Tishbite, from Tishbe** who swore by Yahweh that neither rain nor dew would fall until *he* ordered it. Elijah's address to Ahab includes his oath by the life of Yahweh, **whom I serve**, which indicates his status. He also reminded Ahab, who served Baal, that Yahweh, not Baal, was the God of Israel. Tishbe was east of the Jordan River, south of Galilee.

Although Elijah is not referred to as a prophet until 18:22 (see also 19:16), he clearly was a prototypical prophet who heard from, spoke for, and obeyed Yahweh. Nonetheless, he was unique in that the drought announcement is presented as his word in contrast to 17:8; 18:1, 15 where Yahweh's word precedes the prophet's work. Compare this also to the introductions of prophets to whom Yahweh's word *happened* before they spoke (Jer 1:2; 2:1; Mic 1:1; Hos 1:1; Zech 1:1). Elijah pronounced a drought; it happened! And rain would only fall when Elijah spoke the word.

Elijah is portrayed with more autonomy than most other prophets, but this is partially due to the nature of the narrative genre by which we know Elijah. In his story, he speaks less and does more than the prophets we know through collections of Yahweh's oracles addressed to God's people through them. Throughout the Elijah/Elisha narratives, we find permeability between the prophets' words and Yahweh's. The entire contest between Yahweh and Baal narrated in 1 Kgs 18:16-40, which was the outcome of Elijah's drought pronouncement, seems to be at Elijah's initiative.

Baal, whom Ahab had established as a god with a temple and altar in Israel, was worshipped by Canaanites as the god who caused rain and fertility of land and people. And so also he was worshipped by Israelites, through Jezebel and Ahab's influence. Yahweh and Elijah begged to differ.

Some scholars believe that Elijah's abrupt appearance at 17:1, without previous notice of Yahweh's initiating address, indicates that the first part of the Elijah source was lost. If so, we might assume that Yahweh sent him to Ahab with these words. Yahweh's word *happened to* Elijah in 1 Kgs 17:8 and 18:1 to announce the end of the drought over two years later. Certainly we can affirm that Elijah initiated this contest by pronouncing a drought with Yahweh's support, for they were one in their disgust with Baal worship. The fulfillment of the words of Elijah's living and active God is a focus of 1 Kgs 17—22.

■ **2-6** That Yahweh was behind or completely complicit in the drought Elijah announced is shown when he cared for Elijah by directing him away from Ahab and danger to hide by a brook near his hometown, Tishbe. There Yahweh commanded *ravens* to feed him meat and bread! Yahweh spoke; it happened. Yahweh controlled nature represented by the ravens, but he was not ready to make rain.

■ **7-9** When **the brook dried up**, Yahweh did not send rain or otherwise intervene with the water supply to replenish it (v 7). Instead he directed Elijah to a city of Phoenicia, Jezebel's nation, to receive food from a widow there. Yahweh's power over Baal must be demonstrated in Phoenicia. Here the prophetic formula—**and the word of Yahweh happened to . . .**—appears (v 8).

Zarephath was far to the northwest of Tishbe, just south of Sidon. Just as Yahweh had **commanded ravens to feed** Elijah near his home (v 4), so also he commanded a Phoenician widow **to feed** him there (v 9).

■ **10-12** Elijah obeyed Yahweh's command to go to her. Her region was also suffering from the drought, which indicates that Baal, the rain god, had not provided for them. She and her son were about to eat their last meal. Elijah's residency there showed that Yahweh could provide for those outside of Israel/Judah, who, like the widow, recognized Yahweh and obeyed his commands. She swore to the stranger by Yahweh's life, just as Elijah had sworn to Ahab in v 1.

■ **13-16** Elijah promised rain from Yahweh while assuring the widow that Yahweh words that her oil and meal would never run out would indeed come to pass. Again we see promise and fulfillment in caring for basic needs. Compare this account to 2 Kgs 4:1-7 featuring Elisha.

■ **17-20** Events take an ominous turn when the widow's son sickened and died or nearly died. Calling Elijah **man of God**, she blamed his visit and her own suffering or sin for her son's grave illness (v 18), in spite of the provisions that endured for the household while Elijah was there. He in turn immediately took the son up to his own room and cried out against Yahweh, questioning whether Yahweh was the cause of this crisis, this evil against the woman with whom he stayed.

■ **21-23** Elijah's intervention was necessary, for, after hearing Elijah's cries, Yahweh restored the son to health and to his mother. Notice the Phoenician widow did not turn to Baal, but to the man of God whose prayers to his god, Yahweh, did not go unheeded. This stage of the contest between Yahweh and Baal foreshadows the one in the next chapter. In Baal's own territory, Yahweh supplied sustenance and restored health through the prophet, whose authority is further established through these life-death crises in Phoenicia. The textual attack on Baal is not subtle.

■ **24** The widow's **now I know** concerning the authenticity and authority of Elijah after receiving her restored son reminds the reader of Jethro's response to the signs that accompanied the exodus in Exod 18:11. Both are outsiders to Israel who proclaim the power of Yahweh over all gods. The great Egyptian Pharaoh did not know Yahweh (Exod 5:2), but the priest of Midian and the widow of Zarephath did.

This statement is the purpose of the narrative: that receivers of the text will know, as the widow did, that Elijah is truly a man of God and Yahweh's words come true. Jesus' first message recorded in the Gospel of Luke recalled Elijah's visit to the widow of Zarephath in Sidon, provoking the Nazarenes to murderous rage. They were offended by Jesus' references to their own Scriptures' describing outsiders who were touched by God (Luke 4:24-30).

3. Elijah Reveals the Power of Yahweh and Anoints Elisha (18:1—19:21)

■ **18:1-2** The time finally came for Yahweh to send rain, but first Yahweh ordered Elijah to appear before Ahab, who was needed for the impending contest. This verse represents the standard prophet transmission formula and demarcates the next stage in the Elijah narrative that led to the climatic Yahweh-Baal match that would be no match at all. Yahweh spoke; Elijah obeyed. It also demonstrates that Yahweh was indeed the source of rain, and it would come when Yahweh chose to send it.

■ **3-6** The severity of the famine in the capital and all Israel is shown by Obadiah's role in helping Ahab find pastureland. The narrator explains that even as Obadiah managed Ahab's palace, he was devoted to Yahweh, hiding and feeding one hundred prophets of Yahweh. His name means "servant of Yahweh."

One servant of God, Obadiah, had the position and resources to preserve the life of one hundred other servants of God, indicating how endangered they—and Elijah—were during the rule of Ahab and Jezebel. Throughout the drought, the prophets of Yahweh were persecuted and exiled, while the prophets of Baal were well fed (v 19).

■ **7-8** When Obadiah was away from the palace in search of springs and grass for animals, he encountered Elijah, who was on his way to appear before Ahab. Obadiah recognized him and called Elijah his **lord**; Elijah called Ahab Obadiah's lord. Obadiah must arrange the encounter between prophet and king.

■ **9-14** Obadiah was wary. Through his response to Elijah, we learn the extent to which Ahab had searched for Elijah, the "withholder of rain" (see 17:1), and the peril he had avoided by hiding with the Phoenician widow at Zarephath. Obadiah feared for his own life should Elijah disappear again. Like the widow earlier, Obadiah swore by the life of Yahweh, Elijah's God, and questioned if some sin of his had caused Elijah to endanger his own life.

■ **15-16** Elijah assured him that he would stay in one place, swearing by Yahweh's life that he would meet Ahab that day. Thus Obadiah functioned as the messenger who arranged the meeting. Notice that King Ahab went to Elijah. The repeated oaths taken in Yahweh's name underscore the authority of Yahweh in a land dominated by the worship of Baal, a rain/storm god who had not bothered to end the drought.

■ **17-18** Calling Elijah **troubler of Israel** indicates that Ahab blamed Elijah for the drought and for withholding rain, as well he should, given 17:1. But this is ironic, for if Ahab believed that Elijah and Yahweh withheld rain, why would he not turn to Yahweh and pray for relief from the drought? The narrator intended to provoke this question. The receivers of this text are supposed to react by realizing that it only made sense for Israel to serve the true God who controlled nature. It made no sense to worship Baal, whom both Ahab and, according to Elijah here, his father Omri worshipped. Although 1 Kgs 16:25-26 does not add Baal worship to Omri's sins, Elijah implicated Omri in this. And indeed, Omri may have arranged the marriage between his son and the daughter of Ethbaal of Sidon. Thus Omri and Ahab, not Elijah, were the troublers of Israel!

Unlike the ravens, the widow, Obadiah, and Elijah—who obeyed the commands of Yahweh—Ahab's family had abandoned them by following the Baals. The plural form is used, indicating the multiple regional Baals, each associated with places and towns where they are served (as place names indicate). Seven Baals are listed in the Ugarit tablets. (→ Behind the Text for 1 Kgs 16:29—22:53 [22:54 HB] and 2 Kgs 1:2.)

■ **19-20** Here Ahab obeyed Elijah's demand that he summon to Mount Carmel all Israel and the prophets of Baal and Asherah who were fed by Jezebel. Thus, Ahab was instrumental in setting up the forthcoming match between his god and Elijah's. This compliance indicates Ahab's suspicion that Elijah and Yahweh could indeed send rain to end the deadly drought. The prophets of Asherah are juxtaposed here with the prophets of Baal, but they do not appear again in this story. (→ Behind the Text for 1 Kgs 16:29—22:53 [22:54 HB] and "Asherah" sidebar, above.)

Mount Carmel is northwest of Samaria on the Mediterranean coast and part of a cave-filled range that separated Israel from Phoenicia, an appropriate place for a contest between Yahweh of Israel and Baal of Phoenicia. Already in Zarephath of Phoenicia the power of Yahweh to save lives was revealed. Perhaps Obadiah hid the prophets of Yahweh in two of these caves and they emerged to witness Elijah's match between the gods and to help him in the aftermath.

■ **21** This was Elijah's challenge to Israel put in no uncertain terms. He determined, by this gathering, to demonstrate which god was worthy of worship as he confronted the people with their equivocation and syncretism. They were ***hopping/limping on two opinions*** or ***branches*** (the terms sound alike), a pun that also referred to the prophets' practice of prancing to get Baal's attention (see 18:26). Elijah's demand that Israel choose either Baal or Yahweh went unanswered. This contrasted with Israel's response to Joshua's demand that they choose Yahweh or the gods of the land they had entered. At that time, Israel chose Yahweh (Josh 24:16-18). Before Elijah they stood silent.

■ **22** This forced Elijah's hand. If the people would not choose, he would demonstrate the power the living God through a contest in which he stacked the deck against Yahweh. Elijah proceeded to name the contestants: one man for Yahweh against 450 for Baal, ignoring the 400 prophets of Asherah who are dropped from the scene. Elijah also failed to mention the other one hundred prophets of Yahweh he had heard about through Obadiah, but there were good reasons for this; they were in hiding and may have been killed if he had called them out or even alluded to them. Also, he was purposely giving the Baal prophets an advantage: one against many for greater effect.

■ **23-25** Elijah called for the implements of the contest: two bulls and two piles of wood. He allowed the Baal men to choose the bull they preferred to slaughter, again emphasizing their advantages in the contest. The order not to light a fire as well as Elijah's specific instructions indicate that this is what the contest was all about; lighting the fire in response to the prophets' petitions was the task of the respective contestants: Baal and Yahweh. All of the people agreed to these terms. Whoever ignited the bull was the *always-living* God, in contrast to Baal who was thought to be dead during the winter season, but rose in spring (→ Behind the Text for 1 Kgs 16:29—22:53 [22:54 HB]). Baal adherents must have believed that Baal had remained dead for over two years, never rising to bring the spring or fall rains.

■ **26-29** The practices of Baal worshippers are shown here: desperate cries, dancing, limping, and self-gashing until they were covered with blood. Similar rituals are reported in Ugarit texts and Hellenistic contexts (→ Behind the Text for 1 Kgs 16:29—22:53 [22:54 HB] above and Sweeney 2007, 228). The motivation for slashing their bodies until the blood flowed may have been to identify with a seasonally dead Baal who must be stimulated to arise and bring rain. In the mythology, Baal was resurrected in response to the appearance of his consort, Anat.

It was all to no affect. No sound, no response, nothing; not to the shouting, not to the prancing, not to the slashing and gashing, not to the flowing blood (v 26 and repeated in v 29). In the midst of a long day, Elijah could not resist mocking them and Baal by suggesting that their god must be conversing, otherwise engaged, traveling, or sleeping.

And the Baal prophets responded by shouting even more loudly; if Baal was living, he must be roused. Still Baal made no appearance; he did not consume their offering because he was not. The day's passing was marked by notice of the arrival of the hour of the evening sacrifice (*minḥâ*).

■ **30-32** Elijah may have been egging them on and heaping ridicule with scornful chuckles, but he was deadly serious. Their time was up; they had had all day. At the moment of the evening sacrifice it was his—and Yahweh's— turn, although there was little left of the day. This is another way Elijah handicaps Yahweh in the contest.

His preparations for his offering were at once symbolic, deliberate, methodical, and contrived to present irrefutable evidence of Yahweh's life and power. After calling all the people close to him and repairing a previously damaged Yahweh altar, Elijah made his altar with twelve stones as Moses did in Exod 24:4 and Joshua's memorial in Josh 4, referencing Gen 35:10 when Jacob's name was changed. Elijah made his altar to represent all of the tribes of Israel, including Judah and Benjamin of the southern kingdom. His demonstration is truly for all Israel.

■ **33-35** Elijah filled his trench with twelve jars of water and thus made it harder for Yahweh to ignite his bull. Since water was scarce and therefore dear, it is all the more poignant that he used it in this way.

■ **36-37** Elijah's prayer was impassioned but short and simple compared to the antics of the Baal prophets. He implored Yahweh of the patriarchs to respond to him in order to show all Israel that Yahweh is the living God and that Elijah had been obeying his words.

■ **38** His succinct prayer and his extensive preparations were not for naught. Yahweh reacted and overreacted! Everything associated with the altar was utterly consumed by Yahweh's fire, even the stones, the dirt, and the water. The loss of water by Yahweh's fire was not to be mourned however, for rain was coming!

■ **39** The desired effect was achieved. When Yahweh's fire fell on the altar, they fell on their faces. The people were fully convinced that Yahweh—not Baal—was the Elohim (*the God*) and confessed Yahweh as God alone. (See Deut 4:35, 39; 7:9.)

■ **40** Elijah lost no time in requiring his recent converts to detain the beaten and bleeding prophets of Baal and bring them to the nearby Kishon River where he slaughtered them. The Kishon played a role in Deborah and Barak's defeat of Sisera of Hazor in Canaan (Judg 4:7, 13; 5:21).

The term for slaughter (*šāḥaṭ*) is used most often for ritual killing, sacrifice. Elijah's slaughter of his opponents aligned with devotion to Yahweh alone according to Deuteronomistic principles as expressed (Deut 13:13-15 [14-16 HB]). Ahab is not mentioned. He was clearly outnumbered by "all Israel" and did not attempt to thwart the consequences of the contest. At this point, Ahab may have been fully convinced himself that Yahweh alone was God.

■ **41-42** Whereas Ahab had been a silent bystander throughout the day, Elijah now turned to him and ordered him to *go up* to eat and drink in preparation for the rain, the next consequence of Yahweh's clear victory over Baal. The order to *go up* may mean that Ahab was down in the brook with those slaughtering the Baal prophets.

On the one hand, Elijah was thinking of Ahab's nourishment, because the king must eat before returning to Jezreel before the impending rainstorm (note v 44). On the other hand, telling Ahab to go up to eat signals covenant celebration and is another allusion to Sinai of Exod 24:9-12 when the elders of Israel went up to eat and drink after Israel had fully committed to keeping the covenant commands of Yahweh. Israel under Moses, like Israel in Elijah's time, had just experienced dramatic displays of the power of Yahweh in fire and smoke (Exod 19:18).

Elijah's order to Ahab also demonstrates Elijah's certainty that rain was on the way. He said: *for there is a sound of the great rain* or *the great sound is the rain*. **Sound** (*qôl*) is a term and concept repeated throughout the Elijah narrative. Baal made no sound in response to prophets' cries; Elijah heard approaching rain even though no cloud had yet appeared in the sky; and later in 1 Kgs 19:12, Elijah would hear the "sound of sheer silence" (NRSV) before Yahweh gave him his next orders.

■ **43-45** Meanwhile Elijah climbed to the top of Mount Carmel with his servant to wait for rain. The text does not say he was praying or causing the rain to come through his posture. He may simply have been very tired, while anticipating that the great sound he heard heralded first the tiny cloud, then the storm. His order to Ahab to leave Carmel again indicates the certainty of rain. Ahab complied as the downpour fell.

■ **46** The Carmel contest narrative concludes with the strange scene of Elijah running by the strength of Yahweh before Ahab's chariot all the way to Jezreel, which was at the headwaters of the Kishon River near Carmel. Ahab probably continued further to Samaria, his capital (20:1-2). The regions of Jezreel and Samaria bordered each other according to 1 Kgs 20:43—21:1. (See Map 5, p. 118.)

FROM THE TEXT

The mighty works and commands of God from the past should be sufficient to compel the continuous obedience of the people of God throughout all generations. We are to remember and transmit such commands and stories to our children; we must avoid serving what our culture venerates and acclaims as worth our time, money, and attention. Nonetheless, the first part of the Elijah cycle of narratives shows that God is and was not opposed to performing signs and wonders for living generations who stray in their devotion or to providing what they need.

Often God's ways are revealed through spokespeople and those to whom God's word comes or ***happens***. Elijah was available to be God's covenant partner to orchestrate Israel's repentance after God showed up. Moses and others preceded him, Jesus and others followed him in revealing the ways and works of God (see Mark 9:2-8). God continues to need faithful friends willing to hear and speak, observe and follow God's ways for the sake of the salvation of the world. As we shall see in the next section, God chooses alternate ways of being with people, sometimes with fire, earthquake, and smoke, sometimes through prophetic words, and sometimes through quiet—even silent—stillness.

IN THE TEXT

■ **19:1** Jezebel must have been in Jezreel when Ahab recounted Elijah's contest and Elijah's subsequent slaying of her defeated Baal prophets. Perhaps Ahab failed to emphasize how Yahweh had triumphed over Baal and portrayed Elijah as a murderer of hundreds of her supporters. Elijah's presence nearby suggests that he hoped Ahab would lead a Yahweh alone reform.

■ **2** In any case, if she knew of them, Yahweh's fireworks did not impress Jezebel as it had the Israelites. She fixed on Elijah's slaughter of the Baal zealots and threatened him with the same death. Whereas Elijah and the Phoenician widow had sworn by Yahweh's life, Jezebel swears against her own life to kill Elijah. Ahab stood by. Notice that she sent a messenger with the threat, instead of having Elijah arrested and executed. This gave him time to flee. Perhaps Ahab had some mitigating influence, but we must also consider the possibility that the narrator incorporated the threat to advance the story.

■ **3** *And he saw* [understood] *and he rose and he fled for his life and came to Beersheba of Judah.* Elijah took Jezebel's threat to heart. He fled the Jezreel area with his young man, but left him at Beersheba. Traveling alone deep into the southern wilderness of Judah, he ran far from Jezebel and Jezreel of western Israel. His flight and fear are plausible—Jezebel was the queen and had executed other prophets of Yahweh. However, Elijah has been portrayed as Yahweh's man, speaking his words, doing his work, without fear. Now the difference between Elijah and the God he served is demonstrated. Elijah was tired and afraid, even though he had been the agent of Yahweh's provision, healing, signs of power, and rainfall, as well as Yahweh's directions and explanations.

■ **4** Ironically, Elijah ran for his life when Jezebel threatened it, but then prayed that Yahweh would take it. Jonah did the same, but with even less cause—his shade plant had died (Jonah 4:8). Elijah said: *It is too much!* He wished for the end of his service, the end of his life, recognizing that Yahweh's spectacular victory over Baal was not sufficient to convert Israel's monarchs. Thus, he could not expect a better end than his ancestors and sought to follow them in death, albeit far away from their tombs. To die at the hand of Yahweh in the wilderness meant that he would be separated from the dead of his people.

■ **5-9a** Yahweh had more work in mind for Elijah, however, for an angel fed him twice after he slept (recall 1 Kgs 17:1-16) and told him his next journey would be **too much** unless he ate. Indeed, the journey lasted forty full days (see Exod 24:18; 34:28). Neither the angel nor Yahweh told him where to go, but he stopped in a cave at the mountain of God in Horeb, with which we are familiar from the Horeb/Sinai setting for Moses and Israel's dramatic encounters with Yahweh in Exod 19:1—Num 10:11 (see especially Exod 3:1; 33:6; Deut 1:6; 4:10). Although no one is certain that Jebul Musa in the southern Sinai peninsula is identical with biblical Horeb (the name of the mountain in Deuteronomy), this site could be reached in a forty-day journey from southern Judah.

■ **9b** The word of Yahweh happened to him in the cave as a question: *What is there for you here, Elijah?*

■ **10** Elijah quickly responded, expressing the reason for his flight to the cave at Horeb, and we sense his despair at what appeared to be the ineffectiveness of his efforts on Yahweh's behalf. *I have striven zealously on behalf of Yahweh the God of hosts, because the children of Israel abandoned your covenant; your altars they have torn down and your prophets they have killed with the* *sword, and I alone am left and they seek my life to take it.* Elijah spoke for Dtr to whom the Sinai/Horeb covenant Yahweh made with Moses and Israel demanded Israel's continued allegiance (Exod 20—24). Elijah called Yahweh ***the God of hosts***, a term for God used by the writers of the books of Samuel, Kings, Isaiah, Jeremiah, Hosea, Amos, Micah, Nahum, Zephaniah, Haggai, Zechariah, and Malachi. In the Pentateuch "hosts" (*sĕbāʾôt*) is not used for Yahweh but for companies of Israel (Exod 6:26; 7:4; 12:41; Num 10:15, etc.).

Elijah's response was a brief—and revised—version of Israel's recent story that did not mention Obadiah's prophets who were faithful to Yahweh, or that Jezebel, not Israel, had killed other prophets of Yahweh (1 Kgs 18:4). Nonetheless, Ahab, if not other leaders of Israel, was implicated in the slain prophets and broken altars, for Ahab permitted, at the very least, Jezebel's murders.

Still, so much is left unsaid. Did Elijah come to Horeb to hear a word from Yahweh on the same mountain that Yahweh had transmitted his covenant with Israel to Moses? Did the angel implicitly direct him to retrace Israel's steps? At Horeb they had been landless but determined to follow Yahweh; Israel of Elijah's time was landed but apostate. Or did Elijah come to die in what he may have considered sacred space?

■ **11-12** Yahweh's reaction to Elijah's answer was an order to come out of the cave and stand before him on the mountain, ***for behold, Yahweh is passing over***. A great wind, earthquake, and fire shattered the mountain. But unlike the signs of Yahweh's presence that Moses experienced at Horeb/Sinai, Dtr emphasizes that Yahweh was not in the great wind, earthquake, or fire, although these natural events occurred ***before Yahweh***. Elijah stayed in his cave.

19:11-17

■ **13** When Elijah heard ***a sound/voice of faint silence***, the prophet wrapped his face in his mantle, which became a significant marker of the fulfillment of Yahweh's forthcoming words (compare 1 Kgs 19:19; 2 Kgs 2:8, 13, 14). Only then did he come out as Yahweh had commanded. Somehow he knew that this silent sound indicated the holiness of Yahweh's presence and that it was time to hear a new word. Yahweh had promised he would be passing through, and since he was not in nature's uproar, Yahweh was in this silent sound—a paradox, to be sure. ***And to him there was a sound/voice*** (*qôl*) that asked him the same question that Yahweh had asked a moment earlier: ***What is there for you here, Elijah?***

■ **14** Elijah answered with the exact words he used when Yahweh asked him the same question (v 9). Was Yahweh hoping for a different answer, one that reflected Elijah's recognition that he had just encountered Yahweh, the God of hosts, the covenant-making God of Moses and his fathers?

■ **15-17** This time Yahweh had a lot to say. Yahweh's presence was embedded in his directives to Elijah, just as Yahweh had been immanent in his words to Elijah and other prophets previously. This narrative indicates a progression away from Yahweh moving nature in order to promote belief in fence-sitters and now means that the prophetic word-event-act would take on even greater significance in the future. Elijah was to anoint named successors to the kings of Syria and Israel and to Elijah himself. God told Elijah to go back into the dangerous thick of things, to the scenes of conflict he had fled.

Sermons and commentaries have claimed that Elijah's despair, depression, and "lack of faith" led to Yahweh replacing him earlier than he would have otherwise, but I take another view. First Kings 19 shows that Yahweh met and directed his prophet where he found him; indeed, the angel provided for Elijah in his emotional and physical state on his journey. Yahweh may have led him to Horeb to address him there. The text is silent on that matter. Even if Elijah had not fled in fear from Jezebel and Jezreel, Yahweh's commands to him would likely have been the same: appoint Hazael as king of Syria, Jehu as king of Israel, and Elisha as prophet to succeed him. Implicit in this series of succession notices was death as further judgment on Israel's Baal worshippers, as the next verse indicates.

■ **18** Yahweh had heard Elijah's repetition that he was the only one left and corrected him: seven thousand people had avoided service to Baal, who was no god at all. Elisha, who would be his new companion, was one of them.

■ **19** The last task listed was the first task accomplished by Elijah; albeit with some variance: Elijah did not anoint Elisha with oil, but threw his mantle over him. As it turned out, Elisha performed the other two directives Yahweh gave to Elijah, showing the certain passing of the prophetic mantle from the older to the younger man (2 Kgs 8:7-15; 9:1-13, esp. v 3). Elisha, not in essence, but in action, became Elijah. It did not matter to Yahweh who did it, but that it was done! This also indicates how fully Elisha filled the shoes of Elijah.

Yahweh had told Elijah that Elisha was from Abel Meholah, which he encountered by returning the way he had come. Compare this to the young prophet from Judah who was required to return by a different way (1 Kgs 13). Abel Meholah is on the Jordan River south of Beth Shan (see Judg 7:22; 1 Kgs 4:12). Elijah found Elisha before he made it further north to the wilderness of Damascus of Syria (Aram). Elisha's twelve pairs of oxen indicate that he was a wealthy farmer, and they recall Saul's two oxen in 1 Sam 11, which he slaughtered when called to save Jabesh Gilead. The robe or mantle has been the symbol of prophets in Samuel–Kings since the time of Hannah, when she dedicated her yet to be conceived son to Yahweh, then lent him to Yahweh by means of priestly service and made him a new robe every year (1 Sam 1—2).

■ **20** Elisha understood that this symbolic act of throwing the mantle was an anointing for discipleship and service. He agreed to go with Elijah after bidding his parents good-bye. Elijah granted this request. The surface meaning of his question: **What have I done to you?** belies its deep significance. Elijah's act compelled Elisha's momentous change of vocation, venue, and relations for the rest of his life.

■ **21** Elisha gave himself an enormous good-bye feast, using not only all his oxen but his plowing equipment and followed Elijah. No doubt, during this party, he bid his parents farewell.

FROM THE TEXT

The mighty works and commands of God from the past should be sufficient to compel the continuous obedience of the people of God throughout all generations. We are to remember the covenant God made with our ancestors and transmit its commands and stories to our children. We must review our own covenant with God and rely on it in order to avoid serving what our culture venerates and acclaims as worth our time, money, and attention, even necessary to our survival. We are responsible for teaching our children this covenant so they are not swayed by the vagaries of nature, the economy, and government.

Although our traditions and past experiences with God are sufficient for our continued faithfulness, chs 17—18 in the Elijah cycle show that God is not averse to performing signs and wonders for living generations who stray in their devotion or lose their first love. However, ch 19 demonstrates that God does not always jump to our demands for dramatic signs. God comes to us quietly through stillness and through specific orders to be obeyed.

We have seen that God chooses alternate ways of being with us and demonstrating his presence. In response to the prophet's simple prayer at Mount Carmel near Phoenicia, God swiftly acted with lightning, fire, and smoke in a way that recalled Sinai in Moses' time. After the spectacle at Carmel, however, God found Elijah at Horeb and passed by with quiet—even silent—stillness, followed by specific action steps for the anxious prophet.

Throughout these passages, Yahweh's directives gave Elijah and the widow who cared for him opportunities to obey and overcome their fear of death. As the widow had given a stranger her last meal, so Elijah returned to the region where his life was threatened by its rulers (19:2; 21:20).

Elijah was available to be God's covenant partner to provoke Israel's repentance in a variety of ways throughout his life. And this was not a safe road to travel. He was both courageous and afraid. Moses and others preceded Elijah in doing what they were unable to imagine doing. Jesus and others followed Elijah to reveal the ways and works of God to rebellious people in the midst of threats to their lives. God's thoughts are still revealed through spokespeople, those to whom God's word comes or **happens**. God uses faithful friends willing to hear and speak what God says to those who then have the choice to obey.

4. Ahab Defeats the Arameans (20:1-43)

IN THE TEXT

Yahweh is the hero of both battle narratives, and the prophet who brings Yahweh's word plays the pivotal part. In the first narrative (20:1-22), Yahweh's word triumphs as an obedient Ahab and Israel put the attacking Arameans to flight.

■ **1-8** Meanwhile, Ben-Hadad was still king of Aram/Syria. With thirty-two other kings with whom he was allied, he besieged Samaria, Israel's capital city. King Ahab acquiesced—with words—to his demands for the fairest of his family and silver and gold, as tribute to avoid destruction. But he refused to verbally agree to let Ben-Hadad take everything that he and his officials valued. Ahab's agreement to the former demand was a formality to show subservience, but he and his elders would not go so far as to actually let Ben-Hadad take all of their treasures without a fight. Ahab's apparent willingness to submit to Ben-Hadad at first indicates a characteristic that is repeated in the Ahab cycle.

■ **9-12** Ahab ostensibly stuck with his submissive and deferential first response but showed backbone with his second. He was being more than reasonable. As messengers relayed the posturing oaths and blustering threats of Ben-Had and the retort of the more realistic Ahab, Israel and Aram prepared for battle in unusual ways.

■ **13-14** Ben-Hadad was drinking when he ordered his attack on Samaria, while Ahab was listening to an unnamed prophet who told him how to defeat Aram and witness—again—the power of Yahweh: go on the offensive with 232 elite young guards of the provincial governors. In spite of the judgment Israel was inviting for forsaking Yahweh's covenant, Yahweh was even more intent to demonstrate his vital concern for Israel.

■ **15-21** Israel initiated the attack as Yahweh had ordered (v 14). Seven thousand troops marched out behind the 232 young officers at noon while Ben-Hadad and the 32 other kings were drunk. Each Israelite killed an Aramean soldier and the rest fled, with Ahab riding after and overcoming them. The word of Yahweh through the prophet came true, demonstrating the effectiveness of prophets and the power of Yahweh. Ahab's reaction is not recorded, but this incident further implicates Ahab for his previous and later faithlessness. Yahweh's care for Israel and his power could not be more obvious.

■ **22** The prophet returned to tell Ahab to be prepared for another Aramean attack in the spring.

■ **23-25** Ben-Hadad's officials presented three pieces of advice that he followed: (1) fight on the plains, for Israel's God must be a God of the hills because they defeated them there near Samaria; (2) get rid of those useless kings and replace them with our own officers; (3) replace the armies that were lost last year. The military observations and counsel were astute, but Dtr is setting up this portrayal of their theology for ridicule. Yahweh is not confined to hills and mountainous terrain or any geographic region whatsoever.

■ **26-28** As they drew up for battle the next spring, the narrator contrasts Israel and Aram; Israel is like **two small flocks of goats, while the Arameans covered the countryside**. Any victory for Israel will surely be Yahweh's once again, so that Ahab and the Arameans (like Pharaoh, Jethro, Rahab, and Israel time and again) would know the strength and presence of Yahweh. As the prophet proclaimed to Ahab, no longer would the Arameans be able to claim that Yahweh was not the God of the plains, for Yahweh would deliver *this mob into your hand.*

■ **29-30** Similar to the seventh-day fall of Jericho (Josh 6:12-21), the Arameans were crushed, first by Israel's forces, then by the city wall of Aphek. Ben-Hadad himself found shelter in the innermost room of a house.

■ **31** Recognizing that they were in no position to negotiate, Ben-Hadad's servants set out to shrewdly do just that, suggesting to their king that he allow them to appeal to the mercy (or treaty-keeping propensity; see DeVries 1985, 242) of Israelite kings.

■ **32** The Arameans, enacting captivity by their nakedness and coils of rope (sackcloth on their loins was the attire of captives), begged for their king's life. Ahab must have been unduly impressed by their show of servitude, for he called his enemy **my brother**. In any case, his conciliatory treatment of the drunken king who had demanded Ahab's wives and children, silver and gold, and that of his officials was inexplicable.

■ **33-34** At Ahab's **my brother**, Ben-Hadad's servants recognized that they had saved their king's life and brought him to Ahab, who pulled him into his chariot. The Aramean king promised to return to Israel the cities his father had taken from Ahab's father (Omri) and allow Israelite bazaars (outside shops/booths) in Syria's capital, Damascus. Although he was in no position to do so, Ben-Hadad also released Ahab from any obligations of a former treaty between the two countries. With this new treaty, Ahab *sent him away*. Ben-Hadad was still calling the shots, even though Ahab had soundly defeated him. Although Ahab's decision seems merciful, it was not wise. If Ahab had imprisoned or killed him, would Elijah have then anointed Hazael to take the throne of Aram?

■ **35-41** This section is the rest of the story. Releasing Ben-Hadad was clearly not what Yahweh expected to be the aftermath of his intervention to give Israel victory. Unnamed prophets, members of a guild of prophets, a group of men who ran together, dramatized the consequences for Ahab and Israel of Ben-Hadad's release. Ahab's response, which we shall see repeated, is to become sullen and angry.

■ **42-43** Something Yahweh had determined, Ben-Hadad's destruction (he was banned or condemned: *ḥermi* from *ḥerem*) did not happen, because of the wits of the Arameans and Ahab's decision to make a deal with them. Because Ahab let Ben-Hadad go, Ben-Hadad still ruled Syria (for a time) and Ahab and Israel would suffer.

5. Jezebel Murders Naboth and Gives His Vineyard to Ahab (21:1-29)

BEHIND THE TEXT

This penultimate story about Ahab depicts Jezebel as the orchestrator of Naboth's murder to satisfy Ahab's want of a vineyard near his palace. Nonetheless, Yahweh and Elijah laid the blame at Ahab's feet (v 19), as does 2 Kgs 9:7-10, 25-26, which is the earlier kernel of this chapter's version. Jezebel is also condemned in both accounts, but Yahweh through Elijah implicated the king of Israel for presuming to snatch Naboth's property upon hearing of the latter's death, without regard to tribal and family rights. Ahab's entire dynasty (sons and grandsons) would be eliminated by Jehu, conceived as punishment for this grievous sin as well as for Ahab's apostasy, which was also spurred on by his Phoenician wife (1 Kgs 21:25-26). Like many biblical narratives, this one is easily imagined as a performance, with a succession of scenes, most of them with dialogue between two characters. In the final scene, Elijah and Ahab face each other for the last time.

Notice, as it unfolds, how Ahab's landgrab parallels David's taking of Bathsheba, disposing of her husband Uriah, and Nathan's condemnation of David in 1 Sam 11—12. This story is founded upon an awareness of the Torah's instructions regarding tribal property rights and displays other evidence of being written much later than Jehu's reference to Naboth's vineyard in 2 Kgs 9 (White 1994, 66-76; Rofé 1988, 89-104).

IN THE TEXT

■ **1-2** *After these things*, the introduction to this narrative, implies that the story is an important tradition that must be included in the Ahab-Elijah cycle. This story further augments Dtr's indictment of Ahab as deserving of condemnation and compels the removal of the Omride dynasty from the throne of Israel. Its insertion here between the second and third wars of Ahab with Aram indicates it occurred during the three-year period of peace before Ahab initiated the battle to recapture Ramoth Gilead from the Arameans.

Jezreel was the home of Naboth, as well as of Jezebel and the site of one of Ahab's palaces. Jezreel functioned as his second capital, protecting the Jezreel valley from invasion. Excavations of Jezreel show that the Omride dynasty fortified it in the mid-ninth century BC (Hunt 1992, 850). Jezreel was in the land of the tribe of Issachar (Josh 19:18), which signifies that Naboth and his ancestors were from that tribe.

Ahab, however, is pointedly called **king of Samaria**. Samaria was the city his father built up to be the main capital of Israel in the territory of Manasseh (Josh 17:1-13). For Ahab to desire Naboth's vineyard was to wish to take more of Issachar's land for the royal family than Ahab had already acquired for his palace there. Even if Naboth and his heirs had agreed to the transaction, other members of the tribe of Issachar could have legitimately objected and blocked the sale. (For tribal allotments, see Lev 25:8-31, esp. v 23; Num 27:1-11; 36:7-9; Josh 14—21; Issachar: Josh 19:17-23.)

Although Ahab offered to pay a fair price or make an exchange, his request reeked of imperiousness. He openly expressed the reason he wanted Naboth's vineyard (vineyards take years to establish), and replace it with an annual vegetable garden, because *it is near my house*.

■ **3-4** Naboth had no interest in selling Ahab his family's vineyard; he said: *Far be it from me by Yahweh that I should give the inheritance of my ancestors to you.* In Israel, the king did not have the right to annex the land he desired from his subjects. The structure and stress of his reply (NRSV translates: "The LORD forbid that I should give you my ancestral inheritance"! would have communicated: "I would never give it to *you*!" Naboth's refusal was final, and Ahab accepted it as such, making an exhibit of his ire. He went to bed, *turned his face, and refused to eat*. Ahab's reaction of sullen anger was the same as when the prophet denounced him for saving Ben-Hadad of Syria (20:43).

■ **5-7** Naturally Jezebel noticed Ahab's sulking. She did not care about tribal boundaries or about Israelite principles of inheritance even though such rights were also apparent in the laws of other ancient Near Eastern nations (Andersen 1966, 49-50). She was incensed that her husband, a king, should be refused even a minor whim by one of his Israelite subjects. Ahab did not bother to inform her that Naboth was within his rights or tell her that Naboth had invoked the God of Israel in rejecting his offer. Her exclamation: *You are now the governing royalty of Israel!* became ironic, for she, not Ahab, then engineered the fate of Naboth and his vineyard. She, Ahab, and their offspring ultimately suffered severe penalties for her machinations.

■ **8-10** In its depiction of Jezebel's actions, this account shows the author's awareness of laws that also appear in the Torah. Jezebel, though indifferent to tribal property rights (as expressed in the Torah), attempted to assemble a "legal" way to dispose of Naboth and acquire his vineyard. Nonetheless, although Exod 22:28 [29 HB]; Lev 24:13-23; and Deut 17:6; 19:15 prohibit blasphemy, these verses say nothing about taking the property of the supposed blasphemer.

Proclaiming a fast to isolate and extract sinners was used in the case of Achan (Josh 7). "Thus Jezebel found a special procedure with a prompt condemnation and execution, a kind of lynch law of ancient times" (Rofé 1988, 92). Jezebel used Ahab's name and his seal to send legal documents to Jezreel's elders and nobles, who inexplicably complied. (On cylinder seals, see Sweeney 2007, 250.) Jezebel's actions parallel David sending a message to Joab by

Uriah's own hand to dispose of him so that David could take Bathsheba for his wife (2 Sam 11:14-27).

■ **11-14** Joab, David's general, had showed reluctance to have Uriah slain and severely, albeit subtly, criticized David after he had obeyed David's orders (2 Sam 11:18-21; 12:27-28). These elders, neighbors and kinsmen of Naboth, did not. They obeyed Jezebel's instructions to the letter without protest, all of them colluding with her in this murderous deceit that Naboth blasphemed God and king. They stoned him after a mock trial and reported their multiple acts of cowardly submission to Jezebel. The narrator does not suggest their motives, but the effect of his narrative is disgust.

■ **15-16** Jezebel simply reported to Ahab that the Jezreelite who had refused to comply with his wishes was dead and he may take the vineyard. Considering that Naboth would have had heirs, with whom Ahab must contend, leads us to the Jehu version of the story, which reports that Naboth's children's blood was also seen by Yahweh in Naboth's plot (2 Kgs 9:26). However, the producer of this account hastens to the dénouement, without speaking of Naboth's family: Ahab's confrontation with Yahweh through his prophet Elijah.

■ **17-19** Yahweh's simple and direct oracle to Elijah fell on the heels of Naboth's murder: Ahab was designated for destruction (compare 1 Kgs 20:42). Just as Naboth died ignominiously (the reference to dogs licking the blood means no proper burial) so would Ahab (but see 1 Kgs 22:40). Yahweh's message is fulfilled when Ahab dies in battle and the dogs lick up his blood that drained into his chariot in 1 Kgs 22:29-38 (although this occurred in Samaria instead of Jezreel).

■ **20-24** When Elijah met Ahab in the vineyard, however, he embellished Yahweh's words of judgment, adding Ahab's entire family and Jezebel. Elijah referred to prophetic pronouncements of destruction against the dynasties of Jeroboam and Baasha using the same terminology against the males, all possible successors to the throne (1 Kgs 14:9-11; 16:1-4). This version of the judgment oracle is fulfilled by Jehu in 2 Kgs 9 and provides justification for Jehu's massive bloodletting. (But see Hos 1:4-5, where Jehu is condemned.)

■ **25-26** Dtr reiterates the apostasy and other injustices of Ahab and Jezebel in support of Elijah's denouncement of them, comparing them to the Amorites, doomed to destruction, and reminding us of Yahweh's resolution against Ben-Hadad (1 Kgs 20:42).

■ **27-29** Ahab's serious show of contrition caused Yahweh to speak again to Elijah, his friend, and console him concerning his delay in judgment against Ahab. In the next section, we will examine this unexpected show of mercy from a theological, literary, and historical perspective.

FROM THE TEXT

This chapter is an insertion in the accounts of Ahab's wars with the Arameans. Because Elijah was the prophet that Yahweh sent to denounce Ahab, this narrative must be presented *after* readers have gained a sense of how **Ahab sold himself to do evil, spurred on by his wife, Jezebel** (21:25), but *before* Elijah exits the longer narrative. This pericope in the Ahab-Elijah cycle expresses the heartless lengths to which Ahab and Jezebel stooped to defy the God of Israel, who continued to act on behalf of Israel (e.g., ch 20). Yet God saw Ahab's self-abasement in response to Elijah's condemnation. Ahab's repentance delayed God's judgment, a delay explained to Elijah (and us).

Ahab's humility and God's gracious response raise questions that emerge when villains elude their just deserts, as well as about the function of prophecy and God's freedom. Ahab clearly deserved punishment. His death was repeatedly threatened by no less that God himself through his servants the prophets. And yet, even for the murder of Naboth, over which the reader is left reeling, and for which Ahab was held responsible, he was granted a reprieve because he utterly humbled himself. As much as we wish God to be merciful, when he is, we wonder about justice. Was justice served by the promise that Ahab's son should suffer for his father's sins?

We must also ponder what this tells us about prophecy. In most cases, prophecy does not describe what must happen but what could happen if the listeners do not take heed and repent. Ahab did. God responded and granted pardon even to the most evil king of Israel so far. Theologically, this shows the power of repentance *and* the function of prophecy—to produce repentance so that God might change his mind and show mercy.

We saw that God did not wish Ahab to show mercy to Ben-Hadad (ch 20), for he had condemned him to destruction. But when Ahab repented (like the Ninevites in Jonah), God showed mercy to him. Theologically, this says that God is free to show mercy in response to repentance to whom he will and/or to delay the promised judgment.

Furthermore, from a literary-historical angle, the traditions about Jezebel and Ahab's later deaths *do* correspond to both sets of prophecies expressed in this chapter. In the next chapter, Ahab died as promised by Yahweh's oracle to Elijah in 21:19. In 2 Kgs 9, Ahab's dynasty was wiped out during his son's day as promised by Elijah's message to Ahab in 1 Kgs 21:21-24. As noted above, 1 Kgs 21:21-24 aligns with the elimination of previous dynasties of Israel and appears to justify Jehu's massacre of all males of the house of Ahab, something the prophet Hosea disparaged.

6. Ahab Wars with the Arameans and Dies (22:1-40)

BEHIND THE TEXT

Teaching on the nature of prophecy is expanded in this chapter through the story of another prophet in Israel, Micaiah, also a nemesis of Ahab. It has two scenes or episodes. The first is the threshing floor in Samaria where two kings sat to hear what the royal prophets—and Micaiah—said about Ahab's desire to fight his third war with the Arameans, this time over Ramoth Gilead (22:2-28). The second is the battle itself, in which Ahab was killed in fulfillment of Yahweh's words in 21:19, something that did not have to happen, as this passage demonstrates (22:29-38). The first scene could be performed to powerful effect by a few actors intoning the annoyance, sarcasm, and passion of the words of each principal figure.

Ramoth Gilead was the same city that Joab had besieged and coerced David to take the credit for conquering (2 Sam 12:27-28). It is just west of the Jordan and ten miles east of Jezreel, but over twenty miles northwest of Samaria, where Jehoshaphat and Ahab were sitting on thrones in their regalia (1 Kgs 22:10).

IN THE TEXT

■ **1** This chapter returns to the final war that Ahab fought with Aram after a peace of three years, a peace sealed by the victory Yahweh enacted on Israel's behalf (ch 20).

■ **2** The occasion for a rekindling of hostilities was the king of Judah's visit and Ahab's remark that Ramoth Gilead belonged to Israel. King Jehoshaphat *came down* from Jerusalem, because every Israel-Judah region is *down* from Zion's holy hill in the perspective of the Judahite redactor. Jehoshaphat's regnal account is in 1 Kgs 22:41-51 [41-52 HB], which reports that he was a good king who made peace with the king of Israel (v 44 [45 HB]). John Wesley wrote: "It is strange, that so good a man would be so closely connected with a king revolted from the worship of God! But he appears to have been of too easy a temper, which betrayed him to many inconveniencies" (*Notes on the Bible*, 1 Kgs 22:2).

■ **3-4** As if they were discussing what they should do for sport, Ahab asked Jehoshaphat if Judah would join Israel in battle for Ramoth Gilead and he said "of course." This interaction implies that Jehoshaphat's Judah was a vassal of Ahab's Israel.

■ **5-7** Jehoshaphat suggested that they first consult Yahweh (as a good king would do), so Ahab gathered 400 royal prophets together, a gathering reminiscent of the 450 prophets of Baal in the contest on Mount Carmel. These were purported to be prophets of Yahweh, but Jehoshaphat was not convinced by the way they concurred with what Ahab wished to do and with each other. He asked for another prophet of Yahweh, indicating his suspicion of the many yes-men.

■ **8** Ahab knew of another prophet, heretofore unmentioned. His attitude toward Micaiah mirrored his enmity with Elijah, with which we are familiar. Ahab's hatred of Micaiah set him up as the protagonist before he entered the scene. Since he normally prophesied disaster against the apostate Ahab, Micaiah, like Elijah, was a true prophet of Yahweh.

■ **9-12** When Jehoshaphat insisted, the latter reluctantly sent for Micaiah while the two kings watched the guild of prophets enact skits with props to demonstrate how effective Ahab's battle against the Arameans over Ramoth Gilead would be. Zedekiah (his name means **Yahweh is righteous**, but he is called **son of Canaan**) claimed to hear the oracles of Yahweh, and so did all the rest.

■ **13-14** Either Ahab had told the official messenger to say this to Micaiah or he applied pressure to Micaiah on his own. In any case, Micaiah's response to the messenger's admonition demonstrates that he was a true prophet of Yahweh (compare Num 23:12, 26; 24:13). Like the widow of Zarephath, Obadiah, and Elijah, Micaiah swore by the *life of Yahweh* (1 Kgs 17:12; 18:10, 15).

■ **15-16** Micaiah's tone is important here. Ahab could tell he was giving a rote response: what the other prophets had said and what Ahab wanted to hear. Ahab himself adjured Micaiah to tell the truth, even though he knew he would not like it. Ironically Micaiah had sworn by Yahweh's name to tell nothing but the truth.

■ **17-18** And so he did: a vision in which Israel had lost their king. Ahab interpreted this correctly—it meant disaster for himself. And he petulantly reminded Jehoshaphat that he had told him so. Perhaps this explains Jehoshaphat's willingness to go to battle: Ahab had been right about Micaiah's consistent negative messages, so this may have devalued Micaiah's warning in Jehoshaphat's eyes.

■ **19-22** Micaiah went on. His vision of Yahweh in his heavenly court surrounded by the host of heaven and messenger spirits at Yahweh's bidding transparently demonstrated that anyone who told Ahab to go up to battle was deceiving Ahab so that he would die in battle. The truth is that Ahab would die if he fought; he would be utterly unsuccessful, and Micaiah conveyed this truth openly. This passage cannot be construed to mean that Yahweh is deceptive when it is the way that Yahweh clearly revealed what lay behind any "prophet" who predicted that Ahab would be successful. Wesley wrote: "This is not to be grossly understood, as if God were at a loss to find out an expedient to accomplish his own will; but only to bring down divine things to our shallow capacities, and to express the various means which God hath to execute his own designs" (*Notes on the Bible*, 1 Kgs 22:20).

22:9-24

■ **23** But Yahweh did speak disaster concerning Ahab, and this was a warning to him. By openly relaying the vision and its details, Micaiah and Yahweh showed that Ahab, though seemingly marked for death, was not predetermined to fight and to die. He would die only if he listened to **a deceiving spirit in the mouths of all these prophets**. If he heeded Micaiah's warning, like he did after Elijah's prophecy in the previous chapter, Ahab may have again experienced Yahweh's mercy and died a natural death.

■ **24** Zedekiah was not to be outdone. He struck Micaiah, incensed that Micaiah's message contradicted his own, which he believed was Yahweh's spirit. Of course, Micaiah had already explained why Zedekiah's message was different—it was from Yahweh, but it was an intentional lie, fully uncovered by Micaiah.

■ **25** Micaiah crudely answered Zedekiah that the latter's spirit or wind was not from Yahweh, but what Zedekiah experienced in his private chamber or would experience in captivity (compare Sweeney 2007, 259, with DeVries 1985, 268).

■ **26-27** In his freedom, Ahab chose to respond to Micaiah's revelation of Yahweh's vision by imprisoning Micaiah. **Son of the king** can refer to a king's officer as in Zeph 1:8; 2 Kgs 10:1-11. Ahab may have been worried that by merely speaking disaster against him, Micaiah could bring it to pass, a dynamistic notion of prophecy that the narrator did not share (DeVries 1985, 269).

■ **28** For the benefit of all who wish to know the criterion of true prophecy (***all you peoples***), Micaiah contravened Ahab's claim that he would return in peace by saying that if he did, his own words were false. He was clearly convinced that they were true, knowing from whence they came.

■ **29-30** Jehoshaphat not only was coerced into going to battle with Ahab (king of the stronger nation) but also complied with Ahab's order to wear his royal robes, while Ahab disguised himself. Ahab's assumptions about Jehoshaphat's naïveté were verified. Ahab must have been worried over Micaiah's words and sought to break their power by using Jehoshaphat for a decoy. The Arameans would think Jehoshaphat was the king of Israel and seek to kill him.

■ **31** Although Ben-Hadad is not named as the king of Aram here, according to 2 Kgs 5, he is still on the throne and had not yet been displaced by Hazael. In the previous war with Ben-Hadad, thirty-two commanders had replaced the same number of governors from the first war. Ben-Hadad was the king that Ahab had defeated and released. (See 1 Kgs 20:1, 24, 30-34.) Now the king of Aram whom Ahab had called "my brother" specifically targeted Ahab for death.

■ **32-33** The captains of the Arameans assumed that the one in royal robes was Ahab, but Jehoshaphat's cry informed them he was not. This shows they knew Ahab by sight and that their king's order against Ahab saved Jehoshaphat's life. Ahab's mercy to Ben-Hadad was answered by the latter's order to his warriors to kill him.

■ **34** Meanwhile, a random arrow struck between the buckles of Ahab's armor, a fatal wound. Ahab, the aggressor, was the single target of the Arameans, but the soldier who killed him did not know it was him.

■ **35-36** The narrator does not feign to know what Ahab was thinking about Micaiah's warning as he asked to be propped up in his chariot so that he could watch the battle and support his soldiers. If they knew their king was wounded, they may have panicked. His wound was not treated, and he slowly bled to death in his chariot. He may have seen Israel defeat the Arameans a third time. Either the shout (v 35) was one of victory or the battle could have been a tie. Sunset signaled the time for all soldiers to go home. However, sending each man home recalls Micaiah's vision of Israel as scattered sheep without a shepherd, which the soldiers were. For, although they did not know it yet, Ahab was dead. Ahab of Israel and Josiah of Judah died in a similar way (2 Kgs 23).

■ **37-38** Although Ahab was brought to Samaria and not to Jezreel, **the dogs licked up his blood** as Elijah had threatened would happen as a result of Naboth's murder over his vineyard (1 Kgs 21:19). His death also fulfilled the vision and message from Yahweh that Micaiah had relayed. Although the text is silent, we presume he was released since Ahab did not return in peace.

■ **39-40** The narrator provides a concluding formula that refers to Ahab's ivory palace, the cities he built, and his burial with his fathers. He was succeeded by his son Ahaziah. Clearly, burial with one's fathers did not mean a peaceful death for Ahab, but a reference to the family tomb. A king who died in battle would have been buried with honor. Ahab reigned from 869 to 846 BC (according to Sweeney 2007, 263) and 874 to 853 BC (according to DeVries 1985, 182, following Thiele 1983; see 1 Kgs 16:29).

Excavations at Samaria have uncovered ivory figures in a ninth century BC courtyard that may be part of a royal complex. Furthermore, inscriptions of Shalmaneser III of Assyria refer to a war he fought with the Arameans who were allied with ten thousand Israelites led by Ahab in 853 BC. But such an alliance against the Assyrians does not mean that Israel and Aram did not fight each other, for nations had reasons to fight each other when they did not have a common enemy. As these narratives indicate, they often battled over cities and land.

7. Jehoshaphat Rules Judah and Ahaziah Rules Israel (22:41-53 [41-54 HB])

22:37-49

IN THE TEXT

■ **41** This section returns to Judah's current king, who was part of Ahab's death story. Jehoshaphat, the son of Asa, was introduced in 1 Kgs 15:24 after a brief description of Asa's reign in vv 8-24. Asa was the grandson of Rehoboam and the son of Abijam, who both failed to follow Yahweh alone (see 14:21-24; 15:3). But Asa was one of the good kings, though he failed to tear down the shrines (15:11, 14).

■ **42-44 [42-45 HB]** The same is true for Jehoshaphat, and, as we have seen; he was at peace with the kings of Israel, Ahab and his sons.

■ **45-47 [46-48 HB]** Like the many other references to the annals of the kings of Israel and Judah, this one infers that much more might be learned about Jehoshaphat's reign there. Edom had become subject to Judah during this time, a fact also supported by 2 Kgs 3:8-9, which describes Edom joining Judah and Israel against Moab. Edom revolted later (2 Kgs 8:20-22).

■ **48-49 [49-50 HB]** However, Jehoshaphat had learned a lesson, it appears, by agreeing to join in Ahab's war against the Arameans to restore Ramoth Gilead to Israel. The royal robes Ahab insisted he wear to battle led to Jehoshaphat's near death (1 Kgs 22:32-33). His independence from and possible mistrust of Israel is reflected in the fact that he did not agree to allow Ahab's son's sailors join his own in the ill-fated ships he built.

■ **50 [51 HB]** This brief review of Jehoshaphat of Judah's reign during the time of Ahab and the two sons who succeeded him (Ahaziah and Joram) follows the Judahite formula, including the notice of his death. Second Kings' narratives about Israel, Elijah, Elisha, and Jehu's coup, will show that Judah under Jehoshaphat and his son, Jehoram, was affected by what happened in Israel.

■ **51-53 [52-54 HB]** The formula focusing on Ahaziah, Ahab's son, who provoked Yahweh to anger sets up the opening narrative of 2 Kings. He followed his parents in worshipping Baal and he also made pilgrimages to Bethel and Dan, the shrines Jeroboam I had set up, making Israel sin.

Kings and Prophets—Divided Kingdom 931—586 BC

The LXX provides a different chronology. Scholars working on the chronology of the kings propose dates that vary +/- ten years.

Year BC	Northern Kings	Northern Prophets	Year BC	Southern Kings	Southern Prophets
931/930	Jeroboam Dyn.			Rehoboam 17	Shemaiah
	Jeroboam 22	Ahijah			
	Nadab 2			Abijam 3***	Iddo
			912	Asa 41*	
910	Baasha Dyn.				Azariah
	Baasha 24				Hanani
	Elah 2	Jehu			
	Zimri 7 days				
886	Omri Dyn.				Eliezer
	Omri (Tibni) 12				
875	Ahab 22	Elijah	871	Jehoshaphat 25*	
	Jehoiada				
	Ahaziah 2	Micaiah	849	Jehoram 8 m. Athaliah	
	Jehoram 12	Elisha	842	Ahaziah 1	
841	Jehu Dyn.		841	Athaliah 6	
	Jehu 28		835	Jehoash 40 (Joash)*	
					Zechariah
	Jehoahaz 17		796	Amaziah 29*	
	Joash 16	Jonah	776	Azariah (Uzziah) 52 (783-742)*	
791	Jeroboam II 41	Hosea			
	Zechariah 1/2	Amos			
	Last Kings				
749	Shallum 1/12		750	Jotham 16	Isaiah
	Menahem 10				
	Pekahiah 2	Oded	735/731	Ahaz 16	
737	Pekah 20				
	Hoshea 9				
722	Fall of Samaria		715	Hezekiah 29**	Micah
	(Assyrian Kings)		697	Manasseh 55	
	Sargon II				
	Sennacherib				
	Esarhaddon		642	Amon 2	
640			640	Josiah 29**	Jeremiah

612	Fall of Assyria to Babylon battle of Carchemish	(621 Reform)		Huldah
605		609	Jehoahaz ¼	Habbakuk
		609	Jehoiakim 11	
		598	Jehoiachin ¼	Ezekiel
593-573		597	Zedekiah 11	
		586	Fall of Jerusalem to Babylon (Nebuchadnezzar)	
		539	Fall of Babylon to Cyrus of Persia	
		538	Edict of Cyrus allowing exiles to return	
		537	The return under Zerubabbel	
		515	Temple rebuilt	Haggai/Zechariah
		445	Suggested date for Nehemiah's return	
		430	Suggested date for Ezra's return	

*Trusted Yahweh
**Reformers (see 2 Kgs 18, 22—23)
***Chronicles rates highly (Chronicles includes flaws in the reigns of Uzziah and Jotham)

(For another version of the kings' chronology, see Kitchen 2003, 30-31.)

THE BOOK OF SECOND KINGS

D. Prophetic Ministries of Elijah and Elisha (2 Kgs 1:1—13:24)

BEHIND THE TEXT

As explained in the Introduction, 1 and 2 Kings were originally on a single scroll and considered an undivided book. That the present break to form two books occurs amid the writer's attention to Ahaziah is further evidence of this fact, as is Elijah's continuing role as Yahweh's prophet in 2 Kgs 1. The break was made in the Septuagint, the Greek version of the Hebrew Bible, followed by the Latin Vulgate and then the later English versions.

Second Kings continues to show that kings were responsible for events that blessed or brought adversity to their people and that prophets were sent by Yahweh to restore faithfulness to him alone. The oracles of Yahweh and specific directives spoken through the prophets revealed the ways in which king and people should walk, but, if they went astray after other gods, disaster would strike and even innocents would suffer, as fully reiterated in Deut 28. As mentioned in the Introduction, 1 and 2 Kings were redacted several times; an existing edition that knew the sad fate of the second law-abiding, reforming king of Judah, Josiah, was redacted a few decades after the 586 BC fall of Jerusalem to Babylon. No parallels exist in 2 Chronicles to 2 Kgs 1:1—8:15. In fact, the stories of Elijah and Elisha do not appear in Chronicles.

I. Elijah Denounces Ahaziah before Ascending to Heaven (1:1—2:12)

a. Elijah Denounces Ahaziah (1:1-18)

IN THE TEXT

■ **1-2** The setting for Ahaziah's story is Moab's rebellion against Israel that will be expanded upon in 2 Kgs 3 and is addressed in the ninth-century BC Moabite Stone (→ 2 Kgs 3:4-8 and sidebar "Moabite Stone" following that section). The death of a king signals vulnerability, and Moab successfully took advantage of it when Ahab died and his sons came to the throne (Joram, who followed Ahaziah, was the latter's brother). As we have seen with Ahab and others, kings were their people's military champions; they were warriors. Ahaziah's injury disabled him from fighting and compounds Israel's military decline.

Instead of inquiring of Yahweh, as even the wicked kings Jeroboam I and Ahab had sometimes done, Ahaziah requested a prediction from Baal-Zebub, the god of a Philistine city. Although Elijah and Yahweh had together shown that Yahweh was indeed God in Israel and that Baal was nothing at all (1 Kgs 18), Ahab and Jezebel's son Ahaziah believed that **Baal** was a healing god. So Ahaziah consulted the "god" **Baal of the fly** at Ekron, one of the five major cities of Philistia, about his health. This god (some think this should be spelled Baalzebul, "lord of exaltation") may have been associated with healing, as Mark 3:22 indicates. (For an in-depth discussion of Baalim, → Behind the Text for 1 Kgs 16:29—22:53 [22:54 HB].)

■ **3-4** Yahweh was incensed at this latest snub and sent Elijah to provide the answer to Ahaziah's inquiry, but not the one he hoped to hear. Had Ahaziah inquired of Yahweh, the answer would have been different! This is shown by **therefore** of v 4 (*therefore the bed you went up on*) and the clear causal statement of v 16 ("because you have done this"). Although Elijah had anointed Elisha to be his replacement, he still functioned one final time as Yahweh's prophet to the house of Ahab, son of Omri.

■ **5-8** Obvious to Ahaziah was the fact that his messengers had not made it to Ekron; they returned too quickly and reported the exact words of Elijah. Their description of the man, unknown to them, confirmed Ahaziah's suspicion as to his identity: **He is Elijah the Tishbite** (v 8).

■ **9-12** Ahaziah's perpetuation of the apostasy of his parents provides further reasons for the elimination of the Omrides by Jehu and also paves a foundation for Israel's eventual ruin by the Assyrians. Twice in this section he sent a commander and fifty men to order and bring Elijah **down** from the top of a mountain. Both generals acted arrogantly, and their companies were consumed by fire from the heavens. This is reminiscent of the wet altar at Mount Carmel, proving, as per Elijah's words, that he was indeed a man of God. In Hebrew, the wordplay is obvious: **If I am a man** [*'îš*] **of God, . . . let fire** [*'ēš*] **come down from heaven** (v 12).

■ **13-15** The third commander of fifty that Ahaziah sent was frightened and did not order Elijah to come down but climbed up to him and kneeled before him, pleading for his life and the life of his men. His humility (and survival instinct) was rewarded when the angel of Yahweh assured Elijah that he could **go down** safely with this commander (v 15), the one who did not even politely suggest that he come down but appealed to Elijah for mercy. This commander shows true fear of Yahweh, based upon his experience with what had previously happened. He is a model for listeners and readers of the Bible.

■ **16-17** Elijah repeated Yahweh's words of judgment to Ahaziah's face when he came down and entered Ahaziah's bedchamber. His death (he would not

come down from his bed [v 16]) would be the result of his inquiry to Baal-Zebub of Ekron. This was Elijah's last prophetic act, his last words to a king; they were fulfilled.

Ahaziah's brother Joram, a younger son of Ahab, ruled in his place in Samaria. The dating of Joram's reign to the second year of the reign of Jehoram the son of Jehoshaphat is mistaken. It contradicts 1 Kgs 22:51 [52 HB], which says Ahaziah began to reign in the "seventeenth year of Jehoshaphat," as well as 2 Kgs 3:1, which says Joram then took Israel's crown in Jehoshaphat's "eighteenth year."

■ 18 The LXX adds several statements that reconcile chronological problems in the Hebrew version of Joram's reign. It claims here, among other things, that Joram removed the pillars of Baal that his father had made but walked in the ways of Jeroboam I, which is found in the Hebrew text at 2 Kgs 3:2-3.

b. Elijah Ascends to Heaven (2:1-12)

IN THE TEXT

■ 1 The narrator specifies the starting point for what is about to happen: Elijah and Elisha were together leaving Gilgal (near the Jordan, about one mile north of Jericho). He gives away at the beginning the most unusual climax to this story: Yahweh will take up Elijah **in a whirlwind** or storm-wind. Storm and wind theophanies in the Prophets (Isa 29:6; 40:24; 41:16; Jer 23:19; 30:23; Ezek 1:4; Zech 9:14) and Job 38:1—42:6 also employ this imagery of Yahweh's power or context for speaking. Yahweh did not speak here, but the whirlwind took Elijah to heaven (2 Kgs 2:11).

Israel, led by Joshua, Moses' successor, camped at Gilgal, just after crossing the Jordan on dry ground. It is the site of their "second circumcision," from which the name "Gilgal" came (see Josh 5:2-9).

■ 2 Elisha's refusal to remain behind in Gilgal reminds us of Ruth's refusal to let Naomi leave Moab without her (Ruth 1:10, 16-18). Elisha swore by **Yahweh's life**, as did Ruth and other characters in the Elijah narratives, including Micaiah (→ 1 Kgs 22:13-14 and 17:10-12; 18:9-14, 15-16). Elisha also swore by Elijah's life—**as Yahweh lives and as you live**. Ultimately he would swear this way three times that he will follow Elijah. This shows Elisha's determination to become all that Elijah and Yahweh had in mind for him. He is given three chances by his own master to withdraw from his prophetic role, but he adamantly spurns them. We cannot help but think of Peter, who was given three chances to admit his relationship to Jesus, but denied it (Luke 22:54-62).

■ 3 Three times Elijah silenced the prophets who came out from their respective places to tell him that he would lose Elijah that day. They literally said that Yahweh would take Elisha's lord ***from over your head***, meaning "from leading him." "I know! I know," Elisha snapped: "Why do you think I'm following him around so closely? And if you know, why would you think I don't know? Hush up!"

■ **4-6** The same thing happened when Elijah and Elisha left Bethel for Jericho and from there when they arrived at the Jordan. This builds suspense in the sense that the Elijah, Elisha, and the prophets knew that Yahweh would take Elijah from Elisha that day as Yahweh sent him (them!) from place to place, but no one (in the world of the story) knew when, where, or how. (The reader is told how in v 1.) **The two of them *went*** recalls Isaac and Abraham walking on together toward the place God would show Abraham, the place he would bind his son Isaac and take the knife to slay him (Gen 22:6-12). Elijah and Elisha were bound together in this same way.

■ **7-8** At the Jordan, Elijah took his prophetic mantle, struck the river, and the two of them crossed from the west bank to the east bank on dry ground (recalling Moses' rod of Exod 14:16, 21-29 and Joshua who crossed the Jordan from the east to the west in Josh 3—4). The east bank of the Jordan is near the place Moses transferred leadership to Joshua (Deut 31—34).

■ **9** Elijah confessed what they both knew by asking Elisha to make a request before he was taken away from him. A double portion was the inheritance of every firstborn son (Deut 21:17) and refers to an extra allotment. If there were three sons, then the inheritance was divided into four portions, and the firstborn received two portions, while the others got one. Elisha's full embrace of his future prophetic role is underscored by his request for the firstborn's portion of the spirit of Yahweh from his soon-to-be-departed "father." Yahweh's spirit was involved in the commissioning of Joshua as well (Num 27:18-23).

■ **10** It was a bold, difficult request. Elijah's reply can be paraphrased: "Can you watch me, cling to me, through the last moment when I am taken from you?" Again we see similarities between this and Jesus' request that his disciples watch with him in his last hours. They fell asleep, but Elisha did not (Mark 14:32-42).

■ **11-12** **A chariot of fire and horses of fire** flew between **the two of them**, forcing them apart. Then Elijah went up into the skies in the whirlwind while Elisha was looking. In 1 Kgs 18:12 the prophet Obadiah claimed that the wind/spirit of Yahweh was capable of carrying Elijah here and there, and thus he was afraid to tell Ahab that he could connect with Elijah at any certain place. Here the chariots and horsemen of fire precede the whirlwind that took Elijah to heaven and left Elisha behind. Elisha could not go with him. Divine fiery chariots appear again in 2 Kgs 6:8-23. Second Kings 13:14 depicts the scene wherein King Jehoash cried out at the time of Elisha's death just as Elisha cried out seeing Elijah whirl up and away from him. Watching until Elijah was out of sight, Elisha ***tore his clothes into two tearings***.

2. Elisha Dons the Mantle of Elijah, Helps Prophets and Mothers, Confronts and Replaces Kings (2:13—9:13)

BEHIND THE TEXT

Elisha had become Elijah's disciple-companion when Elijah threw his mantle over him at Elisha's farm in Abel Meholah as described in 1 Kgs 19:19-21 (→). None of the intervening narratives, however, have represented them together. Elijah acted alone in the previous narrative regarding Ahaziah, king of Israel at Samaria, as he had with Ahab. And Micaiah was the working prophet in 1 Kgs 22. These intervening narratives were necessary to Dtr's shaping of Israel's story and mark Ahab's reign more or less chronologically. The bands of prophets that appear in this story affirmed that Elijah and Elisha were known to have been master-disciple by members of these prophetic communities.

As this narrative opens with the news that it was time for Elijah to depart in a most unusual way, recall his challenging question to Elisha in 1 Kgs 19:20: **What have I done to you?** Elijah's anointing mantle not only compelled Elisha's momentous leave-taking and his role as prophet apprentice but also was the basis for continual tests and tasks that shaped Elisha into a prophet like Elijah. Because Elijah had done so much to Elisha by throwing his mantle over him, and because Elisha had clung to Elijah throughout his final circuit and departure from Israel, Elisha became a prophet like his master: an intense loner, ready for the summons of Yahweh.

As this section unfolds, it continues to address the nature of prophets and prophecy and raises troubling questions. Remember that Elijah had performed only one of the tasks Yahweh had set out for him when they were speaking at the mouth of the cave of Horeb; he had anointed Elisha, but not Jehu or Hazael (see 1 Kgs 19:15-17). Elijah had done this principal and most profound task.

a. Elijah's Authority Resides in Elisha (2:13-25)

IN THE TEXT

■ **13** After Elijah ascended to heaven, Elisha gathered up the prophetic mantle Elijah had left for him, struck the water just as Elijah had, and walked through the Jordan riverbed on dry ground. Just as Joshua repeated signs and wonders of Moses, confirming Yahweh's selection of him as Moses' successor, so did Elisha.

■ **14-18** It is not clear in the Hebrew whether *the sons of the prophets* from Jericho were watching him split the Jordan with Elijah's mantle, but they could see when he came near Jericho that Elisha retained Elijah's spirit. They showed him obeisance by bowing before him. They wished to know if the whirlwind had deposited Elijah or his body somewhere in the region and Elisha finally allowed fifty men to scatter and search for three days, knowing all the while that Elijah had ascended into heaven; there was no body to be found.

■ **19-22** Other men from Jericho appealed to Elisha for help with their water, an occasion for Elisha to work a miracle that helped the Jerichoites. ***The waters were healed until today***, a reference to the time of the writer. This is the first of a series of miracles, all of which demonstrated Elisha's possession of a double portion of Elijah's legacy: the spirit of Yahweh. This validated Elisha's role without regard for the curses on Jericho to which 1 Kgs 16:34 alludes (see Josh 6:26).

■ **23-24** To go **up to Bethel** was to continue to retrace the steps Elisha had just taken with Elijah. The primary point of this pericope is to contrast the young lads from Bethel who jeered at Elisha with the prophetic community from Jericho who bowed to him (in recognition that he possessed Elijah's spirit) and townsmen who asked him to heal their water supply. Following his curse in Yahweh's name, two bears **broke open** forty-two boys, which sounds fatal, but most translations use **mauled**, which may or may not be mortal. Elisha's judgment seems harsh for juvenile insolence. The story warns against insulting the prophet of Yahweh.

The tendency of many interpreters has been to harmonize these troubling tales to purge them of their dark understories. For example, some interpreters defend the violence even though the recipients did not seem to be deserving of death. One way of doing this is to insist that Elijah's taunters were not young/small boys, but young men, and to claim they were urging Elisha to worship at the altar at Bethel (Mercer 2002, 171-74). Ultimately, argues Mercer, they would not have been cursed if they were not deserving of a curse. But this is circular. While we should attempt to turn around such a story every which way to discover explanations, sometimes no excuses exist, and we are left with a primary point—don't mess with Elisha!

■ **25** Elijah and Elisha were loners in spite of the guilds of prophets to be found here and there who honored them. Elijah and Elisha together had traveled from Gilgal, ten miles west to Bethel, then ten miles east to Jericho, then about five miles to the Jordan, and finally they crossed it to the east bank on dry ground. From there Yahweh took up Elijah in the whirlwind after a chariot of horses and fire came between him and Elisha.

After watching Elijah ascend to the skies, Elisha went back to Jericho, back to Bethel, then all the way up to Mount Carmel (fifty miles northwest of Bethel) and finally to Samaria, the capital of Israel, which was between Bethel and Mount Carmel. All of these sites were important settings for Elijah's prophetic service. Elisha's return to Samaria indicates that Elisha would complete the tasks Yahweh had given Elijah: to anoint Jehu to become king of Israel in order to overthrow the dynasty of Ahab and his father Omri (1 Kgs 19:19-20; 2 Kgs 8:7-15; 9:1-13) and to anoint Hazael to succeed Ben-Hadad.

FROM THE TEXT

Clearly, Elijah was a unique prophet of Yahweh, and his move from earth to the skies is both more and less mysterious than Moses' death. Moses died, as all creatures do, and no one saw or knew the exact place; he was buried by Yahweh (Deut 34:5-6). Elijah was taken up; he did not die, but Elisha saw what happened: ascension accompanied by chariots and horses of fire that separated the two men. Explicit mention of ascension to heaven is known otherwise only in the case of Jesus (regarding Enoch, Gen 5:24 says "Enoch walked faithfully with God; then he was no more, because God took him away"). Yet Jesus is to be revered over Moses and Elijah. Mark 9:2-8 indicates that Jesus' words and acts are to be obeyed even over the Law (represented by Moses) and the Prophets (represented by Elijah). If and when one perceives conflicts between the Scriptures—the Law and the Prophets—and Jesus' commands, follow Jesus' way.

Elisha's curse on the young boys who mocked him has troubled interpreters more than Elijah calling down fire from heaven on two commanders and one hundred soldiers or his slaughtering of 450 prophets of Baal. Yet all of these incidents in the Elijah-Elisha narratives make the same point; they show the power of the prophetic word, even over wild elements of nature such as lightning and female bears.

In these tales about the kingdom prophets, the authors are emphasizing their radical and rough streaks and the strength of their words. In most cases, the authors were concerned about human life; Yahweh's prophets provided for Israel and those outside of Israel such as the Phoenician widow and her son. They delivered Israel from the Arameans and purified the water for the people of Jericho. On the other hand, stories such as Elisha and the bears, like Uzzah and the ark of God (2 Sam 6:6-9), intentionally strike fear in observers both within and outside of the world of the story, recommending the humility and trust of the people of Jericho in contrast to the jeering of boys of Bethel.

b. The Revolt of Moab (3:1-27)

IN THE TEXT

■ **1-3** Dating Joram's first year this way lines up with 1 Kgs 22:51-53 [52-54 HB], but not with 2 Kgs 1:17, which may be a scribal error. However, Thiele (1983, 100) suggests that this reference may reflect a co-regency, which Jehoram shared with Jehoshaphat beginning in the latter's seventeenth year. The formulaic introduction to Joram's reign refers to his parents, Ahab and Jezebel, to say that he was not as evil as they; he removed the Baal pillar, but he continued to sin like Jeroboam I had sinned at Bethel and Dan. Though this praise is faint, the fact that Joram avoided Baal worship and consulted Yahweh at 2 Kgs 3:10-12 is an enormous religious improvement.

The Dtr's disgust with Bethel and Dan is consistent (Jerusalem is the only place to worship in Dtr's view). Jeroboam did not want his constituency to make pilgrimages to Jerusalem for festivals there, so he built shrines at the borders of Israel to substitute. The result may have eventually been the establishment of a new sort of religion, especially in the eyes of the Judahite Deuteronomistic redactors. Dtr's formulaic accounts of the kings' reigns imply that Baal worship was separate from offerings made at the shrines of the calves at Bethel and Dan. Jezebel and Ahab sanctioned and supported Baal worship in Israel. See 1 Kgs 16:29-33, then refer back to 1 Kgs 12:25-33; 15:26, 34; 16:19, 25-26; 22:52 [53 HB]; and 2 Kgs 3:1-3.

■ **4-8** Mesha, king of Moab, which was directly east of Judah, had been forced by Israel to pay tribute to Israel with lambs and wool, indicating Moab's vassal status (David had subdued Moab [2 Sam 8:2]). Judah was also in a vassal status to Israel during the time of Omrides, which explains why Israel gained the wool of Moab and why Jehoshaphat was obligated to support Israel's armies against Moab. Edom, in vassal relation to Judah, joined them. As noted at 2 Kgs 1:1, Moab rebelled after Ahab's death at the hands of the Syrians.

Moabite Stone

What the biblical text does not mention is found in the Moabite Stone, also known as the Mesha Stele, where an account of Mesha's victory over the Omride dynasty was inscribed. It claims that Mesha advanced into southern Israel, which would have been into the tribal allotments of Reuben and Gad just north of Moab's northern border. The rebellion of Moab cited in 2 Kgs 1:1 and 3:5 resulted in a Moabite presence in Israel and was the reason Israel and Judah marched around to Edom and the weaker south side of Moab to attack.

The Mesha Inscription was discovered in 1868 on the northern border of Moab at ancient Dibon and can be seen in the Louvre, Paris, France. It claims that Israelite inhabitants of Nebo were under the ban, a parallel to the biblical concept of *ḥerem*. (For picture, English translation, and bibliography, see Hanson 2012.)

■ **9-10** Joram's strategy to circle east, then south all the way around Moab into Edom to enter Moab from the south may have helped bring Edom into the fight, but the journey through the desert wilderness meant no water for the soldiers and their animals (see Map 5, p. 118). Joram despaired, claiming it was Yahweh's will that they would all be defeated by Moab. Joram seems pessimistic, but he may well have been aware of Elijah's pronouncements against Ahab's dynasty that would be fulfilled in his son's days, meaning *his* days. Ahaziah, his brother and predecessor to the throne of Israel, had already succumbed (1 Kgs 22:37; 2 Kgs 1:17). Joram's fear that Moab could be the downfall of all three kingdoms (and thus fulfill the word of Yahweh against the Omrides) indicates Joram's reverence for the word of Yahweh, unlike his parents and brother Ahaziah.

■ **11-12** Just as in the Micaiah narrative of 1 Kgs 22, it was Jehoshaphat, king of Judah, who asked for a prophet of Yahweh in response to Joram's foreboding. The kings were referred to Elisha, the servant of Elijah, by one of Joram's servants. The reference to water not only indicates Elisha's service to Elijah but also underscores the drought the armies of the three kings were facing in Edom's desert. Jehoshaphat also affirmed the status of Elisha as a true prophet of Yahweh. So the three kings went to him at an unnamed location. They did not send servants to bring him to them (they are encamped for battle) but indicated their respect for him by visiting him themselves.

■ **13-14** Elisha immediately conveyed his disdain for Joram, son of Ahab and Jezebel, and bitterness toward them for their support of Baal. Joram confirmed his fear that it was Yahweh's will that Moab defeat Israel, Judah, and Edom. Only out of respect for Jehoshaphat did Elisha agree to seek Yahweh for them.

■ **15** Requiring music to inquire of Yahweh was not used by Elijah or mentioned in the case of other prophetic oracles. Yet the structure of prophetic oracles is poetic or songlike throughout the Scriptures. In this case, while an instrument was played, Yahweh's hand ***happened upon him***. And Elisha began speaking with the prophetic messenger formula.

■ **16-17** The Zered brook (Wadi el-Hesa) flows west from beyond (east of) the Jordan to the Dead Sea, forming the border between Edom and Moab. The water that would fill the pools of the wadi would slake the thirst of men and animals.

■ **18-19** Not only that, but Moab would fall to the three kings who were ordered to utterly ruin the land and its water supplies. This contradicts Deut 20:19-20, which prohibits cutting down trees in wartime. Chronologically, the reverse is true, for Deuteronomy was written later than this narrative, which was later reworked into the Deuteronomic History (see Sweeney 2007, 283).

■ **20** The armies were at the northern border of Edom, southern border of Moab. Thus the water came from the south into the border at the Zered brook/wadi without a storm and filled the pools of the wadi visible to the Moabites.

■ **21-25** Moabite boys and men thought the morning sun on the water was blood and that their invaders had destroyed each other. Red sandstone dominates this area and orange-red pools at sunrise during the rainy season are a common phenomenon. But in this case, there had been no wind or rainstorms (2 Kgs 3:17); pools of what appeared to be blood covered land that the Moabites knew to be dry desert. Therefore, they concluded it was time to collect the spoil. All Israel's army had to do was strike Moab's army when the latter came into their camp, then chase them back and deface the land of Moab.

■ **26-27** In a last-ditch effort, Moab's king attacked Edom. When that failed, he sacrificed his firstborn son, the crown prince, on the wall in the sight of Israel, whose anger and disgust (***great wrath***) led them to withdraw. Yahweh had helped them achieve victory over Moab from the southern border up to the city of Kir Haresheth on the King's Highway. But here Israel withdrew in response to the human sacrifice they witnessed. This text would hardly insist that Israel suffered the wrath of the Moabite god, Chemosh, or of Yahweh, who had told the three kings they would have victory. But they were deeply affected by the extremes to which Mesha resorted to save himself. In 2 Kgs 16:3, King Ahaz of Judah is denounced for subjecting his own son to the fire as a sacrifice.

Child Sacrifice

Child sacrifice was known and practiced by Israel and its neighbors. Texts from Phoenician and Ugaritic cultures indicate that the son was sacrificed in place of the father for the sake of the entire kingdom in time of war. Elus of Phoenicia arrayed his son in royal apparel before he was sacrificed. In one Ugaritic tale the son survived the crisis offering to the delight of his father. The motif of the beloved son is held in common by all of these stories, including Gen 22 (see Levenson 1993, 26-37).

Child sacrifice was forbidden in Deut 12:29-32 [29—13:1 HB] and was denounced in the name of Yahweh by the prophets Jeremiah (19:5), Ezekiel (20:31), and Micah (6:7-8). This is problematized by Gen 22:1 and Exod 22:29 [28 HB], but these are mitigated by understanding Gen 22:1 and the rest of the chapter as Yahweh's test of Abraham's devotion and not something Yahweh actually desired. These Genesis and Exodus passages must be compared to Exod 13:12-13 and 34:20, which state the firstborn sons must be redeemed with a lamb; Yahweh did not want them killed. The Torah makes it clear that the Levites took the place of the firstborn sons as set apart for Yahweh for ritual service (Num 1:47-54; 3:11-13; 18:15-20). (For a thorough discussion of child sacrifice in biblical times, see Levenson [1993] and Winslow [forthcoming 2017].)

BEHIND THE TEXT

The narrative shifts from the battle scene that included Mesha publically sacrificing his son to a series of encounters between Elisha and individual Israelites in chs 4—8. Elisha had prophesied military success, but Israel had nonetheless withdrawn from Moab. These pericopes about provision and healing include women, servants, and *the sons of the prophets*. They are similar to portions of Elijah's story that depict the prophet supplying life and health to ordinary people. Yahweh used both Elijah and Elisha to meet their needs, as well as to direct, challenge, and help royalty.

c. The Destitute Widow (4:1-7)

IN THE TEXT

■ **1-2** The destitute Israelite widow *from the wives of the sons of the prophets* (her husband had been one of *the sons of the prophets*) saw Elisha as a source of help, as had the men of Jericho for their poisoned water supply. Obviously these prophetic communities included families, but no one had helped her save her children from debt slavery (see Exod 21:1-11; Deut 15:12-18).

This and other references to **the sons of the prophets** show that Elisha associated with them on a regular basis and was considered their master (2 Kgs 6:1-2). Of the eleven times this term is used in the OT, all but one are in the Elisha stories (see, for example, 2 Kgs 9:6-10; the exception is 1 Kgs 20:35). **The sons of the prophets** are depicted as needy, inept, and sometimes foolish (see Bergen 1999, 57-60, 108).

Amos (from Judah) told the priest at Bethel (in Israel) that he was not "a prophet nor the son of a prophet" (Amos 7:14). Amos thus denied that he was a prophet by profession with a locale in which to prophesy. Neither was he part of a community like the one depicted in 2 Kings. In other words, he had no previous experience as a spokesman for Yahweh and did not associate with known prophets or groups of prophets. Yahweh had called him to speak his word to Israel, but not because he was part of a group of prophets. (See Hobbs 1985, 25-27.)

■ **3-4** Elisha first asked the widow what *he* could do, but immediately set a plan in motion to help her, similar to Jesus' response to his mother at the wedding of Cana when wine ran out (see John 2:1-12). By borrowing empty vessels, she could store the oil that was forthcoming. By shutting the door, no neighbor need know about the origin of her oil supply.

■ **5-7** With every available storage vessel full of oil, she stopped pouring from her original jar. Elisha explained how this oil would pay her debts, save her children from slavery, and support them. Like Elisha, Jesus found a way to fill empty vessels and thus resolve a crisis for ordinary people, although the widow's crisis was much more serious. This widow and orphan story is meant to remind us of the widow in Sidon for whom Elijah supplied meal and oil so that she and her son survived the drought (1 Kgs 17:8-24).

d. The Shunammite and Her Son (4:8-44)

BEHIND THE TEXT

The next Elisha pericope provides a parallel to the second part of the story of the hospitable Sidonian widow in Elijah's day (1 Kgs 17:7-24). As Elijah had been a vessel of Yahweh to save her nearly dead son, so Elisha saved the son of a wealthy woman who gave him a place to stay. The plot unfolds here to show that Elisha was like Elijah, just as Joshua was like his predecessor Moses (see Josh 1—5).

Furthermore, Elisha's assistance to the mother and her son in 2 Kgs 4:8-44 may be fruitfully compared to the next one about the healing of Naaman, the Aramean general in ch 5. There are parallels regarding motifs of greatness, desire to give or take gifts, pursuing compensation, concern for others' welfare, and "standing before" authorities. The young man Gehazi who served Elisha has a significant role in both stories.

IN THE TEXT

■ **8-10** Yahweh continued to intervene in Israel during the divided kingdom period through Elisha's ministry to a **great** (*gĕdôlâ*) woman of Shunem, a town of Issachar opposite Mount Gilboa and north of the city of Jezreel (home of Naboth, as well as Jezebel and Ahab [1 Kgs 21]). This was not far from Mount Carmel and the Kishon River.

Translators have chosen **well-to-do** or "wealthy" (NRSV) for **great** (*gĕdôlâ* [v 8]), because the woman and her husband owned a farm and had the means to feed Elisha and build him a room (v 10). Furthermore, they served him and did not seem to need his help. Nonetheless, this woman's greatness stemmed from her hospitality and her recognition that Elisha was **a holy man of God** (v 9). The woman offered him not only meals, but eventually a walled upper bedroom (or roof room). Her husband stayed in the background. She is the one who initiated Elisha's room, and he serves the narrator as someone to hear her plans, as a way of informing the reader.

■ **11-14** Gehazi is introduced as Elisha's **servant (*young man*)** who accompanied Elisha on his travels. Elisha sought to do something to show his gratitude for the meals and lodging. He first spoke to his hostess through Gehazi, even though she stood before him. Her response was a polite way of saying: "No, thank you; I do not need anything; I am at home; my own people will care for me." Her comfortable context contrasts with that of Elisha; she made a lodging place for him because he was itinerant. Undeterred, he wished to bestow something upon her to show his gratitude and perhaps his power. Elisha addressed Gehazi to indicate his wish to express his gratitude. Knowing she had no son and her husband was old, Gehazi implied that Elisha could offer something that could ensure that her property and person were secure when her husband died (i.e., not taken by male relatives [Deut 25:5-10]).

■ **15-16** To her face, Elisha assured her that she would have a son within a year, *in due time*. Recall the three men (Yahweh) who promised Sarah a son *in due time* (Gen 18:10, 13-14). This future mother did not laugh as Sarah did, but her response was stern: ***Do not deceive me*** (*kāzab*). She charged him to be serious! Her remark would resurface when the child grew older.

■ **17** Too good to be true became too good not to be true. A child was born to this woman *in due time* just as Isaac was born to Sarah *in due time* (Gen 18:14; 21:1-3).

■ **18-25a** While Isaac's life was threatened (Yahweh asked his father to offer him up as a whole burnt offering in Gen 22), this long-awaited son actually **died** (see also 2 Kgs 8:1-6). Many commentators suggest that he had sunstroke in the fields that rendered him unconscious, but the text says that he *died* in his mother's lap, at which time she took him to Elisha's bed.

This mother did not even tell his father about their son's death, only that she needed a donkey and a servant to go to Elisha, **the man of God**, at Mount Carmel. Whereas Sarah was absent in the story of the binding of Isaac, here *the father* was overtly left out of his wife's mission to revive her son. Here the father serves the narrator's purpose to show the mother's haste and desire to be on her own in this. His response that there was no reason to go to the prophet since it was not the Sabbath or a new moon festival may show that she or they visited Elisha on those festivals. It could mean that the husband was mistaken, or it may indicate that the husband considered Elisha to be more like a priest than a prophet, that his holiness came from his celebration of regular festivals rather than bringing Yahweh's word. This may well have been this family's experience with Elisha, for he is not pictured as proclaiming Yahweh's words, but more as a wonder-worker (see Bergen 1999, 99).

More importantly, his question emphasizes that he was unaware how ill the boy was when he sent him to his mother and also unaware of his subsequent death. His wife kept him ignorant. Her response, **That's all right** (*šālôm*), or *it is well*, says that this was entirely her affair; she did not want him involved in the resolution.

▪ **25b-26** Elisha is referred to as **the man of God** throughout this passage until v 32. Clearly, he was most concerned over the welfare of this unnamed family, asking after the wellness or *peace* (*šālôm*) of each family member. She refused to tell Gehazi about her son's death or why she came to see Elisha. She told the servant that all was well (*šālôm*); she wanted to confront Elisha with the bitterness of her loss.

▪ **27-28** Her posture of calmness: *all is well* (*šālôm*) fell away when she saw Elisha. She cast herself down to his feet and grabbed them, a move of utter anguish. Gehazi's move to disentangle her was rebuked, for Elisha was aware of her distress and cared for her. He observed that Yahweh had concealed her state from him, as she also had until this moment. She reminded him of her reply to his announcement that she would bear a son (*do not deceive me* [v 16]). Here she said that she had said: do not tease me or neglect me, or *do not be casual with me* (*šālâ*). Clearly, this recent loss of her child filled her with such sorrow that she suggested it was almost worse than never having one.

▪ **29-31** Elisha sent young Gehazi to run with his staff and instructions to lay it on the boy's face, obviously hoping that the staff would carry healing power. He knew that the youth could run to the boy more quickly than he and the mother could. She refused to return without Elisha himself. The staff in Gehazi's hand did not work; the child did not revive. This emphasizes the significance of Elisha's own presence, his bodily contact as well as showing that neither his staff nor his servant Gehazi was useful as Elisha's representative.

▪ **32-37** Elisha himself revived the boy by going into the room alone, praying to Yahweh, and lying upon him, face to face, hand to hand. The mother's instincts were correct. Elisha's person, his body and breath, had the desired life-giving effect: the return of her son to her. Elisha's way of saving this dead son was similar—but not identical—to Elijah's reviving of the widow's son in 1 Kgs 17:21-24. Yahweh and his prophets overcame death, and the two boys join the few people in the Bible who rose from the dead. The others are in the NT: Lazarus, Jesus, and those whose graves were opened when Jesus died (John 11:38-44; Matt 27:52). We will meet this mother and her son again in 2 Kgs 8.

Although Elisha prayed to Yahweh, we should notice that neither Elisha nor the mother overtly credited Yahweh as the source of the healing, as is the case for his other miracles. The fact that Elisha possessed the firstborn's double portion of the spirit of Elijah, on account of whose prayer Yahweh healed the widow's son (1 Kgs 17:22-24), may imply that Elisha was centered within the stream of Elijah/Yahweh. On the other hand, as Bergen sees it, this may imply that Elisha was another step removed from Yahweh. Indeed, Yahweh's role in the stories of Elisha is much more subtle than in the stories of Elijah. Yahweh is sometimes mentioned, but Elisha was the one who acted and worked wonders. In contrast to the many times Yahweh spoke to Elijah and Elijah to Yahweh, these stories never record any direct speech from Yahweh to Elisha (Bergen 1999, 100 and passim).

■ **38-41** Elisha's journey from Mount Carmel to Shunem continued with a return to Gilgal near the Jordan. He stayed with prophets during a time of famine. The stew was based on herbs of the field, but the man who gathered them and threw them into the pot included one of the poison gourds that grew in the countryside. The stew's resulting flavor indicated its potential toxic or at least harmful effect on those who ate it. The stew would have been wasted had Elisha not thrown meal into the pot. This appears as another one of Elisha's ways of providing for the pressing needs of ordinary people.

■ **42-44** In a similar vein, and foreshadowing Jesus' feeding many people with a meager amount of food, Elisha fed one hundred men with twenty loaves and a few ears of corn that were brought to him from Baal Shalishah as an offering of firstfruits. The skeptical words of Elisha's servant, like those of Jesus' disciples, underscored the miraculous provision (see Matt 14:13-21; 15:32-39; Mark 6:30-44; 8:1-10; Luke 9:10-17). The stories of Elisha, like those about Elijah, show that Yahweh—not Baal—provided for the people! Yahweh used Elijah and Elisha to give life, not simply words of judgment or calls to repentance. Elijah's story served as a polemic against Ahab, Jezebel, and their progeny, who promoted Baal worship, but all of these figures are curiously absent in the stories of Elisha.

e. The Healing of Naaman, the Aramean (5:1-27)

BEHIND THE TEXT

The story told in 5:1-27 about Naaman the commander of the armies of Aram, his servants, Elisha, and his servant parallels that of the Shunammite mother in the previous chapter through the use of terms and themes. Its purpose is to again emphasize Yahweh's concern for people of all nations and the ubiquitous nature of his favor. It also extolls servants and outsiders to Israel for trusting Yahweh and for *knowing* that he is greater than all gods and alone has the power to heal. Elisha, Yahweh's servant, also *knows* many things. (→ 2 Kgs 4:8-44.)

Jesus cited Elisha's healing of Naaman the Aramean at the beginning of his ministry in Nazareth along with Elijah's provision for the Sidonian widow in 1 Kgs 17:7-24. In Luke 4:26-30, Jesus was acclaimed by his listeners in his hometown, but, because of his bold reference to the ministries of Elijah and Elisha to outsiders, his neighbors attempted to kill him!

IN THE TEXT

■ I An abrupt scene shift from Israel to the commander in chief of the Aramean armies brings the **great** (*gādôl*) and **highly regarded** Naaman onto the stage. This verse is a reminder of the previous battles between Israel and Aram when towns of Israel were besieged and Ahab was killed (1 Kgs 20—22). Naaman's greatness also reminds us of the ***great*** (*gādôlâ*) woman of Shunem that recently benefitted from Elisha's intervention.

The narrator claims that Aram's victories, including those over Israel, were wrought by Yahweh! (Micaiah's prophecy and fulfillment at the hands of the Arameans in 1 Kgs 22:17-36 must be associated with Elijah's prophecy against Ahab in 1 Kgs 21:20-26, albeit having been mitigated for a time because of Ahab's repentance.) As unwelcome to Israel as Jesus' reminders of Yahweh's aid to outsiders, this claim affirms that Yahweh was also involved in the success of the armies of the Arameans and his involvement with all nations. (See Amos 9:7 and Isa 10:13.)

The name of the Aramean king before whom great Naaman stood in such favor is not given, just as the king of Israel is not named later. These identities are not important to the story, but the surrounding pericopes provide some clues (if they are in chronological order). The Aramean king may have been Ben-Hadad I (or II) and the Israelite king may have been Joram (849-842 BC). (See Hobbs 1985, 63, 79.)

As many biblical scholars note, Naaman had a flaky skin disease that is often translated as leprosy, but this is not modern leprosy, also called Hansen's disease, that disfigures. Naaman's condition did not isolate him from his king or anyone else in the story. Those who suffered from this disease were not permitted access to the sanctuary; they were regulated by the rules of Lev 13. Priests diagnosed it and determined whether it had been successfully treated. Thus, as Frank Spina notes, Naaman was a highly accomplished enemy outsider with a disease that put him "at the farthest remove from Israel and Israel's god" (2005, 78). This information provides the setting and the problem that needed to be resolved, which is a structure common to the Elisha stories, although this story is more complex than most of them (Hobbs 1985, 61-62).

■ **2-3** During one of their plundering raids, the Arameans had captured a ***little girl*** from Israel to serve Naaman's wife. While Naaman was a great man who ***stood before*** (served) his lord, the king of Aram, this little Israelite girl ***stood before*** [served] **Naaman's wife.** In spite of her lowly status, she was the first one to speak in this story, and thus she initiated the action. She spoke words of trust in the prophet of Samaria's ability to heal her lord. This began a chain of events recounted in this story of servants, kings, Naaman, and Elisha.

■ **4-5** The antecedent of ***he came and told his lord*** is Naaman, while the antecedent of ***his lord*** is the king of Aram, for this king immediately sent Naaman with a letter to the king of Israel. Israel's king was an unlikely recipient, not simply from the reader's point of view, but from his own! The little Israelite servant girl had not mentioned *a king* in Samaria but a prophet! She hoped in Elisha (albeit unnamed) for healing, while Naaman and the king hoped in the king of Israel. Their hopes were misplaced or at least reflect misunderstanding of the king's relationship to the prophet and of the source of potential healing. Naaman took an enormous gift, which demonstrates not only his hope but also that healing can be bought or at least the healer rewarded. All of these movements are the result of the little girl's remark and indicate the Aramean's reliance on her testimony.

■ **6** Enough information about this formal letter between these kings is given to indicate that it followed ANE letter forms (Hobbs 1985, 64). Its primary message was that Israel's king must cure Naaman of his skin disease. If Naaman told his lord exactly what the little girl told his wife about "the prophet who is in Samaria" (v 3), the Aramean king may have assumed that any prophet was subject to the king and must heal whomever he was told to heal. Recall Jezebel's view that King Ahab had a right to Naboth's vineyard.

■ **7** In any case, the Israelite king took the letter at face value, assuming that *he* was supposed to do the healing. Since he could not, he concluded that Aram's king was **trying to pick a quarrel** with him. He was so distressed that he tore his garments, a sign of lament throughout the Scriptures. He knew that God could kill and bring back to life, but he did not remember Elisha, Yahweh's prophet (compare Deut 32:39). The reports provided in previous narratives indicate that this king, one of Ahab's sons, would have been well aware of Elisha. However, instead of seeking him for help in a crisis, the king fell apart in a display of fear and forgetfulness of the power of Yahweh and his prophets.

■ **8** Somehow **Elisha the man of God heard** of the king's reaction to his visitor's letter and came to his aid. Elisha contacted the king, challenging his forgetfulness and ingratitude, which is worse than the ignorance of the Arameans. Elisha's message was that if **the man** would **come to me, he** would **know that there is a prophet in Israel!** Knowledge would come to the Aramean commander from experience with the Israelite prophet. This is a subtle critique of the king of Israel, the only one in the Elisha cycle of stories, which contrasts sharply with Elijah's vivid denunciation of Ahab.

■ **9** Naaman immediately went with his entourage to Elisha's home. Just as the Shunammite woman had stood at the door of Elisha's room in her own home after he had summoned her to do something for her (2 Kgs 4:11-15), so Naaman stood at the door to Elisha's house, expecting healing.

■ **10** Elisha did not even come out to speak to the great and highly regarded military general. Instead, he **sent a messenger** with a strange order, something Naaman must do, instead of something Elisha could do. Elisha said that Naaman's *flesh would return to him pure* if he would go many miles from Samaria to the Jordan and **wash . . . seven times**.

■ **11** Naaman felt insulted! He went away angry, speaking his inner thoughts so that his reasons are made clear to us. He presumed that Elisha would **come out . . . call on the name of Yahweh his God, wave his hand over the *place and heal [him] of [his] skin disease***. This implies Naaman's faith in Israel's God, even though he was disgruntled when his opinions about how his healing should happen were thwarted. He was expecting the prophet to enact a certain ritual and then he could get on with his life.

■ **12** We also might expect Elisha to follow a ritual like this and so sympathize with Naaman stalking off in a heated rage. Except, we wonder: did he not wish to be healed? Had he not come in desperation with gold and silver and ten sets of garments? The absurdity of the ordeal required by Elisha led Naaman to affirm the beautiful rivers near Damascus, his home, and decry the futility of his journey to Israel. The Abana is the Barada River whose source is twenty-three miles northwest of Damascus; and the Pharpar is the el-Awaj River, whose source is on Mount Hermon (Sweeney 2007, 300). Mentioning these rivers to disparage Israel's Jordan River sets up Naaman to be humbled.

■ **13** His servants immediately approached him, calling him **my father**, to reason with him. As in the case of the little Israelite servant girl, so with these Aramean servants. Naaman listened again. He responded to their logic that doing a little thing should not be more difficult than doing a **great thing**, which he would have done. The fact that it is what the man of God in Israel said to do is the important factor. The Aramean servants showed more sense and understanding of the prophet than the Israelite king.

■ **14** So he went down and dipped himself . . . *according to the word of* the **man of God**. And according to the reasoning of *his servants*. Naaman's dipping seven times in the Jordan satisfied Elisha's prescription that he wash. Going to the Jordan was the last essential step of a journey that began when he listened to the little girl who served his wife. **And his flesh *returned* [was restored] like the flesh of a little boy**. This is a purposeful allusion to the little Israelite girl who started this **great man before his lord** on the circuit from having skin marred by disease to having the flesh of a little boy. ***He was cleansed*** (*ṭāhēr*).

181

Although we know that Naaman had been healed (this was his reason for coming to Israel, indeed, this was the demand his king made of the Israelite king), the writer used the term for returning, which is also the term for repentance (*yāšāb*), and cleansing (*ṭāhēr*), a ritual term for what happened to Naaman because he obeyed and dipped in the Jordan.

■ **15** Naaman's flesh **returned** [*yāšāb*] **like the flesh of a little boy** (v 14) and thus he **returned** (*yāšāb* [v 15]) to Elisha. This time he stood before Elisha himself and not at his door, speaking directly to the prophet. There he confessed, **"Now I know that there is no God in all the world except in Israel."** Naaman's firsthand experience with healing led him to faith in Israel's God. His faith confession parallels the faith confessions of other outsiders: Jethro (Exod 18:11), Rahab (Josh 2:9-11), and the Sidonian widow (1 Kgs 17:24). They also begin by saying "now I know" or "I know," which is the purpose of such signs throughout the Scriptures. From the time of Israel's Egyptian bondage, Yahweh performed signs and wonders so that Israel, Egypt, and all the earth might know Yahweh, his deliverance, his power, that the earth belongs to Yahweh, that there is no one like Israel's God (Exod 9:29-30; 14:4; Josh 2:11; see also Exod 5:1; 6:7; 7:5, 17; 8:10, 22 [6, 18 HB]; 9:14; 10:2; 11:7; 16:6-12).

Naaman did not vocalize gratitude or regret for being so angry; he simply confessed that Israel's God was the only god and urged Elisha to **accept a gift**, calling himself Elisha's **servant** (see Spina 2005, 83-85). The point here is not to show how Naaman was transformed from a proud, angry man to a humble, grateful one but to show that he became a convert to Israel's God through his healing. Certainly his humility and gratefulness are implied. On the surface, Elisha was healer, but the effect was to turn Naaman to the worship of Yahweh, emphasizing Yahweh's role.

■ **16-17** Elisha swore by the **life of Yahweh** (as had the Sidonian widow and Elijah) that he would never accept anything. He added **before whom I stand** (v 16), underlining Yahweh's role in the restoration of Naaman's skin. So Naaman asked for something else: ground or soil (*'ădāmâ*) from the land of Israel for the sake of worshipping Yahweh alone in his own land. Although he confessed that the only god was in Israel, he knew he could worship Yahweh in his own land. His request for Israel's soil or ground was a reversal of Naaman's attitude toward Israel's Jordan; he had not wanted Israel's water, but after his conversion, he wanted Israel's soil (*'ădāmâ*). He would build an altar with it, reflecting the narrator's awareness of Exod 20:24, a Torah teaching about sacrificing on altars of soil (*'ădāmâ*). This does not imply Naaman knew the Torah but rather that the narrator presents Naaman as compliant with Israel's covenant (Spina 2005, 86).

To take something from Israel was acceptable, but Elisha would not permit Naaman to be in the position of giver. Naaman must receive the blessings of Yahweh to demonstrate that Yahweh's prophet and the Aramean commander were not and could never be on equal grounds. In fact, the latter had become *like . . . a little boy* (v 14).

■ 18 While determined to offer sacrifices to Yahweh alone on Israelite land carted back to Aram, Naaman recognized he must continue to help his king worship in the **temple of Rimmon**, another name for Hadad, the Aramean storm god. He sought Yahweh's forgiveness in advance through Elisha. The narrator thus exhibits a tolerant attitude toward outsiders who must continue to live in their homelands and serve in their prescribed roles, even though they have converted to the worship of Yahweh alone.

■ 19 Elisha understood and blessed Naaman's departure.

■ 20 The focus on gift exchange and the power differentials that gifts represent continues in the next movement of the story about Naaman. The narrator reveals Gehazi's annoyance with Elisha because the latter *prevented that Aramean Naaman from having his gift accepted*. It seems that Elisha's heretofore helpful young servant (see 2 Kgs 4:11-16) was concerned for the rebuffed commander, but Gehazi's thoughts and actions indicate he was dazzled by the array of gifts offered to his master by Naaman and wanted something for himself (5:5, 15-16). Knowing Elisha's adamant refusal of a gift, Gehazi did not inform Elisha of his plans, swearing by the life of Yahweh to **get something from** Naaman. Elisha had just sworn by Yahweh's life that he would *not* accept a gift (6:16). Gehazi, however, did not say *before whom I stand* as Elisha had.

■ 21-22 Naaman showed concern and respect for Elisha's servant by stopping and dismounting his chariot. He could not tell that Gehazi was lying about Elisha sending him to get goods from Naaman, even though Elisha had sworn by Yahweh, whom he served, to refuse Naaman's gifts.

■ 23 Operating out of gratitude and goodwill, Naaman wrapped more than Gehazi requested and sent his own servants to carry it for him until Gehazi turned them back. But this shifted the blessing order; Naaman was to be freely blessed without compensation to anyone in the land of Israel. Gehazi had obtained Aramean goods by deceit, a sour turn to the story of Elisha's free gift of healing to Naaman.

■ 24 Gehazi and Naaman's two servants went as far as **the mound**, or **the hill** (*'ōpel*), **and set up** or **appointed his house**. This could also mean that Gehazi visited with his household before sending Naaman's servants back to him. Although his household may not have known of Gehazi's deception and greed, this verse may suggest that they were complicitous in accepting goods that Gehazi gained fraudulently. The term *'ōpel* is normally used for a fortified hill in Jerusalem and implies theologically symbolic significance to Gehazi's actions. The narrator is not implying that a servant of Elisha who lived in Samaria was connected with Jerusalem.

■ 25 Returning to his place and his role of servant, Gehazi **stood before his master, Elisha** who gave him the opportunity to tell the truth about his recent errand. But he lied again, even though his experience with Elisha should have disabused him of any notion a lie would be undetected.

■ **26-27** Elisha claimed that his *heart went with [Gehazi] as Naaman jumped down to greet [him]*. Elisha's awe over Naaman's cleansing and conversion is evident in his heartfelt address to his servant. Not only was this a time of judgment for Gehazi's greed, but Elisha's address indicated that he was not indifferent to the work of Yahweh in Naaman's life. We can also sense his regret over Gehazi's attempt to use this extraordinary time to acquire the assets. Gehazi fell under Elisha's sentence: he and his family would acquire Naaman's *flaky, like-snow skin disease* instead of Naaman's gifts (see Exod 4:6 and Num 12:10).

Just as Naaman had left his lord, the king of Aram, to come to faith in Israel's God, so Gehazi left his lord, the man of God, Elisha, to be cursed with the skin disease that had initiated Naaman's journey of faith. As Spina points out, the Aramean outsider—through obedience to the man of God—became an insider to the community of those devoted to Yahweh alone. The Israelite insider failed to understand the ways of Yahweh as exemplified by Elisha, his lord. Thus, through deceit and greed, Gehazi was struck with a disease that marked him an outsider to the sanctuary of God's people (Lev 13—14). Although the characters are Israelites in the world of the story, the Judahite narrator acknowledges the primacy of Jerusalem's temple. In the canonical setting, Gehazi continued to serve Elisha, but he and his descendants are rhetorically cast from God's presence (Spina 2005, 91).

FROM THE TEXT

The writer was concerned with what is at the heart of a person of God. Humble obedience and repentance led to the cleansing of a skin disease that once marked a man who was an outsider, who, as a leprous enemy general, was at the farthest distance from Yahweh. This story also shows that an insider, the aide to God's man, Gehazi, could be utterly ignorant of God's ways in spite of serving God's servant Elisha. His eyes toward this world's goods symbolically caused him to be cast into the role of the outsider, even though he continued as Elisha's servant in the world of the story.

The Scriptures, especially many passages in the OT, have been accused of being ethnocentric, creating outsiders and marking boundaries against outsiders to Israel. Genealogies represent links between the patriarchs, and other passages advocate the removal of those whose gods Israel would serve. Nonetheless, many biblical stories demonstrate the authors' concerns to show that people from other places and cultures were models of faith for Israel. These "outsiders" recognized the ubiquitous nature of Israel's God and his mighty works. In desperation, they used reason and wits to serve or be served by God's people, confessing faith in Israel's God. They thus became the faithful people of God.

Christians are members of faith, cultural, and ethnic communities. Like many groups of people we develop "us-them" attitudes at conscious and unconscious levels, deciding from whom we should learn and who we should love. The Scriptures' lessons about outsiders to Israel challenge our boundaries, proclaiming them permeable, showing God's concerns for all the peoples of the earth, even and especially those who have been cast out or set aside as aliens and others. (For further reading, see Spina 2005 and Winslow 2005, 2012 and bibliographies there.)

f. The Lost Ax Head (6:1-7)

BEHIND THE TEXT

In the previous chapter Elisha received Naaman, the commander of the armies of the Arameans, into the community of Yahweh worshippers. This was the consequence of Naaman's healing, brought about by his willingness to obey the prophet's directive to dip seven times in the Jordan River. By healing Naaman, Elisha also helped the kings of Aram and Israel to extend this interval of peaceful relations between them.

The next pericope also involves the Jordan River, yet it features Elisha returning to the rural world of *the sons of the prophets* and their troubles. Resolving problems concerning a borrowed ax (6:1-7), poison stew (4:38-41), hungry people (4:42-44), and foul water (2:19-22) are part of the domain of Elisha, who works wonders on a small scale as well as raising to life a Shunammite boy, healing an Aramean commander, and enacting words and deeds that affect the armies of Israel, Moab, and Aram. This, and the subsequent pericopes through 2 Kgs 9:13, are all examples of Elisha's powers to help others and convey Yahweh's power to deliver.

IN THE TEXT

■ **1-2** Elisha was residing with or near *the sons of the prophets* when they desired a larger home near the Jordan River. Asking his permission indicates once again that they consider him their master, their "father." In this story, the other prophets act like children, his children.

■ **3-4** After obtaining his approval, they requested his presence as they logged trees and built the structure. While they may have considered him a sort of talisman, or beneficent presence, they also recognized that he was astute in practical matters, like a father would be. He had made their poisoned stew edible by adding meal to it (4:38-41), and he had put salt into the foul water of Jericho as he claimed Yahweh's words of cure over it (2:19-22).

■ **5-7** Naturally, the distressed logger sought Elisha's aid to retrieve the **borrowed** and then submerged ax head. Elisha readily followed him to the place in the river and threw in a piece of wood, which somehow made the iron ax (*barzel*) float. He told the logger to pick it up, again appearing like a resourceful father to an upset son.

This is another story that shows how the prophets with whom Elisha associated relied on him for practical help that was supplied with a miraculous twist. The case of the widow and her children resolved by the miracle of the oil in ch 4 was far more serious; the case of the stew less so, while this one seems petty and almost comical. Still, Elisha's comrade is disturbed and he runs to help. Like previous and subsequent pericopes, the floating ax head shows the prophet's support for his companions and attendants, as well as his interactions with kings and commanders.

g. Chariots of Fire (6:8-23)

BEHIND THE TEXT

Like the other traditions in chs 4—6, this narrative in the cycle of Elisha stories is not understood as chronologically placed, but rather as one in a series of memories about this man of God. The initial *waw* (conjunctive) is rendered "once when" in the NRSV of 6:8 and "while" in the NJPS, which indicates the looseness of the timing of this story that is lost in the NIV's "now," which implies that this is the next thing that happened. Neither the king of Israel nor the king of Aram are named, further underscoring that the story represents a tradition about an Aramean offense against Israel of indefinite timing, mitigated here by Elisha's prophetic performance and concluding in a lull in clashes between Aram and Israel. At first Elisha is simply called "the man of God."

Unnamed servants and attendants play significant roles as servants do in other Elisha tales. The use of the labels "king of Israel," "king of Aram," and "man of God" shows that, although a king of a nation is great (greater than a person of Israel or Aram), no king of any nation can measure up to the *man of God*! And this is the purpose of this collection of stories about the prophet Elisha.

IN THE TEXT

■ **8-10** Without specifying how, the narrator shows that the man of God knew what Aram's king said to his servants. When the king planned camps for attack at specific places, Elisha warned the king of Israel to avoid those areas, which the latter did after verifying Aramean presence. This advice to the king clearly shows that Elisha is supportive of him and Israel. Later in the story, the king would blame Elisha for the crises caused by an Aramean siege (v 31).

■ **11-14** So obvious and infuriating was this intelligence transmission that Aram's king summoned his servants and demanded to be told who was reporting his war camp sites to Israel's king (the Hebrew term *'ăbadîm* is used for these men who surrounded the king). One of these servants (*'ebed*) immediately identified the informant as the prophet Elisha. An Aramean close to his king assured him that Elisha knew the words the king spoke, even in his bedroom;

such was Elisha's reputation, even among enemy soldiers. Recall the Israelite servant girl who told her mistress, the wife of the Aramean general Naaman: **If only my master would see the prophet who is in Samaria! He would cure him of his leprosy** (5:3).

Aram's king then determined to capture Elisha and stop these transmissions of his strategy to Israel's king. At this time, Elisha was in Dothan, twelve miles north of Samaria, at the south entrance to the Jezreel valley. In Gen 37:17-20, an unnamed man wandering in the fields helped Joseph find his brothers in Dothan and there they threw him into a pit before selling him to slave traders who took him to Egypt. The pit at Dothan was a place of preservation for Joseph. Even though he lost his father, family, freedom, and favored status (for a time), the pit preserved his life while his brothers decided not to kill him. In this story, the lives of Elisha and his attendant were also endangered in Dothan, but their lives were preserved. In fact, in an ironic and comedic twist, the *Aramean soldiers* were taken captive by Elisha!

■ **15-18** Elisha's unnamed attendant is called *mĕšārēt* (minister) and *na'ar* (young man/boy) as Gehazi is in ch 5, not *'ebed* (servant). When he saw the Aramean armies, horses, and chariots, he turned to his master, who spoke the formula of prophetic reassurance: ***do not fear***. Elisha then prayed, not for deliverance, but that his young man would *see* the mountain full of **horses and chariots of fire**! The opened eyes of the boy contrast to the blindness that Elisha then prayed would strike the advancing Arameans (see Gen 19:11, in which the angels blind the men of Sodom to the effect that they cannot find the door to Lot's house). In these verses, the Aramean soldiers do not realize they cannot see. "They persist in trying to find Elisha and fail to recognize that the stranger offering to help them is the very man they seek. Elisha easily tricks them and frustrates their plans" (LaBarbera 1984, 643).

Horses and chariots of fire took Elijah to the heavens in the sight of Elisha (→ 2 Kgs 2:11-12; 13:14). Like Elisha's young helper, we must also focus on what may be unseen: the fiery armies of Yahweh standing at the ready against our foes. This story and others like it confirm the reality of God's salvation all around us even when we cannot see them.

■ **19-20** As a result of Yahweh hearing Elisha's prayers, the Aramean offense was blinded so that they could not see that Elisha himself was leading them the twelve miles to Samaria, Israel's capital, the home of Israel's king. The tellers and receivers of this story would delight in the absurdity of enemy warriors led to their potential doom by the very prophet they sought to capture and take to their king. Only when Elisha prayed that their eyes be opened, did they see that they were captives in Samaria, at the mercy of Israel, and realize that Elisha had led them there.

■ **21-22** The Aramean troops were Elisha's captives, trapped in Samaria and led to the king by Elisha's prayers and wit. Israel's king called Elisha **my father** when he asked permission to kill Elisha's captives and obeyed when Elisha insisted that they be fed and released instead. This was a lesson for everyone. The Arameans were not to be killed as if they had been taken through the prowess of the king's sword and bow.

That the king called the prophet **father** again underscores Elisha's place in the eyes of Israel; not only did his disciples among the prophets call him "father," but so did the king of Israel. The king respected Elisha when things went well for Israel, especially when his connection to Yahweh was so obvious, but the king blamed Elisha and Yahweh when things went wrong.

■ **23** The king (Joram) did not just give them bread and water, he gave them **a great feast** and let them return to their king. He went from one extreme to the other! The result of this escapade proved to be an end to the attacks against Israel by Arameans, for a time at least. As in the other Elisha tales, the meanings are conveyed through lively dialogue between the few characters involved, a format that would have been easy to perform and reenact and thereby transmit to delighted Israelites. Elisha is the hero again in this section of 2 Kings.

h. Famine in Israel Caused by Ben-Hadad's Final Siege (6:24—7:20)

BEHIND THE TEXT

In this narrative that continues throughout ch 7, the king of Aram is named. Ben-Hadad last appeared named in 1 Kgs 20. Even if it appears likely that he was the king in the previous accounts, it is important to ponder why the narrator chose not to name the Aramean king there and consider how this may allude to the narrator's unwillingness to specify a particular historical context.

In 1 Kgs 20, Ben-Hadad attacked Israel but ultimately was defeated by them. King Ahab allowed Ben-Hadad to live but was rebuked by a prophet for letting the man go whom Yahweh had devoted to destruction. "He said to Israel's king, 'This is what [Yahweh] says: "You have set free a man I had determined should die. Therefore it is your life for his life, your people for his people"'" (v 42). (See 1 Kgs 20:2, 13, 14; Ahab is usually called "king of Israel" in this chapter.)

Clearly, Yahweh had expected Ben-Hadad's reign and life to end at this point, but now Israel would suffer great disaster as a result of Ahab's unpredictable and unprecedented release of his enemy. When Ahab went on the offense to gain back Ramoth Gilead, he was specifically targeted by the king of Aram but killed by a random Aramean arrow (1 Kgs 22:29-38). Aram's king proceeded to raid Israel intermittently.

IN THE TEXT

■ **24-25** Second Kings 6:24—7:20 provides the dénouement to 1 Kgs 20. King Ben-Hadad again gathered all his troops against Israel, this time against the king's city, Samaria, an ungrateful reaction to the mercy shown him by Ahab, who had once had Ben-Hadad's life in his hands. Ben-Hadad's siege against the city of Ahab's successor (his son Joram [2 Kgs 3:1; 8:16]) obstructed any trade or food imports so that the people not only paid dearly for **a donkey's head** (unfit to eat [Lev 11; Deut 14]), but some were forced to eat their children!

■ **26-29** The desperate plight of the Samarians was demonstrated to the king by the woman seeking his help. Although his grain stores were fully depleted and he assumed this was what she wanted from him, he finally permitted her to explain the pact she had made with her neighbor to eat their sons. Her own son had already been eaten, but the other mother refused to kill and eat her son. This recalls the dire curses of Deut 28:15-68, especially vv 52-53, which threaten Israel with such famine that people will eat their own offspring should they be unfaithful to the covenant of Yahweh. This catastrophe also recalls the mothers who appeared before King Solomon, one with a live son and one with a dead one (1 Kgs 3:16-28). In this case, any "justice" would be a mockery of the concept. How could the king order the other mother to kill her son and eat him, even though this was the agreement and the plaintiff's son was already dead? This was a far greater dilemma than the one Solomon faced.

■ **30** Because this so tragically demonstrated the plight of his people, it pushed the king over the edge. He despaired of any help from Yahweh and threatened the life of Yahweh's most famous prophet of the time. The king tore his clothes and thus showed that he was in mourning over the impoverished city and possibly was humbly seeking help from Yahweh.

■ **31** His oath, *May God (Elohim) do thus to me and more if the head of Elisha the son of Shaphat remains on him today*, shows that he blamed Elisha for the siege and famine just as Ahab had blamed Elijah for the famine in his days (1 Kgs 17:1; 18:16-17). Whereas Elijah told Ahab rain depended on Elijah's word, Elisha had claimed no responsibility for the Aramean siege and resulting famine. In addition, this king of Israel must be the same king (Joram) who knew that Elisha had helped him avoid Aramean ambushes (6:8-10), who fed the Aramean soldiers whom Elisha had captured (vv 20-23), and who sought Elisha at the start of his reign (3:4-27) when Moab rose up against Israel, resulting in Israel's control of the battle (vv 21-25). Here, the same king blamed Elisha (and Yahweh) for Samaria's starving residents, thinking that Elisha somehow controlled the situation. Once again, Joram may have had Yahweh's words to his father on his mind: "Because [Ahab] has humbled himself, I will not bring this disaster in his day but I will bring it on his house *in the days of his son*" (1 Kgs 21:28-29).

Instead of seeking Elisha to pray for Yahweh's intervention, the king sought the prophet to take his life. If the famine is seen by Dtr as a consequence of Israel's leaders' unfaithfulness, innocent people were clearly suffering. We can understand the despair of the king, his sackcloth, and tearing of his garments. But his determination to kill someone—the man of God, Elisha—was perverse.

■ **32-33** Elisha, while consulting with elders, realized that a messenger sent by the king was coming to take his head. He called the king *the son of a murderer*, referring to Ahab who killed the prophets (2 Kgs 6:32; the NIV and NRSV lack "son of," but it is present in Hebrew). The Hebrew text here does not specify the king came in person and spoke to Elisha; the official **messenger** came and spoke (v 33), conveying the hopelessness of the king. The message was: **This disaster is from *Yahweh*. Why should I wait for *Yahweh* any longer?** However, Elisha expected the king or the power of office to harm him. When this incident and dialogue were repeated the next day, the narrator says that the king came down and Elisha spoke the words of Yahweh to him. Nonetheless, the passage could just as easily mean that Elisha's words were told to the king by a messenger (see 7:17-20).

Recall that Joram had good reason to be pessimistic if he knew the prophetic pronouncements against his father's house. However, when he was certain that Yahweh would destroy the armies of Israel when they went up against Moab (2 Kgs 3—4), he was proved wrong. He also should have known that Yahweh relented from the punishment Ahab deserved when Ahab repented (1 Kgs 21:20-29). If Yahweh would accept Ahab's repentance, how much more would he relent from planning disaster against Ahab's son. Joram did not have to choose to walk in the ways of his parents. Indeed, Joram *was* something of a reformer, for he removed the Baal pillar his father had erected, but not the calves of Jeroboam, which was a primary measure of faithfulness to Yahweh for the Judahite writer (2 Kgs 3:1-3).

■ **7:1-2** The messenger sent to arrest Elisha for immediate execution prompted the word of Yahweh to come, then and there. Elisha announced Yahweh's deliverance by means of prophetic oracle to the effect that scarcity would be replaced by plenty, prices would go down because of the great supply. The city gate would be the place of buying and selling again. This meant that the siege would be over on the morrow; impossible to imagine on human terms. The gate of the city continues to appear throughout the rest of this story.

In v 2, we are given the identity of the messenger from King Joram: his nearest aid (lit. *the third man on whose hand the king leaned*). The term "the third man" originally referred to the king's armor bearer but was used to mean a high-ranking official, one of the king's top three advisers or military leaders. Naaman was the one on whose hand the Aramean king leaned (2 Kgs 5:18).

The messenger's words that this could not happen even if Yahweh made **windows in the heavens** may reflect sheer wonder, as have many other responses to the seemingly impossible work of Yahweh. On the other hand, he sounds sarcastic and fully imbued with the king's hostile attitude toward Elisha (see LaBarbera 1984, 647-48). After all, he was the man sent to take Elisha's head from him. In any case, his incredulity came with a price. He would see the surplus of cheap grain *at the gate*, but would not eat from it.

The royal messenger returned to the king without Elisha or his head. As LaBarbera writes, this pericope "has the function of showing the ineffectiveness of the Israelite king. His military power is thwarted, his wisdom is non-existent. He cannot provide food for his people and he cannot even successfully orchestrate the assassination of Elisha" (646).

Perhaps we should give the king's official messenger some credit for not arresting Elisha and consider that Elisha's words concerning him may have impacted him to the effect that he left Elisha alone. LaBarbera thinks this official worshipped Baal, claiming that "windows of heaven" assumes Baal worship (647-48). But this argument is not compelling, for this phrase is used by Israel at Gen 7:11; 8:2; and Mal 3:10.

■ **3-5** This narrative abounds in wordplay that can only be heard or seen in the Hebrew text. The reversal of which Elisha spoke came, not by heaven's windows (*ărubbôt*) but by the feet and reasoning of four (*'arbā'â*) lepers who sat outside the doorway of the city gate, which must have been closed on account of the siege. These men were unfit for the army (see Lev 13—14), the lowest of the low, on the opposite end of the social spectrum from the king. (→ 2 Kgs 5:1, about the skin disease of lepers.) They say: **Why do we sit here until we die?** The outcasts were no great heroes, simply reasonable men, who decided it could not hurt to desert to the Aramean camp where they might be allowed to live and eat.

When they arrived at the camp after twilight the lepers only found food and provisions, no Arameans! Their good sense to desert to the Arameans shows up the king, whose despair led him to condemn God's man, who was always and only supportive of Israel. Later the king would refuse to believe the lepers' account or verify it without the advice of his servants.

■ **6-7** Here we learn what happened. Yahweh had caused the Arameans to hear the sounds of great armies coming against them—also at twilight—so they fled, assuming that Israel had hired foreign armies of Hittite and Egyptian kings to come to their aid. Although the timing was right, the text does not say the Arameans heard the outcasts' approaching footsteps magnified, only loud noises that Yahweh made them hear. We (along with Elisha and Elisha's attendant) know that the fiery horses and chariots and armies of Yahweh can go anywhere and do anything at Yahweh's bidding (6:8-23).

■ **8-9** The four men foraged through the Aramean tents, eating, carrying off and hiding valuables, moving through the deserted camp until they were struck with guilt should they wait any longer to share the good news with their fellow Samarians. It is ironic that men unfit to be soldiers discovered the lifting of the siege, while they were deserting, "the most unsoldierly act of all" (LaBarbera 1984, 648).

■ **10-12** When they reported to the king in Samaria, he assumed the worst: the Arameans were drawing them out of the city to ambush them, which is a great plan, but such was not the case. Joram's lack of trust in the deliverance that Yahweh promised is consistent with his pessimism elsewhere (2 Kgs 3:4-13; 6:31).

▪ **13-14** The king's unbelief and suspicion is frustrating for readers. Like the king, we were stunned at the extremity of the famine; mothers agreeing to kill and eat their own children. We now want the Samarians to feast as the lepers had. Like the lepers, we know the Arameans were long gone, but the king would not believe and let anyone go out. Consider the words of Isaiah to King Ahaz of Judah in Isa 7:9: "If you do not stand firm in your faith, you will not stand at all." This is another case of a faithless king who ignored the assuring words of Yahweh through his prophet. The Samarians continued to languish and die for at least several hours.

A servant of Israel's king was wise enough to suggest that the report be verified by using a few remaining horses. The horses would die anyway, he pointed out, just as the lepers had reasoned about themselves. This servant's remarks to their king are reminiscent of those of Naaman's servants who urged him to try what Elisha suggested: dip in the Jordan seven times; it is simple and what can it hurt? Again, we see that wise servants (*'ăbadîm*) are crucial to the story. The king agreed; he turned his servant's suggestion into a command: *go and see!*

▪ **15-16** The resulting search all the way to the Jordan River (a good distance of twenty miles) produced only more Aramean plunder, no Arameans. Elisha's words from Yahweh came true on the very next day as he had predicted; the provisions in the Aramean camp and the breaking of the siege led to cheap prices for life-sustaining grains for the Samarians.

▪ **17** The king appointed the same official messenger that he had sent to take Elisha's head to control the gate (his close attendant), who was then trampled by the hungry people at the gate.

▪ **18-20** The narrator provides the reason for this death. Reasons are given more in DtrH (Deuteronomistic History) than in other parts of the OT, but this is still unusual. When Elisha had announced deliverance, the king's official was incredulous (for good cause) and Elisha predicted his demise. The repeat of the dialogue at Elisha's door from 6:32-33 may be interpreting his death as punishment for unbelief. However, it also may prove to verify Elisha as a true prophet once again; for his prediction came true (see a test of a true prophet as expressed in 1 Kgs 22:28). Just as Elisha knew that prices would fall and the famine would end, so he knew the end of this man. Many other hearers of wonderful things do not die (for example, Abraham, Sarah, Samson's parents, Mary). Nonetheless, as mentioned earlier, this man represented the unbelieving king, who sought Elisha's life instead of Elisha's prayers.

FROM THE TEXT

This pericope reminds us of the case of the prophet from Judah in 1 Kgs 13, whose life and death became a parable for rebellious King Jeroboam, who had refused to listen to Yahweh's words through several prophets. That messenger-prophet suffered death for failing to keep one particular command. Even after hearing that he was killed by a lion after eating and drinking with the old prophet in Israel, the king, Jeroboam, did not repent. Similarly, in this story, King Joram did not turn to trust in Yahweh and respect his prophet Elisha after his official messenger died as Elisha had predicted. Second Kings 6:24—7:20 also reminds of 2 Kgs 5, the story of Naaman, the general on whom the Aramean king leaned for personal assistance as well as his military prowess. The Aramean commander took dirt from Israel and committed to worship Yahweh in his own land, while the royal Israelite official and messenger bore the brunt of his—and his king's—unbelief.

These are stories about learning from our own and others' experiences. This includes lessons from our traditions, from our Scriptures, stories and parables, and history. These things were written for our instruction that "we might have hope" (Rom 15:4). The psalmist writes that he will open his mouth in parables: "I will utter dark sayings from of old, things that we have heard and known, that our ancestors have told us. We will not hide them from their children; we will tell to the coming generation the glorious deeds of the LORD, and his might, and the wonders that he has done" (Ps 78:2-4, NRSV).

i. Restoration of the Shunammite's Land (8:1-6)

BEHIND THE TEXT

The story about restoration of the Shunammite's land is told as another example of Elisha's great powers. It may be out of order chronologically, but its place in the text here is the proper order for the purposes of the narrator, who also shows what happened to Gehazi as well as King Joram's unstable attitude toward Elisha. Gehazi figured in our introduction to the Shunammite and her son in 2 Kgs 4:8-37 (→ 2 Kgs 4:8-37; 5:19-27).

IN THE TEXT

■ 1 Clearly, Elisha was personally attached to the Shunammite woman and her son, whose birth he had promised and whose life he had restored (2 Kgs 4:8-37). He warned *her* and not the myriads of other Israelites about a coming famine. He said she could go wherever she chose, but she must quickly leave to escape Yahweh's famine. Because 2 Kgs 4:36-37 claims Elisha instructed her to take her son and leave (her own home?), which she did, some commentators believe this story reflects Elisha's directive then. However, since the dead, then revived, boy was in Elisha's room in their house, he was likely telling them to go out of his room.

A Yahweh-decreed famine in Israel fulfills Deut 28:15-68. Since Israel had rejected Jerusalem and its temple, offering instead sacrifices to Jeroboam's calves at Bethel and Dan, they suffered the curses of Deuteronomy all along, even before the Assyrian crisis. In the Elisha-Elijah tales, famine and war riddle Israel as Deut 28:20-25 threatens.

■ **2** The Shunammite woman and her whole household went to Philistia, the nemesis of Israel during the periods of the judges and early monarchy.

Although Solomon received tribute from Philistia (1 Kgs 4:21 [5:1 HB]), it was the target of Israelite attack during the reigns of Nadab (son of Jeroboam) and Zimri (see 1 Kgs 15:27; 16:15). The coastlands were not as subject to famine as the inland hilly regions, which naturally had less rain. Even so, Elisha made it clear the coming famine was called for by Yahweh. It is likely that she picked her refuge on the basis of its freedom from famine.

■ **3** Because she had been gone so long, she lost her house and land and petitioned to the king to have it restored. Her timing was perfect!

■ **4** Gehazi, identified as **the servant of the man of God**, just happened to be recounting tales of Elisha's great actions in the king's presence—at the king's request! Gehazi had left "Elisha's presence" with Naaman's affliction (2 Kgs 5:27), punished for his greed and his lies. Placed here, it shows that Gehazi was summoned from his duties with Elisha by the king or he moved to the king's court. His skin disease did not inhibit him from entering the king's presence, just as Naaman also appeared before the kings of Aram and Israel while suffering from the same malady.

■ **5-6** The Shunammite may not have had much of a case, given the length of her absence, but the king restored her land—and all its income—*because* Gehazi, Elisha's servant, had just told him that Elisha had brought her dead son to life. The Shunammite woman, not her husband, is the primary actor here as in 2 Kgs 4:8-37. Though not without a husband, she was the one that appeared before the king to regain her property. Recall that it was her idea to house the prophet in 2 Kgs 4:8-37.

j. The Murder of Ben-Hadad (8:7-15)

BEHIND THE TEXT

This pericope about Elisha, Ben-Hadad II, and Hazael continues the story of 1 Kgs 19:9-18 (see esp. vv 15-16) and 20:13-43 (see esp. vv 32-34 and 41-42). Recall that Yahweh told Elijah to go to Damascus of Aram and anoint Hazael, then Jehu, then Elisha (1 Kgs 19:15-16). But Elijah only anointed Elisha before leaving in fiery chariots while Elisha watched (2 Kgs 2). Furthermore, Yahweh had determined Ben-Hadad should die, but Ahab had released him (1 Kgs 20:41-42). Here, in 2 Kgs 8, we see how Yahweh's last orders to Elijah and plans for Ben-Hadad unfold.

The Kings Named Ben-Hadad

The name Ben-Hadad means "son of Hadad." The rain god Hadad was a popular deity in the ANE. The Canaanites referred to him as Baal, "lord," or Baal

Hadad. Several kings of Damascus were named Ben-Hadad. When Baasha, the king of Israel, attacked Judah, Asa bribed Ben-Hadad I (ca. 885-870 BC) to attack Israel from the north (1 Kgs 15:16-22). The account of the assassination of his son Ben-Hadad II (ca. 870-842 BC) by Hazael is described in this passage. Ben-Hadad III (ca. 802-798 BC) was the son of Hazael and ruled during the time of Jehoash, king of Judah (2 Kgs 13:24-25) (Bright 2000, 234, 240, 256).

IN THE TEXT

■ **7** Having replaced Elijah as God's man and spokesperson, Elisha finally went to Damascus of Aram, as Yahweh had ordered Elijah in 1 Kgs 19:15. The narrator connects his visit to King Ben-Hadad's illness. Ben-Hadad was the king who raided and attacked Israel repeatedly. Most recently he had kept them under siege until many starved to death, but earlier he was the one Ahab let get away (1 Kgs 20).

■ **8** Ben-Hadad recognized Elisha's prophetic role, asking Hazael to seek out Yahweh through Elisha to learn if he would recover. The king of Aram's consultation of Yahweh through Elisha contrasts to the consultation of Baal-Zebub of Ekron by Ahaziah, king of Israel. This angered Yahweh, who sent Elijah to tell Ahaziah that he would surely die (2 Kgs 1:1-4).

We know of Hazael through Yahweh's word to Elijah as the one he should anoint to be the Aramean king (1 Kgs 19:15). Elijah never made it up to Damascus before he left, but his successor Elisha, over whom Elijah threw his mantle, did—at this time. In either case, we must pause to consider the meaning of Yahweh's involvement in the politics of another nation when, as we see next, the Elisha-anointed Aramean king would bring disaster on Israel.

■ **9** Notice the cryptic way the account unfolds; the text does not say that Elisha went the distance to Damascus in order to anoint Hazael in obedience to Yahweh's word to Elijah, but the task fell to him when Ben-Hadad sent Hazael to Elisha with a request and camels loaded with gifts. Ben-Hadad clearly assumed that Yahweh, the God of Israel, could be consulted regarding his own health. Hazael called Ben-Hadad Elisha's son, indicating respect and honor for the prophet. This king must have been the same Aramean king who tried to capture Elisha in Dothan (2 Kgs 6:11-14).

■ **10-11** Elisha did not actually anoint Hazael the Aramean but told him that Yahweh revealed that Ben-Hadad would surely die, yet to report to the king that he would live. Recall that Yahweh had determined Ben-Hadad's destruction, but Hazael would not be a peaceful king. Elisha *severely set his face to the point of shame and he wept.*

■ **12-13** While his face was set, Elisha recognized the terrors (*evil*) Hazael would bring to Israel. Hazael thought he was much too lowly—a **dog**—to be worthy of *this great thing*! What the man of God called evil, Hazael called great.

According to inscriptions of Shalmaneser III, Hazael was a commoner ("son of a nobody") who seized Ben-Hadad's throne between 848 and 844 BC (Sweeney 2007, 319, 331-32). The same inscriptions claim Jehu came to the throne of Israel at about the same time.

■ **14-15** Hazael returned to Ben-Hadad, his master, with the exact words Elisha told him to say. Then, the next day, Hazael took matters into his own hands and smothered his king on his sickbed. He must have had the military and other leaders on his side, for he succeeded Ben-Hadad as king. This was done according to the word of Yahweh (1 Kgs 19:15-18).

Yahweh had expected Ahab to kill Ben-Hadad when Yahweh gave Israel victory over Aram in 1 Kgs 20, but, since he did not, Israel had suffered further at the hands of Ben-Hadad for many years. Now one of Ben-Hadad's own men killed him. Whereas Israel was beleaguered and harassed under Ben-Hadad, things would not get better with Hazael at the helm. Neither would the new king of Israel, Jehu, bring relief from bloodshed. At this point, the story shifts briefly to the kings of Judah.

FROM THE TEXT

Elisha interacted with kings and outcasts, wealthy women and starving widows. Some of these stories are about the most marginalized of people who were helped by Elisha and/or who helped him: servants, lepers, widows, and a childless then bereaved woman. Other accounts depict Elisha sought out by kings, either to seek a word from his God or to take his life. Often servants and other lowly characters are shown to be far more reasonable or more trusting than their commanders and kings.

As we have seen, Elisha's role included a number of practical works to help people that involved strange elements. To help the men among the school of prophets with whom he was associated, Elisha added salt for the bad water and the meal for the poisoned stew. He required that Naaman dip in the Jordan seven times, a procedure that led to Naaman's healing, even though the Aramean general had expected him to wave his hands and call on his God (2 Kgs 5:11).

Elisha performed some great miracles similar to those of Elijah, but with a bit more difficulty (compare 1 Kgs 17:17-24 with 2 Kgs 4:32-35). No one had yet surfaced among the **sons of the prophets** who might be a successor to Elisha as he had succeeded Elijah. (For further reading on Elisha's effect on the office of prophet, see Bergen 1999, 124-27 and passim.)

Both Elijah and Elisha are complicated characters, but so are most of the biblical figures whose stories are traced over the course of their lives. We must also recognize the playful quality of some traditions that were transmitted about the prophets' lives before being preserved as Scripture. As Clark Pinnock points out,

We are not bound to deny the Bible the possibility of playful legend just because the central claim is historical, as if to admit a few mythical elements into the biblical story as a whole would automatically classify the Christian story itself as myth. Unquestionably, Jesus' Resurrection had to happen for the gospel story to be true; but the same does not hold for Elisha's axe head or the fate of Lot's wife. (1990, 161-62)

In any case, just as the incidents and the resulting traditions became lessons for those who experienced or heard them, so also, as Scripture, these texts are lessons for us. God uses many ways to help us, as formidable as fiery horses and chariots, as clear as direct words, or as still and subtle as promises recalled at random moments. Even though we may suffer while waiting, God's deliverance will come.

k. The Kings of Judah, Jehoram and Ahaziah (8:16-29)

BEHIND THE TEXT

As is the custom throughout 1—2 Kings beginning with 1 Kgs 14:21, the redactor shifts to Judah to summarize the reigns of the kings there. Since the narrator's focus has mostly been on Israel since 1 Kgs 13, the information provided on Judah has been mostly formulaic or representing how kings of Judah interacted with Israel. Not until 2 Kgs 11—12 is there a lengthier presentation of events in Judah.

IN THE TEXT

■ **16-17** The summary of Jehoshaphat's reign is in 1 Kgs 22:41-47 [41-48 HB]; he reigned for twenty-five years in Judah, beginning in the fourth year of Ahab's reign. The reign of Ahab's son Joram of Israel had begun in the eighteenth year of Jehoshaphat, and Joram reigned for twelve years (2 Kgs 3:1-3). The king of Israel and the king of Judah shared the same name and their reigns overlap about seven years, for we learn here that in the fifth year of Joram of Israel's reign Jehoram, son of Jehoshaphat of Judah, began to rule. Jehoshaphat must have initiated a co-regency with his son Jehoram that lasted about two years. The narrator shortens the form of both kings' names here and there, but to distinguish them, I will call Israel's king Joram and Judah's king Jehoram. The formula for Jehoram of Judah's reign varies from most of the kings of Judah in that his mother's name does not appear (compare 1 Kgs 14:21; 15:2, 10; 22:42). We discover in the next verse the name of his wife.

■ **18** Jehoshaphat had created alliance between Judah and Israel through the marriage of his son Jehoram to Ahab's daughter. In 8:26, we learn that this was Athaliah, daughter of Ahab and mother of the next king of Judah, Ahaziah. The narrator blames Jehoram's wife, Athaliah, for the fact that he walked in the evil ways of the kings of Israel. Athaliah's rule and murders of her own grandsons are described in 2 Kgs 11. Jehoram died when he was forty, perhaps in the battle against Edom described in 8:20-22.

■ **19** The narrator assumes that walking in these evil ways was worthy of destruction, but Yahweh withheld judgment because of his promise to David concerning his sons' lasting dominion. The Hebrew term *nîr* is usually translated as if it was *nēr* (**lamp**), but *nîr* means political dominion (Sweeney 2007, 320).

■ **20-22** Nonetheless, the revolt of Edom and Libnah, vassal states of Judah, indicates judgment, lack of thriving, and perhaps Jehoram's death as a relatively young man. Earlier in 2 Kings, Edom joined Israel and Judah against Moab (ch 3; see also 1 Kgs 22:47 [48 HB] and 2 Kgs 14:7). David had brought the Edomites under Judah's control (2 Sam 8:13-14; see their connection to Esau [Edom] in Gen 25—28; 32—36). Libnah is a Levitical city in southern Judah (Josh 10:29; 21:13). No explanation is given for a city of Judah rebelling against its own king, but 2 Chr 21:10 justifies Libnah's revolt against Jehoram ***because he had abandoned Yahweh the God of his fathers***.

■ **23-24** The formula that wraps up Jehoram of Judah's reign matches that of other Judahite kings, but such is not the case for his son Ahaziah, for whom there is no concluding regnal formula. He was assassinated by Jehu on his rampage against Joram of Israel in 2 Kgs 9—10.

■ **25-26** When Jehoram of Judah died at age forty after ruling for eight years, his son, Ahaziah, the son of Athaliah, daughter of Ahab, granddaughter of Omri, began to rule. The biblical text here, like other ancient texts, reaches back to the founder of the Omride dynasty to identify Athaliah. We know from 8:18 that the daughter of Ahab was Jehoram's wife and thus Ahaziah's mother. This formula follows the pattern of other Judahite kings.

■ **27** The Judahite Dtr continues in the formulaic manner to describe Ahaziah's short reign in terms of his ***walk*** or ***path***, which was evil like that of Ahab. He was a grandson of Ahab since Athaliah was his mother and thus was the nephew of King Joram of Israel, the son of Ahab. Ahaziah is called *ḥătan*, to the house of Ahab, which means a legal relation, bound by marriage or other legal means. Depending on the context, the Hebrew term *ḥătan* is translated husband, father-in-law, brother-in-law, or son-in-law. It is a kinship bond created by other legal rituals such as circumcision (see Winslow 2005, 49-52). In Ahaziah's case, he was biologically related to Ahab's house through his mother. The marriage alliance of Jehoram and Athaliah made by Jehoshaphat with Ahab meant the new king of Judah was also legally allied to the dynasty of Omri, Ahab, Jezebel, and their descendants.

■ **28** Ahaziah's close alliance with Israel is seen in the fact that he joined his uncle Joram (son of Ahab) against the new king of Aram, Hazael. Joram was wounded at Ramoth Gilead, a contested city. First Kings 22 describes Ahab's plan to attack that city, the prophet Micaiah's protest, and Ahab's death in that attack. (See 2 Sam 12:27-28; → 1 Kgs 22:3.)

■ **29** After King Joram of Israel returned to Jezreel to recover, so also his nephew, King Ahaziah of Judah, went to Jezreel to visit him. This becomes the setting for what follows.

I. Jehu Anointed King of Israel (9:1-13)

BEHIND THE TEXT

The section 2 Kgs 9—10 includes one of the last actions of Elisha, the man of God in Israel. Elisha last appeared in Damascus when Hazael of Aram went to see him, sent by his king, Ben-Hadad, who was ill. Elisha did not "anoint" Hazael at that time (1 Kgs 19:15-17) but told him that Ben-Hadad would die and recognized that Hazael would be the next king, which occurred when Hazael killed Ben-Hadad (2 Kgs 8:7-15). In this section, he initiated the appointment of Jehu to the throne of Israel. Elisha lived to see the judgment Elijah had pronounced against the house of Ahab executed by Jehu.

Jehu's name means *Yah is he*. As noted in the Introduction (D4. Inscriptions), Jehu appears in Assyrian documents where he is called "Jehu son of Omri." This is ironic to later readers, for we know that Jehu destroyed the house of Omri, but "Omri" is the Assyrian name for Israel, demonstrating the international significance of Omri's dynasty. In the Black Obelisk (841 BC), Jehu is depicted as prostrate in front of Shalmaneser III, king of Assyria. The obelisk claims that Jehu severed his alliances with Phoenicia and Judah and paid tribute to Assyria. The Tel Dan inscription, found by Gila Cook of Abraham Biran's team in 1993, is relevant to this era as well. It is described in the Introduction (D4. Inscriptions) and will be discussed in the Behind the Text section for 2 Kgs 9:14—10:36.

IN THE TEXT

■ **1-3** Elisha sent a young prophet to the site of the ongoing battles at Ramoth Gilead to anoint Jehu with oil to be king of Israel by the word of Yahweh. Yahweh had initially directed Elijah to do this (1 Kgs 19:16), with two other tasks: anoint Hazael to be king of Aram and Elisha to be a prophet in Elijah's place. These tasks were fulfilled in reverse order and with variations. Elijah immediately found Elisha, who said his good-byes and followed Elijah. Elijah did not perform the other tasks; they were left to his successor, Elisha, who took over the king-making task. He did not anoint Jehu in person but ordered one of his followers to privately anoint and proclaim Jehu king of Israel. Again we see flexibility in prophetic performances. Neither Elijah nor Elisha had direct contact with Jehu.

■ **4-5** With no kings commanding the armies or even present on the battlefields of Ramoth Gilead, the time was ripe for Elisha to make his move. This compelled Jehu to make his, even if it had never occurred to him before. The young prophet went to Ramoth Gilead, found Jehu with other commanders, and called him to go inside, away from the rest.

■ **6** Jehu responded, left the other commanders outside, and went inside with the young messenger, who poured the jar of oil over his head. He pronounced him king of Israel with far more words than Elisha is reported to have told him to say. The biblical message motif is often this way; the message spoken to the target is more elaborate than the one the sender told the messenger. Compare what Yahweh told Elijah to say to Ahab in 1 Kgs 21:19 with what Elijah said in vv 20-24.

■ **7-10** Although Elisha had told him to say, "**Yahweh** says: I anoint you king over Israel" only, the young prophet added that Yahweh is "the God of Israel" (2 Kgs 9:6) and also repeated *Elijah's* announcement of Yahweh's judgment to Ahab in 1 Kgs 21. Elijah had delivered this judgment oracle to Ahab after Ahab and Jezebel had murdered Naboth and dispossessed his family of their vineyard (1 Kgs 21:21-24). Second Kings 9:8*b*-10 are the same words used in 1 Kgs 21:21-22*a*, 23. However, 2 Kgs 9:7-8*a* are not the same but carry the intention of 1 Kgs 21:21-24. Here: **You are to destroy the house of Ahab your master, and I will avenge the blood of my servants the prophets and the blood of all Yahweh's servants shed by Jezebel. The whole house of Ahab will perish.** Compare 1 Kgs 21:24: "Dogs will eat those belonging to Ahab who die in the city, and the birds will feed on those who die in the country." After Elijah's announcement of judgment, Yahweh noticed Ahab's repentance and delayed this judgment until his son's day.

■ **11** When Jehu returned, his fellow army officials (***servants of his lord***) asked why the ***madman*** came to him, and Jehu tried to put them off. Calling the young prophet who acted for Elisha a ***madman*** indicates their view of prophets—they were madmen, given to strange behavior, trances, visions, and ecstatic utterances (1 Sam 10:5-13; Hos 9:7). But this is ironic, for what happened next demonstrated *that they implemented* this ***madness***, based on the prophetic word.

■ **12-13** When they heard that the man said that Yahweh pronounced Jehu king of Israel, all of them thought it completely sensible to blow the *shofar*, make a royal carpet out of their garments, and proclaim Jehu king, following the words of the one they claimed was a madman. As army officers, they had the clout to support Jehu's overthrow of the house of Ahab. Clearly, none of them retained a shred of loyalty to King Joram. Both warrior kings (wounded Joram and young Ahaziah) had gone to Jezreel in Israel, leaving the Ramoth Gilead battle to the commanders, including Jehu. The weakness of the kings— one ill, one young, and both away—set the perfect stage for a coup.

3. Jehu Slaughters Ahab's Family, Judah's Royalty, and Baal Worshippers (9:14—10:36)

BEHIND THE TEXT

This section completes the story that began with events that occurred during the days of Elijah as described in 1 Kgs 17—22: Jezebel's murder of Yahweh's prophets, the contest on Mount Carmel that Elijah set up between Yahweh and Baal, the murder of Naboth, and the consequent curses against Ahab, his wife, and his descendants. It describes Jehu's usurpation of the throne of Israel from the dynasty of Omri, his purging of Ahab's descendants, and his subsequent reign over Israel. It is a violent beginning for Jehu and raises the question of the timing of this material. Under whose reign did the Jehu history emerge?

Given that chs 9—10 defend Jehu's bloody rise to power as Yahweh's way to punish Ahab's establishment of the Canaanite god Baal, they fit with the equally violent anti-Baal stance of 1 Kgs 17—19. Thus, scholars think 2 Kgs 9—10 was combined with 1 Kgs 17—22, to which the originally separate traditions of 2 Kgs 1 and 2 Kgs 2—8 were added.

Since Israel was not secure in the hands of the Jehu kings until the reign of Jeroboam II (789-757 BC), many believe that this combination of sources, called the Jehu history, transpired during that time. Later, this text was incorporated into the Judahite Hezekian Deuteronomistic History (Sweeney 2007, 331). As such, this section of DtrH condemned devotion to Jeroboam I's calves at Bethel and Dan. Because Israel rejected Jerusalem's hegemony, Israel was constantly at war with Aram and subject to coups and chaos.

All in all, the final form of the Jehu history shows Dtr's view that the northern kingdom should have been under Judah's control. It further shows his reasons that Judah fell into idolatry under Manasseh, who after all, was also a descendant of Ahab through Athaliah, who married into the dynasty of David and Judah.

The Tel Dan inscription's speaker was a king of Aram, probably Hazael. There he expressed success in conquering named kings of Israel and Ahaz of the "house of David." (→ Introduction, D4. Inscriptions.) The biblical text attributes these killings to Jehu, but the inscription provides an extrabiblical witness to their deaths and to "the house of David" at the time of Hazael's rule in Aram.

The Tel Dan Inscription

The Tel Dan inscription, written in Aramaic of the ninth-eighth century BC, includes three fragments that are legible enough to reconstruct. Dan was a territory in the north of Israel, but Aram encroached upon it throughout the tenure of the kings of Israel. The only kings of Israel and Judah slain at the same time were Joram and Ahaziah, whose names in the original Hebrew forms are Yoram A'ehoram and Ahaziyahu. Hazael was reigning in Damascus when they were killed, and he had met Elisha (2 Kgs 8:7-15), who sent another prophet to anoint Jehu king of Israel. "Hadad" refers to the god of the Arameans. Although royal inscriptions are known to exaggerate military victories, this one sparks a question about the possible connection between Hazael, Elisha, and the Jehu rebellion. This reconstruction is found in Berlyn (2007). See also Schniedewind 1996, "Tel Dan Stela."

> Hadad made me king. And
> Hadad went in front of me.
> [...] [...] ram
>   son of [...] king of
> Israel, and [...] killed
> [...]yahu son of [...]g of
>   the House of David. And
> I set [...] their land into
> [...] other [...] led
>   over Is[...] siege upon [...]

IN THE TEXT

■ **14 So Jehu . . . conspired against Joram.** This claim by Dtr puzzles readers who know how the events unfolded: Yahweh had told Elijah to anoint Jehu as Israel's king and implied that Jehu would bring judgment on Baal worshippers, especially the house of Ahab (1 Kgs 19:16-17). Elisha had just sent the young prophet to anoint Jehu privately. Jehu seemed reluctant to divulge what had happened, and the other commanders had to compel him to tell. While these foundational steps may not be considered conspiracy, Jehu and his companions were all too eager to make his rule a reality from the prophet's visit forward. Thus, they took the necessary steps forward and **conspired against Joram.**

Even apart from the prophetic performance, the absence of their wounded king and the king of Judah signaled a need for new leadership that was fueled by their ambition. In any case, this military revolution against the ruling king occurred while Joram's forces were attempting to secure the contested city, Ramoth Gilead, against Hazael, the new king of Aram.

■ **15-16** Jehu's first order was to enforce secrecy; to prohibit the news reaching Joram, who was recovering in Jezreel. The second was to ride to Jezreel himself.

■ **17-20** The dialogue between the watchman and the king, as they watch the messengers meet and join the approaching party, suspends the plot. We know what Joram did not know: Jehu was after the throne of Israel. Joram was expecting the approaching party to bring news of the battle with Aram. The messengers who were ordered by Commander Jehu to join him would not have been disloyal to their king since they would not have realized that he was pursuing Joram's throne and his life. Once the king and the watchman realized it was Jehu, they assumed he was still a loyal army commander. Otherwise, Joram and Ahaziah would not have ridden out to meet him.

■ **21-23** The reader understands the significance of Jehu halting in Naboth's vineyard more than Joram did, for he simply asked: **Peace, Jehu?** Jehu answered harshly, recalling the recent words of the young prophet in the inner room. When he referenced Joram's mother's harlotries and sorceries, Joram understood—too late—that this was treachery.

■ **24** Joram had reigned for twelve years, but now his reign—and his life— were brought down by Jehu's arrow through his back as he fled, an arrow that was shot so forcibly, it protruded through his chest. He was the last king of the Omride dynasty.

Even though the narrator does not give the assassinated king a concluding regnal summary, given his assassination, we shall look back on his reign. From Joram's first appearance in 2 Kgs 3, he had been worried about disasters, real or potential, assuming Yahweh was against him (3:13-14; 5:7; 6:24-33). He was likely aware of Elijah's prophecy against the house of Ahab for his parents' murder of Naboth; Jehu certainly was (9:21-26). The introductory royal formula of 2 Kgs 3:2 says that Joram took down the Baal stone his father had made but that he continued supporting the pilgrimages to Jeroboam's calves. From this we know that Joram was *not* a Baal worshipper. He had a mixed relationship with Elisha, calling him "my father" in 2 Kgs 6:21 but seeking his life during the time of the great famine reported in 2 Kgs 6. Joram was the king who worried over an Aramean threat when Naaman was sent to him for healing instead of Elisha. He spent most of his reign in conflict with Arameans, which may not have been necessary had his father Ahab terminated Ben-Hadad instead of releasing him (1 Kgs 20:13-43).

■ **25-26** Jehu's orders to his crewman concerning Joram's body provide new information that Jehu and Bidkar had been riding together behind Ahab when they heard a different version of Yahweh's oracle against Ahab (than the one found in 1 Kgs 21:20-24). First Kings 21 does not specify that Ahab would die on Naboth's property (but dogs would lick his blood in the same place they licked up Naboth's) or inform us that Naboth's sons were killed with him. Still, if they had survived him, his vineyard would have gone to them and not to Ahab. Since Elijah met and cursed Ahab as the latter went to take possession of it, Jezebel must have found a way to kill Naboth's sons as well. Elijah's oracle had prophesied the deaths of Ahab and Jezebel's male descendants, one of whom was Joram, whose body was cast on Naboth's ground. Other sons would be slaughtered in Jehu's sweeping coup d'état.

It is not clear that Ahab ever took full possession of Naboth's vineyard, for he repented when Elijah pronounced judgment against him. The land is simply called **the portion of Naboth the Jezreelite** in v 21, and v 25 says: **Lift him up, and throw him out on the portion of the field of Naboth the Jezre-**

elite; for remember, when you and I rode together behind his father Ahab how Yahweh lifted up this oracle against him. After repeating a heretofore unheard oracle from Yahweh about the blood of Naboth and his sons, Jehu repeated his instructions to Bidkar (*his third man*; → 2 Kgs 7:1-2): *Lift him up, and throw him out.* Jehu did not mention Elijah as this source of this oracle against Ahab from Yahweh.

■ **27** Ahaziah, the young king of Judah, son of Jehoram and Athaliah of Ahab (→ 2 Kgs 11:1), saw Joram killed by Jehu. He fled toward Beth Haggan, which is southwest of Jezreel. Jehu ordered him to be struck down in a chariot near Beth Haggan, which may have occurred since Ahaziah turned toward Megiddo and died there. Jehu did not explain why he pursued the king of Judah, but Ahaziah was the grandson of Ahab. All of the kings of Judah from Ahaziah on were descendants of Ahab through Athaliah (his sister or daughter).

■ **28-29** Even though assassinated far from home, Ahaziah's servants transported his body in a chariot and buried him with his fathers, kings of Judah, in the city of David. Chariots figure prominently in 2 Kgs 1—9. Although notice of his death is not accompanied by a regnal formula, because Jehu assassinated him, the text cites the year of his ascent to the throne. Here it says it was the eleventh year of Joram, instead of the twelfth as in 2 Kgs 8:25.

■ **30** Jezebel has not been in the story since she acquired Naboth's vineyard for her husband by killing Naboth. The queen mother, a grandmother by this time, reenters the story here, just after Jehu struck down her son Joram in Naboth's field. Upon hearing that Jehu came into the city of Jezreel, Jezebel prepared to receive him and waited for him at her window. *She heard, she put black powder on her eyes, she arranged her head (she made it well or pleasing), and peered out from the window.* She thus prepared herself not only for meeting her son's murderer and successor but also for her burial, a burial that never happened. Jezebel was hardly attempting to seduce him.

■ **31** Jezebel, aware of the death of her son and her similar fate, called out from the window **peace**, or, is everything well? This had been her son Joram's question to Jehu, which was never answered affirmatively. Jezebel continued by calling Jehu, *Zimri, slayer of his lord*, a reference to the commander who killed King Elah, son of Baasha, and became king for seven days until he was killed by Omri, Jezebel's father-in-law (1 Kgs 16:15-20). Jehu, of course, had just killed his lord. By calling Jehu "Zimri," Jezebel also taunted Jehu by claiming that he would have a short reign and come to a similar end (Sweeney 2007, 336). Jezebel's challenge from her upper window recalls Sisera's mother in Judg 5, who waited for her son who had been deceptively—and treacherously—killed by Jael. Jezebel's taunts hastened her death, which may have been her plan. Jezebel was mocking him in her last words.

> As the daughter, wife, mother, mother-in-law, and grandmother of kings, Jezebel would understand court politics well enough to realize that Jehu has far more to gain by killing her than by keeping her alive. Alive, the

dowager queen could always serve as a rallying point for anyone unhappy with Jehu's reign. The queen harbors no illusions about her chances of surviving Jehu's bloody *coup d'état*. (Gaines 2000)

■ **32-33** Jehu heard and **lifted his face to the window, saying: "Who is with me, who?"** Jezebel's eunuchs indicated that they were with him by looking out at him and then obeying his command to throw Jezebel down, where she was trampled by horses. The immediate support of servants and soldiers for Jehu indicates fear as well as possible dissatisfaction with the Omrides or "the house of Ahab," as the biblical text calls the Omride dynasty. Jehu exuded recklessness, coupled with mastery (9:20 and passim). In addition, the prophetic force of these narratives shows that Yahweh was determined to punish the house of Ahab through Jehu, who did not do so without the compliance of others. Such compliance by fearful Israelite officials would go to extreme lengths.

■ **34** Callously eating in Jezreel—in Jezebel's palace—while she was trampled to death, indicates Jehu's extreme contempt for her and his mastery of the palace in Jezreel (compare Absalom's odious actions against David's concubines [2 Sam 16:20-22]). Finally, he told others to bury her because of her royal status in Phoenicia.

■ **35-37** Although parts of Jezebel's body remained, nothing was buried, as indicated by Jehu's recall of Elijah's curse (1 Kgs 21:23). Jehu elaborated on it when he continued—still, as he said, quoting Elijah: **And the dead body of Jezebel will be like dung on the face of the field in the portion of Jezreel, so that they will not say: "This is Jezebel"** (v 37). We do not have a previous record of Elijah expanding in that way, although this would be parallel to Jehu and Bidkar's expanded firsthand witness of the curses against Ahab and sons (vv 25-26).

Although Jehu ultimately concluded that she should be buried because she was a king's daughter, even this did not occur, as Jehu said, to fulfill Elijah's prophecy against Jezebel. It seems strange that Jezebel's skull, hands, and feet were not considered worth burying, but the rest of her body (had it remained) would have been buried.

■ **10:1-3** The Jehu rampage continues in ch 10, and readers grow conflicted, knowing, on the one hand, that Yahweh appointed Jehu to Israel's throne (1 Kgs 19:16), and that Yahweh called for the house of Ahab to be extinguished. On the other hand, we are appalled by Jehu's bloodshed and callousness toward children who were put to death on account of their grandparents' sins. In Deut 24:16 this is prohibited; see also Jer 31:29-30 and Ezek 18:1-32 (which were far later than the time of Jehu). From a prophetic perspective, Ahab and Jezebel were the ones punished by the demise of their dynasty. (→ Behind the Text and From the Text for 2 Kgs 9:14—10:36.)

Jehu remained in Jezreel to implement a strategy of taking over the kingdom of Israel from the house of Ahab, who had **seventy sons** in Samaria; these were King Joram's brothers, sons, and nephews. All these males would be considered descendants of Ahab and were in line for Joram's vacated throne. Jehu wrote to the boys' guardians and the leaders of Jezreel (they were all in Samaria with the sons) to suggest they select a king from among Ahab's house and get ready to defend him.

■ **4-7** But they were too afraid to stand up to Jehu. They not only passively paved the way for his rule by refusing to fight him but also actively slaughtered their charges, the boys they were raising, and sent their heads to Jehu in compliance with his orders. Jehu's letter asks for the *heads of the men of the children of the king*, but *men* may be another way of saying "males." The seventy had guardians who were bringing them up and thus were not fully grown.

■ **8** Again, Jehu shows extreme callousness. Hearing of the arrival of the heads of Ahab's sons, he ordered them divided and placed where everyone would see them at the city gate and then had a good night's sleep.

■ **9** Jehu asked for the "righteous" people of Jezreel to judge concerning the two piles of heads: *You are righteous . . . who killed all of these?* In other words, "You tell me! I own what I did concerning Joram, but can you tell me how this happened?" Although it may seem like it, Jehu was not feigning innocence for these deaths, which occurred upon his orders to the fearful officials in Samaria. It is a thinly veiled threat against those loyal to the house of Ahab in Jezreel, since the Jezreelites knew the boys were decapitated in response to Jehu's threatening words. In most translations, Jehu proclaimed the innocence of the Jezreelites, which was obvious to them, as was the fact that he was responsible for their deaths.

During the first attempt at monarchy among the tribes of Israel during the judges period, Abimelek killed seventy of his own brothers and manipulated the men of Shechem into supporting him as king (Judg 9:1-6).

■ **10-12** Jehu again defended the mass bloodshed by referring to Yahweh's curse on the house of Ahab through Elijah. Then Jehu proceeded to slaughter everyone remaining in Jezreel who had served Ahab, including priests, before riding to Samaria with his fellow soldiers. Yahweh, in Hos 1:4, deplores Jehu's violence: "I will soon punish the house of Jehu for the massacre at Jezreel, and I will put an end to the kingdom of Israel."

■ **13-14** Finding the brothers of the recently murdered king of Judah, he learned they were on their way to visit the Israelite royalty whom he had just had slaughtered. He and his supporters killed forty-two of the royal family of Judah at the pit at Beth Eked, without proclaiming a defense or referring to Yahweh's vengeance on the house of Ahab. Even if some of these men were sons of Athaliah, the oracles against Ahab's house restricted judgment to Israel (see 2 Kgs 9:8; 1 Kgs 21:21).

■ **15-16** *Jehu found Jehonadab coming to meet him*. Again *found* implies that Jehu was looking for him. Jehu knew of Jehonadab and his loyalties to Yahweh, for Jehu confessed that his heart was in accord with Jehonadab's heart. When Jehonadab assured Jehu that his *heart was straight, right in line with* [Jehu's]

heart, Jehu offered him his hand and a ride to demonstrate his zeal for Yahweh in Samaria. Again a chariot figures prominently in the narrative.

In Jer 35:6-18 "Jonadab" son of Rekab is referred to as the leader of the Rekabites who commanded his people to avoid wine, build houses, plant or own vineyards, but to live in tents. The Rekabites were commended by Yahweh for keeping the commands of Jonadab, in contrast to Judah who did not keep commands of their leader, Yahweh.

■ **17** Jehu's zeal for Yahweh meant killing everyone else in Ahab's family remaining after the officials killed Ahab's sons, including women and girls. This probably included those very officials, servants of Ahab, guardians of his sons, who had beheaded them.

■ **18-19** At this point Jehu lied to the Samarians, saying *he* would serve Baal more than Ahab. With Jehonadab at his side, and hearing his stated reasons for killing all that belonged to Ahab (the word of Yahweh), wary Samarians might have suspected his ruse. But Jehu threatened those known to serve Baal with death if they did not appear.

■ **20-22** Hopeful Baal worshippers believed Jehu—or feared for their lives—and gathered to sanctify Baal at the festival. They donned the identifying garments Jehu provided for them.

■ **23** Jehu trusted the ministers of Baal to recognize any servants of Yahweh and cast them out.

■ **24** Jehu *and* Jehonadab offered sacrifices to Baal after warning soldiers to kill anyone (hence the provided garments) who escaped once the slaughter began. Elijah had massacred all of the prophets of Baal in his day (1 Kgs 18:40), but apparently there were enough worshippers remaining to fill the entire temple to be extinguished by Jehu.

■ **25-27** Second Kings 3:2 notes that Joram had removed the Baal stone or pillar that Ahab had made, but here other sacred pillars as well as the entire temple of Baal that Ahab had constructed were demolished and the place turned into a public **latrine** (v 27; see 1 Kgs 16:32). The first notice of the pillar removal by Joram was to demonstrate that Joram was not as evil as his father, Ahab (see 2 Kgs 3:2 and 1 Kgs 16:29-33). Joram's brother, Ahaziah (who reigned for only two years before him), also served the Baals, did not remove any pillars, and was considered as evil as Ahab (1 Kgs 22:51-53 [52-54 HB]).

■ **28-31** A formulaic DtrH evaluation and summary of Jehu's reign begins here and continues in vv 34-36. The narrator twice cites Jehu's failure to remove Jeroboam's calves at Bethel and Dan while praising him for removing Baal worship from Israel. For this Yahweh promised him a four-generation dynasty. Clearly, in spite of Jehu's proven zeal for Yahweh, the calves meant failure to follow in Yahweh's Torah and also brought on the problems described in the next verses. Jehu's devotion to Yahweh coupled with his maintaining the calves is one of the indicators that Israelites may have viewed the calves as a seat for their invisible god, Yahweh, who brought them out of Egypt (compare 1 Kgs 12:25-28 and Exod 32:1-8).

■ **32-33** Israel under Jehu lost control of the Transjordan. These verses, as part of the regnal summary, maintain that this loss of those tribal lands east of the Jordan was a penalty for Jehu's sustenance of Jeroboam's calves.

■ **34-36** As is the custom, the writer refers readers to the annals of the kings for specifics about Jehu's reign, which was twenty-eight years. All that DtrH saw fit to describe from this long hegemony was Jehu's rampage against the house of Ahab. (See, for example, 1 Kgs 14:29; 15:7, 23, 31; 16:5, 14, 20, 27; 22:39, 45 [46 HB].)

FROM THE TEXT

As observed earlier, this section is disturbing. It illustrates the concept of retributive justice by claiming that Jehu was rewarded by God for ***doing what was right in God's eyes according to all that was in his heart to the house of Ahab*** (10:30). The prophets had declared the reasons for the complete destruction of Ahab's entire house: Jezebel had killed the prophets of Yahweh and Naboth and his sons under Ahab's nose, and together they established Baal worship in Israel. Nonetheless, we must ask: Does bloodshed warrant more bloodshed? Is it ***right in God's eyes***?

Hosea 1:4 provides another perspective, deploring Jehu's bloodshed in Jezreel, and pronouncing nonspecified punishment on Jehu that would include "an end to the kingdom of Israel." Hosea, prophesying during Israel's last days under Jehu's descendant Jeroboam II (2 Kgs 14:23-29), expressed God's lament over Jehu's slaughter in the city. Bloodshed would again be part of the punishment and end to Israel. And yet we see God's mercy extended toward Ahab when he repents after hearing Elijah's pronouncement of punishment against him (1 Kgs 21:27-29).

But the merciful delay of punishment complicates matters further. This meant Ahab's sons and extended family would pay the price for his and Jezebel's sins. Joram (Ahab's second son to be king) had removed the Baal pillar, yet was constantly fearful that God was determined to destroy him. His fear was not misplaced, for, after twelve years, Jehu killed him and his entire family, including women, children, and everyone associated with Ahab.

This raises concerns addressed in Deut 24:16, Jer 31:29-30, and Ezek 18:1-32, all of which clearly state that children shall not die for the sins of their parents. Such legal rulings also represent God's justice. Those passages may well have been written in reaction to overweening violence that takes the lives of innocent people, such as Jehu's massacres. While not indiscriminate, they were nearly so and went well beyond punishing the targets of the prophetic word.

These chapters picture events and notions that demonstrate the tension in the Bible between punishment for sin and mercy for those who repent and go God's direction. The traditions were intended to be a deterrent to listeners who should tremble at the result of disobeying God and a reminder that innocent people suffer when leaders shepherd their charges away from God. According to Joshua—2 Kings (the Former Prophets in the Hebrew Bible or the Deuteronomistic History), God brought punishment on both Israel and Judah as nations, viewing the people as a corporate identity. Even the righteous persons in those nations suffered, as did the family of Achan in Josh 7. We understand punishment given to those who are guilty (individualism), but we have difficulty understanding how God could punish the innocent with the guilty; a concern also reflected in Jer 31:29-30 and Deut 24:16. This was also Abraham's concern in Gen 18:16-33.

4. Athaliah Murders Her Grandsons and Claims the Throne of Judah for Six Years (11:1-21 [1—12:1 HB])

BEHIND THE TEXT

The story continues by turning to Judah, first in the early days of Jehu's reign, then skipping forward to his seventh year of reigning in Israel (2 Kgs 12:1). This chapter shows what was happening in Judah during Jehu's coup against the house of Ahab and then seven years later. Jehu reigned twenty-eight years, so he ruled during and twenty-one years after Joash became king in Judah.

The people of Judah had also suffered at the hands of Israel's Jehu, who murdered their king and forty-two of his relatives while they traveled to visit family. The royal houses of Israel and Judah were related on account of the marriage Jehoshaphat and Ahab arranged between Athaliah of Israel to Jehoram of Judah. Chapter 11 forms the background for ch 12, the story of Joash's reform in Judah. In ch 11, we learn how, as an infant, Joash escaped death at the hands of his grandmother because of the swift action of his aunt Jehosheba. We recall the similar fashion by which Moses escaped death at the hands of the king, his soon to be "grandfather." This pharaoh was the father of the princess who delivered him from the waters (at the suggestion of his sister) and mothered him in the royal house of Egypt (Exod 2:1-10). Clever women rescued future leaders for the sake of God's people.

IN THE TEXT

■ 1 The background for the opening verse of this section is 2 Kgs 8—9, especially 9:24-29, the account of Jehu's pursuit and killing of King Ahaziah of Judah. Ahaziah was the son of Jehoram, the previous king of Judah (2 Kgs 8:16-23), and Athaliah (an Israelite princess from the house of Ahab). King Ahaziah had been supporting Joram, king of Israel, in battle at Ramoth Gilead. He then visited the wounded king at Jezreel (vv 28-29). When Israelite army commander Jehu heard through Elisha's emissary that he would be king (9:1-10), he left the battlefield at Ramoth Gilead with a party of soldiers and met the kings Joram and Ahaziah on Naboth's land. Jehu killed Joram (son of Ahab and Jezebel [v 22]) there, and had Ahaziah killed after a chase (vv 11-29).

A generation back, Athaliah had been given in marriage to Judah's crown prince Jehoram to cement an alliance between Ahab of Israel and Jehoshaphat of Judah. Because 2 Kgs 8:18 calls her the daughter of Ahab (see 2 Chr 21:6), while 2 Kgs 8:26 calls her the daughter of Omri (see 2 Chr 22:2), readers have to decide which text is using "daughter" in the general sense. (The NIV changes the latter to "granddaughter of Omri"). It is most likely that Athaliah was Omri's daughter and Ahab's younger sister, for 8:16 is part of the later DtrH redaction of materials, whereas 8:26 is taken from the earlier Judean royal annuals (Thiel 1992, 511-12). Furthermore, Athaliah could be considered a daughter of the house of Ahab in the general sense, for the biblical text frequently uses the term "house of Ahab" to speak of the Omride dynasty but never "house of Omri" (unlike Assyrian royal annals).

As Israel's king, Ahab could easily have married his sister to the prince of Judah, creating the political alliance that was destroyed by the events of this chapter. Second Kings 8:18 blames Jehoram *and* Ahaziah's walking in the evil ways of the house of Ahab on Athaliah, who brought Baal worship to Judah as a result of the marriage alliance created by Jehoshaphat and Ahab. Ever since the birth of Athaliah and Jehoram's son Ahaziah, all subsequent Judahite kings were in the lineage of Ahab, who "did more evil in the eyes of **Yahweh** than any of those before him" (1 Kgs 16:30).

As we have seen, young King Ahaziah, son of Athaliah, was killed by Jehu. Athaliah changed her status from queen mother to ruling queen and **proceeded to destroy the whole royal family**, all her own sons and grandsons, as well as the sons of any other wives of Jehoram and Ahaziah. Although no explanation is given for her monstrous murders of her own grandchildren, Athaliah, like the rest of us, knew that when the eldest son of Ahaziah became king, she would lose power and status. Instead, she grasped power and status by killing all males (or so she thought) in the Judahite royal family.

Athaliah murdered Judah's royal sons just as Jehu had murdered the royal sons of Israel and some of their relatives from Judah (2 Kgs 10:1-14). Athaliah of Ahab's house would have been a likely target of Jehu as well, but she went on the offense, orchestrating senseless bloodshed to her own advantage, for a while.

■ **2** This verse affirms that Jehosheba was a daughter of King Jehoram but does not mention Athaliah as her mother. She may be the daughter of another wife of Jehoram, as Josephus and Jerome suggest, or she thwarted the evil designs of her own mother by saving baby Joash, one of her nephews. Like the pharaoh of Exod 1—2, Athaliah felt threatened by sons, allowing daughters to live, yet it was a daughter who saved a small son, just as daughters saved Moses—his sister, his mother, and Pharaoh's own daughter. This is the only time Joash's name is mentioned in this chapter until the last verse.

■ **3** The MT (Hebrew text) says that Joash *was hidden with her* ("her" meaning his wet nurse mentioned in v 2 or Jehosheba herself, but the former is more likely) for six years. The temple was a sanctuary from foreigners (including Queen Athaliah). Joash was an infant and small enough to be swept away and not missed by the executioners. Jehosheba's quick and sustained actions to preserve life made possible the coup six years later led by Jehoiada, the priest (v 9).

■ **4-8** After waiting six years, Jehoaida called for *the commanders of the hundreds of the Carites and the runners* (the latter is usually translated soldiers, officers, or **guards**), who figure prominently throughout the successful coup to put a son of David, the son of Ahaziah and grandson of Athaliah, on the throne of Judah. Jehoiada **made a covenant with them**, which is described in these verses, and **showed them** young Joash, who is still called **the king's son**, even though his father, Ahaziah, has been dead for six years. Jehoiada's plan was to change that, to make Joash king with the help of those who guard the palace, temple gates, and the temple. He was preparing for anyone who may be loyal to Athaliah by using the time when the guard changed so the greatest number would be present, without calling attention to something unusual.

Carites are not mentioned outside of this chapter (see also v 19), not even in 2 Chr 22:10—23:21, but they may have been the same as the "troops" or army of 2 Kgs 11:15. They are presented here as loyal to Jehoiada the priest and to the house of David.

■ **9-12** They followed his instructions to the letter. At this time, Jehoiada gave them **the spears and shields** of David from the temple, which *would* have aroused suspicion, but the time for action was here (v 10). Apparently, they did not have weapons when they guarded the royal, civil, and sacred structures. The commanders, Carites, and runners were lined up in an arc to protect the boy king's position by the pillar at the entrance of the temple. Jehoiada immediately brought out the six-year-old prince, placed on him the crown and the covenant, and made him king. The tangible covenant would have been stored in the ark of the covenant (Exod 25:22; 40:3; Num 4:5; Josh 4:16). This included anointing, clapping, and public proclamation: *"May the King live"*—a great noise that Athaliah could not fail to hear (compare 1 Kgs 1:38-40 concerning Solomon's ascension to the throne).

■ **13-14** As Jehoiada intended, Queen Athaliah came out to the temple at the sound of **the** *runners* **and the people**. The text leads us to look at this scene with her eyes: **Behold, the king standing by the pillar according to the law with the commanders and the trumpets, and all the people of the land were celebrating and blowing trumpets!** She immediately knew what had happened and was now happening. She knew that the young boy standing with crown and covenant was her grandson who had been preserved to rule Judah in her place. She knew her days—minutes—were numbered. She had one response: **Treason!**

■ **15** Remaining in control of the coup, Jehoiada ordered the ***commanders of the hundreds and the overseers of the army*** to seize her and kill any supporters, certainly a deterrent for anyone who would have stood with her. This is the first time the army is mentioned, so it may be that with the show of force of the Carites and other armed guards, Jehoiada was now inviting the army to support his coup by seizing Athaliah and bringing her out among the ranks of soldiers and away from the sacred temple of Yahweh to be killed.

■ **16** She was brought ***through the way of the entrance of the horses to the house of the king and died there.***

■ **17-18** At this time, ***the priest Jehoiada cut a covenant*** between Yahweh, the boy king, and the people, by which they covenanted ***to be the people of Yahweh, and between the king and the people.*** All the people of the land understood the implications of this; they could not be attached to Yahweh *and* to Baal. They destroyed the Baal temple and killed the named priest of Baal, **Mattan,** established by Athaliah.

■ **19** All of the armed officers, including the Carites, and all the people brought the king down from the temple to the gateway for soldiers at the palace, where Joash sat upon the throne of Judah after being confined to the temple for the first six years of his life. The Davidic dynasty was reestablished after a six-year interval under Athaliah, its only break in Judah's history. The people were fully included by Jehoiada and fully participated; they owned this renewal of the covenant and supported the new king. This could have been an unstable time; the king was a small boy. His lack of prowess could have led to another revolution if the entire army and **people of the land** were not entirely on board. As it was, Joash was backed by everyone.

■ **20** Thus the critical moments had passed. Jehoiada's carefully orchestrated plan, initiated by Jehosheba when she saved the infant Joash from death at the hands of his grandmother, was entirely successful. All the people **rejoiced** and were at peace. Yahweh's covenant ***was cut*** with the people, and they vowed adherence and commitment. The juxtaposition of this summary statement about the peace of the city and the joy of the region with a reiteration of Athaliah's slaying at the king's house suggests that her death was as much a cause for rejoicing and peace as the installment of the new king. The royal palace is never called *her* home; it is always "the house of the king," underlying the fact that she was a usurper of the throne of Judah.

■ **21 [12:1 HB]** The very young age of the king (whose name is now spelled **Jehoash** here and in 12:1, 2, 4, 6, 7, and 18 in the Hebrew text) is emphasized here. The royal (Jehosheba) and priestly (Jehoiada) leaders of Judah deemed seven years as long enough to wait to overthrow the queen mother, once the queen wife, a worshipper of Baal, who had established and propagated Baal worship in Judah. (See 2 Kgs 8:16-27.)

5. Joash of Judah Repairs the Temple (12:1-21 [2-22 HB])

BEHIND THE TEXT

Joash's reign began a new era in Judah's history, one in which the Baal worship established by alliances with Israel had been removed. Jehu of Israel had removed Baal worship in Israel with far more violence. In the next generation, Joash's son Amaziah faced Israel's Jehoash, grandson of Jehu, in battle and was defeated by him (14:8-16).

Joash ruled Judah for forty years and was only forty-seven when he was assassinated by his servants (11:20-21 [11:20—12:1 HB]). His son Amaziah executed his father's assassins. He was a good king also and reigned twenty-nine years before *he* was assassinated by pursuing conspirators (2 Kgs 14:19). At that time, Amaziah's sixteen-year-old son, Azariah, became king and reigned for fifty-two years, walking **straight in the eyes of Yahweh** like his own father, except without removing the high places where people offered sacrifices (2 Kgs 15:1-4).

Azariah is known as Uzziah in Isa 6:1. Because of his separation from the royal courts on account of "leprosy," Azariah's son Jotham ruled with him until he died (2 Kgs 15:5-7) and then on his own for sixteen more years. After Jotham died, his son, Ahaz, became king and reigned for sixteen years as well. Isaiah prophesied within the courts of Jotham, Ahaz, and finally Hezekiah (twenty-nine years), the first reforming king to remove the high places (Isa 1:1).

12:1-3

This short survey accounts for 182 years of Judah's history: Joash (40), Amaziah (29), Azariah (52), Jotham (16), Ahaz (16), and Hezekiah (29). Although Dtr's narrative about the first four kings in this list is more elaborate than a series of formulas, it is brief. Dtr introduces each king, mentions a high point of his reign, if there was one, and noting that these Judahite kings from the line of David (and Athaliah) did not take down the high places. Unlike his ancestors, Ahaz, son of Jotham, followed the worship of the kings of Israel, sacrificed at the high places, and immolated his own son (2 Kgs 16:1-4). Four good kings in a row are followed by one who violates all the covenant obligations. (→ "Kings and Prophets—Divided Kingdom 931—586 BC" following In the Text for 1 Kgs 22:51-53 [52-54 HB].)

IN THE TEXT

■ **1-3 [2-4 HB]** Joash's coronation is described with vivid and staccato plot movements. Here his reign is introduced with variations from the previous Judahite introductory formula. His age is mentioned and then his first year is aligned to the corresponding year within the reign of Jehu of Israel, followed by the length of reign. His father, Ahaziah, is not mentioned, but his mother is named, following the usual Judahite formula. Compare the formula that introduces Jehoash with the one introducing the later Josiah, who was eight when he began to rule (2 Kgs 22:1-2). Both young kings were concerned with repairing and restoring the temple of Yahweh and both died tragically.

Joash's rule is assessed by Dtr as good—*he did right in the eyes of Yahweh because the priest Jehoiada instructed him.* Dtr offers the qualification also added to his evaluation of Joash's direct descendants, the subsequent good kings of Judah: **the high places** where people sacrificed were not taken down. Later both Hezekiah and Josiah removed the high places during their reforms.

■ **4-5 [5-6 HB]** This passage shows that the temple was in disrepair at the time of Joash's coming to age. He had lived in this temple for six years as a young child, unbeknownst to Queen Athaliah, who would have had no interest in maintaining the temple of Yahweh. These verses do not mention when Joash told the **priests** to **repair** the temple with the collected temple tax and donations whenever and wherever repairs were needed (v 5 [6 HB]; see Exod 30:13-16; Lev 27:30-33).

At some point in his reign, long before his twenty-third year when he was thirty years old, he ordered the priests to be guardians of the physical state of the temple. Attention to the temple signifies remembering Yahweh and obedience to his laws, as well as nationalistic reform and throwing off the yoke of stronger nations. In this case, it was Israel and the house of Omri/Ahab, overthrown by Jehu in Israel and now by Jehoiada with Joash in Judah.

■ **6-9 [7-10 HB]** **The priests**, however, including **Jehoiada**, ignored the young king's directives. They continued to collect the temple tax until the twenty-third year of his reign, when Jehu of Israel died, a transition that meant the time for restoring the temple had come. Seeing no reparations, Joash challenged the priests, who had no explanation for their dereliction but handed over the money they had received to the king. By affirming that they would *not* repair Yahweh's house, they were agreeing that responsibility for its restoration and maintenance was now the king's. Joash's twenty-third year coincided with the death of Jehu of Israel and the ascension of Jehu's son Jehoahaz to Israel's throne, the same year that Hazael of Aram began incursions into Israel.

■ **10-13 [11-14 HB]** The king collected further donations, counted them, and gave them to workmen to repair the extensive damage to Yahweh's house. The chest at the right of the altar was unavoidable by anyone approaching the temple.

■ **14-16 [15-17 HB]** The funds were used only for paying the workmen and not for making the temple vessels. **Guilt** and **sin offering** monies were given to the priests for their support (v 16 [17 HB]); these cash offerings associated with sin and guilt of the people did not come into the temple.

■ **17-19 [18-20 HB]** Joash's attempts to reassert Judah's autonomy and worship of Yahweh were crippled when the Arameans rose against Jerusalem and accepted tribute in exchange for withdrawal. Because **Hazael king of Aram** threatened Jerusalem with his armies, Joash was forced to hand over remaining temple funds and other temple and palace treasures (vv 17-18 [18-19 HB]).

Allying with the Arameans in this way also indicated further rejection of Israel's influence over Judah. The Arameans continued to threaten Israel and Judah until the time of Jehu of Israel's grandson Jehoash (son of Jehoahaz) after Elisha's death (2 Kgs 13:20-25).

■ **20 [21 HB]** This could not have been a popular policy, for Joash was assassinated by his own servants and replaced by his son Amaziah. The story of Joash is rewritten by the much later Chronicler who explains his assassination theologically as a consequence of apostasy and murder. According to 2 Chr 24:15-27, Joash was killed because, after Jehoiada died, he was influenced by officials to serve Asherim and idols, and even commanded Jehoiada's son Zechariah to be stoned in the house of Yahweh between the temple and the altar of burnt offering (v 21), a murder mentioned by Christ as the last slaughter of a prophet narrated in the OT (Matt 23:35; Luke 11:51). (Chronicles is the last book of the Hebrew Bible, and Jesus uses these murders as an example of the range of Jewish history.)

■ **21 [22 HB]** None of that is present in 2 Kings, however, where Joash is presented as a good king, embattled by Aram, and then assassinated by his servants, leaving readers to assume his murder was the result of his tribute to Aram. Nonetheless, we recall Elijah's curse against males of the house of Omri, to whom the kings of Judah were descended through Athaliah, a marriage alliance created by Jehoshaphat, descendant of David, and Ahab, son of Omri.

6. Elisha Dies after Prophesying Limited Victory for Israel over Aram (13:1-25)

12:20—
13:3

BEHIND THE TEXT

Chapter 13 begins a longer literary unit that provides Dtr's description of the reigns of four kings: two in Israel (ch 13) and two in Judah (14:1-22). This way of dating one nation's king in terms of the years of the other nation's king continues through 2 Kgs 17, when Israel is brought low by their erstwhile ally, Assyria.

The focus of ch 13 is Jehoahaz and his son Jehoash, Israelite kings of Jehu's dynasty. We expect the condemnation of their worship of Jeroboam's golden calves at Bethel and Dan, but find surprising the Judahite Dtr's affirmation of Yahweh's response to prayer for deliverance and compassion for Israel (vv 4-5, 23). And yet 13:3-8 is cast in the same mold as Israel's story in the book of Judges: sin, oppression, prayer, deliverance, return to sin.

IN THE TEXT

■ **1-3** The introductory regnal formula for an Israelite king begins this chapter about Jehu's son Jehoahaz, who is first mentioned in the concluding regnal formula of Jehu as the son who succeeded him (10:34-36). Dtr had commended Jehu for wiping out Baal—and the house of Ahab—from Israel with the promise of a dynasty comprising four descendants; but he faulted Jehu for retaining Jeroboam's cultic sites (vv 30-31). Jehoahaz is faulted for the same reason, **kindling** Yahweh's anger.

As in the book of Judges, Yahweh **gave them into the hands of an oppressor**. This time they are given to Aram, the familiar enemy, to **Hazael** and his son **Ben-Hadad** (see 1 Kgs 19:15-18). As in much of Joshua—2 Kings (DtrH), the oppressive enemy rises against Israel as the result of Israel's sin.

■ **4** When **Jehoahaz** turned to Yahweh to implore him, Yahweh saw their oppression, the oppression Yahweh had sent (compare Exod 3:9). He heeded Jehoahaz's prayer, which again emphasizes Yahweh's responsiveness to human entreaty, even in contexts such as this.

■ **5** Yahweh provided a savior that meant Israel was not lost to Aram; the people did not lose their homes. Some commentators (such as Sweeney 2007, 357) think that the savior refers to Jehoahaz's son Jehoash, who defeated the Arameans by allying with Assyria when he ruled (→ 2 Kgs 13:15-19, 23, 24-25 below). This savior could also refer to Jehoash's son Jeroboam II (see 14:27).

However, the implication in this verse is that this deliverance happened during Jehoahaz's time; *he* was the king whose prayers Yahweh heeded. In this case, the savior is unnamed or is Jehoahaz himself. Like the charismatic military leaders of the judges period, he rallied troops so that Israel retained their place and their nation.

■ **6-7** And yet, because Jehoahaz kept the calves in Bethel and Dan and **the Asherah pole . . . in Samaria** (v 6), the armies of Israel were depleted by the Arameans, which was Yahweh's doing. Thus, Yahweh is depicted as desiring to deliver Israel from enemies in response to prayer, but using enemies to oppress in response to continued sin. This is Dtr's way of handling realities that are interpreted through the lens of judgment for sin and blessing for obedience, but with an infusion of mercy when Yahweh chose.

As noted earlier, Israel and her kings may have thought they could appropriately worship Yahweh at the Bethel and Dan shrines, but the Judahite DtrH knew otherwise. This is supported by the later account of Jehu, who purged Baal worship from Israel but maintained the calf shrines. However, the prophets who spoke against the shrines in Jeroboam I's lifetime made clear Yahweh's view of the shrines (1 Kgs 13). We have these stories, but did they?

■ **8-9** The concluding regnal formula for Jehoahaz introduces us to his son Jehoash, who succeeded him.

■ **10-13** These formulaic verses about the next Israelite king of the Jehu dynasty, Jehoash, summarize his reign, but they do not tell the entire story. He is featured in the next two sections, which include the story of Elisha's death, an account of his final prophetic activity, the life-giving power that exuded from his grave, and Jehoash's related victory over the Arameans.

■ **14 Elisha** has not been heard from in quite some time, as John Wesley points out in his *Notes on the Bible*:

> [In] all the latter part of his time, from the anointing of Jehu, which was forty five years before Joash began his reign, we find no mention of him, or of any thing he did, 'till we find him here upon his death bed. Yet he might be useful to the last, tho' not so famous as he had sometimes been. (2 Kgs 13:14)

Here Elisha was on his deathbed and Jehoash, the grandson of Jehu, whom Elisha had anointed many decades previously, rushed to his side, weeping, honoring Elisha with his presence, his tears, and his words: *"My father, my father! The chariots of Israel and its horsemen!"*

These words from the king of Israel are the very words Elisha himself had uttered when Elijah was leaving him (2 Kgs 2:12). (See also 6:8-23.) That the king held the prophet of Yahweh in high esteem and functions as a son or disciple to him indicates that Joash (and his father and grandfather as well) did not consider Jeroboam's calf shrines a blight on Israel's worship of Yahweh. Notice that neither Elijah nor Elisha railed against the calves, but rather against Baal worship. The Judahite Dtr despised the calves.

■ **15-19** Elisha asked Jehoash to perform a prophetic pantomime with him as a gracious and final way of confronting Jehoash's greatest crisis at this time: Aram. Because Jehoash heard Elisha's interpretation of the shot arrow, perhaps he should have known to strike the ground more often, but this is unclear. For the other players in the dramas, the meaning of prophets and prophetic activities are difficult to anticipate, and they often walk away endangered, stymied, or sullen (like Ahab in 1 Kgs 20:35-43). Jehoash, who was mourning Elisha's imminent death, must have felt both sad and hopeful. The incident prefigures Jehoash's successful attacks against Aram (2 Kgs 13:25), which thwart, but do not end, the threat Aram poses to both Israel and Judah (15—16). These promises and acts of deliverance for Israel form a motif that binds this larger section of chs 13—14 together (13:4, 23; 14:26-27).

■ **20-21** The great prophet Elisha died, but his power lived on as depicted in this scene, in which a dead man comes to life after his body **touched Elisha's bones** (13:21). The resurrection motif is associated with both Elijah and Elisha (1 Kgs 17:17-24; 2 Kgs 4:8-37). When his time on earth was over, Elijah was taken to heaven. Elisha's dead body remained but gave life to another man. Prophets are defined by their words, by their voicing of Yahweh's words, and by doing what Yahweh requires—living out the divine life before Yahweh's people. Elisha's infusion with the divine life even after he died restored life to another dead man, foreshadowing other resurrections in the Bible. (To review Elisha's powerful prophetic ministry, → 2 Kgs 2—8, 18—19.)

■ **22** This verse may seem to be an abrupt shift, but it turns our attention to **Hazael** of Aram who oppressed Israel during the reign of Joash's father. It thus provides a context for relaying the fulfillment of Elisha's prophecy to Jehoash concerning his striking of Aram under Hazael's son, Ben-Hadad. We recall the final scene of Elisha' life that included the king of Israel and Israel's great enemy, Aram.

■ **23** Dtr shows further sympathy for Israel by affirming Yahweh's compassion for them on account of **his covenant with Abraham, Isaac and Jacob**. This covenant with the fathers was the reason Moses gave to Yahweh in Exod 32:11-14 when he begged Yahweh not to destroy them then. Although this section is peppered with moments depicting Yahweh's attention to Israel and parallels Exodus in this regard, such depictions are rare in DtrH.

■ **24-25** Jehoash's hastening to Elisha's deathbed and his words of honor and grief led to a unique prophetic moment announcing that Jehoash and his armies would attack Ben-Hadad and recover towns of Israel.

FROM THE TEXT

In this section, as elsewhere in the Deuteronomistic History (DtrH), the narrator viewed disaster as the result of covenant-breaking. Any modicum of peace was attributed to obedience, Yahweh's sympathy for his people, or his covenant with Abraham, Isaac, and Jacob (2 Kgs 13:23). In 2 Kgs 11—13, the compassion of Yahweh for Israel is demonstrated as inextricable from his parental concern that they avoid the apostasy of Jeroboam I's calves at Bethel and Dan. In the next chapter, particularly 2 Kgs 14:25-27, Dtr calls Jeroboam II the deliverer of Israel. He was sent by Yahweh, in spite of Israel's continued service to the calf shrines.

Consistently in DtrH, Yahweh used other nations to punish Israel and Judah (for example, 2 Kgs 13:3; 15:37). This is not the only biblical explanation for disaster or harm befalling nations and individuals, however. Other sections of the Bible, including the NT, show that adversity can be the result of evil intentions, nature, mistakes, or occur in order that the work of God can be revealed (John 9:1-3). Yahweh also sent deliverance out of compassion (2 Kgs 14:26-29) or in response to prayer, such as Hezekiah's in 19:14-32.

The consistent references to the annals of the kings of Israel and Judah indicated that Dtr was aware of other material that he did not choose to select. Along with formulaic evaluations and some particular comments about the kings, Dtr chose incidents from the kingdoms of Israel and Judah, the most elaborate showing kings' interactions with prophets, the men of Yahweh. The books of Kings are thus suitably within the division of the Hebrew Bible called the Prophets.

Throughout 1 Kgs 17—2 Kgs 13 Elijah and Elisha physically declared the thoughts of Yahweh to the people to whom they were sent, as Samuel and Nathan had done in their times. Elijah and Elisha also raised the dead to life; contact with Elisha's bones even raised a dead body (2 Kgs 13:21)! Prophets spoke, trekked, challenged, and otherwise embodied obedience to the everlasting Deliverer of Israel. These prophets were defined by what they said and by obeying Yahweh in action—living out the divine life as a model for all of us.

This prefigures the words, walk, touch, and resurrected life of Jesus. Like some of the sayings of Jesus, some of the directives and actions of Elisha were difficult to understand. Some followers left Jesus, bewildered and afraid (John 6:35-69), while others believed and worshipped him (9:38).

E. The Dynasties of Israel and Judah until Assyria Invades (14:1—17:41)

BEHIND THE TEXT

Pertinent to an understanding of these chapters of 2 Kings is an explanation of the escalating power of Assyria and how it affected Israel, Judah, and their northern neighbor, Aram (Syria). The center of Assyria was northeast of Israel and was bordered on the west by the Tigris River, on the east by the Upper Zab River, and on the north by the Kurd Mountains. Assyria's geographic area expanded far beyond these natural features of Mesopotamia through the conquests of its surrounding areas by ambitious warrior rulers. Its great cities were Asshur, Nineveh, and Arbela, which were independent city-states in 2500 BC.

In the second millennium BC, Assyria was infiltrated by Babylonians from the south, the Amorites from the southwest, and the Hurrians/Mitanni from the north. In the mid-fourteenth century BC, the Amarna age, Assyria became a powerful political entity, which suffered temporary declines as a result of people movements and military pressures from the Arameans to the west and Babylonians to the south. Nonetheless, Ashur-resh-ishi I (1132-1115 BC) and his sons restored the prominence of Assyria and expanded it into an empire.

In the eleventh century BC, Assyria was weakened by further incursions by Arameans and Babylonians, and their failure to effectively administrate areas of their empire. However, Assyria revived and thrived under Ashur-dan II and his sons in the tenth century BC, as well as throughout the next dynasty, the Calah kings (883-824 BC). (For further information on the early centuries of Assyrian history, see Grayson 1992b, 732-39.)

One of these Calah kings was Shalmaneser III (858-824 BC), to whom King Jehu of Israel (ca. 842-815 BC) paid tribute, rejecting an alliance with Aram against Assyria (noted in the Introduction at D.4 and comments on 2 Kgs 9:1-13). The Black Obelisk, now in the British Museum in London, depicts Jehu kneeling and paying tribute to Shalmaneser III. It was found in Nimrud in Iraq. Jehu's purge of Baalism naturally severed all connections between Israel and Phoenicia and thus its seaports, for 1 Kings associates Israel's service to Baal with the Phoenician princess Jezebel, who became Ahab's wife and queen of Israel.

Jehu's alliance with Assyria unleashed the fury of Aram upon Israel during the reigns of his descendants. Aram under Hazael wreaked great havoc on

Israel until Assyria defeated the Arameans at Damascus in 802 BC and then turned to menace Israel and Judah. The Assyrian armies backed off at that time, however, because of troubles in their own land (for specifics, see Grayson 1992b, 743-44).

Tiglath-Pileser III (Pul), who ruled Assyria from 744 to 727 BC, returned to the west to enlarge the empire he inherited. Tiglath-Pileser III's annals of 734 BC mention Ahaz of Judah and call Israel the land of Omri (*ANET*, 284). Assyrian inscriptions of Tiglath-Pileser III claim that he placed Hoshea as king over Israel (ibid., 284; Hobbs 1985, 203). Second Kings 15—17 tells the story differently, but also lists Hoshea as the last king of Israel. When Pul died, Hoshea rebelled and refused to pay tribute, which brought the punishing Assyrian armies into Samaria. The annals of Pul's successors, Shalmaneser V and Sargon II, announce the fall of Samaria in 722 BC.

When Samaria fell and Israelites were deported to Assyria, the Assyrians also destroyed Dan (Tel el-Qadi), the site of the four-horned altar from the Iron Age, which is also where the Aramaic inscription referring to Hazael's defeat of a king from "the house of David" was found (→ Introduction D4. Inscriptions and "The Tel Dan Inscription" sidebar at Behind the Text for 2 Kgs 9:14—10:36). In 612 BC Nineveh, the capital of Assyria, was taken and burned by a coalition of Babylonian and Median forces. The Assyrian Empire was subsequently taken over and enlarged by the armies of King Nebuchadnezzar, to include Judah (2 Kgs 24:10-17).

In this section, we will continue to examine Dtr's interwoven account of Israel and Judah, emphasizing the significance of the text as it is ordered in 2 Kings. The interwoven account indicates that although the two nations were separate entities, each one's story must be told in relation to the other. Judah was ruled by sons of David (who, after Jehoram, were descendants of Ahab, Jezebel, and Athaliah), while the kings of Israel through Zechariah were descended from Jehu, the Israelite general who destroyed the Omride dynasty.

1. Judah Has a Few Good Kings (14:1-22; 15:1-7, 32-38); Israel's Kings Follow in the Sins of Jeroboam (14:23-29; 15:8-31)

a. Amaziah's Reign in Judah (14:1-22)

IN THE TEXT

■ 1 Early in the reign of Jehoash of Israel (the king who would mourn Elisha and repossess towns of Israel taken by Ben-Hadad of Aram [2 Kgs 13:14-24]) Amaziah, son of Joash, began to rule Judah. The forty-seven-year-old Joash was killed by his own servants, the reason Amaziah was placed on the throne at this time. Second Kings 12 told Joash's story: he repaired the house of Yahweh, captured Gath, and paid tribute to Hazael to appease him and avert Aram's besiegement of Jerusalem.

■ **2-4** The Judahite royal formula includes Amaziah's age at inauguration, the length of his reign, his mother and her home: Jerusalem, and Dtr's evaluation of his reign. Amaziah is compared to David; he was righteous, but not as righteous as David. Amaziah did right like his own father, Joash. He did not remove the high places, a major concern of Dtr, even if the people were worshipping Yahweh at the high places. David was not censured for not removing high places, because the temple had not yet been built. Solomon, David's son, found guidance from Yahweh at the high place of Gibeon (1 Kgs 3:2-5). After receiving God's promise at Gibeon, Solomon returned to Jerusalem and stood before the ark *there* (v 15). Once the temple at Jerusalem had been built by Solomon, our narrator denigrates any worship outside of it. During the reign of Solomon's son Rehoboam, after Israel had seceded from Judah, the people built more high places, Asherah poles, pillars, provoking Yahweh's jealousy by committing all the abominations of the nations that were driven out of the land (1 Kgs 14:21-24).

■ **5** Once his rule was firmly established, young Amaziah avenged the death of his father by killing those who had murdered him (2 Kgs 12:21). This assumes that for a while Amaziah had to appease those who had conspired against his father and gain support from others in Judah's militia. First Kings 2:46 is similar in that it tells the story of Solomon's early days after his father died, which included killing his enemies.

■ **6** Dtr locates the reason Amaziah did not kill the families of Joash's murderers as grounded in the words of the law of Moses found in Deut 24:16, indicating that the law of Moses was known and appealed to by Dtr. He claims that Amaziah knew and submitted to this law. The reason is given here to Amaziah's credit; he acted **in accordance with what is written in the Book of the Law of Moses**. This statement also indicates that it was somewhat remarkable that whole families were not exterminated for the crimes of some of the members, as happens elsewhere in Israel's story (Josh 7:20-26) and that this law was *written* at the time Dtr wrote. (See Gen 18:16-33; Jer 31:27-30; and Ezek 18:1-32; → From the Text for 2 Kgs 10.)

■ **7** The kingdom was firmly in his hand, and Amaziah was on a roll. He gathered courage from his success against Edom, which had revolted against Judean rule during the days of Solomon (1 Kgs 11:14-22) and Jehoram (2 Kgs 8:20-22).

■ **8** Although this section begins and ends as an account of Amaziah's reign in Judah (14:1-4, 17-18), the midsection (vv 8-14) reads more like a positive Israelite perspective on Jehoash's success over Judah in response to an ill-advised challenge by Amaziah. Some scholars see a Jehu history interwoven into the Judahite Dtr's longer theological story about the two nations (Sweeney 2007, 363).

The king of Judah raised a challenge against Jehoash king of Israel, grandson of Jehu, attempting to throw off northern dominance or at least to renegotiate their relationship to be more balanced, which Amaziah felt was now warranted. At the most extreme, Amaziah may have been seeking to reunite the long-divided kingdoms, returning to the days of Solomon and David, during which all the tribes were ruled from Jerusalem. But, if so, this was unrealistic, given Israel's dominance and vassal relationship with Assyria.

■ **9** Jehoash used an insulting fable to warn Amaziah to be satisfied with his gains and stay home in peace. The fable made the point that Amaziah's challenge was unwarranted, ridiculous, and would worsen Judah's oppression by Israel. "Don't even think you can take us!" said Joash. "You are a bramble, easily trampled and we are a cedar, way out of your league and no 'marriage' is possible." This is reminiscent of Jotham's speech in Judg 9:7-20 and an example of the parable genre used in diplomatic missives as early as the fourteenth century BC (the Amarna period) when King Labayu of Shechem wrote to the king of Egypt in his own defense (Sweeney 2007, 365; Solomon 1985, 114-32).

Second Chronicles 25:6-16 gives another more serious reason for the battle between Amaziah of Judah and Jehoash of Israel. Amaziah did not pay the 100,000 Israelite soldiers loaned to the Judean army to fight against Edom.

■ **10** Jehoash's disdain for Amaziah's challenge may have been the result of his own victories over Aram, as well as his backing by Assyria. In any case, Israel was the more powerful of the two nations, and Jehoash gave Amaziah the opportunity to withdraw the challenge.

■ **11-12** Israel attacked Judah's forces at Beth Shemesh, met Amaziah *face to face* on the western border of Judah, defeated his armies, and captured him.

■ **13-14** Then King Jehoash acted like the conquering armies of Egypt, Assyria, and Babylon by pillaging Judah, taking hostages and goods, harshly punishing Judah for Amaziah's audacity to suggest a union or more balanced contract. He took him back to Jerusalem to see the wall breached and the temple ransacked of its treasures. The process of enemies raiding Judah's temple began after Solomon died when King Shishak of Egypt looted the house of Yahweh and the king's house (1 Kgs 14:25-26). More recently, Joash the father of Amaziah had plundered the temple and sent the treasures to Hazael of Aram, who then withdrew from Jerusalem (2 Kgs 12:18-19 [19-20 HB]). Some mercy is shown, nonetheless, in that Amaziah remained alive to continue to rule over Judah.

■ **15-16** After this, Judah never threatened Israel again. Jehoash's son, Jeroboam II, also a descendant from Jehu, continued Jehu's dynasty, the longest and most powerful dynasty in Israel's history, which rivaled in size of area the kingdom of Solomon.

■ **17-18** The concluding regnal formula for Judah's king Amaziah appears before the explanation for his death, which was not a natural one. Inferred by the reference to the annals of the kings of Judah is that there are more details and reasons listed there.

■ **19** Like his father, Amaziah was conspired against, pursued to Lachish, and murdered by people of Jerusalem who either did not want or were not able to take over the throne themselves.

■ **20-21** Officially brought back to and buried with his ancestors in the city of David, Amaziah's body was given honor in death. The people of Judah (this could refer to the army) put his teenage son on the throne, continuing the Davidic dynasty. The question remains: Were the people of Judah supportive of the regicide or appalled by it? In any case, the consequences for the king killers is not mentioned here or in 2 Kgs 15, the story of Azariah's reign. This implies that the dissatisfaction with Amaziah was widespread, and the people had higher hopes for his son, who was loyal to the next king of Israel, Jeroboam II.

■ **22** Azariah continued the work of his father in strengthening Judah's presence in Edom. He restored Elath, a city and fortress on a major trade route to Judah (see 2 Chr 26:2). Elath is a southern port on the *Sea of Reeds* on the east of the Sinai Peninsula. Under Jehoram, son of Jehoshaphat, Elath was lost to Judah when Edom revolted (2 Kgs 8:21-22). Under King Ahaz (grandson of Azariah), Edom recovered Elath after Judah was weakened by a war with Aram and Israel (2 Kgs 16:5-6; Zorn 1992, 429).

b. Jeroboam II's Reign in Israel (14:23-29)

■ **23** A little more than halfway through the rule of Amaziah, who ruled for twenty-nine years in Judah, Jeroboam son of Jehoash became king in Israel after his father died. His reign was long, coinciding with that of Amaziah for fourteen years, and for twenty-seven years with the rule of Amaziah's son Azariah.

■ **24** The Judahite Dtr introduces Jeroboam II by noting that he continued practicing the sins of Jeroboam I, serving the calves at Bethel and Dan. The kings of the dynasties of Israel were caused to sin by Jeroboam I throughout Israel's existence as a nation. The next few verses offset this formulaic negative analysis by showing Yahweh's hand of deliverance in the reign of Jeroboam II.

■ **25** Jeroboam II restored Israel's border far to the northern reaches of Aram at Hamath and far to the south to the *Sea of Reeds* through his alliance with / dominance over Judah. (→ 2 Kgs 14:22, comment about Elath.) Thus the region of his rule was as extensive as Solomon's; the borders were thus restored, even though these borders comprise two nations: Israel and Judah. All this was prophesied by Jonah, son of Amittai of Gath Hepher, the main character of the book of Jonah (Jonah 1:1).

■ **26** Yahweh saw Israel's affliction during the divided monarchy period, just as he had seen the affliction of the children of Israel as slaves to the Egyptians (→ 2 Kgs 13:4-5 and 23:31-36). Yahweh promised them freedom from Aram through a prophet. Thus Aram, who had troubled Israel for decades, making Israelite lives bitter, was not a threat during Jeroboam II's reign, during which the land had rest.

■ **27** The credit is given to Yahweh, who wanted to preserve Israel in spite of their devotion to the calf shrines. In his deliverance of Israel from the attacks of Aram, Jeroboam II is likened to champions, the charismatic leaders, of the judges era.

■ **28-29** Although this account of Jeroboam II's reign in DtrH is brief and ends with the concluding reign formula, it shows that Yahweh's compassion extended to Israel, and the punishments wrought against them through prophets and enemies were an aspect of Yahweh's desire that they be restored; that they persist and have rest. Nonetheless, Jeroboam II's son Zechariah only reigned for six months (15:8). He was the fourth king of the Jehu dynasty; Yahweh had directly promised Jehu that his dynasty would include four generations of kings (10:30).

c. Azariah's Reign in Judah (15:1-7)

■ **1-4** Azariah's reign overlapped with that of Jeroboam II by fourteen years. (He is called Uzziah in 2 Kgs 15:13, 30, 32, 34; Isa 1:1; 6:1; 7:1; Hos 1:1; Amos 1:1.) He continued to reign for thirty-eight years after the end of the Jehuide dynasty, which ended with the short reign of Zechariah, son of Jeroboam II. Toward the end of Azariah's reign he inappropriately attempted to offer incense in the temple and was struck with leprosy. His son Jotham then became his co-regent (2 Chr 26:16-21).

The formula for introducing the rule of a king of Judah continues with the name of his mother, a Yahwist name, and the positive evaluation of his reign, which concludes with the caveat: **the high places . . . were not removed** (2 Kgs 15:4), which Dtr would have preferred.

■ **5** Azariah's long reign is storied here only by the mention of his leprosy, which was caused by Yahweh. Second Chronicles 26:16-21 attributes this affliction to the king's pride in going before Yahweh to offer incense, as if he were a priest (vv 1-15 describe the earlier part of his reign and his successful ventures). The narratives of 1—2 Chronicles, which recount the story of Judah (mentioning Israel only as it affects Judah), detail Azariah's failure. He was like David in that he started out well and Yahweh blessed him, but his prosperity led to pride, which Yahweh punished. The king could not rule from the palace but, like all lepers, was forced to live separately, while his son Jotham occupied the palace. The implication is that they ruled together until Azariah died.

■ **6-7** Azariah's reign is concluded with the usual formula announcing his death and burial in peace and referring to Judah's royal annals. Azariah died in the year of Isaiah's vision of Yahweh's throne (Isa 6:1). The prophet spoke for Yahweh during the reigns of Azariah, Jotham, Ahaz, and Hezekiah, kings of Judah (Isa 1:1). Among his other prophetic roles, Isaiah confronted Azariah's grandson Ahaz during the Israel-Syrian crisis, a story told in Isa 7, the background of which is explained in 2 Kgs 16.

d. The Reigns of Zechariah, Shallum, Menahem, Pekahiah, and Pekah of Israel (15:8-31)

■ **8-11** The focus switches to five kings of Israel, whose reigns are encapsulated quickly with reference to the details found in the annals of the kings of Israel. Zechariah, the son of the great king Jeroboam II, joined all of his predecessors in sustaining the calf shrines. He only ruled for six months before he was assassinated by a usurper, Shallum, who thus ended the Jehu dynasty.

Scholars speculate that Shallum wished to align Israel with Aram and break its alliance with Assyria, the far greater nation. That alliance had permitted the peace and prosperity of Jeroboam II's reign.

■ **12** The narrator reminds readers that Zechariah's short reign fulfilled Yahweh's promise to Jehu about his four-generation dynasty.

■ **13-15** Shallum only ruled one month before he was struck down by Menahem of Tirzah, who re-allied Israel to Assyria by supporting King Pul (Tiglath-Pileser III) with money from wealthy Israelites (vv 19-20).

■ **16** Tiphsah was the northern reach of Solomon's extensive kingdom (1 Kgs 4:24 [5:4 HB]). Menahem's attack on the (now) Assyrian-held town of Tiphsah on the Euphrates River to the extreme northeast may have occurred while he was a general for Jeroboam II and not during his own reign as king of Israel, whose capital was Samaria, far to the south. If so, the writer included it here to reveal Menahem's ruthless style of siege warfare, an aspect of his military reputation. This story is preserved in Josephus (*Ant.* 9.228) and may explain why he quickly avenged the blood of Jeroboam's son.

Hobbs writes that '*āz* here, followed by an imperfect form, is archival and

> offers not so much a sequence of events as a selection of events . . . it would not be difficult to envisage an earlier Menahem in his capacity as a general in Jeroboam's army fighting on the northern border of the newly created Israelite empire. His capture of Tiphsach would inevitably become part of his military reputation. This tradition of the role of the early Menahem is, in fact, preserved in Josephus (*Ant.* 9.228). If Menahem had been a general in Jeroboam's army, this position would also explain his loyalty to the house of Jehu and the speed with which he came to avenge the blood of Jeroboam's son. (1992, 693)

Here the Hebrew term '*āz* does not mean "then, at that time" but rather "once upon a time."

■ **17-20** The dates of Menahem's reign are usually given as 746-737 BC. When **Menahem** ruled in Samaria, the armies of King Pul of Assyria (same person as Tiglath-Pileser III [744-727 BC]) came to him. This was not a military invasion (Hobbs 1985, 199). Menahem gave him one thousand talents of silver (i.e., cash for the service of soldiers), demonstrating that Israel was a tribute-paying vassal of Assyria, expecting and receiving protection.

The Assyrian annuals of this period mention payments made by Menahem but may not be referring to this particular incident of paying for military protection (ibid., 200). Although King Pul's armies did not remain in Israel at this time, a few years later, during King Pekah's reign, they returned and seized the majority of the land of Israel: the Galilee and the land of Naphtali as well as Israel's holding on the east side of the Jordan (2 Kgs 15:29).

■ **21-26** No one conspired against Menahem; his dynasty continued to include one son. However, Pekahiah's reign was short-lived, only two years. He was killed by the son of one of **his chief officers, Pekah son of Remaliah** (v 25). The narrator makes no explicit judgment against the assassins in this chapter.

As with the case of every other Israelite king, failing to do well in Yahweh's eyes meant that **Pekahiah** did not remove Jeroboam I's calf shrines. He died in his palace in Samaria at the hands of Pekah and fifty men from Gilead, the northern area of Israel, east of the Jordan and immediately south of Aram.

Gilead's geographical proximity to Aram, Pekahiah's alignment with Assyria, and Assyria's punishing takeover of Israel during Pekah's reign implies that Pekah formed an alliance with Aram, called the Syro-Ephraimitic coalition. This is detailed in 2 Kgs 15:37 and 16:5-9, which is the context for Isa 7:1—8:8 and will be discussed below in connection with King Ahaz of Judah, who followed his father Jotham. Both reigned over Judah during the reign of Pekah, while Rezin was king of Aram. Pekah of Israel and Rezin of Aram troubled Judah in an attempt to force Judah to join them against Assyria: "When Ahaz son of Jotham, the son of Uzziah, was king of Judah, King Rezin of Aram and Pekah son of Remaliah king of Israel marched up to fight against Jerusalem, but they could not overpower it" (Isa 7:1).

■ **27** The problematic dating of the reigns of the kings of Israel in ch 15 is discussed at length in Hobbs (1985, 194, 201-3). A twenty-year reign for Pekah is too long to align with Tiglath-Pileser III's various contacts with Israel, references to Menahem in Assyrian inscriptions as occurring in 738 BC, and Hoshea's surrender to Assyria in 732 BC.

■ **28-29** In response to Pekah's rejection of the Assyrio-Israelite alliance effected by Pekahiah, Tiglath-Pileser III invaded Israel and seized much of the land, deporting the inhabitants to Assyria. **Ijon** was on the river by the same name fifteen miles north of **Abel Beth Maakah** (Tell Abil), which is four miles northwest of Dan. **Hazor** is well known, as is **Gilead, Galilee**, and **Naphtali**. The annexation of most of the land to Assyria crippled Israel, for most of Jeroboam II's expanded kingdom became part of the Assyrian Empire at this time.

■ **30** Although this verse claims Hoshea initiated the assassination of Pekah, Assyrian inscriptions of Tiglath-Pileser III state: "They overthrew Pekah their king, and *I* placed Hoshea as king over them" (italics mine; *ANET*, 284; Hobbs 1985, 203). Dtr's attention to Hoshea's reign continues in 2 Kgs 17:1-6. At this stage, Hoshea represented a reversal of the Aram-Israelite (Syro-Ephraimite) alliance and a return to Assyria. But if he was a puppet king, he did not stay loyal to Assyria; when Tiglath-Pileser III died, Hoshea refused to pay tribute to his successor, Shalmaneser V.

■ **31** Thus, the reign of Pekah ended in the same way he had terminated Pekahiah's before him, by assassination.

e. The Reign of Jotham in Judah (15:32-38)

After thus quickly recounting the troubled reigns of five kings of Israel, some of which were very short, Dtr turns to Judah and the reign of Jotham, who co-reigned with and then succeeded his father Azariah.

■ **32-34** Dtr follows the formula for Judah's kings, noting Jotham's mother's name. She may have been the daughter of a priest. Dtr gives **Jotham** a good rating, comparing him to his father, without mentioning any cause for Azariah's leprosy, unlike 2 Chr 26:16-21, which claims Azariah's pride led to his exile from the palace and the temple. Second Chronicles 27 gives an expanded account of Jotham's building projects and describes his defeat of the Ammonites, attributing his power to his walk with Yahweh.

■ **35** Jotham is remembered for rebuilding *the Gate of the House of Yahweh, the High One*. The term *the High One* (*hā'elyôn*) normally refers to the height of the gate and its location: **the Upper Gate**. But the phrase could also mean the gate of **Yahweh Most High**. Second Chronicles 23:20 describes Joash's coronation as a young boy who was marched from the house of Yahweh through the Upper Gate to the king's house to the royal throne. This means it would have been south of the temple. The Upper Gate was also called the New Gate until the end of the reign of Jehoiakim in 597 BC.

A measure of a Judahite king's rightness in the eyes of Dtr was whether he removed the shrines outside of Jerusalem where the people continually sacrificed. Jotham did not measure up. No king removed or will remove these shrines and thus have the full respect of Dtr until Hezekiah (Jotham's grandson) and Josiah ruled Judah.

■ **36-38** This short account of Jotham of Judah's reign ends with the customary reference to the annals of the kings of Judah, his burial with his fathers, and his successor, Ahaz. This is interrupted by the information that during his reign **Yahweh began to send Rezin king of Aram and Pekah son of Remaliah against Judah** (v 37). This harassment reached a peak in the days of Ahaz and Isaiah and led to Isaiah's prophecy about the sign of Immanuel.

2. King Ahaz of Judah Alters the Altar after Submitting to Assyria (16:1-20)

BEHIND THE TEXT

The parallels to this passage found in 2 Chr 28 and Isa 7 offer variations, elaborations, and expansions, while using some of the same terms and phrases.

Second Chronicles 28 diverges in many respects from this account, constructing the story as one of Judah's defeat by Aram, and Assyria's refusal to help (compare 2 Chr 28:20-21 with 2 Kgs 16:8-9).

IN THE TEXT

■ **1-2** Dtr continues the story of Judah by focusing on the reign of **Ahaz**, Jotham's son, who departed from the good ways of his immediate fathers: Jotham, Azariah, Amaziah, and Joash. Instead of mentioning these fathers, however, Dtr contrasts Ahaz's behavior with that of his father **David**. Ahaz abandoned the righteous ways of David to do more evil than any king before him. Rehoboam and Solomon are the only other kings of Judah who are connected to David in this way (1 Kgs 11:4-6; 15:3).

The name of Ahaz's mother is not provided although it is normally part of the formula for introducing Judahite kings. The mother's name is given for every king of Judah except Ahaz and Jehoram, son of Jehoshaphat, husband of Athaliah. By taking Athaliah of the house of Ahab as a wife for Jehoram, Jehoshaphat had allied Judah with Israel, leading to Baal worship in Judah. (→ 2 Kgs 8:16-18, a passage that seems to associate Jeroboam's Bethel and Dan calf shrines with Baalism.)

■ **3-4** Like Jehoram, husband of Athaliah, Ahaz *walked in the way of the kings of Israel.* Like the Canaanites, Ahaz *passed his son through fire* (v 3). Like the people of Israel and Judah who did not respect the central sanctuary at Jerusalem, Ahaz sacrificed *at the outdoor shrines and under every flourishing tree* (v 4). (See Deut 12:2, 1 Kgs 14:23, 2 Kgs 17:11, Jer 19:4-13 and throughout Jeremiah, all examples of Deuteronomistic writing and editing.) For Dtr, the latter activities are associated with the service of Baal and Asherah, but we also know through Dtr that some kings and people sacrificed to *Yahweh* at the shrines. In other DtrH accounts about Judah, "the people continued to offer sacrifices" at the outdoor shrines, *not* the king himself (2 Kgs 15:35). But King Ahaz did!

This three-part sequence of sins parallels the failures of three groups of disparaged people and serves to show the extent of Ahaz's culpability for the disasters that follow for Judah. It also provides a foundation for his subsequent egregious offenses. Ahaz thus was a foil for the reforming kings, Hezekiah and Josiah, and a model for Judah's most evil king, Manasseh.

■ **5** Second Kings 15:37 stated that Yahweh sent Aram and Israel against Judah before Jotham died. However, the juxtaposition of this announcement with the previous list of Ahaz's apostasy implies an association between it and the attack on **Jerusalem**. By besieging Judah's capital, Aram and Israel sought to force Judah to ally with them against Assyria. Israel had been allied with Assyria but broke that alliance to join Aram, their erstwhile enemy.

■ **6** More about the complex relationships among **Aram**, Edom, and **Elath** at this time can be found in 2 Chr 28:5-21. (See also Sweeney 2007, 383.) Provoked to do so by Aram, Edom took control of Elath from Judah and inhabited it *until this day*, which could refer to Hezekiah's era, through Josiah's time, or perhaps during part of the exile, but not afterward.

■ **7** Assyria's interference in the political life of Judah might have been the result of this invitation by Ahaz, but scholars think that they already had maintained a vassal-suzerain relationship. Ahaz's terms of submission, **I am your servant and *your son*,** indicate not a new treaty but a plea for help from a vassal to an overlord (Sweeney 2007, 380; Hobbs 1985, 214-15). Although Israel had recently broken with Assyria (an alliance established during Jehu's reign), Judah called upon Assyria for help when attacked.

■ **8-9** Ahaz's request and extra payment of tribute to **Assyria** for assistance was unnecessary, for Assyria would have besieged Damascus anyway, and thereby protected Judah by forcing Israel and Aram to withdraw from Jerusalem. Assyria was marching westward on its own accord, taking the areas of Gilead, Galilee, and Naphtali during Pekah's reign (2 Kgs 15:29). With Ahaz's formal request and payment, Judah was more deeply obligated to Assyria and forced to pay greater tribute.

Yahweh's advice through Isaiah to Ahaz (Isa 7:1-17) was practical. The oracle of Yahweh during this crisis insisted that in a few short years (the time for the son [Immanuel] of an already pregnant young woman to grow up and know right from wrong) "the land of the two kings you dread will be laid waste" (v 16). Aram and Israel would have abandoned their attack on Jerusalem to protect their eastern borders against Assyria. Tiglath-Pileser destroyed Damascus in 734-732 BC.

■ **10-11** These verses introduce a lengthy passage demonstrating Ahaz's submission to Assyria. His altering of the altar in Jerusalem after a model he found in Damascus may not have been required by Assyria. Assyria demanded monetary tribute from their vassals, but Assyrians did not sacrifice animals nor impose their rituals on conquered nations (McKay 1973 and Cogan and Tadmor 1988 in Sweeney 2007, 384, n. 11). Dtr claims that Ahaz was eager to accommodate the altar and other sacred temple furniture in Jerusalem's temple and its court to an altar he saw in Damascus, which may have been Syrian, not Assyrian.

■ **12-13** Upon returning to Jerusalem, Ahaz offered the full range of Levitical sacrifices to Yahweh on the new altar that the priest Uriah had built according to Ahaz's blueprints. He thereby inaugurated the new altar as David, Solomon, and Jeroboam had done to their new altars. He did not offer incense as Azariah had (a priestly prerogative).

■ **14** Moving **the bronze altar that stood before Yahweh** from the front of the temple to the north side of the **new altar** indicated Judah's subjugation to Assyria. Again, this may or may not have been required by Assyria's king; Ahaz initiated these changes, although v 18 claims that Ahaz made the changes there ***because of the king of Assyria***, and this may apply to the previously

16:7-14

listed changes as well. Hobbs disputes that these renovations demonstrated Yahweh's subjugation to Ashur, Assyria's god (1985, 217).

■ **15-16** Once the king had inaugurated the newly revised altar with the range of temple sacrifices, he ordered the priest, Uriah, to do the same, announcing that the relocated bronze altar would become a place of ***oracular seeking***, or **seeking guidance** (v 15). Again, this is not an indication of accommodation to Assyrian (or Syrian) practice, for 1 Kgs 22:11-20, 2 Sam 2:1, and 2 Kgs 19:1-7 represent a similar practice among Judahites. Uriah never protested the alterations; he always complied.

■ **17** Ahaz stripped the temple furnishings, removing **basins** and frames or **panels**, and rearranging the molten Sea from its support on the bronze bulls, which had been carefully constructed in Solomon's reign (1 Kgs 7:23-39). Dtr's condemnation of all of these moves is understood.

■ **18** *The covered passage of the Sabbath, which they had built in the house, and the king's outer entrance of the house of Yahweh he removed because of the king of Assyria.* The **Sabbath canopy** and the **royal entryway outside the temple** both represented the close relationship between the house of Yahweh, the temple, and the house of the king, meaning both the dynasty of David and the palace. Removing them symbolically cut this connection. The king of Assyria had good reason to associate these fixtures with divine sonship, as the royal psalms indicate (Pss 2; 72; 110). ***Because of the king of Assyria*** may apply to all of Ahaz's physical alterations or to the ones in 2 Kgs 16:18 alone.

■ **19-20** The concluding regnal formula aligns Ahaz with other Judahite kings, while the introductory formula paralleled Ahaz's actions with the sins of the people of the land, the Canaanites, and apostate Israelite kings. Although Dtr refrains from explicit judgment while listing Ahaz's transgressions (vv 7-12), they are pronounced and perverse. He unnecessarily appealed to and paid Assyria, then violated, rebuilt, and rearranged traditional temple structures, finally inaugurating them with sacrifices. The reader understands that Ahaz and his legacies are judged as utterly bereft by these scriptures, especially when read with Isa 7, which indicates that Ahaz ignored Yahweh's words.

3. Assyria Captures Samaria and Deports Israelites (17:1-6)

BEHIND THE TEXT

This section provides a sketch of dire events, from which Dtr derives theological meaning, instruction, and warning in the balance of ch 17. He stresses the prophetic attempts to lead Israel to repentance and prolonged life. Although scholars have considered it exilic or postexilic, which may be contexts for its redaction, concerns related to Josiah's reforming reign in Judah are reflected here. The apostasy of Israel (and Judah) and the syncretism of newcomers to the northern regions of Samaria are contrasted to obeying the Torah, worshipping Yahweh alone, and responding to prophetic correction.

IN THE TEXT

■ **1** The introductory regnal formula for Israelite kings matches the beginning of Hoshea's reign to the twelfth year of Judah's Ahaz (732-724 BC). We know from 2 Kgs 15:30 that Hoshea was not Pekah's son, but a conspirator who assassinated him. Pekah had assassinated his predecessor, Pekahiah son of Menahem, who had eliminated Shallum, the slayer of his predecessor Zechariah, son of Jeroboam II, descendants of Jehu.

General Jehu had destroyed Ahab's entire family, including the king of Judah and other Judahites. He was the first king of Israel to make an alliance with Assyria. (→ Behind the Text for 2 Kgs 14:1—17:41 and comments at 2 Kgs 9 and 11.) Violence marked Israel's transitions from ruler to ruler. Israel's history includes a number of dynasties in contrast to Judah in which a son of David always ruled, except for Athaliah's reign. Hoshea was Israel's last king.

■ **2** Although Hoshea's nine-year reign is introduced according to formula in vv 1 and 2*a*, v 2*b* departs from it radically. Like other Israelite kings, Hoshea **did evil in the eyes of Yahweh**, but Dtr did not write that he walked in the ways of Jeroboam son of Nebat as Dtr did for every other Israelite king (except Shallum, who reigned over Israel for only one month [2 Kgs 15:13]). In fact, Hoshea is remembered as being *less* evil than all of the other kings of Israel, which amounts to faint praise from the Judahite Dtr. Perhaps Hoshea was the only king of Israel who did not worship at the calf shrines in Bethel and Dan. Perhaps his only "evil" is the fact that he did not submit to Judah and Jerusalem. But the text is silent on this matter.

■ **3-4** Governing now only a small territory, Samaria and the hill country of Ephraim, Hoshea became a vassal of Assyria during the latter phase of Tiglath-Pileser III's (Pul) western campaign (733-732 of his 745-727 BC reign). The Assyrians annexed most of Israel and deported Israelites from many regions. (→ 2 Kgs 15:17-20, 29.)

Shalmaneser V (726-722 BC), successor of Pul, **came up *against*** Hoshea after Pul died. This suggests military attack to force compliance and submission. Hoshea paid a vassal's tribute to him until Hoshea decided to stop and seek an alliance with Egypt. Dtr provides no insight into the reasons for Hoshea's daring break with the great nation, Assyria. Hezekiah's later rebellion was inextricable from his religious reform (2 Kgs 18:5-7), but Dtr does not make that claim here for Hoshea.

Scholars now agree that **So** is a place, the city of Sais, which Pharaoh Tefnakht (726-716 BC) had established as his capital several years before. Hoshea's envoys went there to meet the king of Egypt. No help from Egypt is mentioned, only that Shalmaneser V's response was swift: he imprisoned Hoshea.

■ **5** Not only did Shalmaneser V, king of Assyria, capture Hoshea, but he invaded the entire land, patiently besieging Samaria for three years until the well-fortified capital of Israel that Omri had built fell (1 Kgs 16:24).

■ **6** Shalmaneser V led the siege, but he died sometime during or shortly after Samaria fell (722 BC). His brother Sargon II (722-705 BC) claimed the conquest (*ANET*, 284-85) and deported the Samarians not only to sites across Mesopotamia but also to Philistia and Ekron where many four-horned altars have been found (Sweeney 2007, 394).

4. Israel Is Destroyed for Sinning against Yahweh Their God and Ignoring His Prophets (17:7-23)

■ **7** Dtr provides the reason for Israel's fall to Assyria. Israel did not fall because Hoshea stopped paying tribute to Shalmaneser V and sought an alliance with Egypt. Israel did not fall because Assyria had stronger armies sweeping the region or because they cut off supply lines to Samaria. Neither did Israel fall because their God, Yahweh, was negligent, evil, or weaker than Assyrian gods. Israel lost their land, their king, and their nation because they ***sinned against Yahweh their God, the one who brought them up from Egypt from under the hand of Pharaoh king of Egypt and they feared other gods.*** (For detailed discussion of the Deuteronomist's agenda, → Introduction at the end of section A; Behind the Text for 1 Kgs 3—11; and From the Text for 1 Kgs 15:25—16:28.)

17:5-16a

■ **8-12** The list of Israel's specific failures commences as Dtr delineates how Israel **did wicked things that *provoked Yahweh to* anger** (v 11): fearing other gods, worshipping worthless idols, and building high places, sacred Baal pillars, and **Asherah poles** (v 10) everywhere. They sinned by practicing all that Yahweh and his prophets had *repeatedly* warned them to avoid. For example, Deut 16:21 says: ***You will not plant for yourself an asherah, any tree beside the altar of Yahweh your God which you will make for yourself.*** Commands to burn or cut down every Asherah are found in Exod 34:13; Deut 7:5; and 12:3, all of which have features of the Deuteronomistic redactor (Dtr).

There was no place in the land of Israel—city, town, hill, or grove—that the people of Israel did not break the covenant their fathers had made with **Yahweh their God** who delivered them from Egypt and slavery, gave them land, and made them a people with whom he desired to dwell. According to these passages, both Israel and Judah built hilltop and grove shrines at the beginning of their division into two nations. (For an explanation of the pillars and Asherah poles, → Behind the Text for 1 Kgs 16:29—22:53 [22:54 HB] and the "Asherah" sidebar at Behind the Text for 1 Kgs 16:29—22:53 [22:54 HB].)

■ **13-16a** The Israelites consistently pursued the abominations of the Canaanites, whose land Yahweh had given them. Thus, Israel **rejected his [*Yahweh's*] decrees and covenant** (2 Kgs 17:15). Hosea, the prophet to Israel, condemned Israel for these sins. Hosea warned the Israelites—people and priests—who sacrificed "on the mountaintops and . . . hills, under oak, poplar and terebinth, where the shade is pleasant" (Hos 4:13). In 1—2 Kings, Asherah were located at such sites. See 1 Kgs 14:15-23, which condemns Jeroboam and Rehoboam for constructing **asherim upon every high hill and under every luxuriant tree** (compare Jer 17:2).

■ **16b-20** Bowing to **the starry host**, burning their children as sacrifices, worshipping **Baal**, practicing **divination** and sorcery, and otherwise doing **evil** and provoking Yahweh are forbidden throughout Deuteronomy and by the prophets who were sent to condemn Israel's proclivities toward apostasy.

For example:

When you enter the land **Yahweh** your God is giving you, do not learn to imitate the detestable ways of the nations there. Let no one be found among you who sacrifices their son or daughter in the fire, who practices divination or sorcery, interprets omens, engages in witchcraft, or casts spells, or who is a medium or spiritist or who consults the dead. Anyone who does these things is detestable to **Yahweh**; because of these same detestable practices **Yahweh** your God will drive out those nations before you. You must be blameless before **Yahweh** your God. (Deut 18:9-13)

Dtr gets a shot in at Judah here, for Judah also did all of these "detestable practices," as the prophet Jeremiah indicated (Jer 19:3-15).

■ **21-23** To conclude Israel's list of offenses, Dtr returns to the calf shrines outside of Jerusalem, introduced by **Jeroboam** I, the first king of Israel, and maintained by subsequent kings. Jeroboam's insecurity and lack of faith in Yahweh's covenant led him to build these shrines at Bethel and Dan to keep the people from going to Jerusalem (→ 1 Kgs 13). Throughout this entire passage, Dtr addressed the Israelites, repeating that their sins were against Yahweh, his commands, decrees, and his entire **Torah**—meaning "teaching"—given to their fathers and "delivered to you through my servants the prophets." Moses is not mentioned here, although Deut 34:10-12 assures every reader that Moses, "the servant of **Yahweh**" (v 5) was and will always be the prophet of prophets, never forgotten and always associated in DtrH with the Torah and the covenant of Yahweh.

No longer was Dtr merely listing Israel's prohibited behaviors, nor was he restrained in his assessment of them. The most severe of punishments had now occurred: enslavement, exile, and loss of land, autonomy, identity, and life for many Israelites. Dtr knew why. The force of his anger over Israel's apostasy founded his detailed explanation for Israel's demise. In its unwavering understanding that the Assyrian invasion was Yahweh's judgment upon Israel, this section joins other resoundingly Deuteronomistic passages throughout Deuteronomy—2 Kings (DtrH). As noted at 2 Kgs 15:29, 16:9, and 17:6, the Assyrians commonly deported rebel nations, bringing in diverse people groups from around their expanding empire in order to scatter them and thwart any attempts to revolt.

5. Assyria Resettles Israel with Other Captives, and Syncretism Prevails (17:24-41)

■ **24** Dtr now lists the Mesopotamian, Aramean, and Elamite places from which Assyria brought settlers to inhabit the region of Samaria. At this time (722 BC), Babylon was a vassal of Assyria, but, in 130 years, Babylon would conquer the weakened Assyria and take over and expand its empire.

■ **25-26** These people served the various gods they had known. They ***did not fear Yahweh, and he sent lions against them who were killing them***. The people expected each land to have laws of its own god, and they, like Dtr, saw the lion attacks as punishment for failing to observe laws that they did not know. They reported to the king of Assyria that they needed instruction in the laws of the god of the land of Israel.

■ **27** His answer was addressed to a military governor of Samaria (or similar ruling official) responsible for previous deportations, who had the authority to collect an exiled priest and bring him back to teach the outsider settlers the laws of Yahweh.

■ **28** Irony exists in the undertones of this verse in that Dtr's primary message has been to show how *Israel* utterly failed to fear and serve Yahweh. Israel had shown from the outset of their existence as a separate nation that they did not "know" what Yahweh required. Rather, Dtr insists, they *knew*, but they did not *do*, which made them more culpable.

At this juncture, Assyria brought a "non-Levitical" priest (see 1 Kgs 12:31-33) to "teach" the diverse people ***how they should fear Yahweh***! This priest taught the outsiders about the laws of Yahweh, the very laws that Israel's leaders had failed to teach and enforce, leading to their exile.

■ **29-33** The newcomers were a very religious group, exemplifying adaptability and the syncretism so despised by Dtr, who named the various gods of each group and their evil customs, including child sacrifice. (See Sweeney 2007, 396, for details about these gods and goddesses.) If the priest taught them to worship Yahweh alone, they could not grasp such exclusivity and sought the "safer" practice of worshipping as many gods as they knew: Yahweh, the god of the land of Israel, along with all their own familiar gods. Adding another god for the sake of safety and prosperity was not a problem for those relocated to Samaria by Assyria.

Israel was an unusual people group among their neighbors in that their god was a jealous god, requiring exclusive fidelity. Clearly, the behavior of Israel consistently showed that the people did not understand this demand, for like their neighbors, they also served other gods, adapting to their environs.

Like Jeroboam I had done, the new people **appointed all sorts of their own people to officiate for them as priests** (v 32; see 1 Kgs 12:31). The newcomers were not "Israel" and could not remember a covenant made with their ancestors, but they should have learned to worship Yahweh alone, according to Dtr.

■ **34-40** This section confronts traditional Israelites and Judahites with whose ancestors Yahweh had made the covenant in the first place. It prophetically called them to remember Yahweh's deliverances and consequent decrees, which made them his people. However, this section also recognizes and explains the paradox of how the non-Israelite inhabitants of Samaria could fear Yahweh (2 Kgs 17:32-33) while not fearing Yahweh (v 34). People cannot fear and serve Yahweh if they fear and serve other gods as well.

The **covenant** given to the **descendants of Jacob** commanded worship of Yahweh alone, their God who delivered them from **Egypt** and from all of their enemies (vv 34-36). To worship any other god along with Yahweh was to break this covenant at its core and to bring upon their heads the curses of the covenant, which Israel experienced at the hands of the Assyrians. Now, as Hosea had threatened and then demonstrated with the birth and name of his son, they were "not my people" (Hos 1:9). Just as within the Torah itself, the repeated reminder here is **do not worship other gods** (2 Kgs 17:37).

■ **41** The Israelites were dispersed and Israel, as the northern kingdom, was gone—lost on account of their faithlessness to Yahweh. Assyrian records claim 27,290 Israelites were taken. Thus, this section provides a foundation for understanding Jewish antipathy toward the Samarians and later Samaritans, whom the Judahite Dtr saw as a diverse group of syncretists. Dtr admits that the multicultured inhabitants of Samaria learned to fear Yahweh, but at the same time they served their gods and images, and, says the writer here: their descendants *continue to do so until this day.*

FROM THE TEXT

The formula *until this day*, the present time of the writer (2 Kgs 17:23, 34, and 41), refers to the syncretism of the newcomers to Israel/Samaria. This was pertinent to the decades that Judah remained a nation (722—586 BC), as well as during the Babylonian exile (586-536 BC) and afterward. John Wesley wrote: "Unto this day - That is, till the time when this book was written, above three hundred years in all, till the time of Alexander the Great, when they were prevailed upon to call away their idols" (*Notes on the Bible*, 1 Kgs 17:23).

The fall of Israel and Dtr's explanation for it grounded calls for reform to Judahites who engaged in the same practices, as Dtr frankly asserts in 17:19. The reforms of Hezekiah and later Josiah were restorations to the Torah of Moses. Scribes, prophets, and/or priests faithful to God could have written ch 17's summary of Israel's downfall during Hezekiah and Josiah's restoring reigns or in order to subvert the practices of apostate kings such as Ahaz or Manasseh, who led Judah toward the judgment that befell Israel.

Judah's exile to Babylon taught the returning Jews to be monotheists. The Scriptures produced during this time affirm not only that Yahweh is the only god for Israel but also that Yahweh is the *only* God; he created the universe and

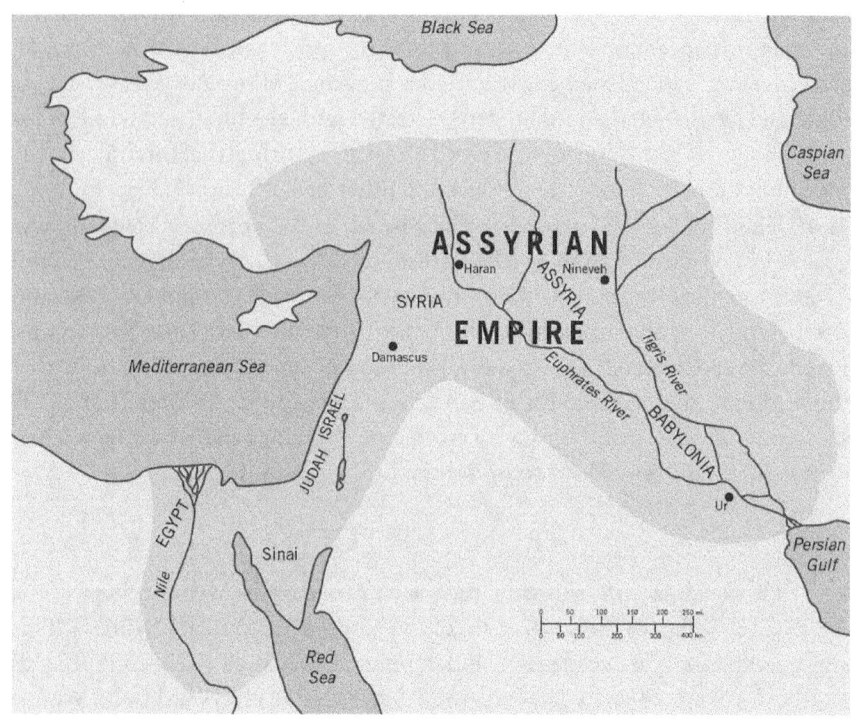

Map 6, Assyrian Empire

all that is in it. Some Jews attempted extreme measures to ensure that their descendants did not serve the gods of the peoples of the land and their neighbors. Ezra, Nehemiah, and a few other officials blamed "foreign wives" who were indigenous women of the land. These wives could have been Judahites, former Israelites, Gentiles resettled into the Persian province of Yehud from outside, and/or intermingled progeny of those groups (Ezra 9—10; Neh 13).

Other Jews understood that wives from outlying nations did not cause Israel to sin; it was the kings, beginning with Solomon and Jeroboam I, who established the worship of other gods and broke their covenant with Yahweh and *who caused Israel to sin* (2 Kgs 13:2; 14:24; 15:9, 24 and passim). Traditions about outsider wives—such as Tamar (Gen 38), Zipporah (Exod 2:21-22; 4:19-20; 18:2-3), Rahab (Josh 2; 6:17-18, 22-23), and Ruth—affirmed that women faithful to God were models to Israel and should not be expelled. Now as then, Christians affirm with the apostle Peter that "God shows no partiality, but in every nation anyone who fears him and does what is right is acceptable to him" (Acts 10:34-35, NRSV).

III. JUDAH TO THE BABYLONIAN EXILE: 2 KINGS 18:1—25:30

BEHIND THE TEXT

During the period 722 BC to 612 BC, Assyria's empire continued to expand to dominate the region, including Judah, but was finally overrun by Babylon in 612 BC. Egypt attempted to resist the westward march of Babylon, and, in the process, controlled Judah from 609 to 604 BC. Through a number of battles, Babylon took over the land that Egypt had won in Mesopotamia (2 Kgs 24:7) and continued to march against the western regions once possessed by Egypt, Assyria, and Judah until 586 BC. At that time, Jerusalem fell to Babylon, and many surviving Judahites were forced to settle there.

The kings of Judah who reigned after the fall of Israel (722 BC) were Hezekiah, Manasseh, Amon, Josiah, and Josiah's sons (Jehoahaz and Eliakim [Jehoiakim]), his grandson, Jehoiachin (who was taken captive to Babylon), and finally Josiah's son Mattaniah (Zedekiah). Each Davidic king was a vassal of and/or rebelled against one or more of the region's superpowers. Egypt, Assyria, and Babylon fought many significant battles during this period. For example, Assyria's Tiglath-Pileser III invaded Babylonia and crowned himself king in 734 BC; Babylon defeated Assyria at Babylon in 626 BC and later defeated Egypt's Pharaoh Necho at the battle of Carchemish in 605 BC, forcing Egypt to withdraw from western Asia.

Babylon's Nebuchadnezzar began to besiege Judah in 601 BC and surrounded Jerusalem in 598 BC, deporting Jehoiachin in 597 BC. But Babylon withdrew after placing Zedekiah on the throne for another eleven years in Jerusalem as a puppet king. Ultimately, pro-Egyptian rebels in Judah provoked Nebuchadnezzar's return to Jerusalem in 588 BC and his breaching of the walls in July-August of 586 BC (9 Tammuz). The city was destroyed, many officials killed, and many more exiled, including King Zedekiah.

Scholars believe that the Deuteronomistic History (DtrH), which includes 1—2 Kings, was produced in Judah after Israel's 722 BC fall to Assyria, using some written sources produced in Solomon and Jehu's time. According to William Schniedewind, these texts were redacted during Hezekiah's rule and under Josiah, in the exilic period and possibly again in postexilic Judah. (See Schniedewind 2004, 64-90.) Other scholars have argued that the DtrH came from the exilic or postexilic period. Schniedewind does not deny the redaction and compilation of earlier sources in these later times, but he argues that, during Hezekiah's and Josiah's reigns, resources and will existed to produce texts from traditions that were incorporated into the Bible.

Other textual sources for the nearly fourteen decades (722—586 BC) that Judah remained a Davidic dynasty are 2 Chr 29—36, Isa 36—39, the book of Jeremiah, and Assyrian and Babylonian annals, including Sennacherib's accounts of his conquest of Judah during Hezekiah's rule. The Assyrian king Sennacherib recorded his western campaigns (705—681 BC) on a hexagonal prism and also upon a limestone relief that paneled a wall in his palace at Nineveh, which depicted his overthrow of the Judahite city Lachish. Both are now located in the British Museum.

Although they have propagandistic elements, the extrabiblical sources provide fixed points for historical events that are explained from a prophetic perspective in 2 Kgs 18—25 and Isa 36—39. Assyrian sources verify Sennacherib's invasion of Judah, demand for extra tribute from Hezekiah in 701 BC, and withdrawal from Jerusalem, as well as his death at the hands of his sons in 680 BC.

Excavations of the city of Nineveh indicate that Sennacherib chose it as his capital, refurbished it, and fortified it. At the city of Ashur he built a new temple devoted to the god Ashur with reliefs that indicate that Ashur, not Marduk, defeated Tiamat, against the Babylonian creation myth *Enuma Elish*. (For more information on the inscriptions and other archaeological evidence of this period, → Introduction, C. History and Geography of the Period.)

The section immediately below, 2 Kgs 18—20, describes events that occurred in Judah during the transition of power from Sargon II (died 705 BC) to Sennacherib. Assyria under Sennacherib was Hezekiah's greatest threat and the reason for Hezekiah's alliance with Babylon (2 Kgs 20:12-15). Hezekiah saw the opportunity to throw off the Assyrian yoke that Ahaz had acquired, as did many other leaders during this season, including Marduk-Baladan king of

Babylon and Egyptian pharaohs. Marduk-Baladan formed alliances with Judah and other nations in order to resist Assyrian domination. His Babylonian envoys and Hezekiah's hospitality to them represents this alliance and prompted Isaiah's prophetic word, claiming calamities would result (vv 16-19).

Sennacherib's armies captured Babylon and destroyed it in 689 BC. When Sennacherib's sons killed him in 681 BC, Esarhaddon, a younger son, became king. Esarhaddon fought a number of battles with Egypt until he died en route to Egypt in 669 BC. Before he died, he assigned one of his sons to the throne of Babylon, and another, Ashurbanipal, to the throne of Assyria. This led to civil war (652-648 BC) and weakened the Assyrian Empire, leading to its decline and eventual fall in 612 BC. After a series of weak successors to Ashurbanipal, the Babylonians under Nabopolassar, allied with Medes, conquered both Ashur and Nineveh and took over the administration of the empire.

The Babylonians continued conquering areas of Mesopotamia in order to expand their empire. This included the 605 BC defeat of Egypt at Carchemish and their advances into Syria-Palestine/Aram-Judah mentioned above. These events are explained in connection to Judah's story from Dtr's theological perspective in 2 Kgs 24—25. At this point, we turn to Hezekiah's story in 2 Kgs 18 and his dealings with Assyria.

A. Hezekiah Serves Yahweh and Is Besieged by Assyria (18:1—20:21)

BEHIND THE TEXT

Although Babylon was the conqueror that brought Judah's tenure as a nation to an end in 586 BC, in Hezekiah's time (716—687 BC), Assyrian armies advanced to the gates of Jerusalem, harassing the city with words and weapons. But Hezekiah was not defenseless; he approached the prophet Isaiah for prayer; he laid out the challenging words of the Assyrians before Yahweh and prayed for salvation. He received Yahweh's answer through Isaiah, and Yahweh's help through a destroying angel (2 Kgs 19). As mentioned above, Hezekiah's court may have been a context for the production of literature that became part of the Bible (Schniedewind 2004, 64-90). Proverbs 25:1 introduces the sayings that follow with: "These are other proverbs of Solomon that the officials of King Hezekiah of Judah copied" (NRSV).

1. Hezekiah Ascends to the Throne of Judah and Does Right like David His Father (18:1-8)

IN THE TEXT

■ 1 Second Kings 16:20 provides the notice of Ahaz's death and Hezekiah's ascension to the throne of David as the concluding formula for Ahaz's reign.

Second Kings 18:1-8 includes the elements of the introductory regnal formula for Hezekiah. As usual, his first year as king is dated according to the year of the reigning king of Israel, Hoshea's third year of nine (732-724 BC). However, 729 BC as Hezekiah's ascension year does not fit with 18:13, which dates Hezekiah's revolt to his fourteenth year. If his ascension year was 715 BC, it would correspond with 701 BC, the secure date of Sennacherib's invasion of Judah. Most interpreters place Hezekiah's twenty-nine-year reign from 715 to 687 BC.

■ **2-3** The introductory formula also includes the length of his reign and the name of his mother and her father. Here information is given about Hezekiah's reign that has not yet been part of the information about other Judahite kings. This time Dtr exclaims that Hezekiah **did what was right in the eyes of Yahweh, just as his father David had done**, a contrast to other Judahite kings, such as Amaziah, who "did what was right in the eyes of **Yahweh**, but not as his father David had done" (14:3).

■ **4** This means that the high places, the sacred stones, and the Asherah poles in the groves of trees were all dismantled. Under Rehoboam, son of Solomon, Judah constructed these sites and continued to use them, committing all the abominations of the peoples that Yahweh had driven out under Joshua (1 Kgs 14:22-24; compare Isa 1:29). Hezekiah is thus affirmed above the several kings of Judah, such as Joash, Amaziah, and Azariah who "did what was right in the eyes of **Yahweh**" but did not remove the shrines outside of Jerusalem at which the people sacrificed (1 Kgs 3:2-4; 11:7; 12:31; 14:23; 15:14; 22:43 [43-44 HB]; 2 Kgs 12:3 [4 HB]; 14:4; 15:4, 35; 16:4; 17:9, 11, 29, 32). Hezekiah's father, King Ahaz, had sacrificed at these places and made a son pass through the fire (16:3-4).

Hezekiah's reform—or restoration—included shattering Moses' bronze serpent to which the people made offerings. The name **Nehushtan**, not given in Num 21:8-9, is based upon *nĕḥōšet* (bronze/*copper*) and *nāḥāš* (serpent). Moses, on the command of Yahweh, had built the fiery (or poisonous) serpent to heal the people who looked upon it for relief from the effects of snakebite. It probably continued to serve for Judahites as an image with healing properties (Handy 1992, 1117). Offering sacrifices to it indicates that the people thought of it as a deity. Wesley wrote: "Nehushtan - [Hezekiah] said, this serpent, howsoever formerly honoured, and used by God as a sign of his grace, yet now it is nothing but a piece of brass which can do you neither good nor hurt" (*Notes on the Bible*, 2 Kgs 18:4).

■ **5-6** Dtr introduces the actions of the new king with no attempt to explain why Hezekiah rose up against the apostasy of Ahaz to trust in Yahweh and follow ***the commandments Yahweh commanded to Moses*** (v 6). As evidence of his devotion to Yahweh, Hezekiah terminated worship outside of Jerusalem.

The fact that the same statement about the reforming king's incomparability—**There was no one like him among all the kings of Judah, either before him or after him** (v 5)—is made about the later reforming king, Josiah, did not trouble the final redactors of the text (compare 2 Kgs 22:2; 23:25; and 1 Kgs 3:12). On a text critical level, however, this remark shows that the statement appeared in a Hezekian edition of the DtrH (see Sweeney 2007, 403). Wesley harmonized the repeated statement in this fashion:

> Before him - Of the kings of Judah only; for David and Solomon were kings of all Israel. The like is said of Josiah, chap. xxiii, 25. Each of them excelled the other in several respects. Hezekiah in this, that he fell upon this work in the beginning of his reign, which Josiah did not, and with no less resolution, undertaking to do that which none of his predecessors durst do, even to remove the high places, wherein Josiah did only follow his example. (*Notes on the Bible*, 2 Kgs 18:6)

■ **7** Ahaz had submitted to Assyria, and, for reasons of his own, had revised the cultic structures in Jerusalem. Hezekiah did the reverse: he restored the commandments given through Moses as the blueprint for worship. *And* he rebelled against Assyria. Wesley was concerned that Hezekiah "rebelled" and explained: "[rebel] doth not necessarily prove this to be a sin. And that it was not a sin in him, seems certain, because God owned and assisted him therein; and did not at all reprove him for it" (*Notes on the Bible*, 2 Kgs 18:7).

The version of Hezekiah's story in 2 Chr 29—31 details Hezekiah's acts of restoration that repaired the temple, restored the Levitical priests and work rotations in the temple, traced genealogies, and reestablished the Passover in Jerusalem.

■ **8** Hezekiah's restoration of centralized Yahweh worship, his attacks upon Philistia, his rebellion against Assyria, and Dtr's positive evaluation of him are all connected. To subjugate Philistia's coast plain would fortify Judah against Assyrian incursions from the south and north.

2. Assyria Captures and Exiles Israel (18:9-12)

■ **9-12** This section is a summary of ch 17 and a reminder that Israel suffered defeat by Assyria **because they did not listen** (*šāmaʻ*) and **they did not do** (*ʻāśâ*) the commands Yahweh gave through Moses. They repeatedly and irresponsibly broke the covenant, whereas Hezekiah reformed Judah according to Mosaic laws. Hezekiah's reforms and devotion to Yahweh gave Judah hope that Yahweh would deliver them from Assyrian might. If Israel had fallen because of their disobedience, how much more should Judah survive because of their return to Yahweh and obedience to Torah.

3. Yahweh Delivers Jerusalem from Assyria (18:13—19:37)

BEHIND THE TEXT

This section should be read with Isa 36—39. The Kings account is prior to and a source for the Isaianic account (see Seitz 1991, 496-502). The few differences between the accounts eliminate Hezekiah's repentance in 18:14-16; 19:35.

This story about Hezekiah's negotiations with Assyria comprises a series of unfolding scenes based upon Hezekiah's reform and revolt (18:4-8). The scenes include (1) Assyrian takeover of Judah (v 13), (2) Hezekiah's repentance and retribution (vv 14-16), (3) Assyrian march against Jerusalem and intimidation (vv 17-36), (4) report to Hezekiah of Assyrian terms (v 37), (5) consultation and response of Yahweh through Isaiah (19:1-7), (6) Assyrian demand for surrender (vv 8-13), (7) Hezekiah's prayer and Yahweh's response (vv 14-34), (8) dénouement: destruction of the Assyrian army by Yahweh's angel (vv 35-37).

This section is not a cobbling together of texts and traditions available to later scribes but rather a carefully orchestrated narrative—a prophetic confrontation story—intent upon showing the unreasonableness of Assyria, the adversary and challenger of Yahweh and Hezekiah. It emphasizes that *even though* Hezekiah fully submitted to Assyrian terms, Assyria *still* came up against Jerusalem and assailed Judah's God, Yahweh. Nonetheless, through his destroying angel, Yahweh validated Judah, Hezekiah, and Isaiah, and his own ability to protect them (see Fewell 1986, 87-90; Sweeney 2007, 412).

IN THE TEXT

■ **13** Sennacherib's invasion of Judah, including his destruction of Lachish, is securely dated to 701 BC, so dating it to Hezekiah's fourteenth year means he became king in 715 BC, not 729 BC (which was Hoshea's third year as king of Israel [v 1]; → 2 Kgs 18:1).

■ **14-16** Hezekiah admitted wrongdoing against Assyria and promised to pay tribute if Assyria would withdraw from Judah. Assyria imposed tribute, which Hezekiah obtained by stripping the temple, as kings before him had done (1 Kgs 14:25-26). Sennacherib claimed to have imposed eight hundred talents of silver and thirty talents of gold on Judah.

■ **17-18** Assyrian forces, however, did not withdraw; they advanced upon Judah from the north, driving south through Phoenicia and Philistia into western Judah and camped in the southwestern city of Lachish. Three high-ranking officials were sent from there to Jerusalem as spokesmen for their king in order to challenge Judah to surrender. The literal translations of the terms for the Assyrian officials are: the general of the army (*tartān*; see Isa 20:1, which says that the Assyrian *tartan* of Sargon II captured Ashdod), the **chief eunuch** [*rab-sārîs*], **and the chief cupbearer** [*rab-šaqēh*]. The latter title applied to the Assyrian king's messenger, a military official or a high-ranking spokesman for the king.

These three were matched by three of Hezekiah's administrative and scribal officials who met them. Hezekiah's representatives included Eliakim, who had replaced Shebna as the manager of the king's household (Isa 22:20-22), the same Shebna now called a **secretary** or **scribe**, and Joah, **the recorder**.

■ 19 The *chief cupbearer*, speaking for the king of Assyria, boldly questioned the basis for Hezekiah's confidence, never addressing the fact that the latter had paid the required tribute. He thus expected the Assyrians to withdraw, not to demand Jerusalem's surrender. The Assyrians had advanced, Hezekiah repented and asked for terms of withdrawal, Assyria gave them, and Hezekiah paid dearly. Yet the Assyrians still moved forward to besiege the city.

■ 20-21 The *chief cupbearer* continued by raising the specter of Egypt, suggesting Egypt was a basis for Hezekiah's nerve to rebel. Although this text does not indicate that Egypt figured in Hezekiah's revolt (he turned toward Babylon [2 Kgs 20:12-13]), Egypt rose against Assyria after the transition from Sargon II to Sennacherib. In addition, Isa 30:1-7, 31:3, and 36:6 speak against Judah's alliance with Egypt while Sennacherib was advancing.

■ 22 Setting aside Hezekiah's possible reliance upon Egypt, the *chief cupbearer* claimed that it was equally foolish for Hezekiah to rely upon Yahweh. He interpreted Hezekiah's destruction of the shrines outside of Jerusalem as an assault upon Yahweh, that Yahweh would thus reject Hezekiah's prayers, even if he was powerful enough to protect Judah.

■ 23 Rapidly shifting gears, the *chief cupbearer* then called for a wager between the two kings. He offered two thousand horses, implying that Hezekiah could not even find two thousand riders for them. This indicates how utterly bereft and hopeless the Assyrians assumed Judah to have been. If they could convince the people of Judah to give up without a fight, the Assyrians themselves would avoid bloodshed.

■ 24 These derisions were intended to undercut the confidence of Judahites in any outside alliance and in their own God, Yahweh. The taunts were designed to portray to all within hearing that Judah should immediately surrender to Assyria. Judah's only hope for peace lay in Assyria's promises of peace and sustenance at home and after they had been deported (v 32).

■ 25 Then the Assyrian taunts took a new form. The *cupbearer* claimed Yahweh himself had sent the Assyrians to destroy Judah. Dtr in 2 Kgs 17—18 claims that Yahweh was behind Assyria's attack on Israel (17:7, 22-23; 18:11-12), as do numerous prophets. However, as this passage shows, this is *not* the case here.

■ 26 Eliakim and the other officials of Judah asked their Assyrian challenger to speak in Aramaic—the language of the empire—so that the nearby Judahites who knew only Hebrew would not hear these taunts. This indicates both the literacy of the Assyrian and Judahite officials—both sets of three knew both languages. More importantly, it shows that the three Judahite officials were frightened and recognized the power of the taunts.

■ 27-32 The *chief cupbearer* refused. He proceeded to mock more loudly in Hebrew in order to frighten and demoralize as many people of Judah as possible. He warned them against trust in Hezekiah and Yahweh and promised that, if they surrendered, they would not suffer the deprivation and death of besiegement. Instead they would have peace in Judah and afterward when they were deported to a region of the Assyrian Empire. His words depict Assyrian language forms and style of negotiation, as well as the Assyrian practice of deporting and scattering conquered peoples. If Judah surrendered, they would **choose life and not death!** (v 32).

■ **33-35** He further demonstrated that trusting in their own gods had not delivered the surrounding peoples from Assyrian advance, destruction, and deportation. The cupbearer meant for his evidence of Assyria's recent victories over other nations—and their gods—to convince Judahites that neither could Yahweh, Judah's God, save Judah.

■ **36-37** Although they did not respond to their Assyrian challengers, the *chief cupbearer's* words had the desired effect on Hezekiah's three court officials, for they returned to him **with their clothes torn**, a sign of mourning and distress, and reported his terms of surrender and other taunts.

■ **19:1** Hezekiah not only tore his garments but also put on sackcloth and thus entered the temple when he heard the Assyrian threats. As noted above, Isa 37 is a nearly identical edition of this passage.

■ **2** He sent his officials, also dressed in sackcloth, including the priests, to the prophet Isaiah and reported to him Hezekiah's message, seeking a word from Yahweh.

■ **3-4** The officials relayed Hezekiah's message, which quoted a proverb to introduce his desperate hope that Yahweh would be insulted enough by the Assyrians' words to punish them.

■ **5-7** Isaiah delivered an oracle from Yahweh immediately with the prophetic formula: **Thus says Yahweh** (v 5). Indeed, Yahweh *had* heard the arrogant words of **the underlings of the king of Assyria** (v 6), was duly insulted, and announced that he, Yahweh, would send the Assyrian king home where he would die.

■ **8** The *chief cupbearer* returned to Lachish to learn of his king's move to Libnah, now Tel Bornat, which was a city in southern Judah five miles northeast of Lachish (Josh 10:29; 21:13). Libnah had revolted against Judah in the time of Jehoram (2 Kgs 8:20-22) but later was returned to Judah's control—until this Assyrian invasion.

■ **9** King Tirhakah of Ethiopia did not rise to the throne until 690 BC, and the events reported here happened in 701 BC. However, this verse concerns rumors and the reason Sennacherib's forces began to disperse and withdraw from Judah. On account of rumors (*a spirit within him so that when he hears a certain report*), Sennacherib would leave Jerusalem.

■ **10-13** Even though the king of Assyria had moved from Lachish to besiege Libnah and was concerned about the Ethiopians, he did not give up his promotion of Assyrian interests against Jerusalem. This time his message was sent in dispatched documents and was shorter than the speech the *chief cupbearer* made in the hearing of Hezekiah's officials and the men on the wall. This message continued the emphasis on previous Assyrian conquests of nearby peoples whose gods and kings did not save them.

■ **14** Hezekiah received the documents from the messengers and spread them before Yahweh in the temple. He directly prayed to Yahweh there instead of reporting his concern to Isaiah.

■ **15** Hezekiah's prayer in the temple refers to the cherubim on the ark and Yahweh's position there, alluding to the heavenly temple (1 Sam 4:4; 2 Sam 6:2; 1 Kgs 6:23-28; Pss 80:1 [2 HB]; 99:1). It emphasized Yahweh as the only God of all earthly kingdoms and Creator of the skies and land.

■ **16** In seeking Yahweh's **ear** to hear Sennacherib's ridicule and his own plea for help, Hezekiah's prayer is similar to numerous psalms (Pss 10:17; 17:6; 31:2 [3 HB]; 71:2; 86:1-2), and he was just as desperate as the psalmists.

■ **17-18** Hezekiah reminded Yahweh of Assyria's success just as Sennacherib and his *chief cupbearer* had reminded Hezekiah. But Hezekiah pointed out that the other gods who could not save were different from Yahweh. They were made of stone and wood and could be destroyed.

■ **19** Hezekiah affirmed that the Creator God, Yahweh, is indestructible and able to save. As Yahweh had used the *smitings* (plagues) in Egypt in order that all the earth would know of Yahweh's might. Here Hezekiah humbly directs Yahweh to once again save his people (Exod 6:7; 8:10, 22 [6, 18 HB]; 9:14, 29; 10:2).

■ **20-22** The prophet Isaiah received Yahweh's answer for Hezekiah and sent it to him. We see here, as in other books of the Former and Latter Prophets (Joshua—2 Kings and Isaiah—Malachi), that Yahweh usually spoke to kings through prophets and not directly to them. Isaiah's oracle from Yahweh showed that Yahweh had heard Hezekiah's prayer, as he had asked. Moreover, Jerusalem could and should mock Assyria's taunts, for Yahweh, the sole God took every Assyrian insult heaped upon Hezekiah as an insult to himself.

19:14-31

■ **23-24** Yahweh's parody of Assyrian boasting parallels the way the Assyrians portray their god, Ashur, in Assyrian pictures and mythologies as flying through the skies (*ANEP*, 536; *ANET*, 278, 284, and 307). In addition, Atrahasis, the Babylonia flood story, depicts humans as created to dig wells so that the gods have water and irrigation.

■ **25-28** In these verses, Yahweh ceased quoting the Assyrians and began to speak for himself. He claimed that Assyrian gods and kings did not have a basis for boasting, for it was Yahweh who planned these things and gave the Assyrians the power to do them. Their arrogant raging against Yahweh and his people, however, caused Yahweh to determine that they should become enslaved.

■ **29-31** Continuing in the manner of other prophetic oracles such as those found in the book of Isaiah, Yahweh addressed Hezekiah to give him a sign (Isa 7:11-14). Like Isa 7, this is an agricultural image about what the land will do and how these seasons indicate the passage of time until Yahweh's promises for a remnant would be fulfilled, which has parallels in Isa 2:2-4; 4:2-6; 9:6 [5 HB]; and 11:1-9.

■ **32-34** Yahweh turned to specifically address Sennacherib in response to Hezekiah's prayers about Jerusalem and the danger it faced. Yahweh's words put a hedge of protection around the city, walls made of divine exclamations: no siege, no arrows, no ramp built, no entrance! And this happened for the city of David **for the sake of David** (v 34) and because of Hezekiah's prayer.

■ **35** The very night of Yahweh's response through Isaiah to Hezekiah's prayer, **the angel of Yahweh** struck the Assyrian armies. They were either at Libnah with the king or at Lachish. In either case, 185,000 Assyrians troops did not awaken in the morning, so those who rose in the morning must refer to the king and his assistants or to the Judahites who awakened to see their enemies slain without a battle (compare Isa 37:36-38).

■ **36-37** Sennacherib **returned to Nineveh** and continued to worship his god, **Nisrok**, at whose temple he was assassinated by two of his sons in 681 BC, a slaying that was part of a rebellion recounted in the Babylonian Chronicle.

The Babylonian Chronicle

The Babylonian Chronicle is a series of cuneiform tablets upon which the history of Babylon and the kings of Babylonia in the late period were described. It includes Babylonian defeats on the battlefield as well as victories and seems more objective than similar annals (Grayson 1992a, 3, 206). The Babylonian Chronicle only records three of the last fifteen years of the Assyrian Empire.

Concerning Sennacherib's untimely death, Wesley wrote: "The God of Israel had done enough to convince him, that he was the only true God. Yet he persists in his idolatry. Justly then is his blood mingled with his sacrifices, who will not be convinced by so dear-bought a demonstration, of his folly in worshipping idols" (*Notes on the Bible*, 2 Kgs 19:37).

This section, 2 Kgs 18:13—19:37, is an exemplar of the prophetic confrontation genre, which sets a king, Yahweh, and/or his prophet against a foe who is then defeated as a fulfillment of Yahweh's words.

4. Yahweh Heals Hezekiah (20:1-11)

BEHIND THE TEXT

This passage appears rearranged in Isa 38 with a prayer psalm of Hezekiah added but with references to the house of David, skepticism, and slight delays dropped. In both cases, the healing of Hezekiah is correlated with the salvation of Jerusalem. The 2 Kings account is the source of the Isaianic account.

IN THE TEXT

■ **1** While the siege of Jerusalem by Sennacherib was threatening, the thirty-nine-year-old king became deathly ill from a boil (20:7). Yahweh announced through Isaiah that Hezekiah would die, so he should **put his house in order**. For a king, this included ensuring a successor. Ultimately, Yahweh decided to give Hezekiah another fifteen years, giving Hezekiah his twenty-nine-year reign, which means that his illness occurred in his fourteenth year (18:13).

■ **2-3** Hezekiah did not accept this; he prayed for Yahweh to remember his good deeds and wholehearted faithfulness and wept. Hezekiah's psalm written after the crisis had passed should be read with this passage (Isa 38:9-20). Second Chronicles 32:31 presents Hezekiah's illness as a test of Hezekiah, ***to know all that was in his heart***, which recalls Gen 22:1 concerning God's testing of Abraham.

■ **4-5** These verses imply an almost immediate answer from Yahweh, retracting the death notice based upon Hezekiah's plea. Isaiah had walked out of the king's room and made it to the middle court when Yahweh stopped him and said, **Go back**. Isaiah 38:4-5 suggests an even more immediate response from Yahweh, who said that he had changed his mind because of Hezekiah's tears and prayer. He would be cleansed of his illness and able to go to the temple **on the third day**.

■ **6** The praying king and the threatened city would be saved by Yahweh for David's sake and for Yahweh's **sake**. Clearly, the events of this chapter occurred at the outset of the crisis represented in chs 18—19.

■ **7** The prophet was practical. Isaiah applied a **fig** poultice to Hezekiah's fatal **boil** so that he lived. The poultice took effect in a couple of days as the means by which Yahweh healed Hezekiah, who could then enter the temple.

■ **8** Asking for signs was encouraged by Yahweh during Isaiah's prophetic ministry (Isa 7:10-14). Although to Yahweh, Hezekiah's healing and the salvation of Jerusalem were intertwined, Hezekiah only asked for a sign of his own healing.

■ **9** Verse 11 of 2 Kgs 20 and Isa 38:7-8 explicate the given sign further. Yahweh would make the shadow cast by the declining sun **on the dial of Ahaz** turn back ten steps. The Hebrew word for ***dial*** (*ma'ălâ*) is normally rendered **steps**. But the ***dial of Ahaz*** was probably a sundial of steps on which a nearby shadow (of a pillar or post) fell as the sun's light passed a window.

■ **10** Hezekiah agreed that a shadow retreating ten steps would be most unlikely, so he chose this for the sign from Yahweh that he would be healed.

■ **11** Isaiah appealed to Yahweh, and Yahweh caused the shadow that had already passed to return on the steps used in the palace as a sundial. In Isa 38, Hezekiah wrote a psalm and then Isaiah prepared the fig poultice.

5. Hezekiah Receives Babylonian Envoys; Isaiah Responds (20:12-21)

■ **12 Marduk-Baladan** of Babylon sent visitors to Hezekiah with gifts and letters because of his illness. Although 2 Kings does not overtly mention Hezekiah's political alliance with Babylon, this incident is indicative of it. Isaiah 39 is nearly identical.

■ **13** Showing the Babylonian officials his treasures demonstrated to them that Judah was a worthy ally. Second Chronicles suggests that they came because they heard of the strange sign accompanying Hezekiah's illness (32:31).

■ **14** The view that Isaiah was a court prophet, associated with Judah's kings, is underscored by these chapters in 2 Kings and Isa 36—39. Although Hezekiah did not consult him in the matter of the Babylonian envoys, Isaiah heard that they had come and questioned Hezekiah.

■ **15** Hezekiah innocently responded with the facts, with no qualms about his utter transparency before Babylon.

■ **16-18** But Isaiah delivered the word of Yahweh concerning what had already transpired. Not only would Babylon take the treasures of Hezekiah's ancestors and himself (see 2 Chr 32:27-29), but they would remove his own sons and make them eunuchs as well.

■ **19** Hezekiah's response was cavalier and selfish, although common among humankind to this day. If Isaiah's picture of impending calamity and exile did not affect *him*, he was content. Isaiah's word implied that Hezekiah's openness to Babylon was the cause of the future disaster, although it may have been an occasion for Yahweh to inform the king of Babylon's increasing power and imperial designs.

■ **20-21** Dtr's concluding regnal formula for Hezekiah includes reference to his famous tunnel, which brought water into the southern edge of the city from the Gihon spring during the time of Sennacherib's siege (compare 2 Chr 32:3-4). The tunnel was dug in haste by two teams working from both ends. An inscription, written about 700 BC and discovered in 1880, describes how the two groups of tunnel carvers, hewing through earth and stone, met each other (see Coote 1992, 24; and Shanks 2008, 52-57).

The Text of the Siloam Inscription
(now on display in Istanbul)

1. [. . .] the tunneling, and this was how the tunneling was completed: as [the stonecutters wielded]
2. their picks, each crew toward the other, and while there were still three cubits to g[o], the voices of the men calling
3. each other [could be hear]d, since there was an increase (in sound) on the right [and lef]t. The day the
4. breach was made, the stonecutters hacked toward each other, pick against pick, and the water

5. flowed from the source to the pool [twel]ve hundred cubits, even though the height of the rock above the heads of the stonecutte[rs] was a hundred cubits!

Completing Hezekiah's tunnel was a great engineering feat. The two teams starting at opposite ends, 150 feet below the surface, burrowed through the bedrock on a zigzag s-shaped curve. Yet they met so near to each other that they could hear each other's hammers and voices. (See Coote 1992, 24; and Tarler and Cahill 1992, 62.)

FROM THE TEXT

Second Kings 20:1-8 affirms that Hezekiah's healing and gift of an additional fifteen years of life was the result of his prayer (and Isaiah's fig poultice). It thus demonstrates how prayer affects outcomes, how God is affected by the requests of his people. This passage joins a long line of biblical texts and thus reflects the overall tenor of the Bible in representing the cooperative nature of divine-human interaction.

God's reversal of an earlier plan is also dramatically stressed in Jer 18:1-12 regarding nations: God's plans for nations could be altered depending on the choices made by the people that comprise that nation. From this we learn that what people say and do affects how circumstances unfold before God.

The stories of Elijah and Elisha in 1—2 Kings are replete with examples of how God moved in response to pleas for help (see, for example, 2 Kgs 4:1-37). Other passages that demonstrate the effectiveness of prayer include Gen 18; Exod 8:12-13, 30-31; chs 32—34; and Num 14. In 1 Sam 15, Saul's prayers did *not* change God's mind; God *became* determined to reject a Saulide dynasty *on account of Saul's disobedience*. God had already changed his mind about Saul's suitability to found a royal dynasty, but he would not change his mind about rejecting Saul (1 Sam 15:29).

In the NT, Jesus often healed in response to specific verbal pleas. A few examples include the Syro-Phoenician woman (Matt 15:21-28; Mark 7:24-30), Jairus, and the "daughter of Abraham" (Matt 9:18-26; Mark 5:21-43; Luke 8:40-56). Our prayers do not control God, and they do not control all circumstances, but we are taught to pray. "You do not have because you do not ask God" (Jas 4:2). For further reading on this passage and subject, see Winslow 2012, 49-51; Varughese 2008, 235-36; and Sanders 1998, 86, 131, 268-79.

B. Manasseh and Amon Abandon Yahweh and Rebuild the Local Shrines (21:1-26)

BEHIND THE TEXT

Although Manasseh's sins were similar to those of Ahaz, his grandfather, (2 Kgs 16:3-4), Dtr details Manasseh's failures much more extensively. Dtr blamed Manasseh for causing the fall of Judah in a manner similar to the way he blamed Jeroboam I for causing Israel's downfall. In Israel's case, Dtr also recognized the additional apostasies of many of the other kings of Israel, whereas Manasseh is denounced as solely culpable for Jerusalem's fall to Babylon (2 Kgs 21:11-13; 23:26; 24:1-4). Other scriptures, such as Jeremiah and 2 Chronicles, blame the generation living during the Babylonian conquest for Judah's ultimate fall and exile (2 Chr 36; Jeremiah passim). Nonetheless all of these agree that idolatrous kings, priests, and people caused the exile; it was not a failure of Yahweh's might.

Manasseh's sins in 2 Kgs 21 are repeated with only a few changes by the Chronicler in 2 Chr 33:1-9. However, the Chronicler's version of Manasseh's story is expanded and includes an account of his repentance, wrought by a forced excursion to Babylon at the hands of the Assyrians against whom he had rebelled (2 Chr 33:10-13). The repentant Manasseh was allowed to return to Judah (vv 14-17). This incident would have fulfilled Isaiah's prediction that Hezekiah's sons would be taken to Babylon (2 Kgs 20:18). In comparison to 2 Chr 33, Dtr's review of Manasseh's reign in 2 Kgs 21 is concise. He is depicted as fully apostate and as the cause of Judah's later subjugation to Babylon, even though his grandson Josiah became fully devoted to Yahweh and sponsored the greatest revival in Judah's history.

Another side to Manasseh's apostate rule may be distilled from accounts of Assyrians and Egyptians who were allied during this period, confining Judah to the borders that Hezekiah had negotiated after his attempt to rebel. Excavations at Ekron (under Assyrian rule) have produced implements of olive oil production *and* Israelite four-horned altars, which means that Judahites labored for this Assyrian industry during this period.

Furthermore, Esarhaddon, the greatest of Assyrian kings, listed Manasseh among a group of twenty-two western kings who were forced to transport building material to Nineveh (*ANET*, 291). (This lends support to the Chronicler's expanded report.) His successor, Ashurbanipal, also listed Manasseh among rulers who paid tribute and helped him conquer Egypt in 668/667 BC (ibid., 294). According to Assyrian annals, Manasseh was always a loyal vassal (Evans 1992, 497).

IN THE TEXT

■ 1 The account of Manasseh's reign begins with the Judahite regnal formula that includes his long reign and his mother's name. Like Joash and Josiah, he became king while still a boy because his father died. Following the ages given in these chapters, Hezekiah was forty-two when Manasseh was born, three years after the illness described in ch 20 when Hezekiah was thirty-nine (fourteen years after he became king at twenty-five). Thus when Hezekiah was ill, he had not fathered any sons who survived him, a fact he did not mention in his prayer, but relates to Isaiah's message from Yahweh announcing his impending death and directing him to get his house in order (name a successor [2 Kgs 20:1]). Hezekiah died when he was fifty-four.

■ **2** Like Ahaz (2 Kgs 16:1-4), Manasseh practiced evil in Yahweh's eyes *according to* the detestable *ways* [tô'ăbôt] of the nations **Yahweh** had driven out before *them*. This reference to Canaanite practices in Joshua's generation (which are described with the same Hebrew term in Deuteronomy and Joshua) is supplemented below by subtle references to Assyrian influence on the small vassal state still ruled by a son of David.

■ **3-5** Like Ahab of Israel, Manasseh built altars for Baal and Asherah. He also established worship of the sun, moon, and stars *in Yahweh's house* (see v 7). He reversed Hezekiah's reforms to restore Judah to Mosaic and Davidic covenantal parameters and to preserve the temple for the worship of Yahweh alone. Manasseh may have found it necessary to mollify the Assyrians in order to preserve the bit of autonomy that remained to Judah (as Ahaz and Hezekiah had done by paying tribute, etc.). Thus the altars for the host of heaven in the temple may reflect submission to Assyria. These moves were abhorred by Yahwistic/Levitical priests, even if they were welcomed by some of the people. Manasseh's long reign indicated that he was sufficiently powerful—because of his submission to Assyria—to squelch detractors (v 16).

■ **6** Deuteronomy 18:9-12 is a direct attack upon Manasseh (and Ahaz):
When you enter the land **Yahweh** your God is giving you, do not learn to imitate the detestable ways [tô'ăbôt] of the nations there. Let no one be found among you who sacrifices their son or daughter in the fire, who practices divination or sorcery, interprets omens, engages in witchcraft, or casts spells, or who is a medium or spiritist or who consults the dead. Anyone who does these things is detestable to **Yahweh**; because of these same detestable practices [tô'ăbôt] **Yahweh** your God will drive out those nations before you.

21:2-14

This scripture uses the same language as that used throughout 2 Kgs 21.

■ **7-9** Manasseh desecrated the temple *and Yahweh's name* by installing the image of Asherah. Yahweh's promise to dwell among his people was conditional, based upon the Mosaic covenant, which they broke, *doing* more evil even than the Canaanite nations (v 9). Dtr depicts Yahweh's disappointment as he recalled this promise concerning the place he had put his **Name forever** (v 7): among his people Israel, their land, Jerusalem, and the temple.

■ **10-14** Even though Yahweh had promised his people that they would not wander from this land (be exiled or driven out), they had failed to keep the covenant. Unnamed prophets pronounced that **therefore** Yahweh had *changed his mind* concerning them (v 12). The prophets and Dtr spoke with one voice, Yahweh's voice, in basing the resulting disasters on Manasseh's **detestable sins** [tô'ăbôt] *causing Judah to sin*. None of this was in Yahweh's earlier plans for Israel; it was determined by Manasseh's initiatives. (See Jer 18:1-12 and → From the Text above.)

Thus, on account of Manasseh and Judah's evil (*rā'â*), during *his* time, Yahweh would bring disaster (*rā'â*) to cause hearers' **ears** to **tingle** (v 12; compare Jer 19:3 and 1 Sam 3:11). The scale of the destruction of the house of Ahab is found in 1 Kgs 21:21: "I will wipe out your descendants and cut off from Ahab every last male in Israel—slave or free." Jerusalem would suffer the same fate as Samaria. This same judgment formula is used in Jer 6:19; 11:11; 18:1-12; 19:3; 42:17; 45:5. Although the implication in this chapter is that Yahweh's judgment was firm, Jeremiah's purpose was to offer repentance during the times of Jehoahaz, Jehoiakim, and Jehoiachin. The passages in Jeremiah are addressed to a later audience, implying that *even after Manasseh* Judah could have repented.

■ **15** Dtr demonstrates Manasseh's culpability in the disasters that followed when Babylon besieged Jerusalem, but this speech also shows Yahweh's longstanding disgust with his people who had been provoking him to **anger from the day their ancestors came out of Egypt until this day**.

■ **16** In addition to Manasseh's apostasy, he slaughtered many innocents. These innocents could have included prophets such as Isaiah, who is alleged to have been "sawn asunder" by Manasseh in *The Martyrdom and Ascension of Isaiah* (first century AD; see Heb 11:37), a Jewish tradition also reported in the Talmuds, *The Lives of the Prophets*, and in patristic writers.

■ **17-18** The concluding formula for Manasseh's long reign claims that he was buried, not *with* his ancestors in the city of David like other Davidic kings, but in the garden of his own house at **Uzza**. Uzza is probably Perez Uzzah near Siloam, named such in 2 Sam 6:8 after Yahweh broke out against Uzzah for touching the ark (Sweeney 2007, 432). The writer does not use this unusual burial place as an opportunity to further censure Manasseh for his sins. The Chronicler can have it both ways by writing: "Manasseh rested with his ancestors [died] and was buried in his palace [at Uzza]" (2 Chr 33:20).

■ **19** Amon's short term of rule is a footnote to the long reign of his father, Manasseh, and a preliminary to that of his son, the reforming king Josiah. The Judahite regnal formula indicates that Amon's mother, **Meshullemeth**, and her father, **Haruz**, were from **Jotbah** of the Negev (see Num 33:33-34), controlled by Assyria.

■ **20-22** When summarizing the reign of Amon (642-640 BC), Dtr again refers to Manasseh's sins. Amon, who also served idols and forsook Yahweh, was born when Manasseh was fifty-five, so he may have had older brothers. They may have been unavailable to succeed Manasseh because the king had **made his son** [possibly the crown prince] **pass through the fire** (2 Kgs 21:6). Others could have otherwise died or had been carted off by the Assyrians (2 Chr 33:11). To be consistent to his account of a repentant Manasseh, the Chronicler points out: "unlike his father Manasseh, [Amon] did not humble himself before **Yahweh**" (2 Chr 33:23). Apart from this verse, 2 Chr 33:21-25 is very close to 2 Kgs 21:19-26.

■ **23** Backed by Assyria, Manasseh had slaughtered many people, indicating a reign of terror against detractors (v 16). Amon, however, was young, new, and vulnerable. Furthermore, movements were afoot in the empire that were beginning to weaken Assyria. Revolts by Babylonians and Elamites, suppressed during this period, drained Assyria's strength. Regional officials ready to revolt against Assyria may have been responsible for Amon's assassination, possibly from the same or associated groups that longed for a return to the worship of Yahweh alone.

Some scholars suggest that older sons may have been behind the assassination of Amon (Cogan and Tadmor 1988, 275), but the text provides no reason for this court conspiracy. Dtr moves quickly to Josiah's reign rather than providing an explanation for young Amon's murder.

■ **24** This revolt against the dynasty of David—and possibly against the Assyrians to whom Judah was subjugated in the mid-seventh century BC—was not supported by the populace. **The people of the land** were Judahites outside of Jerusalem, landowners loyal to the Davidic dynasty (ibid., 275-76). They killed the assassins and returned a son of David to the throne, the young Josiah. According to the ages given throughout this passage and the next, Amon was killed when he was twenty-four and Josiah was eight. Thus, Amon fathered Josiah when he was sixteen.

■ **25-26** Amon was buried in the garden of the Uzza palace with his father, Manasseh; two apostate kings who did not follow in the ways of Hezekiah or David.

FROM THE TEXT

Second Kings is consistent in returning to Manasseh as the cause of Judah's fall (21:11-13; 23:26; 24:1-4). Josiah's later reform could not stop the disaster because of the depth of Manasseh's evil (23:26; 24:3). In contrast, 2 Chronicles and the book of Jeremiah consistently blame the last kings (Josiah's sons) and officials of Judah who did not listen to the prophets Jeremiah and Zephaniah. As noted above, Jeremiah was called by God to speak his mind to Judah mostly after Josiah died. At first, his main message was a call to repentance. For a time it was not too late. Thus, to those writers, Manasseh's sins did not mean it was impossible to thwart the threatened judgment as it does in 2 Kings.

The various biblical documents represent different points of view on the crises that surrounded the fall of Judah. The dramatic differences in the two biblical versions of Manasseh's story—2 Chronicles and 2 Kings—cannot be reconciled, but they can be explained by examining the different purposes of the two writers.

Both writers were accounting for Judah's fall to Babylon, writing theodicies to explain why such evil (disaster) befell God's covenant people. Both agreed that it was not any failure of Yahweh. But the Chronicler's Manasseh was not to blame: he repented (2 Chr 33:13). On the other hand, the Chronicler's Josiah failed to listen to the voice of God through Pharaoh (!) and thus died (35:20—36:1). Nonetheless, even this did not cause Judah's fall to Babylon. Judah was ultimately exiled because the last king of Judah, Zedekiah, and his officials refused to listen to Jeremiah and the other prophets (2 Chr 36:12-17).

Second Kings contrasts Manasseh's great evil and Josiah's great faithfulness but settles on the evil as determinative. The goodness of Josiah was unable to stop the wheels of judgment against Judah set in motion by Manasseh. On the other hand, 2 Chronicles shows the potential for change and repentance provoked by Manasseh's temporary exile to Babylon. This is consistent with other stories in 1—2 Kings and the words of many prophets—up to a point. Time eventually ran out for Judah to be saved from Babylon, but God still sought their repentance and return to him. To listen to his prophets eventually meant submission to Babylon.

God's ways change for particular situations depending on the circumstances. God did not and does not abandon his people, but specific directives depend on how people have responded to previously revealed commands.

C. Josiah Reforms Judah according to the Book of the Law (22:1—23:30)

BEHIND THE TEXT

Josiah reigned from 640 to 609 BC, during which time Judah remained a vassal state of other nations. Throughout the first decade of Josiah's reign, Judah was under the domination of Assyria. During his last two decades, Egypt and Babylon subjected Judah.

The biblical account and texts from Assyria and Babylon are supported by archaeological evidence for the demographics of this period. Judahites of the late seventh century BC moved eastward to the hill country around Jerusalem and away from lands dominated by the Assyrians. The Assyrian Empire experienced civil war (628-626 BC) and consequently declined in strength and influence. Josiah and Pharaoh Psamtik I (664-609 BC) were allied during this time. As Babylon grew stronger, Egypt and Judah supported declining Assyria (Althann 1992b, 1017-18).

According to the Babylonian Chronicle, in 627 BC, three rulers of the Assyrian Empire (Sin-shar-ishkun, Sin-shum-lishir, and the Babylonian Nabopolassar) revolted against Ashur-etel-ilani, successor to Ashurbanipal. By 626 BC, they reconciled by dividing their turf. This distraction allowed Josiah to extend his reform into the former territory of the kingdom of Israel. The Meṣad Ḥashavyahu (Yavneh-Yam) inscriptions indicate that northern Philistia was under Josiah's control (Althann 1992b, 1016), which means Josiah could have entered the northern territory without fear of Assyrian reprisals.

The Babylonian Chronicle also describes how Nabopolassar (626-605 BC) eventually drove the Assyrians out of Babylon (625 BC) and joined Cyaxares, king of the Medes, to capture Ashur (614 BC) and Nineveh (612 BC). Egypt was allied with Assyria against Babylon, which was the reason for Pharaoh Necho's northern march to Megiddo in 609 BC. Alternatively, some scholars believe that Necho and Nabopolassar were fighting with each other to take over Assyrian lands (Hobbs 1985, 339). In any case, Necho killed Judah's king Josiah in the battle at Megiddo. On his way back south, Necho took over Judah and eventually brought Jehoiahaz, the son and successor of Josiah, to Egypt.

In 605 BC, Necho fought Nabopolassar again at Carchemish, where he was defeated by Nebuchadnezzar II, Nabopolassar's son. When Nebuchadnezzar II became king of Babylon (604—562 BC), he led campaigns into northern Syria and Judah to expel Egypt. At this time, Jerusalem was conquered by Babylon and led into exile (586 BC).

Although demographic studies and Assyrian and Babylonian annals have historical relevance to Josiah's reign, its most important underlying *theological* text is the book of Deuteronomy. In Josiah's story in 2 Kgs 22, a book of Torah was found in the temple when the priests were complying with Josiah's orders to restore and renovate it. This scroll is widely considered to be an early form of Deuteronomy, upon which the subsequent reform of Josiah was based.

The discovery of this book of the covenant led to Josiah's program of religious reform that reached into the regions of Samaria with hopes of extending that reform and Josiah's rule into Israel. (→ 1 Kgs 11:26-40; 12:25-33; and 13:1-34 for a discussion of Jeroboam I's golden calves and the prophecy denouncing them that refers to Josiah's reform.) While some scholars are confident that this scroll of Deuteronomy was written in order to support Josiah's program (Sweeney 2001, 139), others consider it older. However, they agree that an earlier version of the present book of Deuteronomy was the basis for the reform because the latter corresponded to the laws found therein.

A number of scholars have seen northern interests behind Deuteronomy, but Sweeney points out that such interests were reformulated to place greater power in the hands of the king—the Davidic Judahite king (ibid., 138-40). Deuteronomy attends to the centralization of the cult and the administration of justice *at Jerusalem*, the city of David, *in Judah* (Deut 12:2-31; compare Exod 20:21-26).

This early form of Deuteronomy was redacted in Josiah's time and again later in the exilic period (see Cross 1973, 274-89; Sweeney 2001, 25-32, and citations there). The final form of Deuteronomy indicates awareness of the exile (Deut 4:27-31; 28:36; 29:27 [26 HB]; 30:1-10) as does the final form of

DtrH (Joshua—2 Kings), a theodicy that attempts to justify the exile in spite of the national repentance and radical reforms of Josiah.

The story of Josiah heightens the tension between the conditional Mosaic covenant and the promises given to David. When first given in 2 Sam 7, the Davidic covenant appeared to be unconditional; it was a forever covenant. Ultimately, 2 Kgs 22—25 weighs in on the side of the conditional Mosaic covenant, because no son of David remained on the throne (contra 2 Sam 7:14-15). Aware of the promises to David and of Josiah's reform on the one hand, the final redactors of 2 Kings were also aware of the many decades of apostasy by Davidic kings and the fact that the exile had happened. They thus attributed Judah's downfall to the failure of Manasseh to keep the conditions of the Mosaic covenant and to walk in the ways of David. (→ Introduction at F. Theological Themes; Behind the Text and From the Text for 1 Kgs 1:1-53; and Behind the Text and comments for 1 Kgs 2:1-46 and 1 Kgs 11:26-40.)

I. Josiah Hears the Words of Yahweh (22:1-20)

IN THE TEXT

■ 1 The efforts of Amon's assassins to implement a new dynasty in Judah were thwarted when the officials were killed and Amon's eight-year-old son was placed on the throne by "the people of the land" (21:24). The aspirations of the assassins are unstated. They may have desired to restore Yahweh alone worship or to avenge Manasseh's rampant bloodshed. In any case, Josiah became king when he was a young boy. No information is given about his advisers as it was for Joash in 2 Kgs 12. Were they "the people of the land," those who had placed him on the throne? This is likely.

■ 2 Like his father David, Josiah **did what was right in the eyes of Yahweh**. Like Moses' successor, Joshua, *he did not turn* aside to the right or to the left (Josh 1:7-8; 23:6). This is also an allusion to Deuteronomy's ideal king, who would not turn aside to the right or the left from Moses' Torah (Deut 17:20) and to the ideal people of God (Deut 5:32; 17:11, 20; 28:14). Dtr gave no other king of Judah, including Hezekiah, this commendation. The entire passage (2 Kgs 22:3—23:25) illustrates how Josiah earned this acclaim. On his own initiative, he began to refurbish the temple, which led to a massive, far-reaching reform.

■ 3-4 When Josiah was twenty-six, he sent **the secretary, Shaphan** to **Hilkiah the high priest** with orders to begin to pay out money to workmen to repair the temple (compare Joash's temple renovations of 2 Kgs 12:4-15 [5-16 HB]). Throughout this story, Shaphan served as an intermediary between the high priest and the king.

■ 5-7 According to the story as it is told in 2 Chr 34:3-17, Josiah first began to seek Yahweh when he was sixteen (631 BC). When he was twenty (627 BC), he removed the Asherah and Baal shrines throughout the land. In 2 Kgs 23:5-8, this activity is described as *subsequent* to his temple reform. As in 2

Kgs 22:3-8, 2 Chr 34:8-14 describes how Josiah restored the temple and thus found the book of the law, the covenant book, when he was twenty-six, the eighteenth year of his reign.

■ **8** While obeying the king's command to repair and refurbish the temple, Hilkiah told the scribe: ***a book of the Torah*** [*sēper hattôrâ*] ***I have found***. The word order emphasizes the significance of the find. Moses referred to "this Book of the Law" (*sēper hattôrâ*) in part of his final sermon to pre-landed Israel before he died (Deut 30:10). There he informed them of Yahweh's promise to restore all exiles to their fathers' land—even those scattered to the heavens (v 4)—if they obeyed his voice "to keep his commandments and his statutes which are written in this book of the law [*sēper hattôrâ*]" (v 10 KJV).

■ **9-10** As Hilkiah no doubt intended, Shaphan approached the king with relevant information about the work. Then, saving the best for last, he reported that Hilkiah gave him **a book** (v 10). Shaphan thus disclosed the recently discovered book and then read it to the king.

■ **11** The king's severe reaction of tearing his clothes was a sign of great mourning. The reason is immediately apparent and shows how much Josiah feared Yahweh and trusted that this book contained his words.

■ **12-13** Sending the high priest and the officials to inquire of Yahweh was not Josiah's way of testing the authenticity of the book to discover if its words were true, or to answer the many questions later readers have about its provenance. He knew it was authentic; he knew it was true; he knew it was from Yahweh. He was well aware that Judah had not been living in the ways prescribed in the book and that they had been doing what it proscribed. At this point, he wanted to hear from Yahweh the consequences for Judah's present generation, whose ancestors had not obeyed the book's words. He cried: **Great is Yahweh's** **anger that burns against us because those who have gone before us have not obeyed the words of this book** (v 13).

■ **14** The high priest, the scribe, and other officials of the king went to a woman prophet whose husband and location are both identified. ***The Second District*** or Quarter (*mišneh*) is part of Jerusalem, west of the city of David, extended to the north by previous Judahite kings (Zeph 1:10). When the king ordered them to inquire of Yahweh, they went to Huldah and ***spoke to her***.

The text gives no sense that to consult a woman prophet was unusual for a king and high priest, or that they sought an oracle of Yahweh from her because male prophets were scarce, busy, or inadequate. Jeremiah was not consulted even though he had been called to be a prophet five years previously. (He was called during Josiah's thirteenth year, and this was Josiah's eighteenth year as king [Jer 1:1-3].) Zephaniah was also a prophet during this time, but neither are mentioned in 2 Kings, although Jeremiah is mentioned in 2 Chronicles.

■ **15-17** Huldah had an immediate response that confirmed Josiah's worst fears. This was the oracle of Yahweh with two presentations of the formula: ***Thus says Yahweh***. The first was directly to the messengers of the king: ***Thus*** *says Yahweh, the God of Israel*. The second was directly to Josiah: **Thus says Yahweh**. As in the case of Num 11:1-3, 33, Yahweh's **burning** anger is stressed. In 2 Kgs 22:15-17 Yahweh's anger was kindled by the people burning incense to other gods. Huldah's oracle from Yahweh recalls his judgment against Jeroboam I (1 Kgs 14:10), the house of Ahab (21:21), and Judah on account of Manasseh (2 Kgs 21:12), a judgment that would stand despite Josiah's national reform. This oracle affirmed the words of the found book without offering the opportunity for repentance or any interchange to change Yahweh's mind. This contrasts to the story of Moses in Exod 32. (→ From the Text for 2 Kgs 21:1-26.)

■ **18-20** The second portion of Yahweh's oracle through Huldah concerned Josiah himself. The events of judgment would occur after he died in peace *because he was responsive and humble* (v 19) regarding the words of the found book, which were indeed Yahweh's words. This moves the burning anger of Yahweh against Judah farther into the future, at least until after Josiah died a peaceful death, which presupposed a long reign and old age.

For many scholars the fact that, as it turned out, Josiah did not die a peaceful death lends credence to this section as part of the original oracle. However, it causes problems for those who believe that what Yahweh announced must be exactly fulfilled. But the story shows that Yahweh had nothing to do with Josiah's violent death; it was not punishment but happened because he confronted Pharaoh Necho. (Compare the Chronicler's version in 2 Chr 35:20-25.)

The words in the book that frightened Josiah are common terms in Deuteronomy and the DtrH, as well as in Jeremiah and Zephaniah. One of these terms, **desolation** (*šammâ*; NIV: **a curse** [2 Kgs 22:19]), is found in Deut 28:37; Jer 2:15; 4:7; 5:30; 8:21; 18:16; 19:8; 25:9, 11, 18; 29:18; 42:18; 44:12, 22; 46:19; 48:9; 49:13, 17; 50:3, 23; 51:29, 37, 43; and Zeph 2:15. This is one of the many reasons that the found book appears to be a form of Deuteronomy (see Sweeney 2001, 137, n. 22).

FROM THE TEXT

Josiah, Hilkiah, and Shaphan were together responsible for the chain of events involving obtaining and revealing the contents of this book. Huldah and God together revealed the significance of this book for Josiah and Judah, *because* Josiah sought God in this regard. Hilkiah's role in the entire process is intriguing. At the beginning of Josiah's story, he told Josiah's scribe that he had found the book, but this may or may not mean it had ever been "lost." He took the opportunity that Josiah's temple cleanup provided to locate or produce *a book of the Torah* and to ensure that the king heard its words (22:4-10). Later, he took it to Huldah to receive an oracle of Yahweh for the king (22:13-14, 20). In 2 Kgs 23:24, Dtr reminds readers that the high priest, Hilkiah, had found this book and thus Hilkiah's involvement in its revelation (and perhaps production) is reiterated and emphasized.

Like elsewhere at critical moments in a story, the biblical text is cryptic regarding this found book. It provokes many questions over which scholars continue to speculate: What was in this book? When was this book written? By whom? Had it been in the temple all this time? Was it created by the high priest who "found" it or by another priest or scribe from Josiah's time or a few years earlier? Or did it originate a few generations before him and had been truly lost? Or was it even older?

Some of these questions are answered by what Josiah did after hearing the book read. He indicated his fear of God's burning anger (expressed in the curses of Deut 28); he centralized the cult in Jerusalem (Deut 12:5, 18; 14:25; 16:6, 11; 17:8; 26:2); he removed all images, idols (Deut 4:19; 5:8; 7:5; 12:3; 27:15; 29:17 [16 HB]), and altars to the sun, moon, and stars (Deut 4:19; 17:3); and he renewed the covenant with a celebration of the Passover. All these things point to Deuteronomy. It was either written by Hilkiah, a priestly predecessor, or had been stored for generations in the temple without being consulted or used.

Josiah feared God in every sense. He was truly afraid of God and what could happen to people who did not fear God enough to keep his commandments. He respected God and his priests. He valued God's house to the extent that he refurbished it, which led to the found book. He did not expect God to pass over the failures and sins of Judah, but he sought God's word from a prophet concerning his situation. Josiah was a model of a true God-fearer who put that awe and respect to work, to bring Judah back into covenant relationship.

Today, even leaders assume they have little power to change the ways of their contemporaries who walk outside of God's ways, so they do not try. But God calls all of us to model righteousness and to warn others against sinning, to offer salvation from sinning and opportunities to know Jesus and his Father in heaven (John 17:3).

2. Josiah Responds to the Words of Yahweh (23:1-30)

BEHIND THE TEXT

In this section, Josiah reversed the apostate establishments of Solomon, Ahaz, and Manasseh (his ancestors) and those of Jeroboam I and Ahab (from whom he also descended through Athaliah of the house of Ahab [2 Kgs 8:18, 26]). Josiah returned to the ways of Moses and Joshua, who were fully obedient to Yahweh's Torah; they also "*did not turn* aside to the right or to the left" (22:2). Like Hezekiah (his own ancestor), he reestablished the worship of Yahweh alone in Jerusalem and tore down the high places. But Josiah went farther than Hezekiah in that he went all through Judah and into Bethel and other towns of Israel to burn to the ground and desecrate all altars, pillars, poles, stones, and shrines. In addition, when he returned, he celebrated the Passover according to the found *Covenant Book*.

This passage is characteristically Deuteronomistic in the manner of Josh 24 and 1 Kgs 8. It repeats certain terms and word order for emphasis such as "all" (*kōl*) to denote the thoroughness of the reform. "All" (*kōl*) Judah pledged to keep the words of the **Covenant Book** (*sēper běrît*). Josiah removed and **defiled** (*ṭāmē'*) all shrines and idolatrous images in the temple, Jerusalem, Judah, and throughout the land in order to conform to "all" (*kōl*) the words of the **Covenant Book**.

IN THE TEXT

■ **1** Josiah assembled **all** (*kōl*) the people in Jerusalem to read to them **all** (*kōl*) the words of the **Covenant Book** (*sēper běrît*) as the first step toward following the commandments therein. The importance of the **elders** would have diminished throughout the monarchic period beginning with David and especially under Solomon's taxation districts that did not follow tribal lines. But the inherited role of elder continued to the degree that even in this late monarchic period they were known and could be gathered to be listed first among those who heard him read all the words of the **Covenant Book**. The listing of elders indicates a return to the ancient ways, to the **Covenant Book**, and the days of Moses and Joshua.

■ **2** *All* (*kōl*) the **priests, prophets,** and **all** [*kōl*] **the people** of every sort gathered before Josiah at the temple. Moses had read the book of the covenant to the people and they promised to keep its words. The significance of these full assemblies cannot be stressed too much. After Moses read the new book of the covenant, all (*kōl*) of Israel's first generation that came out of Egypt responded with a vow to Yahweh (Exod 24:3-8).

Josiah's similar gathering of all the people to renew the covenant based on this scroll is one of the reasons he is lauded by Dtr. Faithful kings and leaders were responsible for their people; ensuring full participation was how they must lead, as good leaders before and after Josiah did. Before and after entering the land, Joshua called a covenant renewal ceremony (Josh 8:30-35; 24:1-28). Later, when the Jews were allowed to return to their land after the exile in Babylon, Ezra read from the book of the Torah of Moses that Yahweh gave to Israel (Neh 8:1-8). The Jews responded by weeping, but Ezra told them to rejoice. Josiah was like Moses and Joshua, and Ezra was like his three predecessors.

Josiah's story demonstrates that the king compelled all the people to gather and confess adherence to the stipulations of a newly found temple book. Repentance was not offered on an individual basis; it was community-wide, demanded and enforced by the king.

■ **3** Josiah stood by his designated royal pillar before Yahweh to renew the **covenant** and lead **all** [*kōl*] **the people** to do the same. The writer repeated that **all the people**—traditional tribal elders, **all** Judahites, **all** Jerusalemites, **all** the people—**pledged themselves to the covenant.**

Everyone followed the king in determining to keep the **covenant** (*bĕrît*), the **commands** [*miṣwâ*], **statutes** [*ʿēdût*] **and decrees** (*ḥuqqâ*) of Yahweh, as outlined in the **Covenant Book**. The list of these terms appears in varied combinations throughout the Torah, Former Prophets (DtrH, or Joshua—2 Kings), and Writings. A few examples are: Lev 26:46; Deut 4:40, 45; 5:31; 6:1, 17, 20; 7:11; 26:17; 27:10; 1 Kgs 3:14; 8:58, 61; 2 Kgs 17:37; 2 Chr 19:10; Neh 1:7; 9:13, 14; 10:29 [30 HB].

■ **4** Even though Josiah's temple renovations had already begun, implements to serve Baal, Asherah, and the hosts of heaven still remained there (Zeph 1:4-6). Josiah had Hilkiah and the priests and doorkeepers remove and burn **all** (*kōl*) of them **outside Jerusalem in the fields** near the **Kidron** stream. This area was thus desecrated.

These "fields" refer to burial sites in the Kidron valley, which is opposite Jerusalem and the place where Solomon erected shrines for Ashtoreth, Chemosh, and Molek (1 Kgs 11:7). King Asa had buried the Asherah image of his grandmother, Maakah (1 Kgs 15:13). The burning of metal implements for idols is reminiscent of Moses' burning of Aaron's golden calf in Exod 32:20. Josiah took the ashes from this destruction to Bethel to desecrate the golden calf altar there. These purges by fire tie together the apostasies of Aaron's golden calf, Baal worship from Elijah's time onward (1 Kgs 18), Jeroboam's calves, and pollutions of the temple at Jerusalem by Ahaz and Manasseh (1 Kgs 12) (see Mare 1992, 37-38).

■ **5** Josiah deposed or retired each ***pagan*** (non-Yahwist) priest (*kōmer*) who had been appointed by Judah's kings to **burn incense** throughout the land to Baal, the sun, moon, and stars. This passage defines the activity of these "priests," the *kĕmārîm*. The designation *kōmer* may derive from the related verb, "to be heated or aroused," an allusion to the rituals of burning incense and also possibly to frenzied practices of the prophets of Baal known from Elijah's time (1 Kgs 18:27-29). The term simply means "priest" in Aramaic and Akkadian, but in the Bible it is used three times to refer to non-Levitical cultic leaders (Hos 10:5; Zeph 1:4). The conventional Hebrew word for priest is *kōhēn*.

23:4-7

■ **6** Josiah's grandfather Manasseh had carved an Asherah pole and placed it in the temple after Hezekiah had removed the one that earlier kings had erected there (2 Kgs 21:7; 18:4). Josiah burned this one to ashes in the Kidron river valley, scattering the ashes on graves of **the common people** or public cemetery. The Hebrew term is literally translated ***children of the people***. The Asherah was thereby defiled and left with the dead. In the story of Elijah, the Asherah was not removed or destroyed when he slaughtered the prophets of Baal. (→ "Asherah" sidebar at Behind the Text for 1 Kgs 16:29—22:53 [22:54 HB], for a discussion of the persistence of Asherah worship among Jews.)

■ **7** The house of Yahweh lodged boys and men (*qĕdēšîm*), set apart or consecrated for temple service. Although the term *qādēš* does not necessitate sexual service in the temple, Deut 23:17 conflates prostitution with temple service. Jehoshaphat had removed the *qĕdēšîm* from Judah in his time (1 Kgs 22:46 [47 HB]). The fact that Josiah **tore down** their **quarters** indicates that they were not serving Yahweh in any acceptable fashion, as do the contexts of other appearances of the term (1 Kgs 14:24; 15:12). In their booths, **women** weaved coverings for Asherah, the activity Josiah targeted here. (For a full discussion of cultic prostitution, see Gruber 1983 and 1986, passim; and Goodfriend 1992, 509-10.)

■ **8-9** These **priests** (*hakkōhanîm*) were not idolatrous; they sacrificed to Yahweh, but did so outside of Jerusalem. Thus, they were not banished but were invited to come to Jerusalem as stipulated in Deut 18:6-8, which does not *require* that they come. They chose to remain with their families in the north.

Josiah set his face to centralize worship in Jerusalem and thus moved forward to ruin and defile (*ṭāmē'*) **all** the high places from the northern border of Geba in Benjamin to the southern border on the Negev, regardless of the focus of their sacrifices. This included the high places established on entrances to the city.

■ **10** Topheth in the Valley of Ben Hinnom (Gk.: *Gehenna*) was the name for the site of child sacrifice to Molek, which Yahweh abhorred (Lev 18:21; 20:2, 3, 4, 5; 1 Kgs 11:7; 2 Kgs 23:10; Jer 32:35). The consonants of *tōpet* derived from an Aramaic term for fireplace, and the vowels points are probably the result of alteration to make the word sound like *bōšet*, "shame." Yahweh sent Jeremiah there with an oracle against it and all of Judah (Jer 19:1-14).

Josiah defiled (*ṭāmē'*) Topheth to make it unusable for child sacrifice. Two decades later, Jeremiah's diatribe against it may imply that some Judahites returned to the practice or he may be referring to the pre-Josianic reform decades under Ahaz (2 Kgs 16:3) and Manasseh (2 Kgs 21:6). (For more reports of child sacrifice in Israel and Judah, see Ps 106:37-39; Isa 57:5; Jer 7:31-32; 19:2-14; 32:35; Ezek 16:20-21; 20:25-26, 30-31; 23:36-39.)

Deuteronomy 12:31 cites the Canaanites as devotees of the cult of Molek, the deity associated with child sacrifice throughout the Bible. Some scholars, such as Weinfeld, hope that "passing one's child through the fire" was a ritual that did not involve the child's death, but this cannot be substantiated. Neither Yahweh nor Jeremiah thought it was a rite that the child survived (Jer 19:2-10). (For further reading on Topheth, see Schmitz 1992, 601; on Molek, see Heider 1992, 897; on both, see Varughese 2008, 123, 245.)

■ **11** Horse and chariot imagery appears in the Bible as metaphors for Yahweh (Pss 68; 104; Hab 3), as well as for natural movements of the sun created by Yahweh, but Josiah knew that previous kings of Judah associated them with solar worship. Thus, Josiah removed these images and figurines as he sought to follow the stipulations of the found book and cleanse his land of all taints of idolatry. Dtr precisely locates them as in the court of a temple official, **Nathan-Melek**.

■ **12** Josiah continued his purge of the syncretism of Kings Ahaz and Manasseh by grinding the unorthodox (anti-Torah) altars and pillars (2 Kgs 21:5) they had constructed in the temple to dust and rubble, which he scattered in the Kidron valley. Jeremiah and Zephaniah prophesied against such rooftop altars made for Baal and the stars and the syncretism they evidenced (Jer 19:13; 32:29; Zeph 1:5).

■ **13-14** Josiah turned to another site on the border of Jerusalem in order to correct the idolatrous establishments of King Solomon, on account of which his kingdom was split and mostly torn from his son (1 Kgs 11:5, 7, 33). Although Dtr firmly denounced Solomon in 1 Kgs 11, the subsequent story does not mention his apostasies until now. The high places, pillars, and Asherah poles Solomon had built to the gods of his wives are listed again here as vile and detestable things (*šiqqūṣ* and *tôʿăbôt*), which Josiah defiled (*ṭāmēʾ*) and rendered useless by desecrating them with human bones. These abominations were built on the **Hill of Corruption** or ***Destruction*** (*har hamašît*).

■ **15** Josiah's reform was not complete until he also confronted and reversed the sins of King Jeroboam of Israel. Josiah destroyed the golden calves **with which Jeroboam caused Israel to sin**. Yahweh had promised the first king of the newly formed kingdom of Israel a lasting dynasty and future as bright as he had promised David, if Jeroboam would be faithful to him. Yahweh's covenant to Jeroboam was clearly conditioned upon Jeroboam's obedience (1 Kgs 11:29-40). But Jeroboam had feared he would lose the devotion of his people if they went to Jerusalem to worship, so he built two calves sites, one in the north at Dan and one in the south at Bethel (1 Kgs 12:25-33). The subsequent kings of Israel followed Jeroboam's lead in sacrificing at the altars of Bethel and Dan.

Josiah's actions here are inextricable from the prophetic activity associated with Jeroboam. The young prophet of Judah came to Jeroboam to warn him of future disaster if he did not repent over making the calf shrines. While Jeroboam stood beside the altar at Bethel to sacrifice at his first self-appointed festival, the young prophet "by the word of **Yahweh** . . . cried out against the altar: 'Altar, altar! This is what **Yahweh** says: "A son named Josiah will be born to the house of David. On you he will sacrifice the priests of the high places who make offerings here, and human bones will be burned on you"'" (1 Kgs 13:2). And indeed, this is what Josiah did. No mention is made of the calf image at Bethel, but an Asherah had been erected here, which Josiah also burned. (→ 1 Kgs 13:1-10.)

■ **16** To further defile this altar and the site on which it had been erected, Josiah removed the bones from the nearby graves (*geber*) and burned them upon it. This fulfills the man of God's predictions (1 Kgs 13:2c).

■ **17** A certain grave marker (*ṣiyyûn*) caught his eye, and Josiah asked the men of Bethel about it. They informed him that **the man of God . . . from Judah**, who had described Josiah's actions more than three hundred years previously, was buried there (1 Kgs 13:1-10).

■ **18** Thus, Josiah did not interfere with the grave of the prophet from Judah or the bones of the other prophet buried near him. The **prophet who had come from Samaria** must refer to the old lying prophet who was from Bethel. The city of Samaria was not built until Omri's time, who lived several generations after Jeroboam. Afterward, in texts, "Samaria" was used for the region, not only the capital city of Israel (see also the reference to "towns of Samaria" in 1 Kgs 13:32). At the time of this writing, Samaria was used to refer to the north, to Israel, in contrast to Judah, from whence the first prophet came.

First Kings 13 describes how the old prophet deceived the Judahite prophet to turn from the directives of Yahweh, which led to his death. The old prophet became convinced of the truth of the first prophet's message against Jeroboam and this altar when the young prophet was killed by a lion. He mourned and buried him in his own tomb and required his sons to bury him with the Judahite who brought Yahweh's words to the king. But still King Jeroboam did not repent (1 Kgs 13:30-33).

■ **19** In obedience to Deut 13:12-18 [13-19 HB], Josiah moved freely throughout towns of Samaria, defiling **all the shrines** in Samaria (Israel) erected by apostate kings. Compare 2 Kgs 23:19 with 1 Kgs 13:32. Although Assyria controlled this region, the Assyrians had problems at home (→ Behind the Text for 2 Kgs 23:1-30), and no one hindered Josiah's unrelenting determination to keep the words of the **Covenant Book**.

Josiah did not simply hear and tear his clothes, or hear and gather all of Judah to pledge allegiance, or hear and cleanse the temple in Jerusalem. He went throughout the far reaches of the lands of the people of Yahweh to destroy the sites and the practices that had **aroused Yahweh's anger.**

■ **20** Up to this point, Josiah's reform had involved burning and destroying objects, sites, and bones; not people. It thus radically differed from Jehu's rampage against Baal worshippers and others (2 Kgs 10) and Jehoiada's slaughter of Athaliah and her priests of Baal (2 Kgs 11:15-18). At this point, however, Josiah **slaughtered** (*zābaḥ*) the priests (*kōhēn* not *kōmer*, as in v 5) of the non-Yahwist shrines of Samaria on the altars there and burned their bones on the altars. The term *zābaḥ* is used for sacrificing, which his action confirms; Josiah sacrificed them on the altars of the shrines and burned their bones to defile these altars. Thus, as in the story of Elijah (1 Kgs 18), Josiah's devotion to Yahweh included bloodshed in the region formerly known as Israel.

These specifics of Josiah's reform in the north are left out of the Chronicler's account in 2 Chr 34—35. There Josiah's activity in the north began in the eighth year of his reign, *before* the **Covenant Book** was found. It included Ephraim, Manasseh, Naphtali, and Simeon (2 Chr 34:6-7), where "Josiah removed all [*kōl*] the detestable idols from all [*kōl*] the territory belonging to the Israelites, and he had all [*kōl*] who were present in Israel serve **Yahweh** their God" (v 33), a far more general description.

■ 21 Upon his return from purging the north of worship sites, Josiah led a national celebration of the Passover in Jerusalem. The Judahites **kept** ('*āśâ*) it **as it is written in this Book of the Covenant.** Whereas the Passover may have been observed in Judah in the past, they had not followed the **Covenant Book** that was found (see Deut 16:1-8 and Hobbs 1985, 337).

■ 22-23 Passover celebrations had been **kept** ('*āśâ*) in Judah since the time of the judges, but they had not been observed in the manner of a national festival in Jerusalem like this one Josiah **kept** ('*āśâ*) in his **eighteenth year.** According to the Chronicler, Hezekiah kept a Passover that was unique since the days of Solomon (2 Chr 30:1-27, note v 26). The last reference to keeping the Passover in DtrH is in Josh 5:10-11, when the people prepared to conquer the lands of the Canaanites. No account of a Passover celebration is included in the book of Judges, but the Chronicler concurs with Dtr's mention of the judges period by exclaiming that no Passover such as Josiah's had been kept since the days of the judge Samuel (2 Chr 35:18). The Passover Josiah led is described in much more detail in 2 Chr 35:1-19.

The entire purpose of the Passover was for later generations of Israel to remember, retell, and symbolically reenact Yahweh's deliverance of Israel from enslavement in Egypt. This national celebration was a climax of Josiah's reform. Because the Passover recalls Israel's triumphant escape from their ancient oppressor, Egypt, this passage provides a subtle link to the dark days that DtrH describes for Josiah and Judah in 2 Kgs 23:29.

■ 24 The coda to this account of Josiah's reform relays that Josiah continued cleansing the land of Judah of people and activities proscribed in the **Covenant Book**, which Hilkiah had found. Hilkiah's role is thus underscored again.

Regarding **mediums, spiritists, household gods**, and **idols**, compare this verse to Deut 12:29—13:18 [19 HB] and 1 Sam 19:13; 28:3-25. Clearly, Josiah remained a consistent disciple of the Torah all the days of his life, Deuteronomy's ideal king who persisted in reversing the evil of Solomon, Jeroboam, Ahab, and all the kings of Israel, as well as the Judahites Ahaz and Manasseh (Deut 17:14-20). Unfortunately, Josiah could not nullify the evil of Manasseh.

■ 25 When compared to 2 Kgs 18:5 about King Hezekiah, this may appear to be one of the inconsistencies in the Bible. But it is not. Biblical writers commonly heap hyperbolic superlatives upon certain characters without fear of being accused of contradiction. Compare Num 12:3 and Deut 34 about Moses with Deut 18:15-20 about the prophet that will arise (see Hobbs 1985, 338).

Even so, this accolade for Josiah stresses the significance of the found Torah as the way by which Josiah surpassed the great king Hezekiah. The difference in the two tributes is clear: ***Josiah returned to Yahweh with all his heart, with all his soul, and with all his very much, according to all the Torah of Moses.*** This is the formula of the Shema ("Hear, O Israel . . .") of Deut 6:4-9. Even though Hezekiah also tore down high places throughout Judah (but not Israel), Josiah was greater than him because Hezekiah did not possess Moses'

Covenant Book that Hilkiah produced for Josiah. He obeyed this Torah in all things. For these reasons 2 Kgs 23:25 and 18:5 do not necessarily support the theory of a double redaction of DtrH, although this is demonstrable on other grounds (Cross 1973, 274-89).

■ **26** Judah's rejection on account of Manasseh's sins is reaffirmed in 2 Kgs 24:3, but not in 2 Chr 35—36. The Chronicler laid the blame for Judah's fall at the feet of Josiah's sons and successors, especially Zedekiah and his officials. (→ From the Text after 2 Kgs 21:1-16 and From the Text immediately below.)

■ **27** This reiterates Yahweh's words concerning Manasseh's sin of desecrating the temple, the place of Yahweh's name (2 Kgs 21:4, 7). Yahweh would still reject Judah, Jerusalem, and the house of Yahweh's name. Manasseh's long, sinful reign influenced the outcome for Judah despite Josiah.

When fully engaged with Dtr's portrayal of the specifics of Josiah's reform and his wholehearted devotion to Yahweh through the Torah, readers will find this notice of Jerusalem's utter rejection to be one of the most disturbing in the Bible. It not only seems incongruous in light of Josiah's reform but also challenges prophetic calls to repentance, which denounce and threaten apostates but seek their repentance (compare Jer 6:29-30). (→ From the Text below.)

■ **28** In the manner of the usual formula for summing up a reign of a king of Judah, Dtr refers readers to the royal annals.

■ **29** In compliance with Huldah's words (2 Kgs 22:20*b*), Josiah died before the curses of the ***Covenant Book*** were fulfilled in Judah. In contrast to Huldah's words, he was killed by Pharaoh Necho of Egypt in a confrontation that Josiah initiated. The similarities to Ahab's death are eerie (compare 1 Kgs 22:29-33), because of the great contrast between Josiah's faithful-to-Yahweh life and Ahab's idolatrous, syncretistic life (1 Kgs 21:17-29; 22:29-40).

■ **30** Whereas Ahab's blood was licked by dogs ***according to the word of Yahweh*** (1 Kgs 22:38), Josiah was gathered into the tombs of his fathers in peace, ***according to the word of Yahweh***. Through Huldah, Yahweh had told Josiah: ***I will gather you to your fathers and gather you to your tombs(s) in peace*** (*běšālôm*; 2 Kgs 22:20*a*). In other places such a pronouncement refers to a natural death after a long life (Gen 25:8). In any case, despite his violent death at Megiddo, Josiah *was buried* in peace. His **servants brought his body** to his fathers' tomb(s) in Jerusalem.

After Dtr's glowing report of Josiah's unswerving commitment to Yahweh and ideal reforming reign, his cryptic summary of his death is remarkable for its flat matter-of-fact tone. The brevity makes Dtr's disappointment almost more evident than if he had effusively rued Josiah's untimely death.

In contrast, the Chronicler's account specifies that Necho conveyed the word of God to Josiah, telling him not to fight (2 Chr 35:22) and other details about Josiah's end. He included how all of Judah, including Jeremiah, formally lamented him and kept records of their laments (vv 20-25). The reticence of

Dtr to explain or understand Josiah's early death in 2 Kgs 23 must be read alongside his repeated explanation for the exile that occurred in spite of Josiah's righteousness: Manasseh's sin.

FROM THE TEXT

Unlike Gideon, Samson, Saul, David, Solomon, all of the kings of Israel, and most of the kings of Judah, Josiah stayed true to the Yahweh and Torah stipulations. Without turning to the right or to the left, he consistently fulfilled the rules for a king found in Deut 17:14-20. Solomon did all that was proscribed there; Josiah did all that was prescribed.

In this he was like Joshua—or Joshua was like him (Josh 1:7-8; 8:30-35; 23:6). Sweeney and Nelson argue that Joshua was modeled on Josiah (Sweeney 2001, 125-36; Nelson 1981, 531-40). Joshua's generation was the ideal generation because of their obedience to Joshua and the Torah of Moses (Josh 24:31; Judg 2:7). So also the Judahites *and* Israelites were thoroughly obedient until Josiah died (2 Kgs 23:3; 2 Chr 34:33). Read in the light of the accounts of Josiah's reign in 2 Kings and 2 Chronicles, the books of Joshua and Judges must be viewed as teachings (Torah) to encourage all surviving people of God to follow him and the Torah of Moses (the **Covenant Book**) as Josiah and Joshua did, but unlike the people of the judges period.

According to the repeated Deuteronomistic pattern (blessings for obedience and curses for disobedience), Judah's repentance should have led Yahweh to forgive them and stop the juggernaut of Babylon. Josiah's choices, however, did not bring the blessings for obedience that the Torah promised. In 2 Kgs 22—23, Dtr's task was to make sense of the exile in spite of Josiah's reform.

23:1-30

The post-Josianic redactors of 2 Kgs 22—25 (Dtr) repeatedly claimed that the exile they experienced occurred because Manasseh failed to remain true to Mosaic covenant obligations and to the ways of David, who "did what was right in the eyes of **Yahweh**" (22:2). The exile occurred even though Josiah led a thorough restoration to Moses' Torah in both Israel and Judah and "**walked** in the ways of his father David." Josiah's correctives for Solomon, Jeroboam, Ahab, Ahaz, and Manasseh's sins did not alter the course that led to Judah suffering the curses of Deuteronomy (Deut 27:15-26; 28:15-68).

The references back to David throughout 1—2 Kings strikes an uneasy note, because readers know that David was not always faithful to Yahweh and to the Torah. He had abused his power to commit adultery and murder. The producers of the text obviously knew this as well. However, David's confession when confronted with his egregious sins by the prophet Nathan made him an example of repentance (2 Sam 12:1-13; Pss 32; 51). Whereas David repented for his own sin, Hezekiah and Josiah led repentance on the national level for the sins of their predecessors, including especially Solomon and Manasseh. Thorough, long-lasting repentance was and is the purpose of prophets and prophecy then and now.

This essential aspect of prophecy and the grace of God integral to it are problematized by the story of the repentant Josiah. Most prophetic messages represented in biblical texts set in preexilic Israel and Judah were demands that listeners turn from their apostasies and thus avoid punishment. (Amos may be the exception to this concept.) The prophets warned Israel/Judah of what could happen if they did *not* repent. Furthermore, the dominant theme of both testaments is that God's love is far greater than his anger, that repentance brings reprieve and restoration, and that God's mercy extends one thousand times further than punishment (Exod 20:4, 6).

The teachings, laws, narrative, and prophecies demonstrating the themes of repentance and God's mercy indicate that God has the ability to change his mind over judgment as well as promises (Jer 18:1-11). As we have seen, according to 2 Kings, God suspended his 2 Sam 7 promise of an eternal Davidic dynasty because of Manasseh and despite Josiah.

According to 2 Chronicles and Jeremiah, God offered Judah new and gracious initiatives and offers to repent through Jeremiah and other late—post Josiah—Judahite prophets. During the first part of Jeremiah's ministry, the people still had the opportunity to repent and thus be delivered from imminent oppression (e.g., Jer 4:1-4); later, Jeremiah told Judah that trust in God must be shown by submitting to Babylon. Even when punishment was announced as directly approaching, the purpose of said announcement was to provoke repentance, which is dramatically illustrated in the book of Jonah concerning Nineveh. As it turned out, God reverted to the judgment of the exile because Judah's last kings (Jeremiah's audience) refused to listen (see Varughese 2008, 269).

Although the dominant biblical message of mercy following repentance is countered by the 2 Kings assertion that the consequences of Manasseh's sins were not altered by his grandson's repentance, the prophetic call to repentance is consistent with the NT. The gospel of John the Baptist and Jesus, as well as the preaching of the apostles, calls listeners to repent to receive forgiveness of sins and deliverance from the coming wrath (e.g., Matt 3:1, 8; 4:17; 9:13; Luke 13:1-3).

Josiah's story is one of faithfulness that could not overcome the evil of his grandfather; one that was unrewarded, although his nation was not exiled in his time. All the more so then, in Josiah we find a person fully devoted to God, who sought God's ways, and who was pure of heart. He instituted a thorough restoration of Torah-based faith and practice in Judah *even though* he was not given any hope that this would avert God's anger. Other biblical heroes received a reward or promise for their faithfulness. For Josiah, doing God's will was the reward in itself. May he be a model for us all.

D. Egypt Controls Judah (23:31-37)

BEHIND THE TEXT

At Josiah's death, Judah lost the freedom that Assyria's decline had afforded them and came under the oppressive hands of Egypt and then Babylon. As mentioned in the previous passage, Pharaoh Necho of Egypt killed Josiah at Megiddo in 609 BC and took over Judah (→ Behind the Text for 2 Kgs 22:1—23:30). Soon after, in 605 BC, Necho was defeated by Nebuchadnezzar II of Babylon at Carchemish. Nebuchadnezzar II was the son of Nabopolassar, the founder of the Chaldean dynasty (626—539 BC). When Nebuchadnezzar II became king of Babylon (604—562 BC), he expelled Egypt from northern Syria and Judah and invaded Judah, tearing its royal family and many people from the land. Jeremiah, Micah, and Uriah regularly brought the word of Yahweh to these kings and thus endangered their own lives (Jer 26:12-24). These were Judah's last days.

IN THE TEXT

■ **31** Jehoahaz's brief reign is introduced according to formula. His name is given as Shallum in Jeremiah (Jer 22:10-11). Libnah, the home of his mother, **Hamutal**, was in the Shephelah southwest of Jerusalem near the regions that had been occupied by Philistines. He was the *younger* brother of Eliakim/Jehoiakim by two years, whom "the people of the land" had bypassed (v 30).

■ **32** For three months **he did evil in the eyes of Yahweh**, but he did not have time to do much damage. Jeremiah called the people to lament Jehoahaz/Shallum (Jer 22:11-12). His older brother, whom Pharaoh placed on the throne of Judah in his place, did evil for the eleven years of his reign.

■ **33 Pharaoh Necho** took control of Jerusalem, bound Jehoahaz, and moved him to **Riblah** . . . ***during his* reign in Jerusalem**. Riblah was north of Jerusalem near Kadesh and appears throughout the story of Judah's last days as a post for the Babylonian king who imprisoned Zedekiah and his officers there as well (2 Kgs 25:6, 20-21; Jer 39:5-6; 52:9-10, 26-27). Later, at Riblah, Zedekiah, the last king of Judah, was forced to watch his sons and nobles slaughtered; then his own eyes were put out. Then he was taken in shackles to Babylon (2 Kgs 25:6-7; Jer 39:6-7).

■ **34** Although Necho rejected the son chosen by "the people of the land" to succeed Josiah (Jehoahaz/Shallum), he set up **Eliakim**, the elder son of Josiah, as king. He changed his name to **Jehoiakim**, from ***God establishes*** to ***Yahweh establishes***. (Jehoiakim had a different mother than Jehoahaz, Zebidah of Rumah [2 Kgs 23:36].) Necho did not confine Jehoahaz to Riblah but took him to Egypt with him. Jehoahaz never returned to his own land; he died in Egypt.

■ **35** The tax Necho imposed on Judah under Josiah's son Jehoiakim was not nearly as excessive as that imposed by Sennacherib of Assyria upon Hezekiah's Judah (18:14-15), but it was a burden for Judah during this troubled time.

■ **36-37** Dtr provides the Judahite introductory formula and regnal summary for Jehoiakim. The Egyptian Pharaoh Necho, who killed Josiah and kidnapped Jehoahaz, established Jehoiakim as king in 609 BC, after Necho's attempt to aid Assyria. Jehoiakim's given age of twenty-five shows that he was two years older than the deposed Jehoahaz who was from a southern Judahite region that was anti-Egyptian. His mother's family was from **Rumah**, fifteen miles west of the Sea of Galilee and about six miles southeast of Nazareth in northern Israelite territory that was probably pro-Egyptian and anti-Babylonian (Sweeney 2007, 454). Jehoiakim **did evil in the eyes of** *Yahweh* for the eleven years of his reign (609—598 BC). The book of Jeremiah provides details about Jehoiakim's rebellion against Yahweh and his abuse of Jeremiah (chs 25—28). During Jehoiakim's eleven-year reign, Babylon trounced Egypt and invaded Judah.

E. Babylon Takes Exiles, Overruns Judah, and Razes Jerusalem (24:1—25:30)

BEHIND THE TEXT

Between 609 and 604 BC, Egypt and Babylon tangled over the then defunct Assyrian Empire. In 605, after the battles of Carchemesh and Hamath, Babylon drove out Pharaoh Necho of Egypt from the western regions, areas that Assyria had controlled for many years (Syria, Judah, and Philistia). Soon after Nebuchadnezzar II succeeded Nabopolassar as king of Babylon (604 BC), he took control of Judah and Syria. Nonetheless, Egypt continued to fight to regain the lost territory. A major battle between Egypt and Babylon at Pelusium south of Gaza in 601 BC was indecisive; both sides suffered major casualties.

This battle apparently gave Jehoiakim confidence that Egypt could force Babylon to withdraw from Judah. Demonstrating this hope, as well as his loyalty to Egypt (who had placed him on Judah's throne), he rebelled against Babylon eight years into his rule (601 BC). King Jehoiakim and the prophet Jeremiah clashed over whether Judah should choose to be allied with Egypt or Babylon. Jeremiah was consistently pro-Babylonian (Jer 21:8-10; 27—29; 38:1-3).

The raiding parties of Chaldean/Babylonian vassals against Judah (2 Kgs 24:2-4) were precursors to Nebuchadnezzar's siege of Jerusalem in 598 BC. Dtr uses the term "Chaldean" (*kaśdîm*) for the Babylonians subsequently in some places in 2 Kings. Comprised of five tribes originally located in southern Babylonia, the Chaldeans had become the leaders of Babylon by the latter eighth century BC. The terms "Chaldeans" and "Babylonians" are used synonymously in texts of the eighth century BC and following (Hess 1992, 886).

Nebuchadnezzar's siege of 598 BC resulted in the death of Jehoiakim at age thirty-six and the deportation of his son and successor, eighteen-year-old Jehoiachin, to Babylon (597 BC). This was the beginning of Judah's exile, even though Jerusalem was still standing, and Zedekiah, a son of Josiah (and David), sat on Judah's throne. He was placed there by Nebuchadnezzar. Twenty-one-year-old Zedekiah was the uncle of Jehoiachin and the full brother of young Jehoahaz (whom Pharaoh Necho had taken to Egypt from his headquarters at Riblah). Zedekiah and Jehoahaz had the same mother, Hamutal of Libnah. Zedekiah was the last king of Judah.

After Jehoiachin and his retinue submitted to the king of Babylon and were exiled, Nebuchadnezzar entered the temple built by Solomon and cut up the gold vessels that Solomon had made for it (24:10-15; compare 1 Kgs 6—7). A few years later, when King Zedekiah rebelled against Babylon, gold and silver vessels and bronze structures created for the temple by Solomon were stripped and taken to Babylon (2 Kgs 25:9-17; compare 1 Kgs 7:27-50). Then the Babylonians burned it (586 BC). David and Yahweh both had warned Solomon that unless he kept the covenant of Yahweh, he and this house would be swept away (1 Kgs 2:1-4; 9:1-9). Solomon did not keep the covenant and neither did many of his descendants. These chapters tell the story of how the temple built for Yahweh was swept away.

Peter Leithart points out that Babylon's plundering of the temple was the seventh time an invading or Judahite king entered the temple to remove its treasures. The first was Shishak of Egypt (1 Kgs 14:26), then Asa and Joash of Judah (1 Kgs 15:18; 2 Kgs 12:17-18 [18-19 HB]), Jehoash of Israel (14:13-14), Ahaz and Hezekiah of Judah (16:7-8; 18:14-16); and finally, a two-part plundering by Nebuchadnezzar and Nebuzaradan of Babylon (24:13-14; 25:13-17). Leithart calls this the "systematic decreation of the temple and kingdom of Judah" (2006, 274). Thus, the temple's final destruction in these chapters was the final stage of a process.

Furthermore, Solomon's temple in Jerusalem seemed doomed even during the reign of the reforming king, Hezekiah. Isaiah told him that the royal treasures viewed by Babylonian visitors would be brought out to Babylon as well as his own sons (20:12-18). This threat was articulated *before* Manasseh had become king and filled Jerusalem with innocent blood along with his apostasies. And yet Dtr consistently affirms that the disaster that would befall Judah at the hands of Babylon was the result of Manasseh's sins (24:3-4; compare 21:10-16).

Nonetheless, the larger context of 1—2 Kings in DtrH continually alludes to apostasies generated by David's son, Solomon, and the resulting reversals that led Judah's inhabitants and treasures back to Egypt, the land of bondage. Judah was also led back to Babylon from whence their ancestor in the faith, Abraham, had come. Further parallels with the Torah, Genesis—Deuteronomy, and Judges abound throughout the latter chapters of Kings, which describe Judah's rebellion and disobedience that led to oppression by Gentiles, to their exile, and their loss of land and king, promise and blessing. Judah's story followed the pattern of Israel fourteen decades before (722 BC).

Elaborated accounts of this disaster appear in Jer 39—44; 52; and 2 Chr 36:11-21. The book of the exilic prophet Ezekiel, who was taken to Babylon during the first deportation with Jehoiachin, presents oracles of warning and hope to Judahites. Within these passages, especially Ezek 17:11-21, aspects of Judah's history from 593 to 563 BC are evident.

1. Jehoiakim and Jehoiachin Face Nebuchadnezzar (24:1-17)

IN THE TEXT

■ 1 Although Jehoiakim served as a vassal for three years, he rebelled against Babylon, expecting the renewed support of Egypt when this nation seemed to be regaining its strength. Instead, Babylon was regrouping and gaining the power to overcome Egypt and Judah.

■ 2-4 Juxtaposing Jehoiakim's rebellion with these raids by Chaldean/Babylonian vassals under the command of Nebuchadnezzar implies his rebellion caused the raids. And on one level they did. However, the passage continues to emphatically clarify that these attacks were caused by Yahweh's reaction to the sins of *Manasseh*, including especially the spilling of innocent blood with which **he had filled Jerusalem** (v 4; compare 21:11-17). This underscores the tension recognized by Dtr between prophetic explanations for judgment and political reasons for disaster.

■ 5-6 Dtr's formulaic summary of the reign of Jehoiakim is brief compared to Jeremiah's colorful depiction of the prophet's interaction with Jehoiakim. According to Jeremiah, the third to last king of Judah had the opportunity to repent and turn the tide of Yahweh's wrath against Jerusalem, but he did not (Jer 22:18-28; 25:1-29; 26:1-23; 28:1-8; 35:12-16; 36:28-31). During Jehoiakim's tenure, Babylon came to stay, with a brief interruption when they withdrew because they heard about approaching Egyptian armies (Jer 37:4-5).

Second Chronicles' depiction of Jehoiakim's reign is also short, but it claims *he* was taken to Babylon with the temple vessels (36:5-8). Second Kings, however, simply notes that he died in Jerusalem (**rested with his ancestors** [v 6]). No mention is made of a deportation to Babylon of either Jehoiakim or temple vessels in his time.

In his prophetic challenges to Jehoiakim, Jeremiah threatened him with an ignominious end: "They will not mourn for him: 'Alas, my master! Alas, his splendor!' He will have the burial of a donkey—dragged away and thrown outside the gates of Jerusalem" (Jer 22:18-19). No mention of this sort of inglorious death is made in 2 Kings. Second Kings 24:6 simply asserts that **Jehoiakim rested with his ancestors**, in the same manner that Dtr concludes the reigns and lives of most other kings of Judah. This is the last time in DtrH that a Judahite reign ends with this sort of report. Jehoiakim's son, Jehoiachin, and brother, Zedekiah, were taken to Babylon; they were not buried in Jerusalem; that is, they did not rest with their fathers (v 12; 25:7).

As his reign concludes, we must recall that Jehoiakim was the older son of Josiah who succeeded his younger half-brother, Jehoahaz, whom "the people of the land" (23:30) had placed on the throne. Jehoiakim may have been assassinated by pro-Babylon Judahites who opposed his rebellion against Babylon (Sweeney 2007, 455). He may have been killed by raiders (24:2) or died of natural causes. No biblical or extrabiblical text states the cause of his death at age thirty-six. In any case, his son, Jehoiachin, the grandson of Josiah, became king for three months (598-597 BC).

■ **7** Babylon's renewed strength confined Egypt to its traditional boundaries. Egypt had once expanded to control the area **from the Wadi of Egypt to the Euphrates River**, which had been ruled by Solomon (1 Kgs 4:21, 24 [5:1, 4 HB]; 8:65; compare 2 Sam 8:3), but now Babylon possessed it.

■ **8-9** Jeremiah called Jehoiachin Coniah (Jer 22:24, 28; 37:1 [NRSV]) or Jeconiah (24:1; 28:4; 29:2). It is more likely that he was eighteen, his age given here, than eight, his age given in 2 Chr 36:9 (NIV mg.), because he had wives (2 Kgs 24:15). In addition, Jeremiah made comments about his offspring (Jer 22:28; compare Ezek 19:5-14). He had at least five sons known to the Babylonians, for they are mentioned in the Babylonian Chronicle (*ANET*, 564). First Chronicles 3:17-18 lists seven sons: "Shealtiel his son, Malkiram, Pedaiah, Shenazzar, Jekamiah, Hoshama and Nedabiah."

Jehoiachin's three-month reign is introduced according to the Judahite formula of providing his mother's name. It parallels those of apostate Israelite and Judahite kings by claiming that **he did evil in the eyes of Yahweh**. Concerning Israel, see: 1 Kgs 15:26, 34; 16:7, 19, 25, 30; 22:52 [53 HB]; 2 Kgs 3:2. Concerning Judah, see: 1 Kgs 11:6 (Solomon); 14:22-24; 2 Kgs 8:16-18, 27 (kings of Judah related to Ahab); 21:2, 20 (Manasseh and Amon); 23:32 (Jehoiachin's father and uncles: Jehoahaz, Jehoiakim, and Zedekiah [24:19]).

■ **10** This is the first mention of the official siege of Jerusalem by Babylon's Nebuchadnezzar.

■ **11** The king of Babylon and his armies went up and came against the city to besiege it.

■ **12** Jehoiachin **surrendered** or "gave himself up" (NRSV). The Hebrew says that Jehoiachin and his retinue **went out against** [*yēṣēʾ ʿal*] **the king of Babylon**. The term is not "to" or "unto" (*ʾel*) but *ʿal* (compare 25:1). The preposition *ʿal* can also mean "over," "among," or "nearby." In any case, he went out to be among the Babylonians. The context suggests surrender, for **the King of Babylon accepted him** in response.

Furthermore, it is unlikely that Jehoiachin would confront Babylonian armies with his mother. Although Jehoiachin would never return to Judah and rule from Jerusalem, the final verses of ch 25 (which conclude DtrH) report that he (Zedekiah's immediate predecessor) was released from prison in Babylon.

Jeremiah consistently told the kings of Judah to surrender to Babylon, which Jehoiachin did (see Jer 22:24-30; 24:1-7; 29:1-11; and Esth 2:6). This first exile of Jerusalemites with King Jehoiachin took place in Nebuchadnezzar's eighth year, according to 2 Kgs 24:12 (597 BC). The Jeremiah account and the Babylonian Chronicle say it was his seventh year (598 BC).

■ 13 This invasion and stripping of the temple by Babylon represents a fulfillment of Isaiah's words to Hezekiah (20:12-18) and to Solomon when he built and furnished the temple as a dwelling place for Yahweh (1 Kgs 9:1-9). Whenever Judah was oppressed by an outside ruler, the temple was raided. Five years after Solomon died, during Rehoboam's reign, King Shishak of Egypt took the treasures of the house of Yahweh, including all the shields of gold that Solomon had made (14:25-26). (→ 1 Kgs 15:18; 2 Kgs 12:18 [19 HB]; 14:14; and Behind the Text for 2 Kgs 24:1—25:30, above.) Rehoboam replaced the gold with bronze (1 Kgs 14:27-28), but later kings may have been able to supply gold vessels from time to time.

■ 14 The king of Babylon *exiled all Jerusalem*. As far as Dtr is concerned, *all* essential inhabitants of Jerusalem were exiled to Babylon at this time: *all commanders, all the mighty young men, exiling ten thousand; each artisan and each worker. No one remained but the poor people of the land.* Exiled (*gālâ*) appears here as a verb and a participle, an action undertaken by Nebuchadnezzar. It will be repeated throughout these last two chapters of 2 Kings before and after Jerusalem fell to the Babylonians. Dtr used the term to describe Israel's exile to Assyria for the first time in 2 Kgs 17:23.

■ 15 The king of Babylon *exiled* (*gālâ*, verb) Jehoiachin (NIV: **took . . . captive**). *His mother, his wives, his eunuchs, and the leaders of the land he made to walk* [*hālak*; "to go"] *into exile* (*gôlâ*). The noun *gôlâ* derives from the verb *gālâ*, "to exile," "to go into exile," or "to be exiled" (*gālâ*), which stems from the verb "to uncover," "lay bare," "remove," or "raze to the ground." It is commonly used in the Bible to indicate deportation and captivity.

■ 16 The first stage of the Babylonian exile continues (597 BC). The king of Babylon also *brought out to exile* [*gôlâ*] *in Babylon seven thousand men of valor, one thousand artisans and workers, and all young men fit for war* (NIV: **deported**). The skilled soldiers and craftsmen would have then served Babylon.

In its summary of the deportations, Jer 52:28 reports only 3,023 Jerusalemite exiles with Jehoiachin and his family in Nebuchadnezzar's seventh year (March 16, 597 BC, in Babylonian records). Whether three thousand or eighteen thousand (2 Kgs 24:14-16), the removal from Jerusalem of its elite, capable, and strong persons was intended to deprive remaining Judahites of any basis for a future rebellion, as well as to supply Babylon with skilled labor. According to Jeremiah, subsequent deportations were far smaller (832 in 586 BC and 745 in 582 BC [Jer 52:29-30]). Many remaining in Jerusalem lost their lives in its destruction.

■ **17** Nebuchadnezzar did not exile Mattaniah, Jehoiachin's uncle, but changed his name to Zedekiah and made him a vassal king. At this time no loss of life is mentioned.

2. Zedekiah Rebels and Jerusalem Falls to Babylon (24:18—25:21)

■ **18** The pertinent events that happened while Zedekiah was king, including his rebellion and how he fled during the resulting siege, was caught, and exiled are told in 2 Kgs 25:1-7, Jer 39:1-10, and 52:1-11. Babylon's burning of Jerusalem and its aftermath are described in 2 Kgs 25:8-26, 2 Chr 36:11-20, Jer 39:8-10 and 52:12-30.

Zedekiah's reign is introduced with the Judahite regnal formula that includes his age at the outset of his rule and his mother's name. He was the younger full brother of Jehoahaz, the first king after Josiah. Jehoahaz (Shallum) was put on the throne by "the people of the land" (2 Kgs 23:30), but Egypt quickly deposed him and took him to Egypt, placing Jehoiakim on the throne. Verse 17 affirms that Zedekiah was Jehoiachin's uncle, and v 18 names his mother as Hamutal daughter of Jeremiah of Libnah, but neither verse reaffirms that he was the son of Josiah (which he was). He would have been ten years old when Josiah died, his brother Jehoahaz made king, then deposed, and his half-brother Jehoiakim became king (1 Chr 3:15 provides conflicting data about the order of Josiah's sons).

24:17-20

■ **19** Zedekiah **did evil** in Yahweh's eyes throughout his eleven-year reign, in the manner of **Jehoiakim**. No contrast to David or Josiah or comparison to Manasseh is made here, although his sins are compared to those of Jehoiakim's eleven-year reign. Dtr will provide no concluding formula for this last king of Judah; he will not sleep with his ancestors.

■ **20** *For Yahweh's anger was against Jerusalem and Judah until he cast them out of his presence, thus* [lit. "and"] *Zedekiah rebelled against the king of Babylon.* In the *exilic* version of DtrH, Yahweh's wrath against Judah was inexorable because of Manasseh's sins, which were the necessary (underlying) cause of Judah's exile. Manasseh's sins made the exile inevitable. Yahweh's wrath had been kindled and could not be doused! In this *preexilic* version, Zedekiah's sins became part of that pattern. Similarly, his rebellion was the political (and sufficient or immediate) cause of the final Babylonian siege that destroyed land, temple, and king, bringing the punishment Yahweh had already determined for Judah (2 Kgs 21:10-15). In other words, Zedekiah's rebellion cannot be separated from Yahweh's wrath; it was the means by which his fury was turned on Jerusalem.

■ **25:1** Zedekiah was a younger brother of both Jehoahaz and Jehoiakim, not brought up to be king. But the Babylonians who placed him on the throne expected his loyalty, which he gave them for nearly nine years. Zedekiah's rebellion provoked the anger of the king of Babylon against Jerusalem. According to the Chronicler and to Ezekiel, Zedekiah had sworn an oath of allegiance to Babylon's Nebuchadnezzar, confirming his vassal status (2 Chr 36:13; Ezek 17:13-14). This is assumed in 2 Kings, given Nebuchadnezzar's treatment of Zedekiah and Judah's officials, but not mentioned.

This final rebellion may have been incited by the powerful pro-Egyptian Judahites that later killed Gedaliah and others before fleeing to Egypt (2 Kgs 25:25-26; Jer 41:1-3, 16-18). Ezekiel 17:13-16 lays blame for this rebellion fully at the feet of Zedekiah. The Babylonian siege began on the tenth day of the tenth month of Zedekiah's ninth year: 10 Tevet (December-January) 587/586 BC.

■ **2-3** Jerusalem was captured in Zedekiah's eleventh year on the ninth of Nisan (March) 586 BC after eleven months of severe famine caused by the siege. Jerusalem was finally invaded and burned when the starvation of its inhabitants made it possible for the Chaldeans (*kaśdîm*) to break through and breach its walls. The terms "Chaldeans" and "Babylonians" are used interchangeably throughout the account of Judah's fall (→ Behind the Text for 2 Kgs 24:1—25:30 and comments at 24:2-4; 25:5-6, 10-11, 13-16, 24).

■ **4** In the MT, the Hebrew does not include "the king" or "fled." If these are added to the text as in NIV and NRSV, it reads that the king and Judah's **men of war** (NIV: **whole army**) abandoned ship and fled to the desert that very night. The general meaning is the same in Jer 39, but 39:4 includes a few lines that seem to have dropped out of the MT of 2 Kgs 25:4: **And it happened when Zedekiah the king of Judah saw them** [the named princes of Babylon (Jer 39:3)] **and all the men of war, they fled, going out at night from the city by the way of the garden of the king through the gate between the walls; and they went out the way toward the Arabah.** In this case the **men of war** are Babylonians with the princes of Babylon.

However, Jeremiah's second version of the story in 52:7 says: **Then the city wall was breached and all the men of war fled and went out from the city at night by way of the gate between the walls, which were around the garden of the king. The Chaldeans were around the city, and they pursued them by way of the Arabah.** This is similar to the way 2 Kgs 25:4 is translated: the **men of war** are Judahites with Zedekiah.

The garden of the king may have been the garden of Uzza in which Manasseh and Amon were buried (21:18, 26). The walls include the old wall around the city of David and the newer wall built by Hezekiah on the south-eastern edge of Jerusalem. Zedekiah's party thus fled toward the Transjordan by way of Jericho and the Jordan River. But they did not make it to safety.

■ **5-6** The Chaldean army pursued Zedekiah to the *Arabah* (plains) south of Jericho, dispersed his men of war, and captured him there. The end of the royal dynasty of David exemplified by the capture of his descendant Zedekiah by the Babylonians occurred at Jericho. Jericho was the site of Joshua's first inroad into the land of Canaan (Josh 6). Thus, the promises to Abraham and all the people led out of Egypt by Moses began to be fulfilled at Jericho, but so also did they end there (Sweeney 2007, 467). After Joshua's conquest, Jericho was cursed against its rebuilding (v 26). Hiel of Bethel rebuilt the city and suffered the curse when Omri became king of Israel (1 Kgs 16:34).

The Chaldeans brought Zedekiah to Nebuchadnezzar at Riblah *who passed judgment upon him*. The Egyptians had briefly held Josiah's first successor, Jehoahaz, at Riblah before exiling him to Egypt (2 Kgs 23:33-35). It became Nebuchadnezzar's headquarters as well, as he sent his general Nebuzaradan to destroy Jerusalem. Riblah was north of Jerusalem, seven miles south of Kadesh along the Orontes River.

■ **7** Nebuchadnezzar's judgment of Zedekiah was cruel and in keeping with the terms of vassal-suzerain treaties made in the era for vassals who broke their covenants: *they slaughtered his sons before his eyes*, blinded him, bound him, and carried him into captivity to Babylon. Jeremiah affirms that he died there. "The king of Babylon . . . put him in prison till the day of his death" (Jer 52:10-11). Thus, the last event that thirty-year-old Zedekiah would have seen was the slaughter of his young children.

The killing of his children implies that Zedekiah's young family was with him when he fled, which would have been natural, but was not mentioned earlier. The account in Jeremiah adds that some officers of the army were killed at that time at Riblah: "the king of Babylon . . . also killed all the officers of Judah at Riblah" (v 10 NRSV). Both 2 Kgs 25:18-21 and Jer 52:24-27 (nearly duplicate accounts) list the executions of specific priests and army commanders after the burning of Jerusalem.

Nebuchadnezzar's ghastly but pro forma treatment of Zedekiah, Jerusalem, and priestly and military elites in reaction to Judah's most recent rebellion (2 Kgs 25:7-21) represents Yahweh's response to Israel and Judah's breaking of their covenant with Yahweh. The curses of Deut 28:15-68 (and Lev 26:14-39) were *fully* fulfilled in Zedekiah's time.

■ **8-9** After the slaughter of Zedekiah's sons, the Babylonian general, Nebuzaradan, entered Jerusalem to destroy it. Whereas vv 1-2 of 2 Kgs 25 aligned Nebuzaradan's siege and breach of the walls of the city to Zedekiah's reign, this verse does not align this invasion, the seventh of Av, 586 BC, to the rule of Zedekiah. Instead it is aligned with Nebuchadnezzar's reign, for Zedekiah is no longer king. The years of his rule were over and the king of Babylon reigned over the Judah he was destroying. The traditional day of Jewish mourning the temple razing (and other great disasters of the Jews) is the ninth of Av. The Babylonian Talmud (*b. Ta'an.* 29a) reconciles this with Jer 52:12, which states the temple was destroyed on the tenth of Av, by stating the temple was burnt on the ninth and fully collapsed on the tenth.

Nebuzaradan's title *rab ṭabbāḥîm* literally means "chief slaughterer" (of animal meat; see 1 Sam 8:13; 9:23, 24). In Babylon, *rab ṭabbāḥîm* was used to mean military commander and chief of the guards (*ṭabbāḥîm*). But its original meaning is appropriate here, for he butchered the people of Jerusalem as he burned the temple, palace of the king, and homes of the nobles. The term *śar ṭabbāḥîm* is used for Egyptian officials, including Potiphar, in the Joseph story of Genesis (Gen 37:36; 39:1; 40:3, 4; 41:10, 12). Other parallels to the Joseph story appear in this last passage of 2 Kings about Jehoiachin's release from prison to eat at the king's table.

In Jer 40:1-6, Nebuzaradan addressed Jeremiah with the voice of Dtr to claim that Yahweh was behind the disaster and devastation by which he, Nebuzaradan, was razing Jerusalem. Jeremiah could go wherever he wished, escorted to Babylon in safety, or stay in Judah with Gedaliah the newly appointed governor of the towns of Judah.

■ **10-11** The besieging army of the Chaldeans broke down all crucial parts of the city walls, and Nebuzaradan exiled the remaining people including the ***fallen ones*** (*nōpělîm*), those who had already ***fallen*** (*nāpal*) to the king of Babylon. The term ***fallen*** seems pejorative here, but the prophet Jeremiah persistently urged leaders and people to submit to Babylon based on the oracles of Yahweh that came to him (Jer 38:2-3).

■ **12** Just as Nebuchadnezzar had left "the poorest people of the land" to farm (2 Kgs 24:14), after the exile of Jehoiachin and Jerusalem elites in 597 BC, so also his captain, Nebuzaradan, left **the poorest people** to farm the land in 586 BC (compare Jer 52:16). However, Gedaliah, who was later appointed governor of Judah by the Babylonians, and Ishmael who murdered him, were both nobility, and they remained in the land. Gedaliah was pro-Babylonian, but Ishmael was of the royal house of David and would have been a Babylonian target if he were not in hiding (Jer 40:7—41:10).

■ **13-16** The passage outlining the stripping of the precious metal structures of Solomon's temple aligns with the details of how he constructed them in 1 Kgs 7:15-50. This literary technique of paralleling their destruction with the construction underscores the reversal of Yahweh's promises as well as the peace represented by the extent and wealth of Solomon's rule.

■ **17-20** Nebuzaradan gave his king the "honor" of killing any remaining Judahites who had any authority over temple or people. The named chief priest and assistant priest, the unnamed temple guardians, surviving military commanders, seven men of the king's cabinet, the leader of "the people's army," and sixty leading men of **the people of the land**, were executed by Nebuchadnezzar at Riblah (the same list is given in Jer 52:24-27). Thus, representatives of all of Judah's people and influential persons not already slaughtered or exiled by Nebuzaradan were executed by King Nebuchadnezzar at Riblah.

Seraiah was the son of Azariah (1 Chr 6:14), who was an ancestor of Ezra (Ezra 7:1). Zephaniah interacted with Jeremiah as priest during Zedekiah's reign (Jer 21:1; 29:25-29; 37:3). The people of the land had normally supported anti-Egyptian kings (Jehoahaz) and thus could have been considered pro-Babylonian to a degree, but this did not save them from Nebuzaradan and Nebuchadnezzar.

■ **21** With this final display of the Babylonian slaughter of leading Judahites in Jerusalem and throughout the land, Dtr declares that Judah was fully exiled from its land. But there was no exile for these men. The equally bloody and disturbing repercussions among those who remained in Judah are described in the final section of the exilic version of DtrH (2 Kgs 25:22-30).

3. The Aftermath of Judah's Exile to Babylon (25:22-30)

a. From Gedaliah to the Flight to Egypt (25:22-26)

■ **22** Gedaliah, whom Nebuchadnezzar appointed to govern the remaining people of Judah, was the son and grandson of two royal scribes in Josiah's time. Shaphan, Gedaliah's grandfather, had brought the book to Josiah after Hilkiah, the high priest, found it. Later, Josiah sent them to consult Huldah, the prophet in Jerusalem, about the meaning of the found book (*sēper hattôrâ*) for his generation (2 Kgs 22:12-13).

The Gedaliah of 25:22 is not to be confused with another Gedaliah, the son of Pashhur, who (with three other lords) persecuted Jeremiah and opposed his oracles about submitting to Babylon during Zedekiah's reign (Jer 38:1-6). The book of Jeremiah alludes to the support of Shaphan's family for Jeremiah (26:24; 29:3; 36:11-18; 40:5-6; and throughout ch 41). Shaphan was the father of Ahikam (father of Gedaliah) and Gemariah, although there is some confusion of names and relationships in Jeremiah. In Jer 36:9-10, Gemariah is called the son of Shaphan, whereas in Jer 29:3, a certain Gemariah is called the son of Hilkiah and Elasah is called the son of Shaphan.

The seal impression found at Lachish that reads "belonging to Gedaliah, the one who is over the house" came from around 600 BC. It may refer to the anti-Babylonian Gedaliah who served under Zedekiah or to the Gedaliah son of Ahikam that the Babylonians later appointed to govern what remained of Judah at Mizpah (Althann 1992a, 923).

■ **23** Men that figured prominently in the rest of the story that follows gathered to Gedaliah at Mizpah (Tel en-Nasbeh), eight miles north of Jerusalem in Benjamin, where damage was minimal (ibid.). At this point, they and their soldiers recognized Gedaliah's authority. But all of this changed within a few months.

■ **24** Loyal to Babylon, Gedaliah urged these parties of survivors to thrive in Judah by serving the Chaldeans, by trusting them. Gedaliah's words here convey the same message that the prophet Jeremiah conveyed to Judahites throughout the book of Jeremiah. Although no mention of Jeremiah is made in 2 Kings, the book of Jeremiah says that Nebuchadnezzar and Nebuzaradan sent Jeremiah to Gedaliah, after releasing him and giving the prophet his choice of residence (Jer 39:11—40:5).

■ **25** Briefly and summarily, Dtr announced that one of these survivors, Ishmael, of the house of David, killed Governor Gedaliah and the Chaldeans and Judahites who were with him at Mizpah. This occurred **in the seventh month**, suggesting these assassinations occurred in the same year as Jerusalem's destruction and the appointment of Gedaliah as governor (in "the fourth month" [Jer 39:2]). However, it could have occurred up to five years later if this crisis led to further deportations by Nebuchadnezzar of Judahites in his twenty-third year (582/581; Jer 52:30; compare Josephus, *Ant.* 10.9 §7).

Jeremiah provides the details of these coups (Jer 40:5—43:7, esp. 40:7—41:18), but the exilic Dtr, in his conclusion of these troubled times, did not include the intrigues behind Ishmael's murder of Gedaliah and the subsequent revenge killing of Ishmael by Johanan son of Kareah.

■ **26** Johanan son of Kareah and his party led all the remaining survivors to Egypt because of their fear of the Chaldeans. Jeremiah 41:16—43:7 answers questions that 2 Kgs 25 raises about the fear and distrust that led to further bloodshed of surviving Judahites by Judahites. For example, Jeremiah explains that Johanan and his men were afraid that they would be blamed by the Chaldeans for killing Gedaliah (Jer 41:17-18), even though Johanan had warned Gedaliah about Ishmael's plot and later sought to kill Ishmael for murdering Gedaliah. After seeking Yahweh's direction through Jeremiah (42:1-6), which emphasized that they should remain in Judah (vv 7-22), Johanan utterly rejected Jeremiah's oracle and forced him to go to Egypt (43:1-7).

Dtr, however, concludes the tragic story of Judah by simply stating that the survivors of the Babylonian siege fled to Egypt because of their fear of the Chaldeans. Thus, God's people returned to Egypt from whence Yahweh had delivered their ancestors through Moses. Forcibly exiled to Assyria (Israel) and Babylon (Judah) and self-exiled to Egypt, the land was left desolate, the city of Jerusalem bereft. The book of Lamentations is a collection of dirges of grief over the loss of the city and its inhabitants.

b. Epilogue (25:27-30)

■ **27** When Nebuchadnezzar died, his son, Evil-Merodach (**Awel-Marduk**), became king of Babylon. During his short reign (562-560 BC), he **lifted the head** [*nāśā'* . . . *'et rō'š*] **of Jehoiachin**, the erstwhile **king of Judah from prison**, who had been imprisoned in Babylon from the time he was eighteen years old, thirty-seven years. This was the twenty-seventh of Adar, 561-560 BC. This passage is nearly duplicated in Jer 52:31-34, but it says these events occurred on the twenty-fifth of the month.

Lifted the head is an idiom for restoration, granting clemency or pardon. As a result the head is no longer bowed in subjection or shame. It is also used for the release of the chief cupbearer from prison in the Joseph story (Gen 40:13; Alter 2013, 851).

Jehoiachin is called the **king of Judah** twice; even though his exile had formally deposed him from the throne of Judah. This shows that Jehoiachin was still the king of Judah in the eyes of the final set of redactors. King Zedekiah, his successor, was taken to Babylon eleven years after Jehoiachin's exile began, but no epilogue was provided for him; he disappeared from the story (2 Kgs 25:7). This notice of Jehoiachin's release indicates that this account was written after Jehoiachin's release but possibly before Evil-Merodach (**Awel-Marduk**) was assassinated by the usurper, Nergal-sar-usar (Berridge 1992, 662; Sweeney 2007, 465).

William Schniedewind argues that Jehoiachin and his family in Babylon are responsible for the redaction of this material that includes the notice of vv 27-29 (2004, 149-64). Even though it was not necessarily grounding for great hope for all exiles or for the inhabitants of Judah, it was certainly good news for Jehoiachin!

Babylonian cuneiform tablets describe the generous provisions for Jehoiachin (*Ya'u-ki-nu* or *Yakū-kinu*), king of Judah (Yahudu, Yaudu, or Yakudu) and his family even before his release. Jehoiachin and his family may have been confined to the South Citadel in Babylon, where he was given five liters of oil, twelve times the amount given to each of his five sons listed there (Berridge 1992, 663). According to 2 Kgs 24:15, Jehoiachin had more than one wife, even as an eighteen-year-old king turned exile. First Chronicles 3:17-18 names seven sons born to the captive king: Shealtiel, Malkiram, Pedaiah, Shenazzar, Jekamiah, Hoshama, and Nedabiah. Shenazzar may be Sheshbazzar, the first governor of Judah in the Persian period ("the prince of Judah" [Ezra 1:8; 5:14]). Zerubbabel, the son of Jehoiachin's son Shealtiel, followed him. (See Ezra 3:2; Hag 1:1; 1 Chr 3:19 in the LXX; but in the MT, in 1 Chr 3:19, Zerubbabel's father was Pedaiah, another son of Jehoiachin [Berridge 1992, 663].)

The Babylonian tablets list provisions during Jehoiachin's *imprisonment* (not for the later period when he was released and dined in the king's presence). A number of other Judeans are also named in these tablets, which date from 595/594—570/569 BC (the tenth to the thirty-fifth year of Nebuchadnezzar).

■ **28** Not only was Jehoiachin lifted out of prison, but he was even exalted. The new king **spoke well to him and his chair was placed above the chairs of other exiled kings.**

■ **29** Like Joseph who was rushed out of prison in Egypt to shave, change clothes, and meet Pharaoh (Gen 41:14), so Jehoiachin changed his prison clothes to **always eat bread** in the new Babylonian king's **presence all the days of his life.** Many scholars consider Jehoiachin's confinement a sort of house arrest, and the fact that he had children in captivity for whom he provided suggests the same. Although the text says that he wore prison clothes until his release, the mention of his changing of clothes may be to stress the remarkable change of circumstances, rather than implying he had been in a prison cell.

■ **30** Perpetual, *day by day provisions were given to him by the king, something each day for the rest of his life*. This refers to the rest of *Jehoiachin's* life. He was fifty-five when he was finally released from Babylonian confinement. He may have died before Evil-Merodach was murdered within two years of coming to the throne of Babylon. Or the usurping king continued to provide for Jehoiachin for many more years.

Although this was a momentous change for Jehoiachin and his family, it provided a dubious foundation for the restoration of Judahite exiles to their land. Jehoiachin, the only Judahite king that survived as far as many exiles knew, was still confined to Babylon. He was in finer circumstances, yes, but still in exile. On the other hand, a number of preserved prophetic oracles provide explicit hope to the exiles for their return to Judah (e.g., Jer 29:1-14; Isa 40:1—41:25; 44:24—45:13; 46; 47—55; Ezek 11:14-25; 16:59-62; 20:33-38).

FROM THE TEXT

Behind the Text explanations join In the Text exegesis and commentary and From the Text discussions to explain the production of these texts, the history of God's people that they tell, and their meanings for then and now. They also explore persistent theological tensions within Scripture that we face today. Together these are guides for serious Bible students as they lead others to deeper engagement with God using the ancient reflections on God's work in the world: the Scriptures. We humbly receive these traditions from our ancestors in the faith; studying them, preserving them, and transmitting them to our children in the faith.

As with the other sections of 1—2 Kings, these last two chapters demonstrate the benefits of considering historical issues, including how these books came to be in their present form. As noted above, the release of Jehoiachin from confinement demonstrates that the final form of 1—2 Kings was penned around the time this happened and possibly before Evil-Merodach (Awel-Marduk) was assassinated by Nergal-sar-usar. Thus, it is an exilic redaction and perhaps produced by Jehoiachin and/or his family with the backing of the king of Babylon. The mention of Jehoiachin's release was not intended to promise a restoration of Judahites (Jews) to their land, and even less that a son of David would return to a throne in Jerusalem. But it did raise the sense of well-being of the Jews exiled there. God spoke hope for return and blessing to survivors in Babylon and the land of Israel during this period through prophets like Ezekiel, Jeremiah, and Second Isaiah.

As is evident from the text itself, the exilic editors preserved Hezekiah's edition of the 1—2 Kings material that showed him as a reforming son of David, who purged Judah with hopes to gather Israel to worship in Jerusalem. Similarly, the exilic editors preserved a Josianic version that demonstrated another son of David beginning to bring Israel into Jerusalem's orbit by eliminating sites and personnel of apostasy throughout the land of Israel. Marvin Sweeney states that the Josianic edition of DtrH was written to convince the remaining Israelites "to reunite with Judah, to return to the Temple in Jerusalem, and to accept Josiah as their righteous monarch" (2001, 316).

This King Josiah, who loved God with all his heart and soul and kept a copy of the Law with him (Deut 17:14-20), could have been the son of David who reigned over a united Israel. Perhaps this potentially reunited Israel would be that blessing to the nations and families around them as promised to Abraham (Gen 12:3). This is not how it turned out. Josiah, nonetheless, was a bright spot in Judah's history, modeling cooperation with the God who created and blessed his people.

The exilic editors of the books of Kings dealt with the post Josianic reality they experienced: the exile. All throughout Deuteronomy—2 Kings, not only in these last two chapters, we sense that the writer/redactors suffered the disasters of exile. They insisted that God's wrath, inflamed by Manasseh's sins, along with generations of covenant violations, led God to use Babylon to wreak havoc upon Judah.

On the other hand, God also used Babylon to preserve God's people both in Babylon and in Judah. The Jews were not assimilated into Babylonian culture, but knew and transmitted their own stories. They held to their identity through practices such as storytelling, Sabbath keeping, and circumcision that they could do anywhere, without land, temple, or king. When they eventually returned to Judah, they constructed a community based on stories, rituals, and other traditions that further preserved their identity and life together as the community of God in Persian Yehud (Judah). The texts *we* receive as comprising the Hebrew Bible were birthed as Scripture among restoration period Jews who also built a second temple with the help of Persia, who allowed them to return their homeland.

The historical factors that influenced the production of Scripture also help us analyze the theological *and* logical problems that emerge from the text for us. One of the continuing theological difficulties we have been examining in latter chapters of 2 Kings has been the tension between the promised results of Torah-keeping and the threatened results of Torah-breaking that occurs throughout Deuteronomy and DtrH (Joshua—2 Kings).

The disaster of exile happened even though Josiah submitted fully to the Torah *after* Manasseh's long reign of broken covenant violations. This stands in tension with a major theme of all of biblical literature: the mercy and grace of God. God is regularly depicted as merciful and gracious, showing steadfast love to the thousandth generation while only punishing to the fourth generation (Exod 20:5-6). God proclaimed before Moses that he maintained "love to thousands, and forgiving wickedness, rebellion and sin" (34:7).

Nonetheless, God affirmed that he would not leave the guilty unpunished, but punish "the children and their children for the sin of the parents to the third and fourth generation" (34:7). Furthermore, throughout the Torah and the Former Prophets, God's wrath was kindled against sin and he flared out to consume sinners. This is the case with the exile as told in 2 Kgs 24—25.

Certainly Exod 20 and 34 metaphorically emphasize that God is much more gracious than punishing (one thousand times to four times). Although a literal approach will detect that the generations after Manasseh lie within the fourth generation, Josiah's sons and grandsons certainly fall within the thousandth generation of those who loved God and kept his commandments (Exod 20:6). This brings us back to the theological tensions of these texts. The left-behind and exiled Jews expressed their struggles with these tensions in Pss 89 and 137. Psalm 89 underscores Yahweh's steadfast love and promise of a perpetual dynasty to David. But the previous praises become the psalmist's basis for interrogating God about Jerusalem's collapse and the removal of Judah's kings. Lamentations takes this further, and the lament of Ps 137 concludes by blessing anyone who shatters the heads of Babylon's infants.

These passages show that not all Jews understood why God deserted his people. Eventually they recognized, with the help of prophets, that he had not abandoned them forever, but held hope out to them. Along with deep, enduring disappointment, the exile provoked new possibilities for God's people. They turned to him with their severe grief, disappointment, and inquiries (see, for example, the book of Habakkuk).

Different Jews expressed this hope in different ways. Some developed a messianic hope in a future scion of David who would deliver them from oppression as he returned to the throne of his ancestors. But, for others, some messianic expectations were dashed, while others were opened as survivors reflected upon what life before God meant in new and reduced circumstances. While hope in a physical Davidic dynasty seems to have soured for some, they emphasized the model of Moses and the teachings of Torah (Sweeney 2001, 320).

The task of the prophets of the exilic and postexilic period was to restore hope in God and instill faithfulness to God alone through keeping the covenant mediated by Moses. Torah—instructions in God's ways—could be taught orally and in writing even without land, temple, and king. They could be practiced by anyone, anywhere, whether the person was royal, priestly, or, in many stories, not even a Jew.

In this way, the last chapters of 2 Kings, with their depictions of the tragedies that befell Israel/Judah, lead us back to the beginning of DtrH and to Joshua, the book and the man. Within the world of the story, Joshua was a model for Josiah. But in the processes of the literary formulations of these traditions, Josiah may have been a model for Joshua. They both effectively dealt with the banned influences of Canaanite religion, especially attractive to northern Israelites. Although Josiah was tragically killed, he remained an example of one son of David who ruled according to the Mosaic covenant. Joshua had led the children of Israel in this same manner. Survivors could look to Joshua as an example of a faithful leader. Joshua was neither a king nor a son of Moses, but he exemplified the law-abiding, successful leader by his compliance with all that Moses taught. Anyone anywhere—to this day—can, like Joshua (Josh 1:7-8) *and* Josiah, keep the book of the Torah and trust in God's presence, regardless of their physical heritage.

Furthermore, 1—2 Kings is not the end of the story for followers of God in Scripture-centered communities. There is a "Rest of the Story!" God restored the Babylonian exiles to their land, and they lived under Persia according to their received Torah as a constitution.

Followers of Christ see the story continue in Jesus of Nazareth, a son of David who fully fulfilled Torah. Like Joshua, Jesus did not sit on a throne during his sojourn on earth, but all the Gospels see him as Israel's king (Matt 27:11, 37; Mark 15:2, 26; Luke 23:3, 38; John 19:19). God declared him to be his Son by his resurrection from the dead; he is both Lord and Messiah (Acts 2:36; Rom 1:2-4). The NT with all of its variety of emphases is remarkably consistent in its view of Jesus as Son of David and King-Messiah (Matt 1:1; 2:2; 9:27). New Testament writers apply royal psalms to his life and work. See, for example, Heb 1:5 (Ps 2:7); Acts 4:25-26 (Ps 2:1-2); and Heb 1:8-9 (Ps 45:6-7 [7-8 HB]).

Jesus was the opposite of Solomon, Jeroboam, Ahab, Manasseh, and the other covenant-breaking kings of Israel and Judah whose stories are told in Kings. Jesus showed that full faithfulness to God and to Torah was possible. Paul said that God's righteousness, attested by the Torah and the Prophets, was disclosed through the faithfulness of Jesus Christ for all who believe (Rom 3:21-22). The basis of Jesus' lordship and perpetual reign, according to Phil 2:8-11, was his obedience. He can never be rejected from his forever throne, for, though tempted like we are, "he did not sin" (Heb 2:18; 4:15).

Since Jesus is "the Rest of the Story" for Christians, we can go forward in faithfulness to the will of the Father, keeping covenant and gratefully accepting grace for failures. We faithfully step forward each day by receiving these Scriptures and learning from them, for they cause us to remember the faithfulness of God and Christ, which is our salvation.

www.ingramcontent.com/pod-product-compliance
Lightning Source LLC
Chambersburg PA
CBHW082103250426
43661CB00079B/2623